Artificial Intelligence in Architecture and Interior Design

Artificial Intelligence in Architecture and Interior Design

Guest Editors

Ewa Janina Grabska
Baohua Wen

MDPI
Basel • Beijing • Wuhan • Barcelona • Belgrade • Novi Sad • Cluj • Manchester

Guest Editors
Ewa Janina Grabska
Department of Design and Computer Graphics
Jagiellonian University
Kraków
Poland

Baohua Wen
School of Architecture and Planning
Hunan University
Changsha
China

Editorial Office
MDPI AG
Grosspeteranlage 5
4052 Basel, Switzerland

This is a reprint of the Special Issue, published open access by the journal *Buildings* (ISSN 2075-5309), freely accessible at: https://www.mdpi.com/journal/buildings/special_issues/782H0X96W9.

For citation purposes, cite each article independently as indicated on the article page online and as indicated below:

Lastname, A.A.; Lastname, B.B. Article Title. *Journal Name* **Year**, *Volume Number*, Page Range.

ISBN 978-3-7258-8225-0 (Hbk)
ISBN 978-3-7258-8226-7 (PDF)
https://doi.org/10.3390/books978-3-7258-8226-7

Contents

About the Editors

Ewa Janina Grabska

Ewa Janina Grabska from the Department of Design and Computer Graphics of the Jagiellonian University in Krakow, Poland, received the title of professor from the President of Poland in 2013. Her research focuses on design theory and computer-aided design using artificial intelligence methods, computer graphics, graph transformations, graph data structure, visual communication, design theory, creativity, and computer games. She collaborated with numerous international institutions, including the University of Erlangen-Nuremberg (Germany), the Faculty of Architecture at the University of Helsinki (Finland), the University of Paisley (Scotland), and George Maison University (USA). Among the most important projects she has participated in are the Polish-German project "Graph-based tools for conceptual design in civil engineering," funded by the Humboldt Foundation as part of joint European research, 2000–2003, and the KBN & British Council project "MAST – Multi Agent System for Structural Design," 2003–2005. She was the project manager for the State Committee for Scientific Research (KBN) project "Graph Transformations in the Construction of Diagrammatic Reasoning Systems," 2003–2006, and the project manager for the "Virtual City Creator for Computer Games" project, funded by the National Centre for Research and Development (NCBR), 2021–2023. She has been giving lectures entitled Computer-Aided Design for twenty years.

Baohua Wen

Baohua Wen, Ph.D., is an Associate Professor and Ph.D. Supervisor at the School of Architecture and Planning, Hunan University. He serves as Principal Investigator for multiple research grants, including the General Program and Youth Program of the National Natural Science Foundation of China (NSFC) as well as the General Program of the Hunan Provincial Natural Science Foundation. He holds editorial positions as Senior Editorial Board member of Journal of Green Building; Editorial Board member of Humanities and Social Sciences Communications, Scientific Reports, and PLoS One. His research interests include contemporary spontaneous green evolution and professional intervention in vernacular architecture; assessment methods and system optimization for green and low-carbon buildings; and green livable village construction along with urban-rural sustainable development.

buildings

Editorial

The Role of Artificial Intelligence in Architecture and Interior Design

Ewa Janina Grabska [1] and Baohua Wen [2,*]

[1] Department of Design and Computer Graphics, Jagiellonian University, 31-007 Kraków, Poland; ewa.grabska@uj.edu.pl
[2] School of Architecture and Planning, Hunan University, Changsha 410082, China
* Correspondence: wenbaohua@hnu.edu.cn

1. Introduction

Design is one of the most creative aspects of human endeavor. Thinking in the design process is, on the one hand, logical and rational, and on the other, intuitive and imaginative. Analysis of design problems reveals that the nature of design is divergent; it assumes multiple perspectives and encompasses numerous possibilities for the design task. However, convergent tasks clearly exist in every design process, in which logical reasoning and the search for more or less optimal solutions are required [1]. Design is characterized by two distinct worlds and the actions that define them. The first internal world is constructed in the designer's mind through perceptual, functional, and conceptual actions. The second external world is created through physical actions, such as drawing, copying, and deleting elements. A physical action in design is a change in the external world that aligns with a goal envisioned in the internal world [2].

Recent research is exploring hybrid artificial intelligence (AI) frameworks that are replacing earlier versions of isolated design tools. We are currently moving from viewing AI as a technical aid to understanding it as an integrated element in the design process. AI supports the designer's internal world, increasing design efficiency and enriching the creative process of finding solutions, while retaining the designer's key decision-making authority.

The past decade has witnessed a paradigm shift in computational design driven by advances in deep learning and neural network architectures. Unlike rule-based parametric systems, modern deep learning models learn implicit patterns from extensive architectural datasets, generating solutions that balance creativity with functional requirements [3]. Generative adversarial networks (GANs) [4], Variational Autoencoders (VAEs) [5], and diffusion models [6] have transformed early-stage design by enabling high-fidelity image synthesis and exploration of latent design spaces. Text-to-image diffusion models, such as Stable Diffusion and DALL-E, have been widely adopted for rapid concept visualization and ideation [7].

Parallel advances in computer vision and 3D reconstruction, including Neural Radiance Fields (NeRF), convolutional neural networks (CNNs) [8], and Vision Transformers (ViTs) [9], are redefining how architects capture, analyze, and model built environments. Large language models (LLMs) now facilitate natural language interaction with design tools, enabling designers to express intentions conversationally rather than through complex coding [10]. Collectively, these technologies expand the boundaries of architectural design and foster interdisciplinary collaboration between computer science and architecture.

 https://doi.org/10.3390/buildings16112106

Although the research focus of this Special Issue is limited to architecture and interior design in the context of artificial intelligence, its aim is more general: to highlight the ongoing enrichment of the framework for the interdisciplinary integration of diverse aspects of design and artificial intelligence technologies.

2. An Overview of the Published Articles

The ten articles published in this Special Issue collectively demonstrate the diverse applications of AI across the entire architectural design lifecycle.

Hong and Choo (contribution 1) address a critical limitation of current text-to-image diffusion models in architectural design: the lack of precise control over architectural parameters. They propose fine-tuning the Stable Diffusion XL (SDXL) model using Low-Rank Adaptation (LoRA) in a dataset of 1000 architectural massing images. Systematic evaluation of training parameters—epoch, batch size, and network rank—demonstrates that LoRA fine-tuning significantly improves the model's ability to generate accurate architectural masses from text prompts, offering practical guidance for domain-specific AI adaptation.

Wang et al. (contribution 2) develop a hybrid multi-criteria decision-making framework to analyze the influence mechanisms of AI-based Architectural Design (AIAD). Integrating Analytic Hierarchy Process (AHP), Decision-Making Trial and Evaluation Laboratory (DEMATEL), Interpretive Structural Modeling (ISM), and Cross Impact Matrix Multiplication Applied to Classification (MICMAC) methods, they identify 18 key factors across technology, organization, environment, project, education, and economy. Technological factors and project execution processes emerge as primary drivers of AI adoption, while learning and time costs act as barriers, offering structured insights for design firms undergoing digital transformation.

The article by Nam and Park (contribution 3) deals with the use of artificial intelligence in assessing the effectiveness of screen façades that are designed with geometric patterns and play a key role in shading. In this study, generative adversarial networks (GANs) and machine learning classification based on convolutional neural networks (CNNs) were applied to the generative method of designing screen facade features and integrating them with daylight simulation analyses. Using StyleGAN3 trained on 664 black-and-white patterns, these models generated 5000 unique façades, classified using CNN-based hierarchical clustering. The proposed daylight simulations revealed that frame ratios of 50-65% optimize daylight and glare reduction. This workflow integrates generative AI with performance simulation, enabling rapid exploration of thousands of alternatives.

Mehraban et al. (contribution 4) proposes an innovative process that enables the generation of semantically and geometrically useful BIM-based models from RGB images captured by standard cameras or unmanned aerial vehicles (UAVs). The proposed solution is based on Neural Radiation Fields (NeRF), artificial intelligence models known for their use in reconstructing detailed 3D scenes from 2D images. In the case considered by the authors, a precision of up to 0.994 and 0.992 Intersection over Union (IoU) were achieved for window and door detection, offering a cost-effective and scalable approach to BIM generation, supporting practical applications such as renovation and facility management.

The article by Zhong et al. (contribution 5) addresses the problem of automatically completing a floor plan from an unfinished design. A self-supervised framework for floor-plan (FP) completion was developed using a Masked Autoencoder (MAE) strategy with Vision Transformer (ViT). Training on the FloorplanNet dataset of 8000 layouts yielded consistent examples of residential layouts. FP-MAE reconstructs missing regions by capturing global structural patterns, accelerating early-stage design and reducing repetitive revisions.

 https://doi.org/10.3390/buildings16112106

The article by Lim and Yoon (contribution 6) demonstrates how image-based deep learning and expert evaluation can help identify trends in residential building design in the post-pandemic era, using over 10,000 interior images. Features extracted by a pre-trained convolutional neural network (ResNet50) reveal transformations in openness, flexibility, and integration with nature, highlighting the evolution of living spaces toward resilience and human-centered design. Although expert assessments largely confirmed the deep learning results, there were also discrepancies. Combining AI-based computational analysis with expert assessment is valuable because it allows for the identification of gaps between design intent, professional expectations, and implemented AI-enabled spatial configurations.

The article by Zhang et al. (contribution 7) explores the challenges of architectural heritage management using a Heritage Building Information Model (HBIM) with intelligent, data-driven decision-making. This workflow integrates 3D laser scanning, UAV photogrammetry, and archival data, with a parametric component library and value-risk model to enable the automated evaluation and real-time visualization of conservation priorities. This framework has been validated in its application to the Suopo Ancient Watchtower Complex in Danba, Sichuan.

The article by Liang et al. (contribution 8) proposes an integrated methodology for automating the identification and analysis of large-scale morphological features in typical residential courtyards. This approach utilizes both deep machine learning based on computer vision and GIS spatial statistics for large-scale morphological analysis of vernacular courtyards in Wu'an, Hebei. Using high-resolution network architectures pre-loaded with weights (HRNetV2) for semantic segmentation on satellite imagery for 134,280 courtyards, spatial statistics revealed regional patterns influenced by climate and topography, offering scalable methods for heritage preservation.

The article by Alana et al. (contribution 9) describes the transformation of architectural education toward human–AI collaboration, examining the impact of AI on six stages of architectural design via mixed-methods research. Evaluating AI across efficiency, creativity, accuracy, integration, adoptability, and environmental impact, student participants reported that AI is most effective in the early stages of design, where it supports idea generation, visualization, and iterative exploration. However, human expertise and critical reasoning remain crucial in later technical phases, as emphasized by the field, which prioritizes AI's analytical and evaluative capabilities, enabling informed decision-making. The contemporary educational task is to convince students that AI works most effectively as a complementary partner, not as a replacement for humans.

The article by Han and Jeong (contribution 10) validates generative AI-generated 360° images for indoor environmental research. Using a three-stage framework, base panorama generation, AI-based greenery integration, and validation, the stimuli exhibited minimal distortions and high visual fidelity, surpassing conventional 3D modeling for research applications. The model offers an alternative to expensive physical photography or complex 3D simulations, particularly for studies requiring precise control of environmental variables. It can be considered an extremely efficient and inexpensive spatial perception research paradigm for future indoor environment research, utilizing AI-generated virtual reality stimuli, enabling more diverse and scalable experimental designs.

3. Conclusions

The articles published in the Special Issue devoted to artificial intelligence in architecture and interior design are characterized by a wide spectrum of research topics and the resulting variety of methodologies. The following main thematic categories are presented:

1. General—searching for a methodology integrated with artificial intelligence, reflecting the contemporary role of artificial intelligence in architectural design.

 https://doi.org/10.3390/buildings16112106

2. Applied—searching for a methodology integrating artificial intelligence methods to solve specific design problems.
3. Educational—transforming architectural education towards human–AI collaboration.
4. Collaborative—identifying gaps in combining AI-based computational analysis with expert assessment.

In other words, this collection of articles provides a comprehensive overview of the current state of AI research in architecture and interior design, highlighting both the significant progress achieved and the important challenges that remain to be addressed. From a more detailed perspective, it presents the transformative impact of AI on the entire lifecycle of an architectural project, from early concept generation through heritage conservation to post-occupancy evaluation.

Looking forward, several key directions emerge for future research in AI and architectural design. First, there is a critical need to develop more controllable and interpretable generative AI models that can better respect architectural constraints and design intent. While current models excel at generating esthetically pleasing images, they often struggle with precise control over functional parameters such as spatial relationships, structural integrity, and building code compliance [11]. Second, further research is needed to develop seamless integration between AI tools and existing BIM and CAD workflows, enabling bidirectional data exchange and preserving design intent throughout the design process [12]. Third, there is an urgent need to address the ethical implications of AI in architecture, including issues of authorship, intellectual property, algorithmic bias, and the potential impact on employment in the design professions [13]. Fourth, future research should explore the potential of AI to address global challenges such as climate change, urbanization, and social inequality by enabling more sustainable, equitable, and resilient design solutions [14]. Finally, there is a need for continued interdisciplinary collaboration between architects, computer scientists, engineers, and social scientists to ensure that AI technologies are developed and deployed in ways that serve human needs and enhance the quality of the built environment [15].

In conclusion, this Special Issue demonstrates that artificial intelligence is no longer a futuristic concept but a rapidly evolving reality that is fundamentally reshaping architectural practice. While significant challenges remain, the potential benefits of AI in terms of increased efficiency, enhanced creativity, and improved design quality are undeniable. As the articles in this Special Issue illustrate, the most promising path forward is not one of AI replacing human designers, but rather one of human–AI collaboration, where each partner contributes their unique strengths to create better, more sustainable, and more human-centered buildings and cities. We hope that this collection of research will inspire further innovation and dialog in this exciting and rapidly evolving field.

Funding: This research was funded by the National Natural Science Foundation of China, grant number 52578016; Natural Science Foundation of Hunan Province, grant number 2025JJ50234; Science and Technology Program Project of Hunan Province, grant number 2025RC3096.

Acknowledgments: We sincerely thank the authors for their valuable contributions and high-quality submissions to this Special Issue. We are equally grateful to the reviewers for their diligent and constructive feedback, which greatly improved every paper. Finally, we extend our appreciation to the editorial team of *Buildings* for their professional support, which was key to the success of this Special Issue.

Conflicts of Interest: The authors declare no conflicts of interest.

https://doi.org/10.3390/buildings16112106

List of Contributions:

1. Hong, S.M.; Choo, S. Systematic Parameter Optimization for LoRA-Based Architectural Massing Generation Using Diffusion Models. *Buildings* **2025**, *15*, 3477. https://doi.org/10.3390/buildings15193477.
2. Wang, X.; Zhao, Y.; Zhang, W.; Li, Y.; Shi, X.; Xia, R.; Su, Y.; Li, X.; Xu, X. Artificial Intelligence-Based Architectural Design (AIAD): An Influence Mechanism Analysis for the NewTechnology Using the Hybrid Multi-Criteria Decision-Making Framework. *Buildings* **2025**, *15*, 3898. https://doi.org/10.3390/buildings15213898.
3. Nam, H.; Park, D.Y. Screen Façade Pattern Design Driven by Generative Adversarial Networks and Machine Learning Classification for the Evaluation of a Daylight Environment. *Buildings* **2025**, *15*, 4056. https://doi.org/10.3390/buildings15224056.
4. Mehraban, M.H.; Mirzabeigi, S.; Wang, M.; Liu, R.; Sepasgozar, S.M.E. Automated Image to-BIM Using Neural Radiance Fields and Vision-Language Semantic Modeling. *Buildings* **2025**, *15*, 4549. https://doi.org/10.3390/buildings15244549.
5. Zhong, J.; Luo, R.; Li, P.; Li T, Zeng, P.; Lei, Z.; Feng, T.; Yin, J. FP-MAE: A Self-Supervised Model for Floorplan Generation with Incomplete Inputs. *Buildings* **2026**, *16*, 558. https://doi.org/10.3390/buildings16030558.
6. Lim, H.; Yoon, H.J. Post-Pandemic Trends in Residential Space Design: An Analysis Using Deep Learning and Expert Evaluation. *Buildings* **2026**, *16*, 589. https://doi.org/10.3390/buildings16030589.
7. Zhang, L.; Tang, C.; Ye, Y.; Yang, J.; Xu, F. Intelligent HBIM Framework for Group-Oriented Preventive Protection: A Case Study of the Suopo Ancient Watchtower Complex in Danba. *Buildings* **2026**, *16*, 995. https://doi.org/10.3390/buildings16050995.
8. Liang, L.; Li, X.; Liu, S.; Guo, Z.; Tang, S.; Wen, B. Integrating Computer Vision and GIS for Large-Scale Morphological Mapping and Driving Force Analysis of Vernacular Courtyard Dwellings. *Buildings* **2026**, *16*, 1118. https://doi.org/10.3390/buildings16061118.
9. Alana, H.; Fikry, M.; Hasan, A. Human–AI Collaborative Design in Architectural Studios: Evaluating Paradigm Shifts Across the Six Stages of the Design Process. *Buildings* **2026**, *16*, 1445. https://doi.org/10.3390/buildings16071445.
10. Han, Y.; Jeong, J. Leveraging Generative AI for High-Fidelity 360° Spatial Images: Methodological Validation for Use as Experimental Stimuli. *Buildings* **2026**, *16*, 1679. https://doi.org/10.3390/buildings16091679.

References

1. Lawson, B. *How Designers Think*; Butterworth Architecture: Oxford, UK, 2001.
2. Suwa, M.; Gero, J.; Purcell, T. Unexpected discoveries and S-invention of design requirements: Important vehicles for a design process. *Des. Stud.* **2000**, *21*, 536–567. [CrossRef]
3. Zhuang, X.; Zhu, P.; Yang, A.; Caldas, L. Machine learning for generative architectural design: Advancements, opportunities, and challenges. *Autom. Constr.* **2025**, *174*, 106129. [CrossRef]
4. Goodfellow, I.; Pouget-Abadie, J.; Mirza, M.; Xu, B.; Warde-Farley, D.; Ozair, S.; Courville, A.; Bengio, Y. Generative adversarial networks. *Commun. ACM* **2020**, *63*, 139–144. [CrossRef]
5. Girin, L.; Leglaive, S.; Bie, X.; Diard, J.; Hueber, T.; Alameda-Pineda, X. Dynamical variational autoencoders: A comprehensive review. *Found. Trends Mach. Learn.* **2022**, *15*, 1–175. [CrossRef]
6. Ho, J.; Jain, A.; Abbeel, P. Denoising diffusion probabilistic models. *Adv. Neural Inf. Process. Syst.* **2020**, *33*, 6840–6851.
7. Yiannoudes, S. Shaping architecture with generative artificial intelligence: Deep learning models in architectural design workflow. *Architecture* **2025**, *5*, 94. [CrossRef]
8. Almaz, A.F.; El-Agouz, E.A.E.-A.; Abdelfatah, M.T.; Mohamed, I.R. The future role of artificial intelligence (AI) design's integration into architectural and interior design education is to improve efficiency, sustainability, and creativity. *Civ. Eng. Archit.* **2024**, *12*, 1749–1772. [CrossRef]
9. Maurício, J.; Domingues, I.; Bernardino, J. Comparing vision transformers and convolutional neural networks for image classification: A literature review. *Appl. Sci.* **2023**, *13*, 5521. [CrossRef]
10. Fernandes, D.; Garg, S.; Nikkel, M.; Guven, G. A GPT-powered assistant for real-time interaction with building information models. *Buildings* **2024**, *14*, 2499. [CrossRef]
11. Bagasi, O.; Nawari, N.O.; Alsaffar, A. BIM and AI in Early Design Stage: Advancing Architect–Client Communication. *Buildings* **2025**, *15*, 1977. [CrossRef]

https://doi.org/10.3390/buildings16112106

12. Kutá, D.; Faltejsek, M. The role of artificial intelligence in the transformation of the BIM environment: Current state and future trends. *Appl. Sci.* **2025**, *15*, 9956. [CrossRef]
13. Oluwagbemiga, A. The role of artificial intelligence in enhancing design innovation and sustainability. *Smart Des. Policies* **2024**, *1*, 6–14.
14. Suleimany, M.; Gonbad, M.R.S.; Naghibizadeh, S.; Niri, S.D. Artificial intelligence as a tool for building more resilient cities in the climate change era: A systematic literature review. In *Artificial Intelligence and Machine Learning Applications for Sustainable Development*; CRC Press: Boca Raton, FL, USA, 2025; pp. 60–81.
15. Onatayo, D.; Onososen, A.; Oyediran, A.O.; Oyediran, H.; Arowoiya, V.; Onatayo, E. Generative AI applications in architecture, engineering, and construction: Trends, implications for practice, education & imperatives for upskilling—A review. *Architecture* **2024**, *4*, 877–902. [CrossRef]

https://doi.org/10.3390/buildings16112106

buildings

MDPI

Article

Systematic Parameter Optimization for LoRA-Based Architectural Massing Generation Using Diffusion Models

Soon Min Hong and Seungyeon Choo *

School of Architecture, Kyungpook National University, Daegu 41566, Republic of Korea; soonmin_hong@knu.ac.kr
* Correspondence: choo@knu.ac.kr; Tel.: +82-53-950-6414

Abstract: This study addresses the systematic optimization of Low-Rank Adaptation (LoRA) parameters for architectural knowledge integration in diffusion models, where existing AI research has provided limited guidance for establishing plausible parameter ranges in architectural massing applications. While diffusion models show increasing utilization in architectural design, general models lack domain-specific architectural knowledge, and previous studies have offered insufficient hyperparameter optimization frameworks for architectural massing studies—fundamental components for expressing architectural knowledge. This research establishes a comprehensive LoRA training framework specifically for architectural mass generation, systematically evaluating caption detail levels, optimizers, learning rates, schedulers, batch sizes, and training steps. Through analysis of 220 architectural mass images representing spatial transformation operations, the study recommends the following parameter settings: detailed captions, Adafactor optimizer, learning rate 0.0003, constant scheduler, and batch size 4, achieving significant improvements in prompt-to-output fidelity compared to baseline approaches. The contribution of this study is not in introducing a new algorithm, but in providing a systematic application of LoRA in the architectural domain, serving as a bridging milestone for both emerging architectural-AI researchers and advanced scholars. The findings provide practical guidelines for integrating AI technologies into architectural design workflows, while demonstrating how systematic parameter optimization can enhance the learning of architectural knowledge and support architects in early-stage massing and design decision-making.

Keywords: architectural AI; diffusion model; LoRA technique; architectural mass generation; human-AI interaction

1. Introduction

1.1. Research Background and Objectives

Recent advancements in AI technology have increased its potential for application across industrial sectors, stimulating related research and development. Carpo [1] describes this progress as "the second coming of AI", emphasizing that technologies once considered impossible are now becoming reality.

In architecture, AI adoption is also accelerating. Platforms such as Spacemaker, an AI-based design environment for multi-family housing development acquired by Autodesk in 2020, exemplify how AI can improve design efficiency while enabling broader participation in the design process [2]. Beyond such platforms, research on automation and AI-driven image generation is expanding, laying the groundwork for AI-based architectural design environments [3,4].

Diffusion models, which generate images through iterative denoising, have gained significant attention in architectural design for their stability and diversity of outputs compared to Generative Adversarial Networks (GANs) [5,6]. These advantages make them suitable for automating early-stage design tasks and exploring diverse alternatives, and they are already being applied by leading firms such as Morphosis Architects, Coop Himmelb(l)au, MVRDV, and Zaha Hadid Architects [7].

However, diffusion models commonly used in design workflows remain limited in handling domain-specific architectural tasks due to insufficient incorporation of architectural knowledge [8]. Fine-tuning approaches such as Low-Rank Adaptation (LoRA) offer a potential solution, but prior studies provide only limited systematic guidance on how to configure plausible parameter ranges in architectural contexts [9,10]. As highlighted in related research, inappropriate hyperparameter settings can lead to unstable learning or outright failure [11].

Architectural massing studies—concerned with spatial relationships, geometric transformations, and formative logic—represent a fundamental medium for expressing architectural knowledge [12]. Yet systematic parameter optimization frameworks tailored to massing applications remain underexplored, despite their central role in early-stage architectural design.

Therefore, this study aims to explore effective ways to learn architectural knowledge related to architectural mass generation using the LoRA technique based on Diffusion models. Rather than simply applying existing methods, this study systematically constructs an architectural mass-specific dataset and optimizes hyperparameters to tailor AI models for early-stage architectural design workflows. The goal is to analyze the impact of LoRA hyperparameters configurations on architectural knowledge acquisition and recommend parameter settings within the experimental scope for architectural mass generation. This is expected to increase the practical applicability of AI technology in the early stages of architectural design and enhance design efficiency through human-AI interaction. The contribution of this study is not in developing a new optimization algorithm but in systematically applying LoRA to embed architectural massing knowledge into diffusion models. This novelty lies in the disciplinary and methodological framing: it provides a structured reference for fine-tuning practices in architectural contexts, thereby serving as a bridging milestone for both emerging architectural-AI researchers and advanced scholars. To this end, the following research question has been established: "How can architectural knowledge be systematically fine-tuned through the LoRA technique so that diffusion models are not only optimized in terms of technical performance but also capable of producing architecturally meaningful massing outputs that support human–AI interaction in early-stage design?"

1.2. Research Scope and Method

This study is confined to architectural knowledge, particularly focusing on architectural mass generation in the early stages of architectural design. It excludes elements such as exterior finishing materials or facades. All outputs generated and analyzed are 2D images, and no 3D models were produced. Evaluations are therefore based solely on visual analysis of 2D architectural mass forms. This clarification ensures that the methodological scope aligns with the objectives of evaluating LoRA-based Diffusion models for image-level generative tasks. The Diffusion model used in this study is the realisticVisionV51_v51VAE model, which is versatile and suitable for architectural research due to its flexibility in parameter adjustment. For generating LoRA checkpoint files, the widely used Python library Kohya_ss was employed.

It should be noted that this study is confined to 2D image-based massing exploration, which is both a limitation and a necessary first step. While 3D models and façade-level applications are excluded from the present scope, these remain essential directions for future work, as evidenced by recent façade-focused research [13]. At the same time, this 2D scope inevitably restricts external validity, since practical architectural massing workflows involve 3D modeling, site constraints, and schematic CAD inputs that are not addressed in the present study.

The RealisticVisionV51_v51VAE model and the Kohya_ss library were chosen for their widespread adoption and flexibility in parameter adjustment, which make them suitable for architectural image experiments and consistent with the objectives of this study.

The research method consists of three main stages:

First, we analyze the theoretical background on architectural knowledge learning for human-AI interaction and review previous studies related to architectural image generation based on Diffusion models, with the purpose of establishing a conceptual baseline for subsequent experiments.

Second, we construct scenarios for the fine-tuning technique LoRA in order to systematically examine the influence of different hyperparameter settings. To achieve this, we perform (a) Caption Level comparison, (b) Optimizer comparison, (c) Learning Rate comparison, (d) LR Scheduler comparison, (e) Batch Size comparison, and (f) Training Steps analysis to derive key elements of the learning scenario.

Third, we comprehensively evaluate the model outputs using both qualitative and quantitative methods, with the purpose of identifying parameter settings that balance technical fidelity with architectural design relevance. Specifically, we conduct (1) quantitative evaluation through CLIP score analysis to measure the semantic alignment between prompts and generated architectural mass images, and LPIPS, which provides a complementary measure of perceptual similarity against teacher images; and (2) qualitative evaluation based on the visual clarity of architectural mass and the reflection of prompts. Additionally, we compare the performance of the fine-tuned LoRA models with that of the original, unfine-tuned Diffusion model (without LoRA) to verify the learning effectiveness of architectural mass-related knowledge.

Through this process, we identify the optimal settings for LoRA parameter settings in architectural mass-related knowledge learning.

2. Theoretical Background and Literature Review

2.1. Fine-Tuning for Architectural Knowledge

Adjusting general AI models to fit specific domains for architectural knowledge learning is essential, and one of the main methods for this is fine-tuning. Fine-tuning is the process of adjusting a pre-trained model to suit a specific task or dataset, adding new knowledge suitable for new data while maintaining the general knowledge learned in the existing model [14]. However, existing research has provided limited systematic guidance for establishing plausible parameter ranges for fine-tuning in architectural contexts, with researchers noting that "in many cases, engineers rely on the trial-and-error method to manually tune hyperparameters" [11].

This fine-tuning is effective and widely used as it can improve performance for specific domains with relatively small amounts of data [15,16]. Yet systematic parameter optimization frameworks specifically for architectural applications remain limited, with building applications demonstrating that "the performance of DRL is highly sensitive to hyper-parameters, and selecting inappropriate hyper-parameters may lead to unstable learning or even failure" [9].

LoRA is a lightweight fine-tuning method developed to overcome the limitations of extensive computational requirements and storage space demanded by traditional fine-tuning techniques. As shown in Figure 1, LoRA proceeds with learning by adding small low-rank matrices while keeping the pre-trained weights intact, instead of updating all parameters of the model [17]. This LoRA technique saves computing resources such as GPU memory, reduces learning time, and facilitates easy switching between various tasks as the learning results are stored as LoRA checkpoint files, eliminating the need to generate the entire model anew. In other words, LoRA can be considered an efficient fine-tuning method that can perform domain-specific learning while maintaining the performance of the existing model [17].

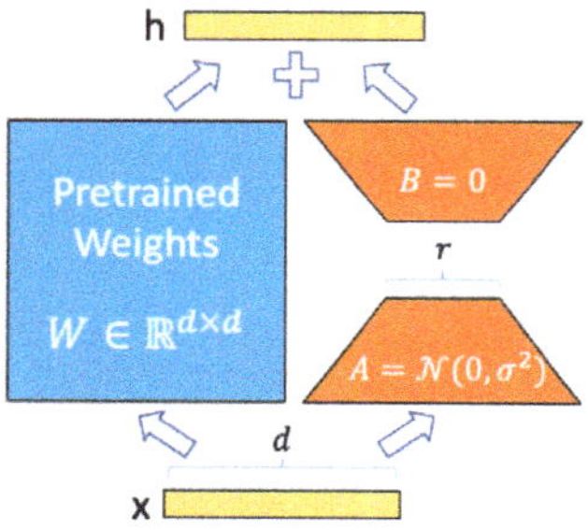

Figure 1. The basic structure of LoRA: only the low-rank matrices A and B are trained. Adapted from He et al. [17].

Compared with other fine-tuning methods such as full fine-tuning, DreamBooth, or ControlNet, LoRA offers clear advantages in efficiency and modularity. Full fine-tuning requires updating all model parameters, which is computationally expensive and less practical for rapid architectural prototyping. DreamBooth and ControlNet provide stronger task-specific control but demand larger datasets and higher computational resources. By contrast, LoRA enables lightweight, domain-specific adaptation with minimal resource requirements, making it particularly suitable for early-stage architectural massing studies.

Given these comparative advantages, digitizing architectural knowledge becomes all the more essential for enabling AI-based design environments. Bernstein [18] emphasized the importance of organizing architectural data and converting it into learnable structures to implement AI-based design environments. This data conversion process forms the basis for AI to effectively learn architectural knowledge and collaborate with architects in the design decision-making process.

Beyond this, computational design theory also provides an important historical context for understanding how design knowledge can be formalized. Shape grammars established rule-based generative processes [19], and parametricism emphasized the role of parameters in structuring design [20]. These approaches resonate with diffusion-based fine-tuning, where captions and prompts function as descriptors that guide generative outputs.

In this study, we further define architectural knowledge as the structured representation of spatial relationships, geometric transformations, and formative logics that underpin design reasoning, as elaborated in Hong [21]. This definition clarifies how LoRA-based fine-tuning embeds architectural reasoning into diffusion models, ensuring that our methodological framework is anchored in a coherent theoretical foundation.

The LoRA technique can fine-tune AI models to suit specific architectural design environments, generating architectural masses and forms in the early stages of architectural design and presenting new design paradigms for human-AI collaboration. Therefore, this study aims to explore effective methods of learning architectural knowledge using the LoRA technique, thereby enhancing creativity and efficiency in AI-assisted architectural design processes and supporting effective human-AI interaction in design workflows.

2.2. *Diffusion Models in Architectural Image Generation*

Diffusion models, a recently emerged deep learning-based generative model, have gained attention for surpassing the performance of existing Generative Adversarial Networks (GANs) in image synthesis [22]. These models are applied to various tasks beyond image synthesis, including machine vision, natural language processing, and multi-modal learning, with active research and technological development in interdisciplinary fields, including architecture [15].

According to del Campo [22], the origin of diffusion models stems from image caption generation research. ImageNet dataset contains 14,197,122 annotated images according to the WordNet hierarchy. Since 2010 the dataset has been used in the ImageNet Large Scale Visual Recognition Challenge (ILSVRC), a benchmark in image classification and object detection. The publicly released dataset contains a set of manually annotated training images [23]. ImageNet laid the foundation for developing algorithms capable of describing images. By 2016, algorithms transitioning from image analysis to generation emerged, presenting the initial concept of generating images from textual scene descriptions [24,25]. This development led to the birth of diffusion models, generally defined as probabilistic generative models that operate by injecting noise into images and gradually removing it.

Diffusion models can be particularly useful tools in the architectural design field for quickly generating images that visualize initial design ideas, helping to concretize or develop creative concepts. Various studies are being conducted using diffusion models in the architectural design field, including text-to-image and image-to-image generation.

Unlike conventional GAN-based generation models, diffusion models offer higher output stability and better prompt controllability, making them more suitable for creative and iterative design processes. Moreover, their structure allows for relatively straightforward integration with fine-tuning techniques such as LoRA and ControlNet, which have enabled their rapid adoption in architecture-related workflows. However, most studies in this domain remain focused on the visual output and creative utility of diffusion models, rather than on systematic learning of architectural knowledge embedded in image-caption data or prompt structures.

A range of studies illustrates how diffusion models are being integrated into architectural workflows. Çelik's [26] research reinterpreted Andrea Palladio's form grammar through text-to-image generation, highlighting AI's potential in conceptual design while also stressing the continuing need for human intervention in functional design aspects. Building on this idea of concept exploration, Horvath & Pouliou [27] leveraged eVolo skyscraper competition data to investigate how prompts influence architectural form generation, reinforcing the role of diffusion models as early-stage visualization tools.

Moving beyond general form generation, Kim et al. [8] proposed the Text2Form Diffusion framework to incorporate architectural vocabulary via fine-tuning, showcasing how dataset construction and parameter optimization could lead to more refined outputs. Complementing this, Wu [28] addressed architectural style generation using the ArchDiff model, which demonstrated enhanced consistency and stylistic clarity by combining image-text pairs in a large-scale dataset.

Subsequent research has aimed to enhance control and customization. Ma & Zheng [29] integrated LoRA and ControlNet into Stable Diffusion to generate text-based architectural facades, balancing stylistic diversity with geometric consistency. Similarly, Yoo & Lee [30] focused on exterior visualization of single-family houses, using generative AI and LoRA fine-tuning to tailor design outputs to specific user preferences.

Collectively, prior research demonstrates that diffusion models and fine-tuning techniques hold considerable promise for early-stage architectural design, offering the capacity to generate diverse and creative alternatives. Nevertheless, most of these studies have remained oriented toward aesthetic visualization or stylistic adaptation, and only a few have provided systematic guidance on how domain-specific architectural knowledge might be formally encoded and optimized within such models. The present study addresses this gap by advancing a structured framework for LoRA-based parameter optimization tailored to architectural massing. In doing so, it explicitly links hyperparameter configurations with the architectural relevance of generated outputs, thereby distinguishing itself from prior approaches and underscoring both methodological rigor and design-oriented significance.

Therefore, based on the importance of digital modeling mentioned by Steenson [31], this study aims to focus on generating architectural masses using AI models. We intend to explore ways to learn architectural knowledge through the LoRA technique and generate architectural mass images reflecting the morphological characteristics of architecture by applying LoRA to diffusion models.

3. Methodology for Architectural Knowledge Learning Using LoRA Technique

3.1. *LoRA Training Method*

3.1.1. Training Environment and Tool

For LoRA training in this study, an AMD EPYC 7352 24-Core Processor (Advanced Micro Devices, Santa Clara, CA, USA) and an NVIDIA Quadro RTX 6000 (NVDIA Corporation, Santa Clara, CA, USA; 24 GB VRAM) were utilized. Model training and data processing were conducted in a Python 3.10.11 environment. The base model employed was RealisticVisionV51_v51VAE, which is based on Stable Diffusion 1.5 (SD 1.5). This model allows for optimized learning in specific domains with minimal data, making it applicable in various fields such as architectural design, medical imaging, and art. Kohya_ss was used for LoRA training. This tool supports dataset preprocessing, hyperparameter setting, and visualization of the learning process. It provides an intuitive learning environment through a Web UI. This configuration was selected to ensure sufficient computational capacity for diffusion model training while remaining accessible and reproducible for architectural researchers.

3.1.2. Training Procedure

The main procedures for LoRA training are illustrated in Figure 2. First, the essential task that must be completed before LoRA learning is building an image dataset. After collecting and preprocessing architectural mass images, an image-caption dataset is constructed through a captioning process that describes the images. Second, in LoRA training, multiple LoRA checkpoint files are generated by setting various hyperparameters such as Caption Level, Optimizer, Learning Rate, LR Scheduler, Batch Size, and Training Steps. In this process, the model is trained by applying various settings, and each checkpoint is learned according to different hyperparameter configurations. Third, architectural mass images are generated using the created LoRA checkpoint files, and the quality of the generated images is compared and analyzed. In this process, the impact of each hyperparameter combination on the generation results is evaluated to derive the optimal settings. Finally, based on the analysis results of the loss graphs, a LoRA checkpoint file specialized for generating architectural mass images is ultimately created through optimized hyperparameter settings.

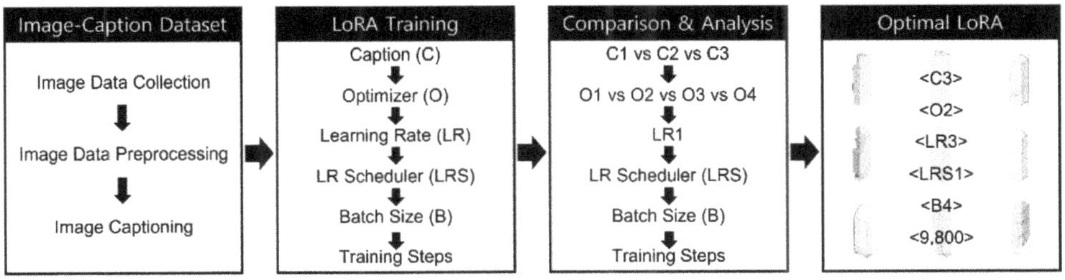

Figure 2. Diagram of the LoRA training procedure.

3.2. Building of Architectural Mass Image-Caption Dataset

3.2.1. Image Data Collection and Preprocessing

In this study, architectural mass images were collected from two sources: Operative Design: A Catalogue of Spatial Verbs by Di Mari & Yoo [32], and Conditional Design: An Introduction to Elemental Architecture by Di Mari [33]. The book Operative Design illustrates the process of architectural form transformation through spatial verbs such as extrude, merge, and twist, represented as geometric mass forms. It explores the investigation of form transformation within the architectural design process. Additionally, Conditional Design focuses on various spatial conditions that arise as a result of operative design. This book addresses changes in mass forms and components, exploring design approaches that respond to surrounding environments and contexts through processes where masses intersect, merge, and spaces connect or gain openness.

The architectural mass images collected from these books effectively illustrate spatial and operative verbs along with mass forms as text-image pairs, making them suitable data for learning architectural knowledge related to building masses. Each collected image was preprocessed to a resolution of 150 dpi and a size of 1024 × 1024 pixels to optimize for learning, resulting in a dataset of 220 images as shown in Table 1.

Table 1. Example of image dataset *.

Expand	Extrude	Inflate	Branch	Merge
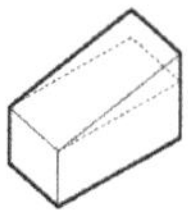	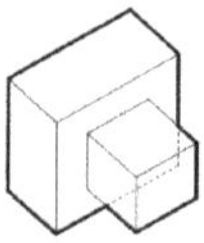	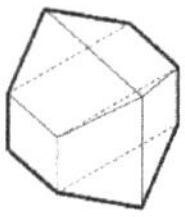	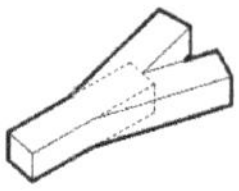	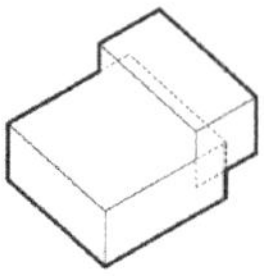
Nest	**Bend**	**Skew**	**Twist**	**Interlock**
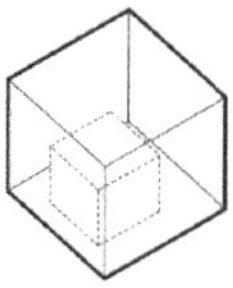	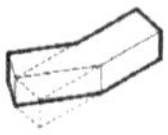	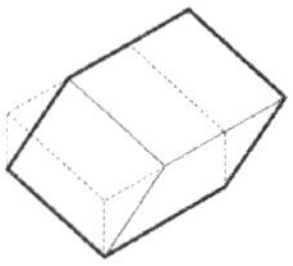	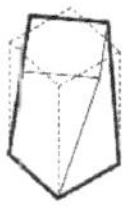	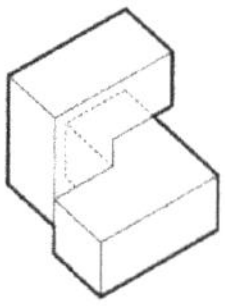
Intersect	**Lift**	**Lodge**	**Overlap**	**Rotate**
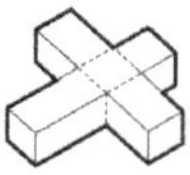	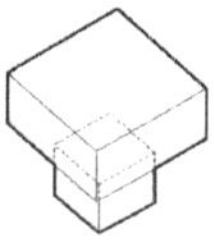	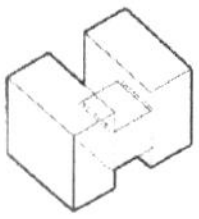	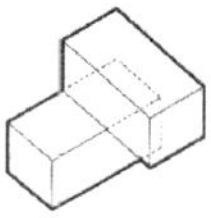	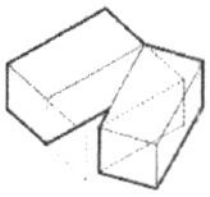
Shift	**Carve**	**Compress**	**Fracture**	**Grade**
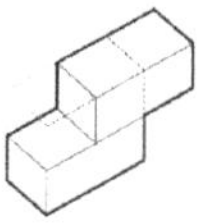	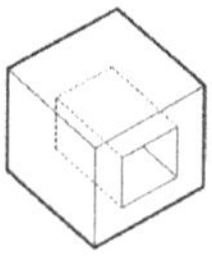	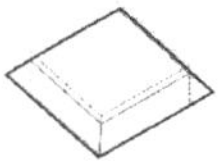	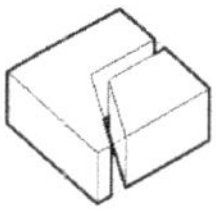	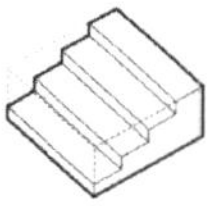
Notch	**Pinch**	**Shear**	**Taper**	**Embed**
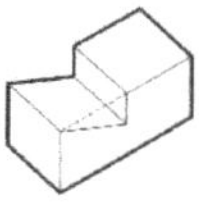	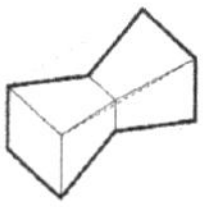	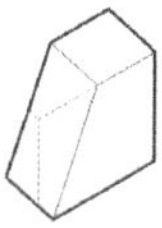	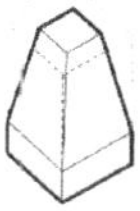	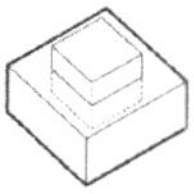
Extract	**Inscribe**	**Puncture**	**Split**	**Reflect + Expand**
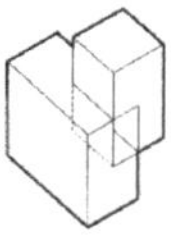	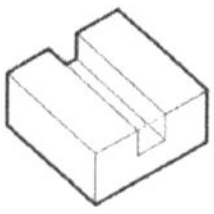	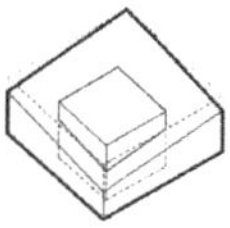	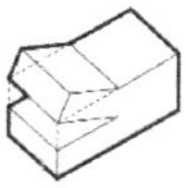	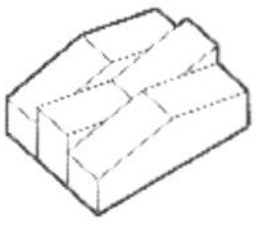
Pack + Inflate	**Array + Stack + Rotate**	**Array + Taper**	**Join + Array + Pinch**	**Join + Split**
	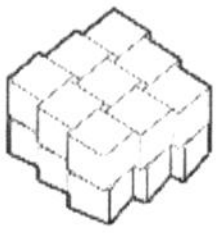	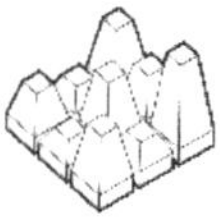	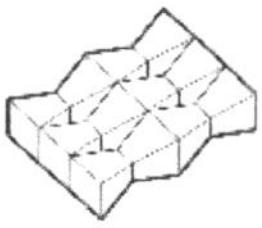	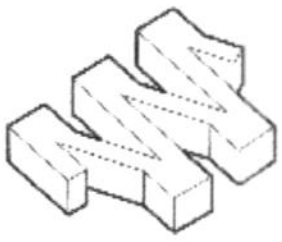

* The images in Table 1 were redrawn and adapted from the original sources to clearly illustrate architectural mass transformations as spatial verbs, with all images preprocessed to 150 dpi resolution and 1024 × 1024-pixel dimensions to optimize them for LoRA training procedures.

3.2.2. Image Captioning

Image captioning assigns textual descriptions to images so models can better interpret them and align prompts with visual elements [34]. Kohya_ss supports AI-based automatic captioning functions like Bootstrapping Language-Image Pre-training (BLIP), allowing for fast and efficient image captioning. However, automatically generated captions have limitations in fully reflecting detailed features and diverse descriptions of images [35]. Therefore, to create more accurate captions, it is necessary to manually complement the automatically generated captions [34].

In this study, initial captions were generated using ChatGPT-4o to produce text based on each image's spatial characteristics. ChatGPT-4o was chosen due to its contextual language generation capabilities, especially for domain-specific captioning in architecture. As shown in Table 2, we uploaded architectural mass images to ChatGPT-4o to generate descriptive captions, then manually reviewed and edited them to ensure terminological and conceptual accuracy. To further ensure reproducibility, we adopted a fixed template of seven descriptive elements—subject, medium, environment, lighting, color, mood, and composition—and applied it consistently across all captions.

Table 2. Examples of image captioning using ChatGPT-4o.

	Expand	**Extrude**
ChatGPT-4o	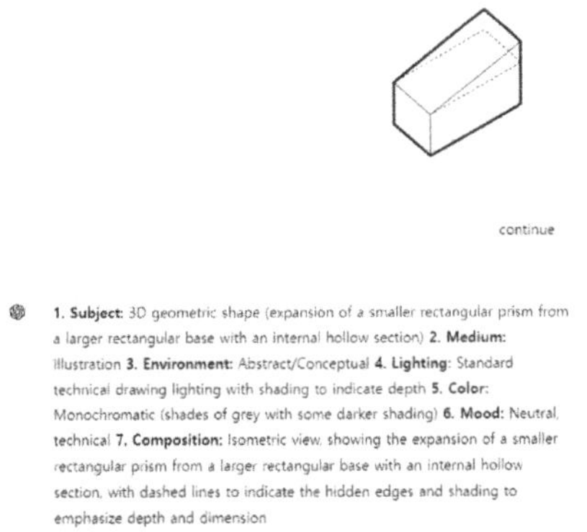	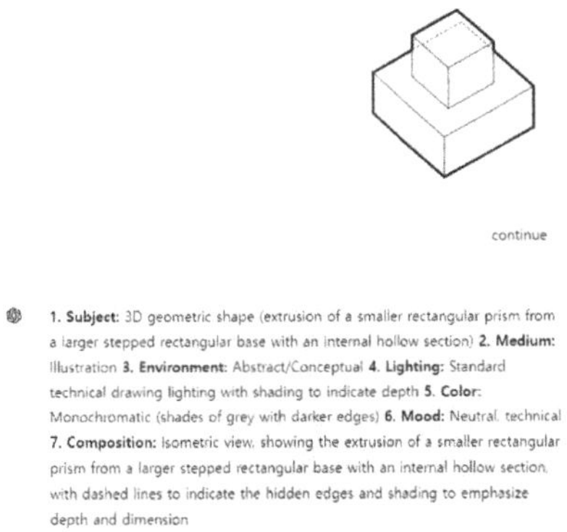
Common	2. Medium: illustration 3. Environment: Abstract/Conceptual 4. Lighting: Standard technical drawing lighting with shading to indicate depth 5. Color: Monochromatic (shades of grey with some darker shading/edges) 6. Mood: Neutral, technical	
Feature	1. Subject: 3D geometric shape (expansion of a smaller rectangular prism from a larger rectangular base with an internal hollow section)	1. Subject: 3D geometric shape (extrusion of a smaller rectangular prism from a larger stepped rectangular base with an internal hollow section)
	7. Composition: Isometric view, showing the expansion of a smaller rectangular prism from a larger rectangular base with an internal hollow section, with dashed lines to indicate the hidden edges and shading to emphasize depth and dimension	7. Composition: Isometric view, showing the extrusion of a smaller rectangular prism from a larger stepped rectangular base with an internal hollow section, with dashed lines to indicate the hidden edges and shading to emphasize depth and dimension

According to Chang & Han [36], in the field of architectural design, it is important to consider various aspects of prompt types and compositions for effective image generation.

These include elements such as Subject, Medium, Environment, Lighting, Color, Mood, and Visual Composition. 'Medium', 'Environment', 'Lighting', 'Color', and 'Mood' were summarized as common caption elements, while 'Subject' and 'Composition', being important items describing specific features of architectural masses, were manually reviewed and modified to improve the accuracy of the captions.

Furthermore, to analyze the impact of image-caption detail level on LoRA learning, this study constructed datasets divided into three levels, as shown in Table 3. The first is a no caption dataset learning only images, the second is a simple caption dataset using brief text, and the third is a detailed caption dataset including comprehensive descriptions. The detailed captions in Table 3 were initially generated using ChatGPT-4o and subsequently edited for clarity and domain accuracy. Through this, we aim to evaluate the performance of the LoRA technique according to the level of caption detail.

Table 3. Examples of image-caption dataset.

Image	Caption Level		
	No	Simple	Detailed
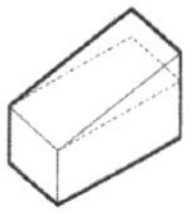	-	expand	expand, expansion of a smaller rectangular prism from a larger rectangular base with an internal hollow section, illustration, conceptual, standard technical drawing lighting, monochromatic, neutral mood, isometric view
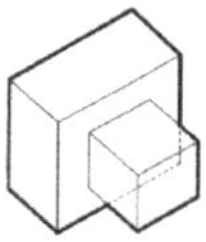	-	extrude	extrude, extrusion of a smaller rectangular prism from a larger rectangular base with an internal hollow section, illustration, conceptual, standard technical drawing lighting, monochromatic, neutral mood, isometric view
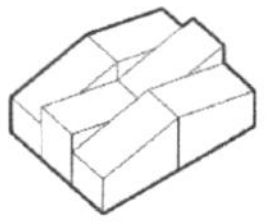	-	reflect_expand	reflect_expand, combination of reflecting and expanding rectangular prisms forming a complex, interlocked structure, illustration, conceptual, standard technical drawing lighting, monochromatic, neutral mood, isometric view
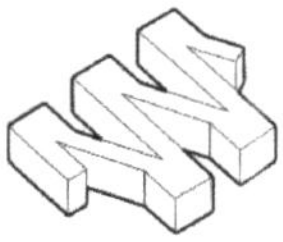	-	join_split	join_split, a joined and split rectangular prism forming a zigzag pattern, extended further, illustration, conceptual, standard technical drawing lighting, monochromatic, neutral mood, isometric view
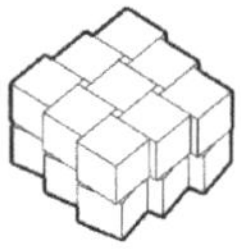	-	array, stack_rotate	array, stack_rotate, combination of stacking and rotating rectangular prisms forming a cubic, interlocked structure, illustration, conceptual, standard technical drawing lighting, monochromatic, neutral mood, isometric view
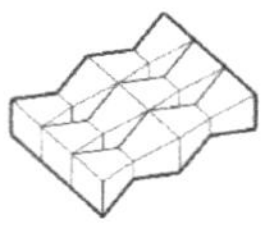	-	join, array_pinch	join, array_pinch, combination of joined and pinched rectangular prisms forming a complex, interlocked structure, illustration, conceptual, standard technical drawing lighting, monochromatic, neutral mood, isometric view

3.3. Setting of Hyperparameters

To optimize the performance and efficiency of LoRA training, we set Optimizer, Learning Rate, LR Scheduler, and Training steps as the main hyperparameters. The Optimizer is an algorithm that adjusts the model's weights to find the minimum value of the Loss Function, while the Learning Rate determines the magnitude of these weight adjustments. The LR Scheduler dynamically adjusts the Learning Rate to promote stable learning. Training steps represent the total number of times the model's parameters are updated, and are directly related to the number of images, repeats, epochs, and batch size [31]. The formula for calculating this is as follows:

$$\text{Total steps} = (\text{Number of images} \times \text{Repeats} \times \text{Epoch}) \div \text{Batch size} \quad (1)$$

Epoch represents the number of complete passes through the entire dataset, Repeats is the number of times each image is learned within one epoch, and Batch size refers to the number of images processed simultaneously in one learning session. In this study, LoRA training was conducted based on the hyperparameters presented in Table 4.

Table 4. Hyperparameter variants for LoRA trainings.

Hyperparameter	LoRA Experiment	Value
Caption	C1	No Caption
	C2	Simple Caption
	C3	Detailed Caption
Optimizer	O1	AdamW
	O2	Adafactor
	O3	Prodigy
	O4	Lion
Learning Rate	LR1	0.0001
	LR2	0.0002
	LR3	0.0003
	LR4	0.0004
LR Scheduler	LRS1	constant
	LRS2	cosine
	LRS3	linear
	LRS4	adafactor
Batch Size	B1	1
	B2	2
	B3	4
	B4	8
Training Steps	Analysis of Loss Graph	5500
		9800
		11,000

The model performance evaluation will be conducted by comparing and analyzing the results generated using img2img and inpaint with prompts set as extrude, branch, and twist, as shown in Table 5. Other LoRA training hyperparameters were fixed as presented in Table 6. In addition, LoRA-specific settings (rank r, alpha, dropout, and target modules/layers) and diffusion parameters (sampler, guidance scale, random seed, and inpaint/img2img strengths) were not the focus of this study and were therefore kept at the default values of Kohya_ss.

Table 5. Prompt and input images used for LoRA-trained model evaluation.

Prompt	img2img	Inpaint	
Extrude Branch Twist		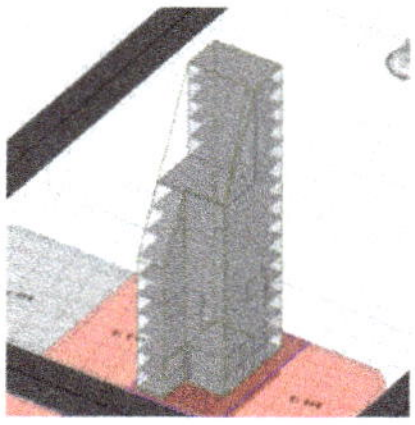	

Table 6. Hyperparameters fixed for model evaluation.

	No. Images	Optimizer	Learning Rate	LR Scheduler	Batch Size	Epoch	Repeats
value	220	Adafactor	0.0003	constant	4	5	20

In this process, it is important to note that the urban background visible in the 3D images is derived from the original input image and not from the prompts used for generation. Since the inpaint function was used to manually select and mask only the architectural mass area within the image, the generation result reflects only the prompt content applied to the selected mass. Therefore, the contextual elements or surrounding environment present in the image had no influence on the generation outcome. This ensured that the generated architectural mass forms were based solely on prompt-driven generation.

3.4. Evaluation Criteria and Metrics

To evaluate the architectural mass images generated under the parameter settings in Section 3.3, both quantitative and qualitative assessments were conducted. For each LoRA model configuration, ten images were generated per prompt, and one image with low visual noise and clearly defined geometry was selected. These selected outputs were then assessed by combining objective numerical evaluation and visual judgment, aiming to determine the most effective parameter setting for learning architectural mass-related knowledge.

The quantitative evaluation was performed using the CLIP score. The CLIP score quantifies the semantic similarity between a text prompt and an image using cosine similarity. This metric objectively measures how well the generated image aligns with its corresponding prompt. In this study, we computed the CLIP score for each image by comparing the prompt with the image features extracted using the CLIP model. The average CLIP scores for each parameter setting were used to compare model performance across configurations (Figure 3).

In addition to CLIP score, this study employed the Learned Perceptual Image Patch Similarity (LPIPS) metric as a complementary quantitative indicator. LPIPS measures perceptual similarity between generated outputs and reference teacher images based on deep feature embeddings, where lower values indicate greater visual similarity. In this study, LPIPS was computed by comparing generated architectural mass images against teacher images corresponding to the prompt operations—specifically "extrude", "branch", and "twist", as presented in Table 1. Because the teacher images are simplified line drawings without shading or background, whereas generated outputs include tonal and contextual variations, LPIPS is reported as a supplementary diagnostic metric rather than the primary decision criterion. Accordingly, CLIP score was adopted as the main indicator of prompt fidelity, while LPIPS provided additional insight into perceptual differences across model configurations.

Figure 3. Examples of CLIP score results.

Qualitative evaluation was conducted based on the visual clarity of the generated architectural masses and the degree to which the prompts were reflected. For each prompt, final images were selected by focusing on cases where the generated architectural masses best satisfied these criteria, and this process can be visually confirmed through the images presented in the following tables of Chapter 4.

4. Generation and Validation of LoRA Model Performance

4.1. Comparative Analysis Based on Architectural Mass Image-Caption Dataset

To analyze the impact of Caption Level on architectural mass image generation performance during LoRA training, three Caption levels were set (C1: No Caption, C2: Simple Caption, C3: Detailed Caption). The architectural masses generated by each model are presented in Table 7.

C1 and C2 produced forms that did not reflect the prompts. The extrusion (extrude) of the mass form was not properly executed, the branch resulted in a form closer to rotation (twist), and the rotation (twist) was not reflected at all. In contrast, C3 showed mass expressions that reflected the forms in the prompts. For extrude, a protruding mass form could be observed; for branch, an expanded form with segmentation was visible; and for twist, a form with applied torsion could be confirmed.

Table 7. Comparative results of Caption Levels (C1: No Caption, C2: Simple Caption, C3: Detailed Caption). C3 produced clearer geometric transformations (extrude, branch, twist) and achieved the highest CLIP score and lowest LPIPS score, indicating stronger prompt fidelity.

Prompt	C1	C2	C3
extrude (CLIP Score) [LPIPS Score]	 (0.2467) [0.350381] 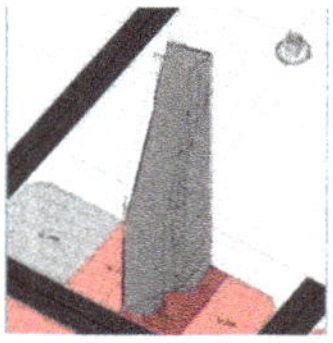 (0.2127) [0.647027]	 (0.2446) [0.346895] 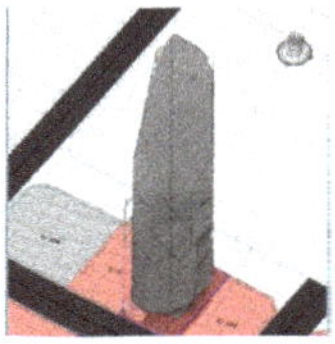 (0.2127) [0.650432]	 (0.2512) [0.353704] 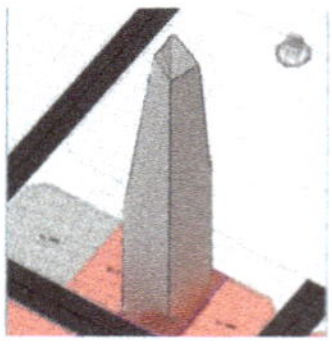 (0.2247) [0.647987]
branch (CLIP Score) [LPIPS Score]	 (0.1979) [0.326616] 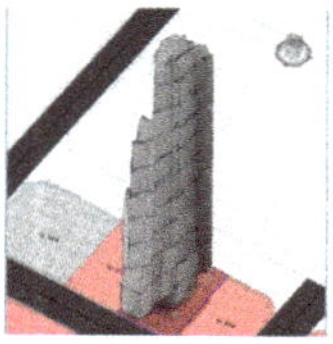 (0.1812) [0.688126]	 (0.2107) [0.333401] 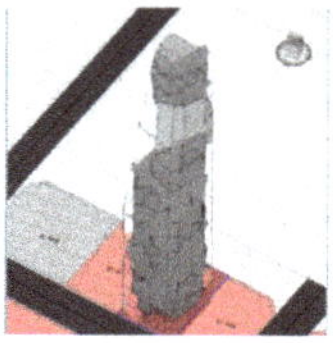 (0.1849) [0.677643]	 (0.2159) [0.326094] 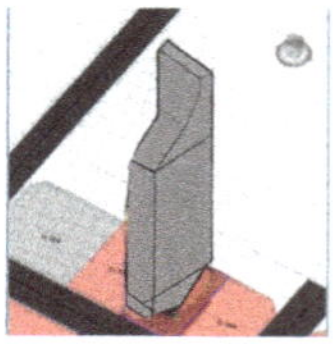 (0.1856) [0.675901]
twist (CLIP Score) [LPIPS Score]	 (0.2038) [0.214463] 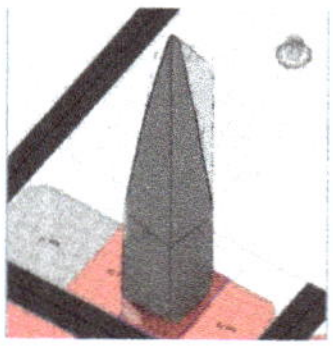 (0.1890) [0.670984]	 (0.2044) [0.191077]  (0.1914) [0.675118]	 (0.2228) [0.197385] 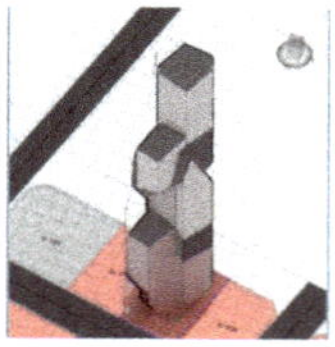 (0.1939) [0.684472]
Average CLIP Score	0.2052	0.2081	0.2157
Average LPIPS Score	0.482933	0.479108	0.481524

Quantitatively, C3 also achieved the highest average CLIP score (0.2159), compared to C2 (0.2081) and C1 (0.2052), indicating stronger alignment between prompts and outputs. By contrast, LPIPS did not follow this trend: the lowest (best) average LPIPS was observed for C2 (0.479108), followed by C3 (0.481524) and C1 (0.482933). This divergence likely reflects the domain gap between simplified teacher drawings and rendered outputs; therefore, we prioritize CLIP as the primary indicator of prompt fidelity and report LPIPS as a supplementary diagnostic measure.

Taken together, these results confirm that Detailed Captions (C3) provided the most effective learning condition. Therefore, for the LoRA training in the next chapter, we decided to select the C3 setting, Detailed Caption.

4.2. Comparative Analysis Based on LoRA Training Parameter Settings

4.2.1. Optimizer

To analyze the impact of Optimizer on model performance during LoRA training, experiments were conducted applying four different Optimizers (O1: AdamW, O2: Adafactor, O3: Prodigy, O4: Lion) as shown in Table 8.

Table 8. Comparative results of four Optimizers (O1: AdamW, O2: Adafactor, O3: Prodigy, O4: Lion). O4 achieved the highest CLIP score but generated distorted masses, while O2 provided the most balanced outputs with greater architectural fidelity, leading to its selection as the optimal optimizer.

Prompt	O1	O2	O3	O4
extrude (CLIP Score) [LPIPS Score]	 (0.2435) [0.343182] 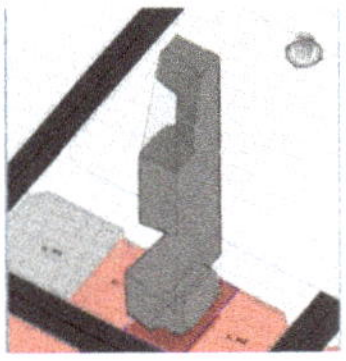 (0.2100) [0.651672]	 (0.2555) [0.349378] 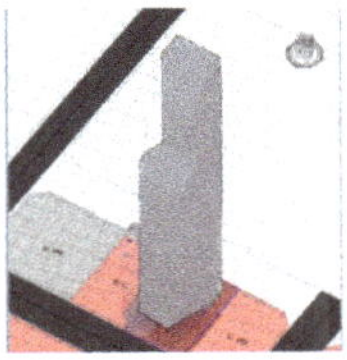 (0.2177) [0.645908]	 (0.2433) [0.354583]  (0.2016) [0.648482]	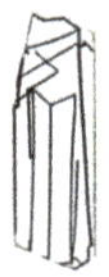 (0.2481) [0.363083] 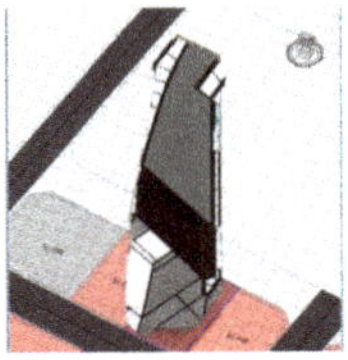 (0.2166) [0.651206]

Table 8. *Cont.*

Prompt	O1	O2	O3	O4
		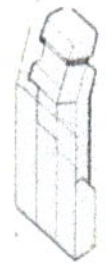		
branch (CLIP Score) [LPIPS Score]	(0.1766) [0.343366]	(0.2135) [0.333571]	(0.1943) [0.337466]	(0.2280) [0.344603]
	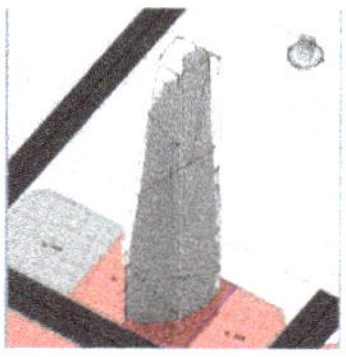		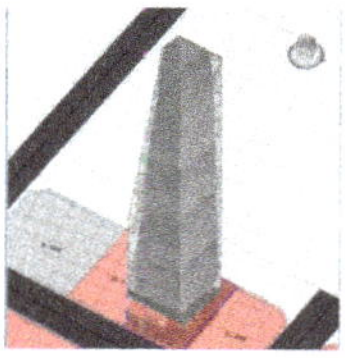	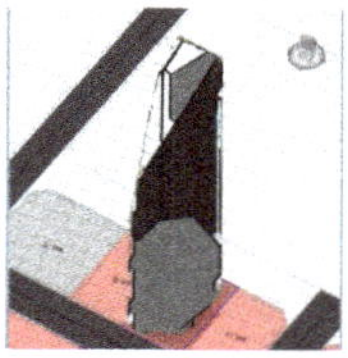
	(0.1905) [0.674829]	(0.1920) [0.677852]	(0.1792) [0.678657]	(0.1913) [0.673498]
	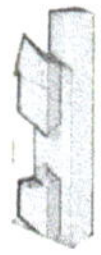			
twist (CLIP Score) [LPIPS Score]	(0.1901) [0.214797]	(0.2165) [0.214462]	(0.1961) [0.212614]	(0.2188) [0.219594]
	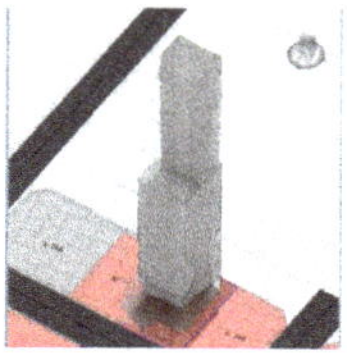	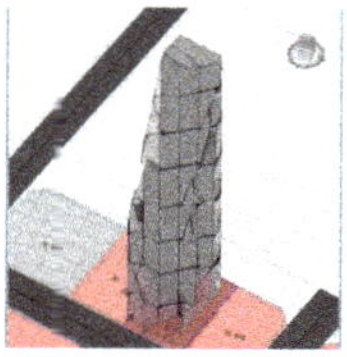	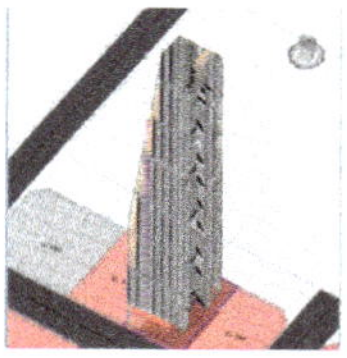	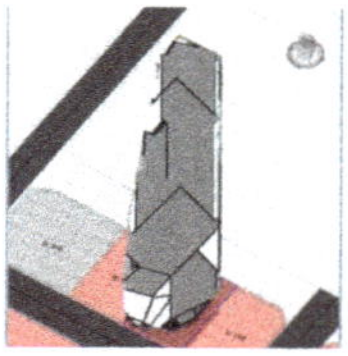
	(0.1813) [0.675989]	(0.1888) [0.676852]	(0.1857) [0.686007]	(0.1950) [0.675635]
Average CLIP Score	0.1987	0.2140	0.2000	0.2163
Average LPIPS Score	0.483972	0.483004	0.486301	0.487936

Analysis results showed that O1 and O3 generated mass transformations that did not clearly reflect the prompts, while O4 produced masses with visually distorted or overly abstracted masses. Although O4 achieved the highest average CLIP score (0.2163), the resulting shapes lacked clarity and did not maintain architectural coherence, making them unsuitable as architectural mass outputs. In contrast, O2 achieved a more balanced result. It successfully generated protruding architectural mass for extrude and torsional shapes for twist, while showing moderate performance for branch. The average CLIP score for O2 (0.2140) was slightly lower than that of O4, but the visual clarity and architectural fidelity of the generated outputs were superior.

LPIPS results further supported the choice of O2. Adafactor (O2) recorded an average LPIPS score of (0.483004), which was lower than O3 (0.486001) and O4 (0.487936), and comparable to O1 (0.483972). These values indicate that, in addition to semantic fidelity captured by CLIP, O2 also maintained perceptual consistency with the teacher images. While the numerical differences among LPIPS scores were relatively small, the consistent trend across both CLIP and LPIPS suggests that O2 produced outputs that better balanced prompt alignment and perceptual similarity.

Based on these analysis results, Adafactor (O2) was selected as the Optimizer for LoRA training.

4.2.2. Learning Rate

To analyze the impact of Learning Rate (LR) on model performance during LoRA training, experiments were conducted applying four different Learning Rate settings (LR1: 0.0001, LR2: 0.0002, LR3: 0.0003, LR4: 0.0004) as shown in Table 9.

Table 9. Comparative results of Learning Rates (LR1: 0.0001, LR2: 0.0002, LR3: 0.0003, LR4: 0.0004). LR3 yielded the clearest architectural transformations and competitive quantitative scores, indicating that 0.0003 is the most suitable learning rate setting.

Prompt	LR1	LR2	LR3	LR4
extrude (CLIP Score) [LPIPS Score]	 (0.2341) [0.350163] 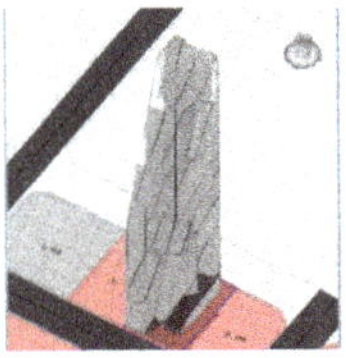 (0.2201) [0.642323]	 (0.2287) [0.350193] 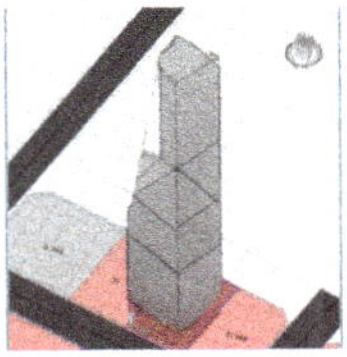 (0.2130) [0.634285]	 (0.2380) [0.351559] 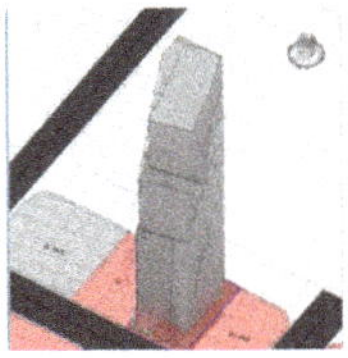 (0.2137) [0.642483]	 (0.2447) [0.342769] 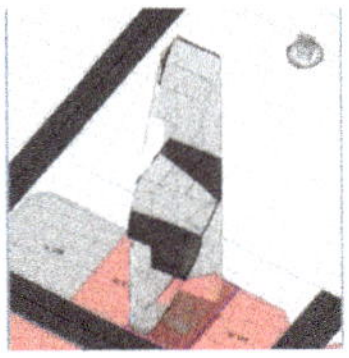 (0.2067) [0.642551]
branch (CLIP Score) [LPIPS Score]	 (0.2037) [0.347179] 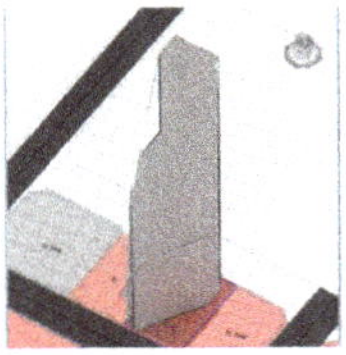 (0.1895) [0.667573]	 (0.2141) [0.340617] 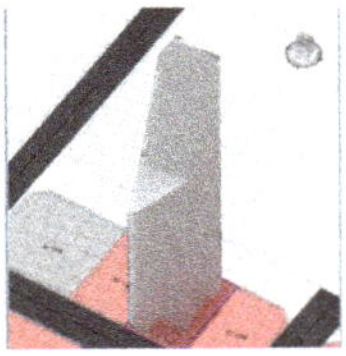 (0.1745) [0.661532]	 (0.2074) [0.333245] 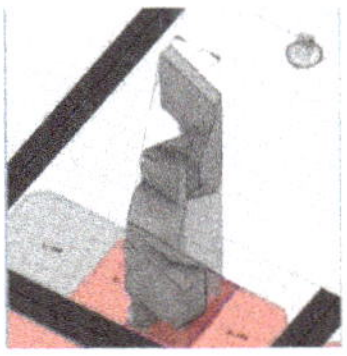 (0.1916) [0.676919]	 (0.2026) [0.333787] 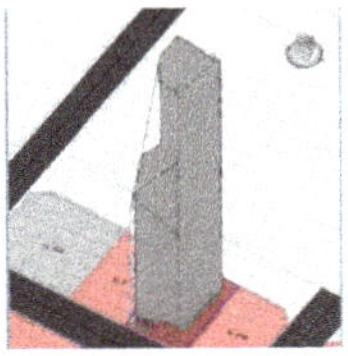 (0.1873) [0.670242]

Table 9. *Cont.*

Prompt	LR1	LR2	LR3	LR4

twist (CLIP Score) [LPIPS Score]	(0.2170) [0.199774]	(0.1947) [0.207238]	(0.2163) [0.211201]	(0.2095) [0.210177]
	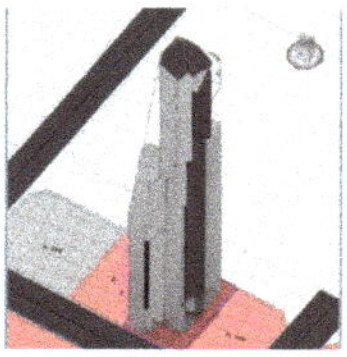	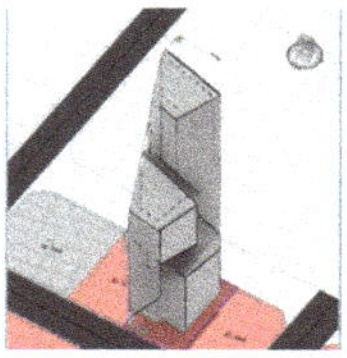		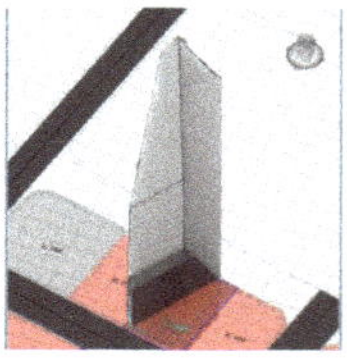
	(0.1827) [0.681593]	(0.1909) [0.676819]	(0.1916) [0.6712]	(0.1921) [0.678881]
Average CLIP Score	0.2078	0.2026	0.2098	0.2072
Average LPIPS Score	0.481434	0.478447	0.481103	0.479749

Visual analysis revealed that LR1 and LR2 produced architectural masses that were either excessively deformed or exhibited insufficient transformation, while LR4 often resulted in unstable and noisy outputs. On the other hand, LR3 demonstrated relatively clear architectural masses that best reflected the prompts: the extrude prompt generated outward-protruding masses, branch produced appropriately segmented and split forms, and twist resulted in dynamic torsional masses.

Quantitatively, the differences in average CLIP scores among the four learning rates were minimal—ranging from 0.2026 (LR2) to 0.2098 (LR3). Still, LR3 exhibited the most consistent architectural coherence and clarity among the compared settings, in conjunction with competitive CLIP performance. LPIPS results provided a complementary perspective. The lowest (best) average LPIPS score was observed for LR2 (0.478447), followed closely by LR4 (0.479749), LR1 (0.481434), and LR3 (0.481103). This indicates that although LR2 was slightly superior in perceptual similarity to teacher images, its outputs were visually less coherent in architectural form compared to LR3.

Taken together, these findings suggest that while LPIPS highlights perceptual closeness for LR2, the balance between semantic fidelity (CLIP) and visual clarity favors LR3. Therefore, the Learning Rate setting of 0.0003 (LR3) was selected for LoRA training.

4.2.3. LR Scheduler

To analyze the impact of LR Scheduler on model performance during LoRA training, experiments were conducted applying four different LR Scheduler settings (LRS1: constant, LRS2: cosine, LRS3: linear, LRS4: adafactor) as shown in Table 10.

Analysis showed that LRS2, LRS3, and LRS4 generally produced geometric masses that did not reflect the prompts. LRS3 and LRS4 in particular generated blurred masses with slight noise. Conversely, LRS1 effectively represented the prompts: extrude produced a protruding mass; twist a rotational transformation; and although branch exhibited some blur, it could still be interpreted as a segmented form.

Quantitatively, LRS1 achieved the highest average CLIP score (0.2127), followed by LRS4 (0.2110), LRS2 (0.2082), and LRS3 (0.2078). In parallel, LPIPS results indicated a slightly different trend: LRS3 recorded the lowest average LPIPS value (0.477515), suggesting relatively higher perceptual similarity with teacher images, while LRS1 (0.478304), LRS2 (0.482184), and LRS4 (0.484317) showed comparatively higher values. Although these LPIPS differences were marginal, the divergence between CLIP and LPIPS underscores their complementary roles—CLIP capturing semantic fidelity to prompts and LPIPS reflecting perceptual resemblance to teacher images.

Table 10. Comparative results of LR Schedulers (LRS1: constant, LRS2: cosine, LRS3: linear, LRS4: adafactor). LRS1 consistently reflected prompts more clearly and recorded the highest CLIP score, supporting its selection as the most effective scheduler.

Prompt	LRS1	LRS2	LRS3	LRS4
extrude (CLIP Score) [LPIPS Score]	 (0.2562) [0.347824]	 (0.2496) [0.360708]	 (0.2446) [0.34897]	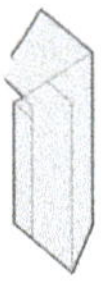 (0.2518) [0.360331]
	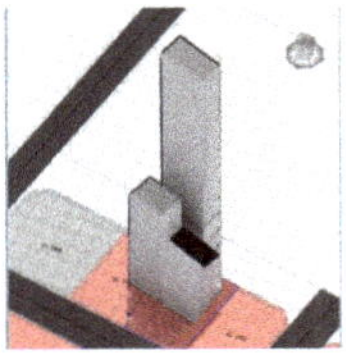 (0.2149) [0.643275]	 (0.2118) [0.640745]	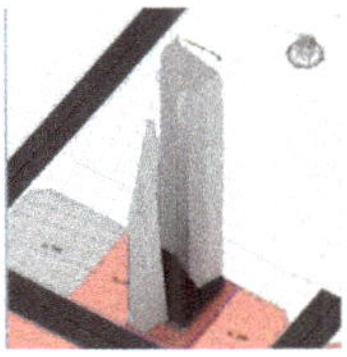 (0.2231) [0.643537]	 (0.2107) [0.634892]
branch (CLIP Score) [LPIPS Score]	 (0.1937) [0.331238]	 (0.1964) [0.336442]	 (0.1931) [0.35139]	 (0.2167) [0.342915]
	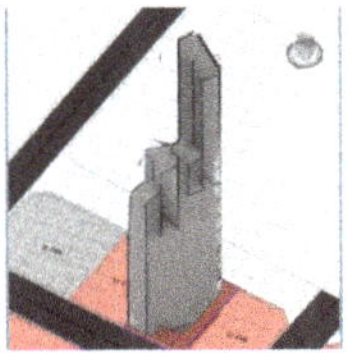 (0.1978) [0.667002]	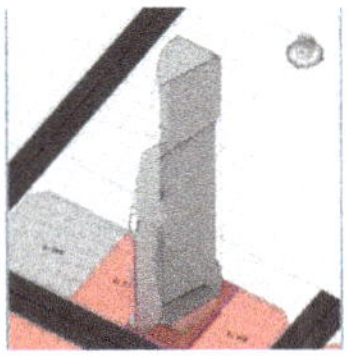 (0.1891) [0.677781]	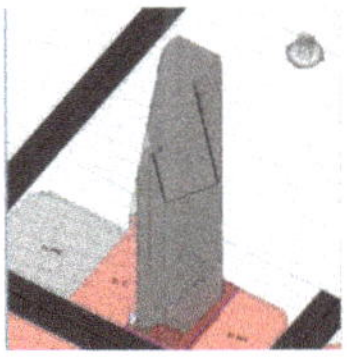 (0.1934) [0.670332]	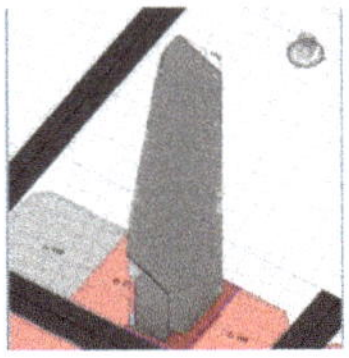 (0.1884) [0.671802]

Table 10. *Cont.*

Prompt	LRS1	LRS2	LRS3	LRS4
twist (CLIP Score) [LPIPS Score]	 (0.2201) [0.198131] 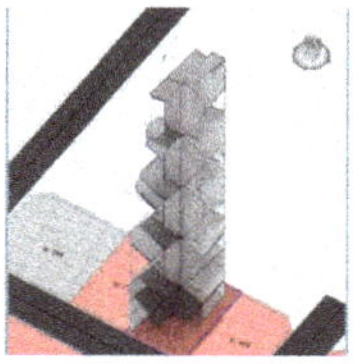 (0.1935) [0.680731]	 (0.2096) [0.202021] 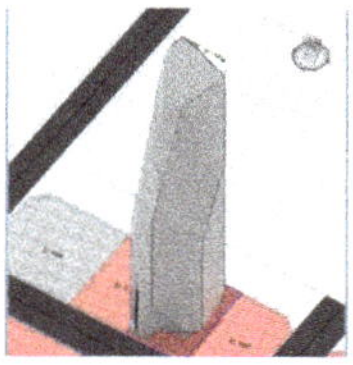 (0.1927) [0.675404]	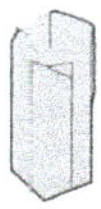 (0.2120) [0.168319] 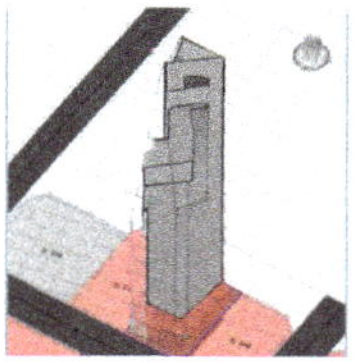 (0.1807) [0.682539]	 (0.2141) [0.212691] 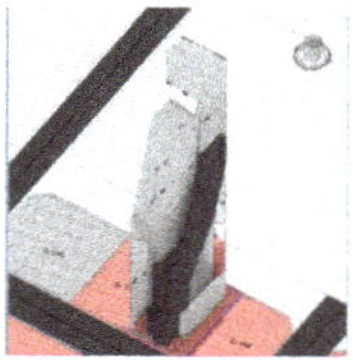 (0.1843) [0.683273]
Average CLIP Score	0.2127	0.2082	0.2078	0.2110
Average LPIPS Score	0.478034	0.482184	0.477515	0.484317

Based on both qualitative and quantitative evaluations, Constant (LRS1) was selected as the LR Scheduler setting for LoRA training.

4.2.4. Batch Size

To analyze the impact of Batch Size on model performance during LoRA training, experiments were conducted applying four different Batch Size settings (B1: 1, B2: 2, B3: 4, B4: 8) as shown in Table 11.

B2 and B4 generated rectangular column-shaped masses that did not reflect the prompts and often exhibited visual noise. B1 produced masses that partially reflected the prompts for extrude and branch, but these effects were not consistently applied, and the twist transformation was weak. In contrast, B3 successfully reflected the prompts: extrude showed a progressively protruded mass, branch produced segmented forms in both regular and irregular configurations, and twist exhibited clear torsional deformation.

Quantitatively, B3 achieved the highest average CLIP score (0.2123), followed closely by B2 (0.2109) and B4 (0.2082). LPIPS results showed a similar trend, with B3 obtaining a competitive perceptual similarity (0.482865), which was slightly higher than B1 (0.475726) and B2 (0.480138) but still consistent with qualitative observations. Although LPIPS differences across batch sizes were relatively small, B3's balance between semantic fidelity (CLIP) and perceptual consistency (LPIPS) supports its selection.

Based on these combined qualitative and quantitative evaluations, a Batch Size setting of 4 (B3) was selected for LoRA training.

Table 11. Comparative results of Batch Sizes (B1: 1, B2: 2, B3: 4, B4: 8). B3 demonstrated the most coherent prompt reflection across extrude, branch, and twist, and achieved the highest CLIP score, confirming Batch Size 4 as the optimal configuration.

Prompt	B1	B2	B3	B4
extrude (CLIP Score) [LPIPS Score]	 (0.2448) [0.350233] 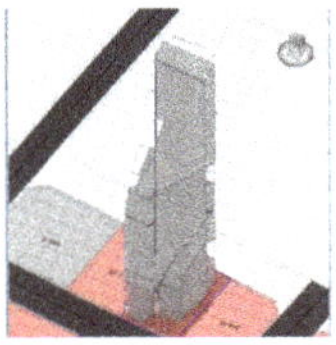 (0.2164) [0.635002]	 (0.2574) [0.359554] 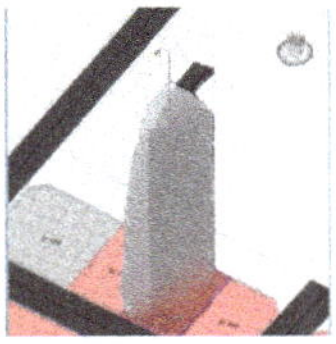 (0.2101) [0.649085]	 (0.2485) [0.350928] 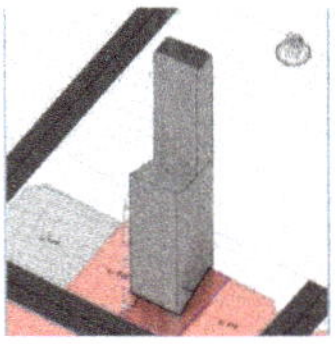 (0.2118) [0.648677]	 (0.2472) [0.356032] 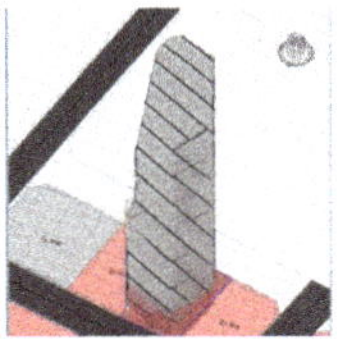 (0.2094) [0.633884]
branch (CLIP Score) [LPIPS Score]	 (0.1988) [0.325867] 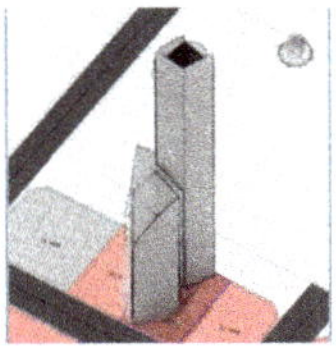 (0.1850) [0.675247]	 (0.2167) [0.336992] 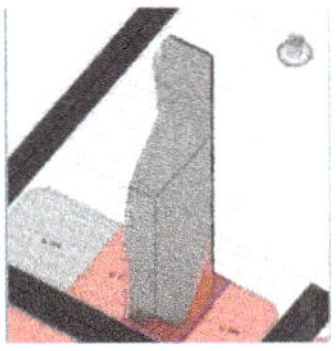 (0.1875) [0.66697]	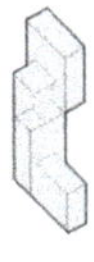 (0.2173) [0.331515] 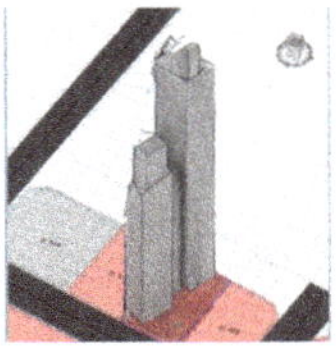 (0.1873) [0.68546]	 (0.2092) [0.342192] 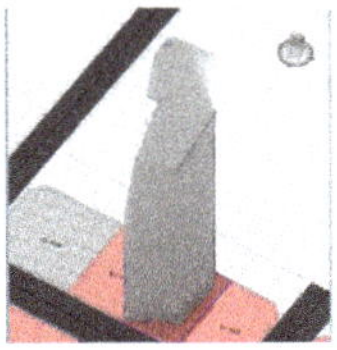 (0.1766) [0.661859]
twist (CLIP Score) [LPIPS Score]	 (0.2134) [0.191182]  (0.1931) [0.676824]	 (0.2116) [0.192647] 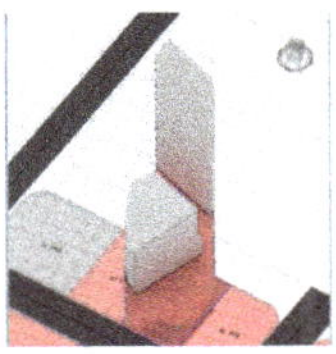 (0.1821) [0.675579]	 (0.2173) [0.206828] 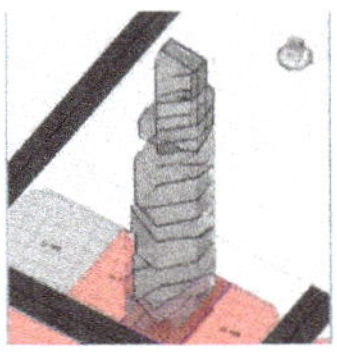 (0.1918) [0.673779]	 (0.2183) [0.204495] 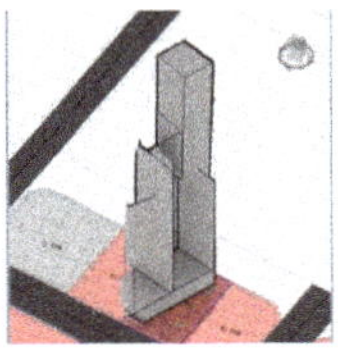 (0.1886) [0.671848]
Average CLIP Score	0.2086	0.2109	0.2123	0.2082
Average LPIPS Score	0.475726	0.480138	0.482865	0.478385

4.2.5. Training Steps

The Training steps for the hyperparameter settings derived so far is 5500, and the LoRA training loss graph is shown in Figure 4. As we can observe an increasing trend in loss values after 5000 steps, we conducted LoRA training with Training Steps set to 11,000 (epoch 10), twice the original value, to find the interval where the loss value converges to zero (Table 12).

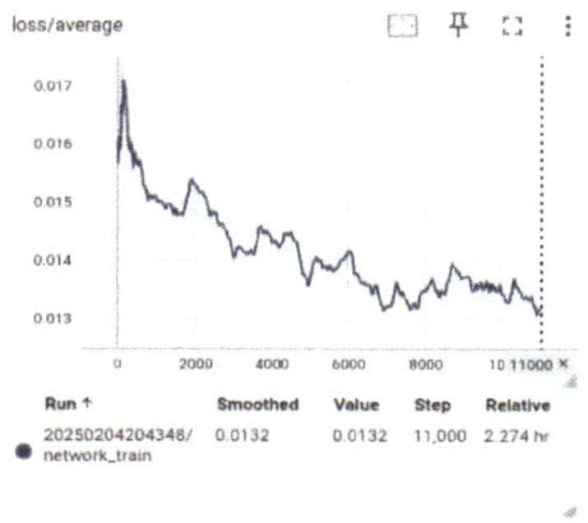

Figure 4. B3's Loss Graph.

Table 12. Hyperparameters for 11,000 training steps.

	No. Images	Optimizer	Learning Rate	LR Scheduler	Batch Size	Epoch	Repeats
value	220	Adafactor	0.0003	constant	4	10	20

The experimental results (Figure 5) show that the loss value converges to zero after passing 0.011 in the 8000–10,000 steps range, and the loss value increases again after exceeding 10,000 steps. In other words, we need to find Training Steps close to but not exceeding 10,000 and derive hyperparameter settings accordingly. The explicit selection rule was to identify the interval where the training loss approached its minimum value, converging toward zero, while avoiding the divergence observed beyond 10,000 steps. Within this convergence range, a step count of 9800 was determined to provide the most stable outcome.

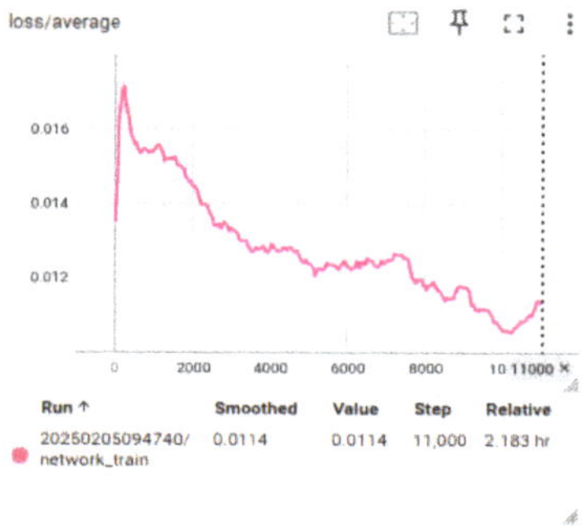

Figure 5. Loss Graph of 11,000 steps.

Finally, the number of Training Steps was set to 9800, and, accordingly, as shown in Table 13, the optimal parameter settings were derived by setting the number of images to 280 and repeats to 14.

Table 13. Hyperparameters for 9800 training steps.

	No. Images	Optimizer	Learning Rate	LR Scheduler	Batch Size	Epoch	Repeats
value	280	Adafactor	0.0003	constant	4	10	14

In order to verify the effectiveness of LoRA fine-tuning, a baseline comparison was conducted using the base diffusion model without LoRA training. Table 14 presents the results of mass generation using the final LoRA model configuration, alongside the output of the base diffusion model. Visual comparison indicates that the base model failed to generate architectural mass images with recognizable form or consistent alignment with prompts. In contrast, the LoRA-trained model consistently generated coherent and differentiated architectural masses that effectively reflected the prompts for extrude, branch, and twist. This baseline comparison serves as a validation of architectural knowledge acquisition through LoRA fine-tuning.

Table 14. Comparison of Learning Rate.

Prompt	Without LoRA	The Optimal LoRA Model		
extrude	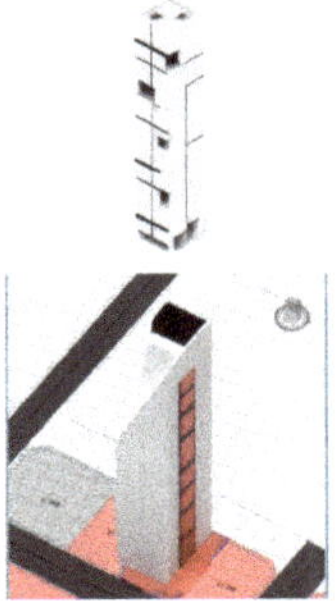	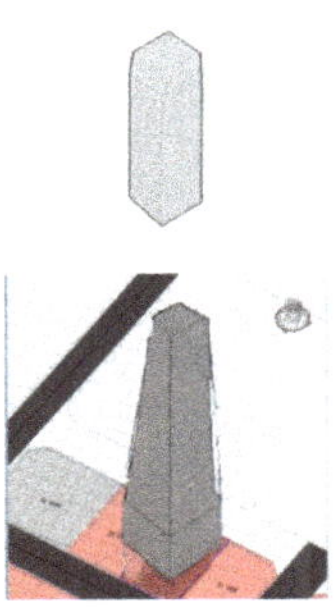	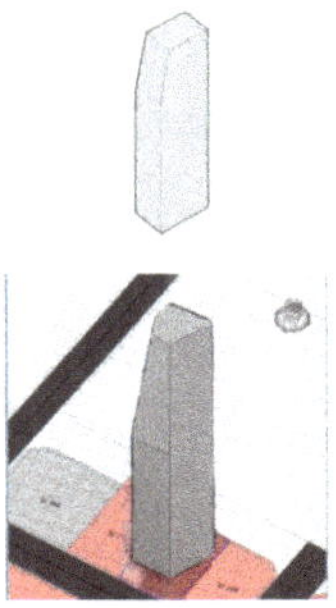	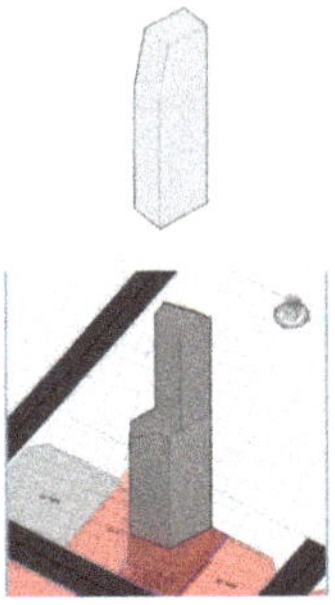
branch	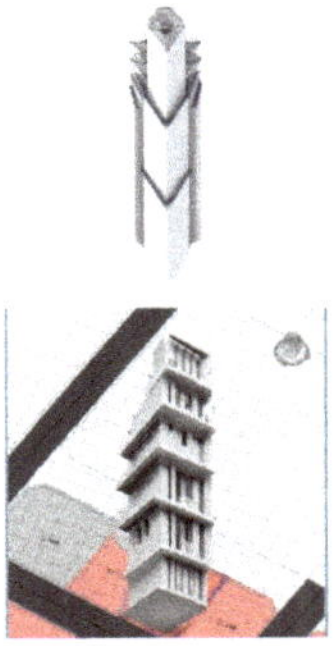	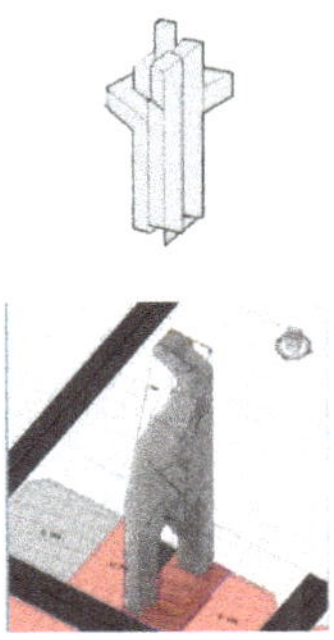	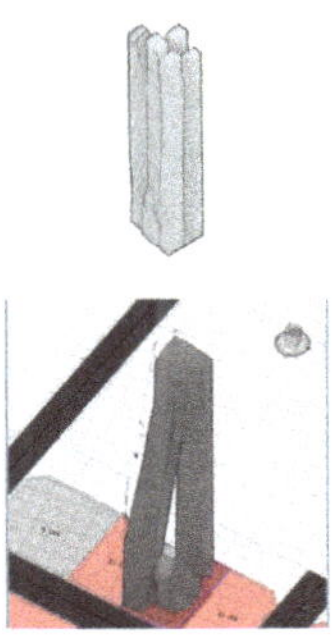	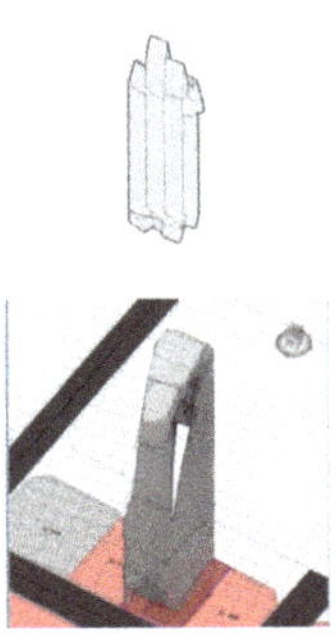
twist	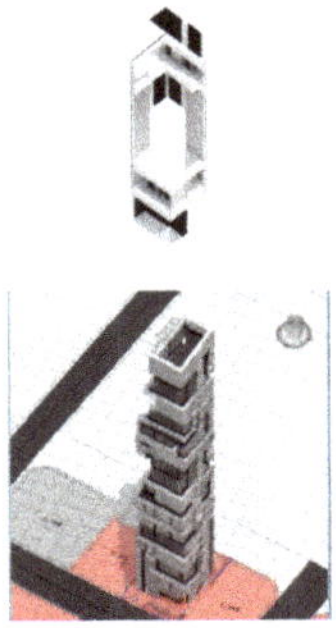	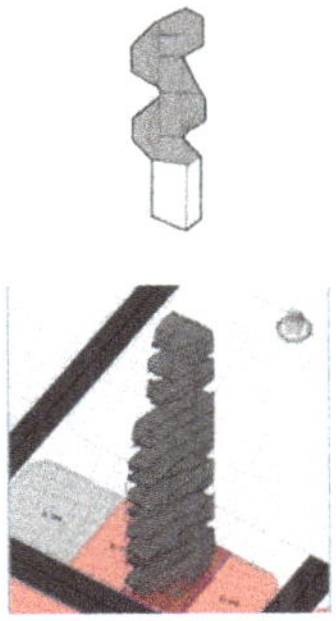	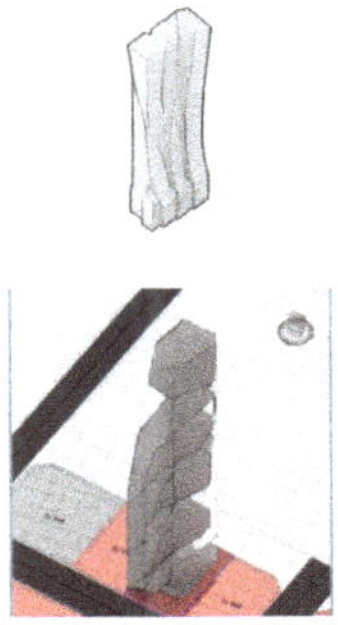	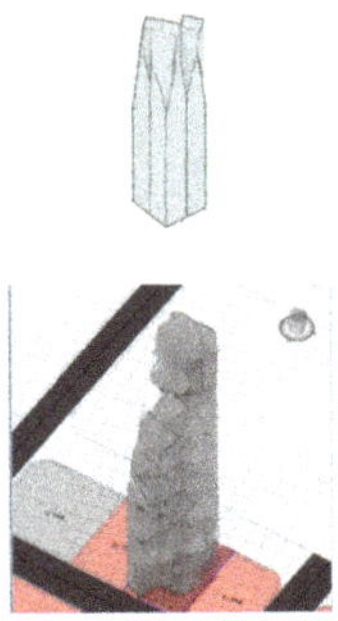

This comparison clearly demonstrates that LoRA fine-tuning enhances the model's capability to generate prompt-aligned architectural masses.

5. Discussion

This study explored how to fine-tune architectural knowledge using the LoRA technique to implement a Diffusion model for human-AI interaction, addressing the limited systematic guidance for establishing plausible parameter ranges in architectural contexts. The results showed that in learning architectural mass-related knowledge, detailed captions describing the corresponding images in the image-caption dataset influenced LoRA's performance. This suggests that AI models can generate forms that better reflect prompts when architectural concepts and specific descriptions of transformations and shapes are included. Additionally, Adafactor was evaluated to be more accurate for architectural mass generation than Prodigy and Lion, which have recently gained attention for their good performance as optimizers. While cosine or linear adjustments of learning rates are generally known to be more effective, we found that constant, which adjusts a fixed learning rate, was more suitable as an LR Scheduler for architectural mass generation.

The novelty of this study does not lie in presenting new AI architectures or algorithmic innovations, but in systematically applying LoRA to architectural massing knowledge, which has been underexplored in prior work. This framing positions the study as a bridging milestone, offering foundational guidance for emerging architectural-AI researchers and structured methodological references for advanced scholars.

These results imply that a different approach from conventional AI learning optimization is needed to learn architectural knowledge. It can be interpreted that stable and consistent learning is based on an image-caption dataset that includes detailed descriptions of the geometric properties, spatial relationships, and formative features of architectural masses, as well as accurate terms denoting mass forms and transformations, positively influences the reflection of prompts. Architectural massing studies represent fundamental components for expressing architectural knowledge, encompassing spatial relationships, geometric transformations, and formal logic that define architectural spatial reasoning.

Furthermore, this study contributes to the broader discourse on human-AI interaction by demonstrating that AI's performance in architectural design tasks can be systematically improved through domain-specific prompt structuring and fine-tuning. Unlike general image generation tasks, architectural mass generation requires an understanding of spatial logic and typological nuance, which this research attempts to capture and quantify. This reflects the importance of curating not only a suitable dataset but also selecting hyperparameters that reinforce architectural reasoning rather than merely visual coherence. Although the generated outputs remain simplified 2D mass forms, they can directly support early-stage design workflows by expanding option spaces and informing subsequent decisions on volumetric articulation and façade development [13]. Recent façade-focused studies reinforce this linkage: Wang et al. [37] demonstrated transformer-based façade feature acquisition from static street view images, and Wang et al. [38] showed that augmentation techniques improve window state detection. While these works emphasize façade-level articulation and openings (e.g., rhythm, window states), our study contributes at the upstream stage by optimizing mass generation. Together, they highlight how massing decisions form the foundation upon which façade composition and functional elements are developed, situating our framework as complementary to façade-oriented research [38,39].

While GANs have been widely explored in architectural image synthesis, their instability and susceptibility to mode collapse limit their reliability for systematic parameter optimization in domain-specific contexts. In contrast, the LoRA-based diffusion framework presented here demonstrates stable learning behavior with modest datasets, making it more suitable for embedding architectural knowledge and supporting consistent analysis of hyperparameter effects.

These findings also extend prior architectural diffusion studies by shifting the focus from stylistic adaptation to methodological rigor. For instance, Kim et al. [8] emphasized curated vocabularies for architectural form generation, and Wu [28] highlighted stylistic consistency through ArchDiff. Similarly, Ma and Zheng [29] and Yoo and Lee [30] demonstrated façade- and style-level customization. In contrast, this study situates LoRA fine-tuning at the massing stage, providing a structured framework for parameter optimization that directly embeds architectural reasoning. This positioning clarifies how our contribution complements, yet diverges from, earlier work in the field.

Rather than presenting novel AI architectures or proposing algorithmic innovations, this study offers a systematic parameter optimization framework that serves as practical guidance for practitioners and architectural researchers newly entering the field of AI. Although the scope of this research is limited to 2D architectural mass image generation and not interactive workflows or 3D modeling, it demonstrates that careful fine-tuning and dataset structuring can lead to meaningful improvements in the alignment between AI-generated outputs and architectural intentions.

By validating the feasibility and effectiveness of LoRA fine-tuning in architectural mass generation, the study adds to the growing body of knowledge that supports AI integration in the architectural design process. It highlights that systematic parameter optimization can play a crucial role in building foundational knowledge and practice for future advancements in the field.

Additionally, the dataset size (220 images) is modest, which limits generalizability; however, this controlled scale enabled a systematic examination of captioning strategies and hyperparameter effects. A limitation of this study is that we did not analyze in detail the changes in model performance according to combinations of hyperparameter settings for Batch Size, Epoch, and Repeats during the optimization process of Training Steps. Particularly, experimenting with different settings for Batch Size and Repeats while fixing Training Steps could have provided insights into how the number of images processed at once (Batch Size) and the number of times the same image is repeatedly learned (Repeats) affect the learning of architectural mass-related knowledge. Therefore, future research should analyze the effects of Batch Size and Repeats when learning the architectural mass image–Detailed Captions dataset to propose a more precise LoRA model optimization method.

Additionally, although this study sequentially tuned hyperparameters such as Caption Level, Optimizer, Learning Rate, LR Scheduler, Batch Size, and Training Steps, potential interaction effects between these variables—particularly between Batch Size and Repeats—were not systematically investigated. Future research will aim to address this limitation by exploring how different combinations of Batch Size, Repeats, and Epoch settings interact under fixed Training Steps. This expanded approach is expected to contribute to a more comprehensive understanding of LoRA-based optimization for architectural mass learning.

Another limitation lies in the evaluation framework. Although CLIP and LPIPS metrics were employed to strengthen the quantitative analysis, these measures remain proxies and cannot fully capture architectural reasoning such as spatial logic or functional coherence. This limitation is acknowledged, and we suggest that future work incorporate expert evaluation to complement quantitative indicators and reinforce architectural validity.

A further limitation concerns external validity. Because all evaluations in this study were conducted on 2D mass images, the findings cannot be directly generalized to architectural massing in practice, which requires 3D modeling, site-specific massing, or schematic CAD-based inputs. Future work will extend the framework to these contexts and test the robustness of LoRA-based optimization on out-of-distribution mass images, thereby enhancing its applicability to practical architectural design scenarios. This limitation also underscores the importance of connecting massing-level optimization with façade-level performance studies. As Wang et al. [37–39] have shown, façade analysis from urban-scale image data depends on reliable upstream massing structures. Extending LoRA-based optimization from simplified 2D forms to schematic CAD or 3D contexts would therefore enable a more direct interface with façade recognition and window state detection pipelines [38].

6. Conclusions

This study investigated the fine-tuning of architectural knowledge for architectural mass generation using LoRA applied to a diffusion model, addressing the systematic parameter optimization gap in architectural contexts where existing AI research has provided limited guidance for establishing plausible parameter ranges. Through a series of experiments, the study identified that the inclusion of detailed, domain-specific image captions significantly enhances prompt-to-output accuracy. It also demonstrated that constant learning rates and the Adafactor optimizer are more suitable in architectural workflows compared to generally favored optimizers or learning rate schedulers.

The findings across different hyperparameter experiments (Caption Level, Optimizer, Learning Rate, LR Scheduler, Batch Size, and Training Steps) were systematically synthesized to identify optimal parameter settings for architectural mass generation. Architectural massing studies, as fundamental components for expressing architectural knowledge, require specialized optimization approaches that maintain spatial relationships, geometric transformations, and formal logic inherent in architectural spatial reasoning.

The research provides foundational insight into how AI models can be adapted for architecture-specific design tasks, marking a shift from generalized image generation toward domain-sensitive modeling. While not claiming algorithmic novelty, the study contributes methodologically by establishing a systematic parameter optimization framework and providing practical guidelines for integrating AI technologies into architectural design workflows while maintaining architectural knowledge integrity.

The contributions of this study can be considered along three dimensions. Practically, it provides structured guidance for practitioners and educators to integrate LoRA-based diffusion models into early-stage design workflows. Empirically, it offers a systematic evaluation of hyperparameter effects using both semantic and perceptual metrics, strengthening the robustness of AI-assisted design research. Conceptually, it clarifies the role of architectural knowledge as spatial and morphological logic, demonstrating how such knowledge can be embedded into generative models and advancing discourse on architectural intelligence.

These findings are expected to aid future developments in intelligent design environments, where AI tools support architects through enhanced responsiveness, data-informed design iteration, and the encoding of architectural reasoning into generative processes. The systematic approach demonstrated in this research establishes a foundation for evidence-based AI adoption in architectural practice, enabling practitioners to implement domain-specific fine-tuning with greater confidence and effectiveness.

Nonetheless, several limitations should be noted. The modest dataset size, the focus on 2D massing rather than 3D or contextual modeling, and the absence of expert evaluation restrict the generalizability of the findings. Future research should expand datasets, incorporate site and 3D contexts, and engage expert assessments to validate architectural reasoning beyond proxy metrics, thereby strengthening the applicability of LoRA-based optimization to architectural practice.

Author Contributions: Conceptualization, S.M.H. and S.C.; methodology, S.M.H. and S.C.; software, S.M.H.; validation, S.M.H.; writing—original draft preparation, S.M.H.; writing—review and editing, S.C.; visualization, S.M.H.; supervision, S.C.; project administration, S.C. All authors have read and agreed to the published version of the manuscript.

Funding: This work is supported in 2025 by the Korea Agency for Infrastructure Technology Advancement (KAIA) grant funded by the Ministry of Land, Infrastructure and Transport (Grant RS-2021-KA163269).

Data Availability Statement: The data presented in this study are available on request from the corresponding author on reasonable request. The data are not publicly available due to privacy policies.

Conflicts of Interest: The authors declare no conflicts of interest.

References

1. Carpo, M. *Beyond Digital: Design and Automation at the End of Modernity*; MIT Press: Cambridge, MA, USA, 2023.
2. Bao, Y.; Xiang, C. Exploration of Conceptual Design Generation Based on the Deep Learning Model—Discussing the Application of AI Generator to the Preliminary Architectural Design Process. In Proceedings of the International Conference on Architecture and Urban Planning, Suzhou, China, 11–12 November 2023; Springer Nature Singapore Pte Ltd.: Singapore, 2024; pp. 171–178. [CrossRef]
3. Luhrs, M. Using Generative AI Midjourney to Enhance Divergent and Convergent Thinking in an Architect's Creative Design Process. *Des. J.* **2024**, *27*, 677–699. [CrossRef]
4. Almaz, A.F.H.; El-Agouz, E.A.E.; Abdelfatah, M.T.; Mohamed, I.R. The Future Role of Artificial Intelligence (AI) Design's Integration into Architectural and Interior Design Education is to Improve Efficiency, Sustainability, and Creativity. *Civ. Eng. Archit.* **2024**, *12*, 1749–1772. [CrossRef]
5. Cao, Y.; Abdul Aziz, A.; Mohd Arshard, W.N.R. Stable diffusion in architectural design: Closing doors or opening new horizons? *Int. J. Archit. Comput.* **2024**, *23*, 339–357. [CrossRef]
6. Sadek, M.M.; Hassan, A.Y.; Diab, T.O.; Abdelhafeez, A. Creating Images with Stable Diffusion and Generative Adversarial Networks. *Int. J. Telecommun.* **2024**, *4*, 1–14. [CrossRef]
7. Leach, N. *Architecture in the Age of Artificial Intelligence: An Introduction to AI for Architects*; Bloomsbury Visual Arts: London, UK, 2022.
8. Kim, F.; Johanes, M.; Huang, J. Text2Form Diffusion: Framework for learning curated architectural vocabulary. In Proceedings of the 41st Conference on Education and Research in Computer Aided Architectural Design in Europe (eCAADe), Graz, Austria, 20–23 September 2023.
9. Li, S.; Su, S.; Lin, X. Optimizing the hyper-parameters of deep reinforcement learning for building control. *Build. Simul.* **2025**, *18*, 765–789. [CrossRef]
10. Manmatharasan, P.; Bitsuamlak, G.; Grolinger, K. AI-driven design optimization for sustainable buildings: A systematic review. *Build. Environ.* **2025**, *310*, 112707. [CrossRef]
11. Ma, Z.; Cui, S.; Joe, I. An Enhanced Proximal Policy Optimization-Based Reinforcement Learning Method with Random Forest for Hyperparameter Optimization. *Appl. Sci.* **2022**, *12*, 7006. [CrossRef]
12. Gero, J.S.; Jupp, J. Strategic use of representation in architectural massing. *Build. Res. Inf.* **2003**, *31*, 429–437. [CrossRef]
13. Park, J.; Hong, S.M.; Choo, S.Y. A Generation Method and Evaluation of Architectural Facade Design Using Stable Diffusion with LoRA and ControlNet. *J. Archit. Inst. Korea Plan. Des.* **2025**, *41*, 85–96. [CrossRef]
14. Panigrahi, A.; Saunshi, N.; Zhao, H.; Arora, S.K. Task-Specific Skill Localization in Fine-tuned Language Models. *arXiv* **2023**, arXiv:2302.06600. [CrossRef]
15. Rombach, R.; Blattmann, A.; Lorenz, D.; Esser, P.; Ommer, B. High-resolution image synthesis with latent diffusion models. In Proceedings of the IEEE/CVF Conference on Computer Vision and Pattern Recognition (CVPR), New Orleans, LA, USA, 18–24 June 2022; pp. 10684–10695.
16. Yang, Y.; Bhatt, N.; Ingebrand, T.; Ward, W.; Carr, S.; Wang, Z.; Topcu, U. Fine-Tuning Language Models Using Formal Methods Feedback. *arXiv* **2023**, arXiv:2310.18239. [CrossRef]
17. Hu, E.J.; Shen, Y.; Wallis, P.; Allen-Zhu, Z.; Li, Y.; Wang, L.; Chen, W. LoRA: Low-Rank Adaptation of Large Language Models. *arXiv* **2021**, arXiv:2106.09685.

18. Bernstein, P. *Machine Learning: Architecture in the Age of Artificial Intelligence*; RIBA Publishing: London, UK, 2022.
19. Stiny, G.; Gips, J. Shape Grammars and the Generative Specification of Painting and Sculpture. In Proceedings of the IFIP Congress, Ljubljana, Yugoslavia, 23–28 August 1971; North-Holland: Amsterdam, The Netherlands, 1972.
20. Schumacher, P. Parametricism as Style—Parametricist Manifesto. In Proceedings of the 11th Architecture Biennale, Venice, Italy, 14 September–23 November 2008.
21. Hong, S.M. Development of an AI-Based Architectural Mass Design System for Enhancing Creative Thinking. Ph.D. Thesis, Kyungpook National University, Daegu, Republic of Korea, 2025.
22. del Campo, M. Ontology of diffusion models: Tools, language and architecture design. In *Diffusions in Architecture: Artificial Intelligence and Image Generators*; del Campo, M., Ed.; John Wiley & Sons, Inc.: Hoboken, NJ, USA, 2024; pp. 44–54.
23. Russakovsky, O.; Deng, J.; Su, H.; Krause, J.; Satheesh, S.; Ma, S.; Huang, Z.; Karpathy, A.; Khosla, A.; Bernstein, M.; et al. ImageNet Large Scale Visual Recognition Challenge. *arXiv* **2014**, arXiv:1409.0575. [CrossRef]
24. Ahmad, I.S.; Siddiqui, N.; Boufama, B. A Comparative Study of Text-to-Image Generative Models. In Proceedings of the 2024 IEEE 12th International Symposium on Signal, Image, Marrakech, Morocco, 21–23 May 2024., Video and Communications (ISIVC). [CrossRef]
25. Sudha, L.; Aruna, K.; Sureka, V.; Niveditha, M.; Prema, S. Semantic Image Synthesis from Text: Current Trends and Future Horizons in Text-to-Image Generation. *EAI Endorsed Trans. Internet Things* **2024**, *11*. [CrossRef]
26. Çelik, T. Generative design experiments with artificial intelligence: Reinterpretation of shape grammar. *Open House Int.* **2023**, *49*, 123–135. [CrossRef]
27. Horvath, A.S.; Pouliou, P. AI for conceptual architecture: Reflections on designing with text-to-text, text-to-image, and image-to-image generators. *Front. Archit. Res.* **2024**, *13*, 593–612. [CrossRef]
28. Wu, Y. ArchDiff: Streamlining Architectural Design with Diffusion-Based Style Generation. *Lect. Notes Comput. Sci.* **2024**, *14871*, 300–315.
29. Ma, H.; Zheng, H. Text Semantics to Image Generation: A Method of Building Facades Design Based on Stable Diffusion Model. In *Phygital Intelligence, Computational Design and Robotic Fabrication*; Springer: Berlin/Heidelberg, Germany, 2024.
30. You, Y.; Lee, J. Generative AI-Based Construction of Architect's Style-trained Models and its Application for Visualization of Residential Houses. *Soc. Des. Converg.* **2023**, *22*, 103–116. [CrossRef]
31. Steenson, M.W. *Architectural Intelligence: How Designers and Architects Created the Digital Landscape*; MIT Press: Cambridge, MA, USA, 2017.
32. Di Mari, A.; Yoo, N. *Operative Design: A Catalogue of Spatial Verbs*; BIS Publishers: Amsterdam, The Netherlands, 2013.
33. Di Mari, A. *Conditional Design: An Introduction to Elemental Architecture*; BIS Publishers: Amsterdam, The Netherlands, 2014.
34. Steen, J. Bridging the Gap Between Generative Artificial Intelligence and Innovation in Footwear Design. Master's Thesis, Delft University of Technology, Delft, The Netherlands, 2024.
35. Lin, H.; Hong, D.; Ge, S.; Luo, C.; Jiang, K.; Jin, H.; Wen, C. RS-MoE: Mixture of Experts for Remote Sensing Image Captioning and Visual Question Answering. *arXiv* **2024**, arXiv:2407.02233.
36. Chang, Z.-Y.; Han, J.-W. Analysis on prompt engineering structure of AI-generated architectural/interior design images. In Proceedings of the Korean Institute of Interior Design Spring Conference, Bucheon, Republic of Korea, 18 May 2024; Volume 26, pp. 150–154.
37. Wang, S.; Korolija, I.; Rovas, D. Development of Approach to an Automated Acquisition of Static Street View Images Using Transformer Architecture for Analysis of Building Characteristics. *Sci. Rep.* **2025**, *15*, 29062. [CrossRef] [PubMed]
38. Wang, S.; Korolija, I.; Rovas, D. Impact of Traditional Augmentation Methods on Window State Detection. In Proceedings of the 14th REHVA HVAC World Congress CLIMA 2022, Rotterdam, The Netherlands, 22–25 May 2022. [CrossRef]
39. Wang, S.; Korolija, I.; Rovas, D. Transformer-Based Building Façade Recognition Using Static Street View Images. In Proceedings of the European Conference on Computing in Construction (EC3), Crete, Greece, 10–12 July 2023. [CrossRef]

buildings

MDPI

Article

Artificial Intelligence-Based Architectural Design (AIAD): An Influence Mechanism Analysis for the New Technology Using the Hybrid Multi-Criteria Decision-Making Framework

Xinliang Wang [1], Yafei Zhao [2,*], Wenlong Zhang [2], Yang Li [2], Xuepeng Shi [3], Rong Xia [4], Yanjun Su [5], Xiaoju Li [5] and Xiang Xu [6]

1 School of Economics and Management, Huainan Vocational and Technical College, Huainan 232001, China; h2314@hnvtc.edu.cn
2 School of Smart City Engineering, Qingdao Huanghai University, Qingdao 266427, China; wenlong0523@163.com (W.Z.); 18810618713@163.com (Y.L.)
3 School of Architecture and Urban Planning, Qingdao University of Technology, Qingdao 266033, China; shixuepeng@qut.edu.cn
4 College of Civil Engineering and Architecture, Zhejiang University, Hangzhou 310058, China; sharon.xia@zju.edu.cn
5 School of Design and Architecture, Zhejiang University of Technology, Hangzhou 310023, China; 202005540910@zjut.edu.cn (Y.S.); 221124150105@zjut.edu.cn (X.L.)
6 School of Architecture, Tianjin University, Tianjin 300072, China; xuxiang@tju.edu.cn
* Correspondence: zhaoyf@qdhhc.edu.cn

Abstract: Artificial Intelligence (AI) has emerged as a transformative force in the field of architectural design. This study aims to systematically analyze the influence mechanisms of Artificial Intelligence-based Architectural Design (AIAD) by constructing a comprehensive hybrid model that integrates the Analytic Hierarchy Process (AHP), Decision-Making Trial and Evaluation Laboratory (DEMATEL), Interpretive Structural Modeling (ISM), and Cross-Impact Matrix Multiplication Applied to Classification (MICMAC). Based on the previous quantitative literature review, 6 primary categories and 18 secondary influencing factors were identified. Data were collected from a panel of fifteen experts representing the architecture industry, academia, and computer science. Through weighting analysis, causal mapping, hierarchical structuring, and driving–dependence classification, the study clarifies the complex interrelationships among influencing factors and reveals the underlying drivers that accelerate or constrain AI adoption in architectural design. By quantifying the hierarchical and causal influence of factors, this research provides theoretical findings and practical insights for design firms undergoing digital transformation. The results extend previous meta-analytical studies, offering a decision-support system that bridges academic research and real-world applications, thereby guiding stakeholders toward informed adoption of artificial intelligence for future cultural tourism development and regional spatial innovation.

Keywords: artificial intelligence-based architectural design; AIAD; influence mechanism; multi-criteria decision-making; digital transformation; future cultural development

1. Introduction

As a revolutionary technology, artificial intelligence holds the potential to foster economic growth and enhance productivity [1], profoundly influencing multiple industries, including the construction industry and the architectural design field addressed in this study. Serving as a bridge between the physical and virtual worlds [2], artificial intelligence plays a significant role in advancing the intelligence and digitalization of the architectural design process. Over the years, researchers have conducted studies on artificial intelligence tailored to architectural design. The adoption of artificial intelligence technologies in this field not only directly reduces economic costs and improves efficiency but also offers multiple potential advantages.

Therefore, both academia and industry in the architectural design field require a multidimensional analytical model and a set of feasible solutions to enhance productivity while addressing existing challenges in the industry. However, current research remains limited, often focusing on narrow applications or specific artificial intelligence methods, or being substantially influenced by subjective biases, lacking comprehensive analyses capable of responding to the fundamental transformations brought about by artificial intelligence in the construction sector. This study seeks to broaden the perspective, conducting a thorough and multifaceted investigation and exposition to examine the mechanisms of influence, adoption intentions, and implementation strategies of artificial intelligence in the field of architectural design.

On the basis of identification and summarization of the influencing factors of AI-based architectural design, this research will further study the relationship between the influencing factors, and analyze the potential complex relationships between weight ranking, causal relationship, hierarchical structure, driving force and dependence. Meanwhile, the importance of each factor is evaluated, so as to quantify the influence of current AI technologies at the level of influencing mechanism and clarify the influencing mechanism in the field of AI-based architectural design.

The remainder of this paper is organized as follows. Section 2 presents a comprehensive literature review, establishing the theoretical foundations from both architectural and computer science perspectives. Section 3 defines the research questions and aims. Section 4 introduces the integrated methodological framework combining Analytic Hierarchy Process (AHP), Decision-Making Trial and Evaluation Laboratory (DEMATEL), Interpretive Structural Modeling (ISM), and Cross-Impact Matrix Multiplication Applied to Classification (MICMAC). Section 5 reports the analysis results, while Section 6 discusses the methodological implications and key findings. Finally, Section 7 concludes the study and outlines directions for future research.

This study makes a meaningful contribution by creating a hybrid multi-criteria decision-making (MCDM) framework that in a systematic way combines AHP, DEMATEL, ISM, and MICMAC to assess the influence mechanisms of Artificial Intelligence-based Architectural Design (AIAD). Previous studies highlighted carefully selected drivers based on either single-factor or qualitative analyses, whereas this study provides a quantitative causal–hierarchical model that outlines distinctive driving and dependent factors contributing to contextual AI adoption in Architectural practice. This study's contribution expands the existing AIAD literature by unifying meta-analytical literature with data-rich decisional models informed by AIAD tendencies.

Emerging artificial intelligence technologies are transforming the traditional architectural design industry. Whether in terms of technology, design processes, personnel management within design firms, or project collaborations with upstream and downstream enterprises, the potential influence of AI technologies is evident. Therefore, analyzing the factors influencing AI-based architectural design has become particularly important. Given that AI technologies are currently in a stage of rapid development, with fast-paced iterations, there has not yet been a systematic analysis of the mechanisms influencing the specific domain of architectural design. Hence, it is necessary to identify and determine the influencing factors from the perspective of architectural design firms and architects, and further analyze the relationships among these factors. At the same time, the impact of AI technologies on architectural design also faces obstacles and challenges. Accordingly, it is essential to further investigate the driving factors and potential complex relationships, assess the importance of the factors along with their causes and consequences, and thereby quantify the influence of AI technologies at the level of impact mechanisms.

This study addresses the following main research questions (RQs):

RQ1: What are the influencing factors of AI technologies on architectural design at the level of impact mechanisms?

RQ2: How are these identified factors interrelated?

RQ3: How can potential mechanisms—such as weight ranking, causal relationships, hierarchical structures, driving forces, and dependencies—be analyzed?

This study will conduct an in-depth investigation into the following issues: identifying and summarizing the influencing factors of AI-based architectural design; analyzing the relationships among these factors; establishing a hierarchical structure diagram of the influencing factors and explaining their causal links; assessing the importance of the factors and their causal relationships; and clarifying the attributes of the driving factors.

This study constructs an impact mechanism framework for Artificial Intelligence-based Architectural Design (AIAD) through the integrated Analytic Hierarchy Process (AHP), Decision-Making Trial and Evaluation Laboratory (DEMATEL), Interpretive Structural Modeling (ISM), and Cross-Impact Matrix Multiplication Applied to Classification (MICMAC) model, revealing the causal relationships and hierarchical structures among technological, organizational, and environmental factors. The significance of this research lies in extending and deepening the outcomes of Artificial Intelligence-based Architectural Design (AIAD): A Meta-Analysis as Quantitative Literature Review (MQLR), transforming a macro-level literature review into an operational causal network and mechanism framework. Building upon this, the study closely connects with Artificial Intelligence-based Architectural Design (AIAD): An Empirical Study on Adoption Intention Based on the TOE-UTAUT Integrated Framework with SEM: the latter translates the causal relationships and mechanism framework developed here into observable variables and empirically validates them in real-world enterprise contexts through surveys and structural equation modeling, thereby testing the effectiveness of the impact mechanisms. At the same time, the causal structures and influence pathways identified in this study also provide essential inputs for Artificial Intelligence-based Architectural Design (AIAD): Dynamic Modeling and Simulation Analysis Using the System Dynamics (SD) Approach), which extends the mechanism logic into a dynamically simulatable system capable of predicting AIAD's evolutionary trends under different scenarios.

In summary, this research serves a key function in the entire research series, acting as a deepening of the previous review and a strong structural foundation for the later empirical and simulation studies. In addition to the connections to architectural design practice, the exploration of Artificial Intelligence-based Architectural Design (AIAD) also has broader implications for cultural and tourism development. As the connections between architecture, culture, and experience design continue to merge, AI-based design intelligence can create new avenues for interpreting regional identity, enhancing spatial vitality and visitor engagement, and creating adaptive and data-informed environments. Therefore, the findings of this research will provide theoretical contribution and practical direction for the future integration of AI technologies into a sustainable development strategy for cultural tourism spaces and the regional innovation ecosystem.

2. Literature Review

2.1. Theoretical Foundations from an Architectural Perspective: Architectural Design Automation Theory

The theoretical origins of architectural design automation are often traced back to Christopher Alexander and his works A Pattern Language and The Timeless Way of Building. Alexander employed the concept of Pattern Language to describe places characterized by consistent cultural activities, while reflecting on the developmental dilemmas of architecture and planning from the perspectives of architecture, design, and philosophy. His approach provided simple, structured, and humanistic solutions for complex design challenges [3] (Figure 1). This method of generating diverse forms and unique layouts implied the possibility of automation in architectural design. Christopher Alexander's work and design knowledge were represented as modular, reusable patterns—conceptually similar to the 'datasets' used in machine learning today. This early typological approach provides a foundational analogy for AIAD, illustrating how design automation evolved from human-curated pattern systems to algorithmically generated solutions.

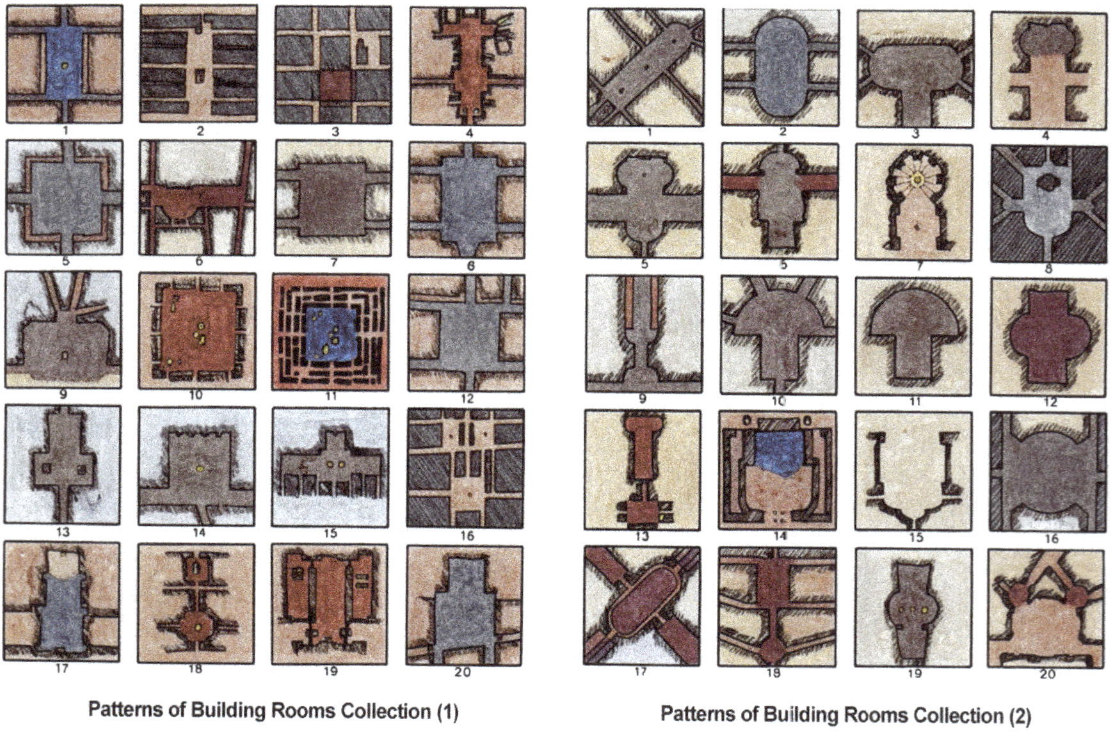

Figure 1. Patterns of Building Rooms: A Typology-based Dataset for Architectural Design Solutions (Source: Original concept from the literature by Christopher Alexander [3], re-drawn by the author).

Since the 1960s, the application of computers in architectural design has begun to develop in an exploratory manner. As architects realized that design and interaction problems were becoming increasingly complex, they sought assistance from computers. In the Sydney Opera House project, Arup pioneered the use of computers for simulation and calculation, pushing beyond the limits of design and engineering technology at the time. In 1963, Sketchpad (also known as Robot Draftsman), developed by Ivan Sutherland, was recognized as the first program system capable of generating line drawings on a computer [4], marking the beginning of Human–Computer Interaction (HCI). This technological breakthrough, capable of representing realistic graphic information, overcame the limitations imposed by insufficient computer power and inspired the development of many subsequent creative applications and computer-aided architectural design software.

During the same period, from the 1960s to the 1970s, knowledge engineering—represented by the knowledge base—provided new tools for the field of computer-aided architectural design. It was capable of addressing the core issue of integrating automation and semi-automation [5], thereby expanding the role of computers in design and enhancing the efficiency of architects and designers.

2.2. Theoretical Foundations from a Computer Science Perspective: Artificial Intelligence Technology

In the 1960s, the focus of artificial intelligence research was on creating symbolic artificial intelligence capable of simulating human intelligence. John Haugeland referred to this as "GOFAI," or Good Old-Fashioned Artificial Intelligence [6]. GOFAI was primarily based on symbolic operations such as manual coding, rules, and logical reasoning, bearing strong resemblance to modern programming [7]. It executed tasks automatically according to predefined rules, but its limitation lay in handling ambiguity and uncertainty. Early artificial intelligence systems were restricted to specific tasks, such as playing chess or solving mathematical equations. By the 1990s, neural networks emerged as a new approach to artificial intelligence, capable of learning from experience and effectively addressing problems involving fuzzy and uncertain data.

Since September 2022, technologies for AI-Generated Content (AIGC) have rapidly proliferated in design, creative, and content industries, undergoing iteration at an extremely fast pace. The refinement of deep learning models, the efforts of open-source communities, and cultural explorations have all acted as driving forces for the development of AI-generated content. In the field of architectural design, AIGC also demonstrates its technical advantages and unique value. For instance, when users input descriptive prompts into Midjourney or DALL·E, the platforms automatically generate architectural renderings consistent with the descriptions for users to select from. This illustrates AIGC's advantage of rapidly and cost-effectively producing large volumes of content.

2.3. Summary of Industry Paradigm Shift Trends

The world's first digital electronic computer, ENIAC, was invented in 1946 as part of a military collaborative research project. In its early stage, computer equipment was highly complex to acquire and operate, serving only companies with military contracts or large research institutions. Today, big data, computing power, and artificial intelligence have evolved and converged, organically integrating into a range of intelligent solutions. As a branch of computer science, artificial intelligence possesses the capacity to interpret external data [8]. It involves the development of general-purpose programs to accomplish tasks requiring human intelligence, including learning, perception, problem-solving, language understanding, and logical reasoning. Artificial intelligence is rapidly opening new frontiers in the discipline of sustainable development [2], accelerating multiple digital revolutions [9], and influencing broader global sustainability trends [2].

In his research, Manzoor describes artificial intelligence as a distributed, statistical, and symbolic technology designed to simulate human behavior or thought in order to complete specific tasks [2]. Bostrom and others classified artificial intelligence into three types: Artificial Super Intelligence (ASI), Artificial Narrow Intelligence (ANI), and Artificial

General Intelligence (AGI) [10–12]. ASI is defined as "intelligence that vastly surpasses the human brain in practical applications," ANI demonstrates intelligent functionality only within a specific domain, while AGI attains and surpasses human-level intelligence with the capacity for rapid learning and reasoning.

In recent decades, interdisciplinary teams of designers, computer scientists, and developers have implemented a variety of AI-based automated design algorithms, some of which remain theoretical while others have been successfully industrialized and commercialized. Scholars have summarized the applications of artificial intelligence in design processes, which primarily include concept design, functional specification, geometric modeling, structural consistency and code checking, optimization, collaborative workflow management, and creative design.

To analyze and address increasingly complex problems and challenges in architectural design, artificial intelligence has been introduced into the field [13]. Computer scientist Herbert Simon, focusing on intelligent design research, proposed the theory of "Design Science" [14]. He argued that design science should be a clearly organized, rational, and fully systematic design approach, rather than a body of simple scientific knowledge manufactured by humans. Design science must follow three principles: how designers work and think; how to establish an appropriate structure for the design process; and how to apply and develop design knowledge. Consequently, many scholars and architects have regarded design as a complex "decision-making process" [15–17]. Artificial intelligence technologies are now exploring new paradigms for analysis and seeking innovative solutions within complex systems.

With the widespread application of artificial intelligence, the entire construction industry is undergoing transformation, leveraging digitalization and intelligent innovations to enhance productivity. Disciplines and fields related to architectural design, such as construction engineering and management, are also experiencing rapid digital transformation, with AI-based solutions becoming a research focus [18]. In addition, Manzoor et al. explored the intersection of urbanization, cultural development, and artificial intelligence [2]. Thus, interdisciplinary research in the era of artificial intelligence is essential. It fosters collaboration and exchange across different disciplines, advances the application and development of AI technologies, and thereby creates greater economic and social value.

2.4. Identified Influencing Factors for AIAD

Through the extensive review of the literature, a range of influencing factors that pertain to AI adoption in architectural design has been examined and organized. These factors were acquired through the examination of several peer-reviewed studies pertaining to technological, organizational, human, educational, project-related, and economic dimensions. To support transparency and traceability, Table 1 presents the prominent factors that emerged from the examined literature, accompanied by their representative sources and thematic categories. This synthesis provides the empirical backing for the subsequent quantitative assessment and modeling procedures.

Past research on the use of artificial intelligence in architecture has mainly highlighted conceptual exploration or thing-based examples without providing a common theoretical model to explain the ways AI technologies interact with aspects of design thinking, adaptations of the organization, and project management. Most of the literature reflects a descriptive or technology-centered view, emphasizing the function of a tool rather than the ways in which human, technological, and institutional variables crop up in the way architecture's design process alters due to technology. This limited scope fails to show how technology, human, and institutional factors work together to contribute to the evolution of architectural design processes. This paper contrasts this narrow focus with a conceptual model that positions Artificial Intelligence-based Architectural Design (AIAD) as a socio-technical system at play. This model combines design theory studies, innovation diffusion, and technology adoption studies to broaden the conversation from tool use to mechanism interpretation. This shift from tool use to mechanism makes it possible for AIAD to transcend disciplinary boundaries, framing a theoretical model to evaluate AI's role in innovation and organizational change in architecture.

Table 1. Summary of Identified Influencing Factors from Literature (Source: Drawn by the author).

Primary Influencing Factors	Secondary Influencing Factors	Citations and Sources
Technology Factors (A01)	Aesthetics (B01)	[19–23]
	Interoperability (B02)	[24–29]
	Frontier Technology (B03)	[30–34]
Organization Factors (A02)	Information Exchange (B04)	[35–39]
	Organizational Governance (B05)	[40–44]
	Manpower and Employees (B06)	[45–48]
Environment Factors (A03)	Rules and Standardization (B07)	[49–55]
	Upstream and Downstream Connection (B08)	[56–59]
	Social Focus (B09)	[60,61]
Project Factors (A04)	Project Condition Basis (B10)	[62–64]
	Project Management (B11)	[65–67]
	Project Execution and Process (B12)	[68–71]
Education Factors (A05)	User Learn to Use (B13)	[72–75]
	External Support (B14)	[76–79]
	Inter-Sector R&D Collaboration (B15)	[80–86]
Economy Factors (A06)	Budget (B16)	[87–89]
	Sustainability Factors (B17)	[90–92]
	Time Cost and Hidden Cost (B18)	[93–98]

Most of the previous literature on AI as a design agent in architecture methodologically depended on singular analytical techniques such as qualitative case studies, a factor survey, and even multi-criteria decision-making (MCDM) modeling. While those can be effective methods of analysis, they fundamentally focus on only one or two dimensions of the underlying ecology of dynamic and interdependent factors on agents' willingness to embrace AI technologies used for design. We advance the methodological considerations of AI as a design agent by proposing a unified hybrid MCDM framework that is composed of AHP, DEMATEL, ISM, and MICMAC approaches that include quantifying weight, causal mapping, hierarchical structuring, and various levels of dependency classification. This hybrid MCDM approach offers an improvement to analytical qualities, and we were able to use it to cross-validate the findings from one model against another, decreasing subjectivity in evaluation and improving interpretation. In addition, providing a linked hybrid MCDM framework allows for a larger consideration of the theoretical tenets of the AIAD framework, which implies that our findings advance the understanding of AI mechanisms in design practices holistically, as compared to relying on past studies that either a model or framework devoted to one or the other. Overall, in relation to previous studies, the contribution offers methodological rigor and theoretical robustness, which enables further methodological advancement through empirical validation of structural equation modeling and potential system dynamics simulations.

3. Research Design and Framework

This study employed a systematic design, combining qualitative analysis with quantitative reasoning. By integrating artificial intelligence with architectural design, the study explored the impact mechanism of the project. The overall logic, from concept to empirical modeling, organically combined expert evaluation with measured data. This research was based on a previously validated literature-based survey. This study uses a hybrid multi-criteria framework to examine the hierarchical relationships and causal relationships between these factors. This approach maintains conceptual and theoretical coherence while ensuring the rigor of this current research, thereby bridging the gap between theory and practice in AI-assisted architectural design.

The overall analysis process consists of three stages. First, in our previous literature review research, we identified six major influencing factors and 18 minor influencing factors. Second, this study applied a hybrid decision model, which includes four frameworks. Finally, after neutralizing these research results, a unified influencing mechanism framework was constructed to identify the key driving factors of artificial intelligence application in architectural design. The data was collected through professionals from the fields of architecture, computer science and artificial intelligence. This integration of theory with measurable evidence provides depth of explanation and quantitative accuracy. Therefore, this research established a coherent logical foundation for the application and dissemination of complex interrelationships that define the adoption and diffusion of AI technologies in architectural design.

4. Research Methodology and Data Collection

4.1. Research Design and Process

This section aims to analyze the influencing mechanisms and interrelationships among the factors influencing the AI-based architectural design via the establishment of a combined AHP-DEMATEL-ISM-MICMAC model (Figure 2). The four models, AHP, DEMATEL, ISM and MICMAC, are commonly used as Multiple Criteria Decision Making (MCDM) methods to evaluate the best decision options or summarize the analysis based on multiple criteria. The combination of these four methods can make the research process more complete, rational and scientific. The purpose of the AHP method is to establish the basic and comprehensive weights of each factor, and DEMATEL is used to analyze the relationship between various factors and construct a matrix. ISM is adopted to build a multi-layer recursive structure model to further analyze the hierarchical structure and overall influencing relationship among the influencing factors. MICMAC is used to identify the driving factors for the adoption of AI technologies, as well as to provide the basis for subsequent analysis and implementation strategies.

Within the combined model, the results of the four models complement each other and are intrinsically related and complementary. For example, DEMATEL complements the scope of the AHP research object, while the MICMAC analysis is based on the ISM calculations. The subsequent research in this study will also be conducted based on the results of the four combined models.

It is also used to identify influencing factors that influence the implementation of AI-based architectural design. In this section, with a meta-analytic quantitative literature review as the basis, 6 primary influencing factor groups and 18 secondary influence factor groups are divided, as shown in Figure 3. The set of influencing factor indicators used in this study was derived from a systematic literature review conducted by the authors, which involved literature collection, screening, and thematic synthesis following PRISMA guidelines. Detailed procedures and source references are provided in a companion review article currently under submission. These established indicators serve as the theoretical and empirical foundation for the quantitative modeling presented in Figure 3.

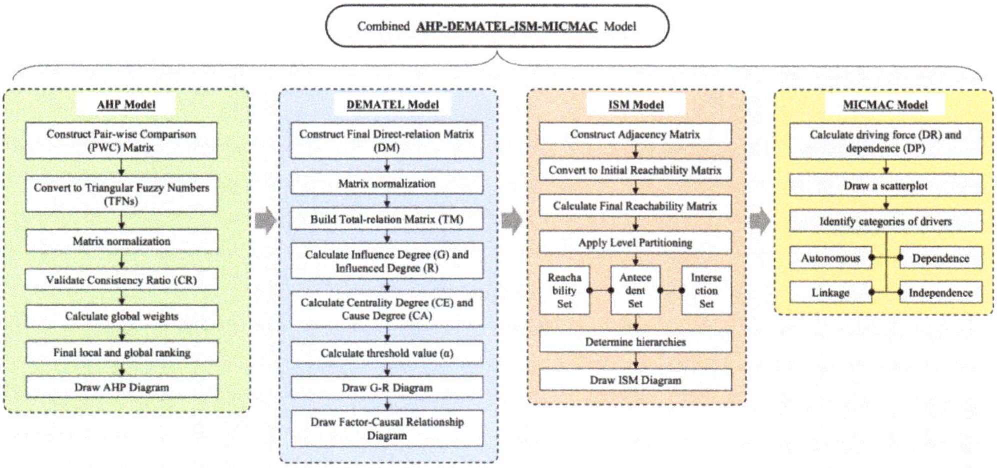

Figure 2. Analysis process of a combined AHP-DEMATEL-ISM-MICMAC model (Source: drawn by the author).

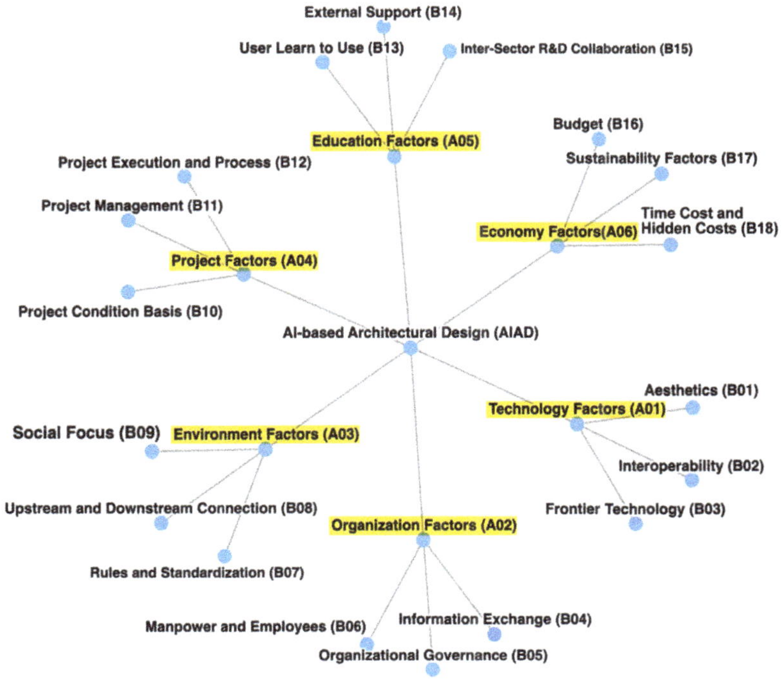

Figure 3. AHP Hierarchy Tree and Influencing Factor Indicators (Source: Drawn by the author).

4.2. Method of Data Collection

The data for this study was collected from a group of 15 experts representing different fields, including the architectural design industry, academia, and the computer and internet industry. The experts were divided into three groups based on their professional domains. Group 1 consisted of experts from the architectural design industry, Group 2 comprised academic experts, and Group 3 comprised experts from the computer and internet industry.

In Group 1, the architectural design industry experts held positions such as Deputy General Manager, Project Manager, Director of Equipment, Chief Architect, and Creative Director. They had an average of 24 years of experience in their respective fields. Group 2 included academic experts from universities and research institutions, with positions ranging from Associate Professor to Professor and Institute Director. Their average years of experience were around 25 years. Group 3 consisted of experts from the computer and internet industry, holding positions such as Project Manager, Technical Lead, Digital Marketing Manager, Software Architect, and Senior Development Manager. They had an average of 28 years of experience.

The diverse expertise and extensive experience of these experts make them valuable contributors to the study. They bring a wealth of knowledge and insights from their respective domains, which will help in understanding the factors influencing AI adoption in architectural design. The inclusion of experts from different industries ensures a comprehensive and holistic analysis of the topic, considering various perspectives and potential interrelationships between factors. The composition of the expert group reflects a well-rounded representation of relevant domains, ensuring the credibility and reliability of the study's findings. The insights provided by these experts will contribute to developing data-driven strategies for architecture firms undergoing digital transformation and addressing the knowledge gap in AI adoption within the architecture industry. The consistency checks will be completed as part of the AHP in Section 5.1.

Based on the professional field of decision makers, the expert group is further divided into three groups, with each consisting of five members. In this part, the Likert Scale and Structural Self-Interaction Matrix (SSIM) are adopted to design the scale and questionnaire.

In this section, the Likert Scale and the Structural Self-Interaction Matrix (SSIM) method were selected for the design of the scales and questionnaires. The Likert Scale is a rating tool used to measure attitudes or opinions, consisting of a series of statements to which respondents indicate their level of agreement using numerical scales or shorthand codes. For the AHP and DEMATEL sections, scores from 1 to 5 correspond to: (1) Equal Importance (EQI), (2) Moderate Importance (MI), (3) Strong Importance (SI), (4) Very Strong Importance (VSI), and (5) Extreme Importance (EXI). In the DEMATEL section, differing from the "importance" comparisons in the AHP part, data are collected to analyze the "degree of influence" among the factors. Scores from 0 to 5 correspond to: (0) No Influence (NI), (1) Low Influence (LI), (2) Moderate Influence (MOI), (3) High Influence (HI), (4) Very High Influence (VHI), and (5) Extreme Influence (EI). The advantage of using the Likert Scale is that it allows respondents to maintain a neutral stance when completing the questionnaire, without immediately expressing opinions that could bias the analysis results. At the same time, it does not compel participants to take a position on a specific topic, allowing them to respond with varying degrees of agreement. For the ISM section, the SSIM-VAXO method of the Structural Self-Interaction Matrix is employed for questionnaire design. These responses are easily quantifiable, thereby enhancing the reliability of subsequent data analysis results.

4.3. Construction of Combined AHP-DEMATEL-ISM-MICMAC Model

4.3.1. The Construction Process of AHP

AHP is a method proposed by Saaty to analyze complex decisions [99,100]. AHP has the ability to quantify the evaluation results of influencing factors into numbers to evaluate different alternatives and to determine the relevance of various elements considered in the analysis. The hierarchy established by the AHP determines the weights of the influencing factors, thus providing decision-making suggestions for the subsequent qualitative and quantitative analysis. The flow chart of the AHP model is shown in Figure 4. To determine the parameter weights via AHP, the following steps need to be followed:

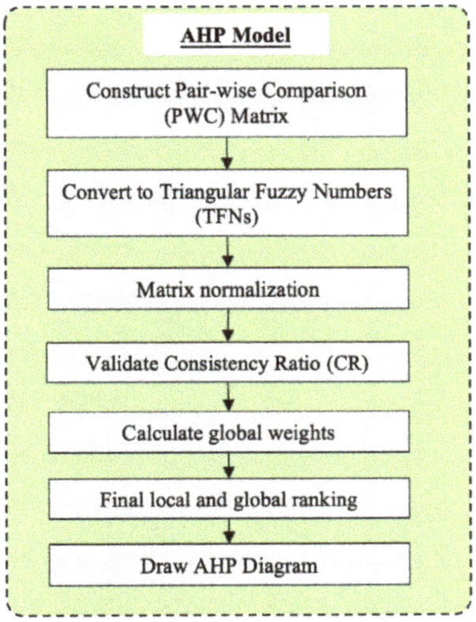

Figure 4. AHP analysis process (Source: drawn by the author).

Step 1: a Pair-wise Comparison (PWC) matrix is established according to Equation (1) $(n_i \times n_j)$. n represents the number of parameters used for PWC. p_{ij} stands for the decision elements of the pair-wise matrix shown. To obtain the final pair-wise comparison matrix, it is necessary to introduce fuzzy theory.

First of all, the experts give their opinions on comparison of primary influencing factors and other influencing factors. After describing the initial paired comparison matrix, showing the qualitative paired comparison. Then the scale will be quantified into Crisp Numeric Values, and the next step is to convert the values into Triangular Fuzzy Numbers (TFNs).

Then, the three original paired comparison matrices obtained by the three expert groups are merged into a paired comparison matrix, thus a summarized fuzzy paired comparison matrix is formed. Following the defuzzification step, the final paired comparison matrix is obtained. The following steps are used to carry out AHP analysis to determine the parameter weights. Equations (1)–(9) of this part of the model come from Saaty and his research work [101,102]. These include the pairwise comparison matrix, normalization procedure, eigenvector computation, and consistency ratio (CR) calculation.

In the paired comparison matrix, if the value of a cell is p_{ij}, the corresponding value p_{ji} in the table cell is $\frac{1}{p_{ij}}$. For example, the relationship between cells p_{12} and p_{21} in Equation (1) can be reflected by $p_{12} = \frac{1}{p_{21}}$ and $p_{21} = \frac{1}{p_{12}}$ respectively.

$$P(n_i \times n_j) = \begin{bmatrix} p_{11} & p_{12} & \cdots & p_{1j} \\ p_{21} & p_{22} & \cdots & p_{2j} \\ \cdots & \cdots & \cdots & \cdots \\ p_{i1} & p_{i2} & \cdots & p_{ij} \end{bmatrix} \quad (1)$$

Step 2: The paired comparison matrix is normalized via the use of Equation (2). N_{ij}^{AHP} represents the influencing factors in the normalized matrix.

$$N_{ij}^{AHP} = \frac{p_{ij}}{\sum_{i=1}^{n} p_{ij}} \quad (2)$$

Step 3: The Priority Vector of each influencing factor is calculated via the use of Equation (3). If the Consistency Ratio (CR) condition is met after the consistency is checked, the Priority Vector can be considered as the final weight of the influencing factors, and w_i^{AHP} represents the weights of each parameter.

$$w_i^{AHP} = \frac{\sum_{j=1}^{n} N_{ij}^{AHP}}{n} \quad (3)$$

Step 4: The last step of AHP is to calculate the *CR* value and check whether it is within $CR \leq 0.1$ or 10%. The following are the steps to perform the consistency checking process.

First, the Weighted Sum WS_i matrix is calculated according to Equation (4).

$$WS_i \begin{bmatrix} WS_1 \\ WS_2 \\ \cdots \\ WS_i \end{bmatrix} = \begin{bmatrix} p_{11} & p_{12} & \cdots & p_{1j} \\ p_{21} & p_{22} & \cdots & p_{2j} \\ \cdots & \cdots & \cdots & \cdots \\ p_{i1} & p_{i2} & \cdots & p_{ij} \end{bmatrix} \times \begin{bmatrix} w_1 \\ w_2 \\ \cdots \\ w_i \end{bmatrix} \quad (4)$$

Then, the Consistency (C_i) of each factor is determined.

$$C_i = \frac{WS_i}{w_i^{AHP}} \quad (5)$$

The average consistency (λ_{max}) is calculated by taking the average value of all consistencies calculated in the previous step.

$$\lambda_{max} = \frac{\sum_{i=1}^{n} C_i}{n} \quad (6)$$

Equation (7) is used for calculating the value of Consistency Index (*CI*).

$$CI = \frac{(\lambda_{max} - n)}{(n-1)} \quad (7)$$

Finally, Equation (8) is used to calculate the *CR* value.

$$CR = \frac{CI}{RI} \quad (8)$$

RI stands for random index, which can be obtained from Table 2 according to the number of influencing factors considered in AHP analysis. If the *CR* value is less than 0.1 or 10%, the paired comparison matrix created in step 1 is consistent, and the weight calculated in step 3 via the use of Equation (3) can be finally determined as the influencing factor weight. If the *CR* value exceeds 0.1, it is necessary to return to step 1 to reconstruct the judgment matrix and paired comparison matrix until the *CR* value is limited to 0.1. For the complete AHP analysis of the 6 primary influencing factors, see Section 4.1 for details.

Table 2. Random index (RI) values (Source: drawn by the author).

n	1	2	3	4	5	6	7	8	9	10	11	12
RI	0	0	0.58	0.9	1.12	1.24	1.32	1.41	1.45	1.49	1.51	1.58

Step 5: After that, the Global Weights of the parameters need to be calculated. The weights obtained from pairwise comparisons in AHP analysis are usually Local Weights. The concepts of Global Weights and Local Weights are applied to the secondary influencing factors, and the Global Weights are calculated using Equation (9).

$$w_{i(global)(sub)} = w_{i(main)}^{AHP} \times w_{i(local)(sub)}^{AHP} \quad (9)$$

The Global Weights of each secondary influencing factor $w_{i(global)(sub)}$ can be obtained if the primary influencing factor weight $w_{i(main)}^{AHP}$ is multiplied by the respective local secondary influencing factor $w_{i(local)(sub)}^{AHP}$. While the following conditions must be met:

Condition 1: $\sum_{i=1}^{y} w_{i(global)(sub)} = w_{i(main)}^{AHP}$

Condition 2: $\sum_{i=1}^{x} \sum_{i=1}^{y} w_{i(global)(sub)} = \sum_{i=1}^{x} w_{i(main)}^{AHP} = 1$

Condition 3: $\sum_{i=1}^{x} w_{i(main)}^{AHP} = \sum_{i=1}^{y} w_{i(local)(sub)}^{AHP} = 1$

Here, x represents the number of primary influencing factors and y stands for the number of secondary influencing factors within the primary influencing factors. It is important to note that the three conditions stated resolve under the assumption of hierarchical independence and consistent judgment matrices. For instance, the same secondary influencing factor may have overlap between different primary categories, which may have a smaller effect on the overall weight accuracy. Furthermore, as attention is put on the experts to make comparisons using the AHP method, the resulting weights may have subjectivity, of a considerable amount when increasing the number of comparisons and level of comparisons. This study will address those limitations by applying fuzzy logic transformation and expert group averaging to increase consistency and eliminate some subjectivity. Finally, the AHP method can be used to calculate the weights of primary and secondary influencing factors, including local weights, local ranking, global weights, and global ranking, all of which are shown in Table 3 below.

Table 3. Final AHP calculation results (Source: drawn by the author).

Primary Influencing Factors	Weight	Ranking	Secondary Influencing Factors	Consistency Ratio CR	Local Weights	Local Ranking	Global Weights	Global Ranking
A01	0.34338	1	B01	0.02694	0.57233	1	0.19653	1
			B02		0.13260	3	0.04553	9
			B03		0.29507	2	0.10132	3
A02	0.12164	4	B04	0.00026	0.55024	1	0.06693	5
			B05		0.27603	2	0.03358	11
			B06		0.17373	3	0.02113	14
A03	0.08017	5	B07	0.00912	0.27977	2	0.02243	13
			B08		0.58715	1	0.04707	8
			B09		0.13307	3	0.01067	17

Table 3. *Cont.*

Primary Influencing Factors	Weight	Ranking	Secondary Influencing Factors	Consistency Ratio CR	Local Weights	Local Ranking	Global Weights	Global Ranking
			B10		0.15396	3	0.03687	10
A04	0.23951	2	**B11**	0.01087	0.57117	1	0.13680	2
			B12		0.27486	2	0.06583	6
			B13		0.17311	3	0.00949	18
A05	0.05480	6	**B14**	0.01579	0.30177	2	0.01654	16
			B15		0.52512	1	0.02877	12
			B16		0.50468	1	0.08100	4
A06	0.16051	3	**B17**	0.00133	0.13130	3	0.02107	15
			B18		0.36402	2	0.05843	7

Step 6: The local and global influencing factors are ranked according to the results of the calculated weights, as shown.

4.3.2. The Construction Process of Decision-Making Trial and Evaluation Laboratory (DEMATEL)

DEMATEL is an analytical method used to analyze the interaction among factors in complex systems and identify the core influencing factors. After the basic weight and comprehensive weight of each influencing factor are established, it is necessary to further analyze the relationship between these factors and identify the key ones. Different from AHP in which the "importance" of influencing factors is analyzed, DEMATEL is mainly used to analyze the "influencing degree" between various factors. The relationship between factors is bidirectional. DEMATEL method needs to be supplemented by Fuzzy Set theory to solve the problems of insufficient data clarity and subjective judgment of respondents [103]. It has been widely used in many fields. DEMATEL technology, based on graph theory, helps decision makers analyze multiple measurement standards into causal groups, thus producing simpler causal relationships [102]. Equations (10)–(18) follow the standard formulation established by Gabus & Fontela [104], with methodological refinements referenced from Ocampo et al. and Chen & Chen [101,103]. Figure 5 are the steps of DEMATEL method:

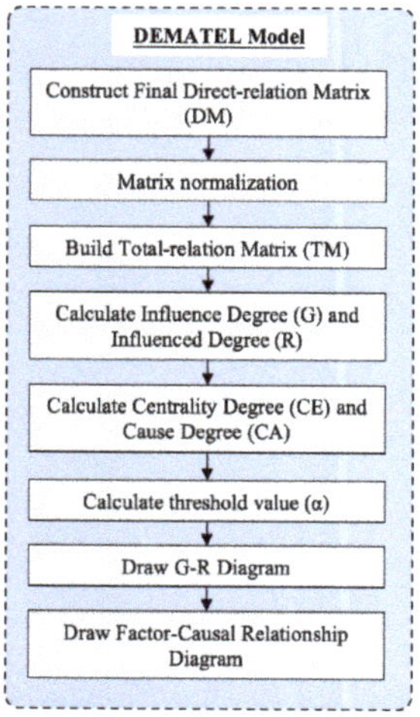

Figure 5. Diagram of DEMATEL analysis process (Source: drawn by the author).

Step 1: A Direct-relation Matrix is constructed based on Equation (10). d_{ij} represents the influencing degree of the I-th factor on the J-th factor. Based on the scale in Table 4, the three direct influence matrices of the three expert groups are quantized, and then converted into triangular fuzzy numbers, and summarized to obtain the Fuzzy Direct-relation Matrix. Finally, defuzzification is performed to obtain the Final Direct-relation Matrix.

$$D(n_i \times n_j) = \begin{bmatrix} d_{11} & d_{12} & \dots & d_{1j} \\ d_{21} & d_{22} & \dots & d_{2j} \\ \dots & \dots & \dots & \dots \\ d_{i1} & d_{i2} & \dots & d_{ij} \end{bmatrix} \tag{10}$$

In Equation (10), the diagonal elements of the direct influence matrix $d_{11}, d_{22}, d_{33}, \dots$ are set to be zero. If there are k (number) decision makers, the final direct influence matrix is considered as the average value of all elements d_{ij} provided by the k decision makers, as shown in Equations (4)–(11) $1 \le k \le K$.

$$D = [d_{ij}] = \frac{1}{K}\sum_{k=1}^{K} d_{ij}^k \tag{11}$$

Step 2: The direct influence matrix D is normalized via Equation (13). Before normalization, it is necessary to calculate the sum of values in each row and column, find the largest number-s in the summation elements according to Equation (12), and then normalize the direct influence matrix according to Equation (13).

$$S = max\left(\sum_{j=1}^{n} d_{ij}, \sum_{i=1}^{n} d_{ij}\right) \tag{12}$$

$$N_{ij}^{DEMATEL} = \frac{d_{ij}}{S} \tag{13}$$

Step 3: A Combined Influence Matrix is established according to Equation (14), and the Total-relation Matrix is represented by Equation (15). t_{ij} Represents the total-relation elements of matrix T.

$$T = N_{ij}^{DEMATEL}\left(I - N_{ij}^{DEMATEL}\right)^{-1} \tag{14}$$

$$T(n_i \times n_j) = \begin{bmatrix} t_{11} & t_{12} & \dots & t_{1j} \\ t_{21} & t_{22} & \dots & t_{2j} \\ \dots & \dots & \dots & \dots \\ t_{i1} & t_{i2} & \dots & t_{ij} \end{bmatrix} \tag{15}$$

Here I is the Identity Matrix of an n-matrix $(n_i \times n_j)$. All diagonal elements are 1, and the other elements are equal to 0, as shown in Equation (16).

$$I = \begin{bmatrix} 1 & 0 & \dots & 0 & 0 \\ 0 & 1 & \dots & 0 & 0 \\ \dots & \dots & \dots & \dots & \dots \\ 0 & 0 & \dots & 1 & 0 \\ 0 & 0 & \dots & 0 & 1 \end{bmatrix} \tag{16}$$

Step 4: The Influence Degree (G_i) and Influenced Degree (R_j) for each influencing factor are calculated according to Equation (17). The Gi is obtained by the summing of values in each row of the combined influence matrix, while the R_j is calculated by the summing of values in each column.

$$\begin{cases} G_i = \sum_{j=1}^{n} t_{ij} \\ R_j = \sum_{i=1}^{n} t_{ij} \end{cases} \tag{17}$$

Step 5: After the Gi and the R_j are confirmed, the Centrality Degree (CE) and Cause Degree (CA) will be calculated. The Centrality Degree (CE) and Cause Degree (CA) will be determined via Equation (18), and both reflect the causal relationship among influencing factors. The calculation results about the CE and CA for each influencing factor are listed in Equation (16).

$$\begin{cases} CE = (G_i + R_j) \\ CA = (G_i - R_j) \end{cases} \tag{18}$$

Centrality Degree $(G_i + R_j)$ value indicates the importance of this factor in the whole system. The higher the value is, the more important the influencing factor is. Cause Degree $(G_i - R_j)$ value indicates the causal relationship, indicating the influence of an influencing factor on other factors. If $CA > 0$, the corresponding factor is a causal factor that has a strong influential effect on other factors. If $CA < 0$, the corresponding factor belongs to a result factor, indicating that the factor is susceptible to the influence of other factors. Based on the calculation results, the centrality is ranked, and the factor attributes are determined by the positive and negative values of the Cause Degree. With the Centrality Degree as the horizontal axis and the Cause Degree as the vertical axis, the "Cause-effect Diagram" is drawn eventually.

Step 6: The "Cause-effect Diagram" drawn in the previous step labels the influencing factors as points on the Cause Degree-Centrality Degree axis. In order to visualize the relationship between parameters, a Digraph in the section will be constructed in the form of arrows to a more visualized presentation. Therefore, it is necessary to calculate the threshold value (α) by using Equation (19) to calculate the average values of all elements of the Total-relation Matrix (T).

$$\alpha = \frac{\sum_{i=1}^{n} \sum_{j=1}^{n} t_{ij}}{n} \tag{19}$$

At this time, the importance of influencing factors is determined based on the threshold value, and the total relation elements t_{ij} in the Total-relation Matrix (T) that are greater than the threshold (α) are used to construct the DEMATEL diagram. The directional arrows in the Section 5.2 indicate the intervention direction and are superimposed on the "Factor-Causal Relationship Diagram" drawn in the previous section to show the strong and weak causal relationship between different influencing factors more intuitively.

Table 4. Linguistic-based importance conversion scale (Source: drawn by the author).

AHP		DEMATEL		Scale Value	Fuzzy Number
Qualitative Terms	**Symbols**	**Degree of Influence**	**Symbols**		
-	-	No influence	NI	0	0, 0, 0
Equal Importance	EQI	Low Influence	LI	1	1, 1, 1
Moderate Importance	MI	Moderate Influence	MOI	2	1, 2, 3
Strong Importance	SI	Hight Influence	HI	3	2, 3, 4
Very Strong Importance	VSI	Very High Influence	VHI	4	3, 4, 5
Extreme Importance	EXI	Extreme Influence	EI	5	5, 5, 5

4.3.3. The Construction Process of Interpretative Structural Modeling (ISM)

Since AHP-DEMATEL can only judge the relationship between the primary influencing factors of a complex system or the relation between all the secondary influencing factors under the independent primary influencing factors. While it cannot judge the relationship between the secondary influencing factors under across-level influencing factors. For example, it cannot judge the relationship between aesthetics (B01) under technological factor (A01) and information exchange (B04) under organizational factor (A02). Meanwhile, it is impossible to divide the structural relationship between influencing factors. Therefore, in order to clearly analyze the hierarchical relationship among the influencing factors in the system and identify the basic influencing factors in the system, the Interpretive Structural Modeling (ISM) and Cross-Impact Matrix Multiplication Applied to Classification (MICMAC) are combined to solve the problem that the importance of each influencing factor in the system cannot be identified. ISM can be used to solve complex system problems, and it is also suitable for system analysis with many variables and unclear structural relationships. The hierarchical relationship diagram obtained by ISM shows the ultimate goal of the system at the top, with the lower hierarchies, respectively, showing the causes of the upper hierarchies. This method makes the analysis results not only intuitive but also precise and reasonable, and it facilitates the understanding and identification of the direct and indirect relationships between specific projects. Equations (19)–(22) are derived from Warfield's original system-structure modeling framework [104]. The ISM steps are described in Figure 6 as follows:

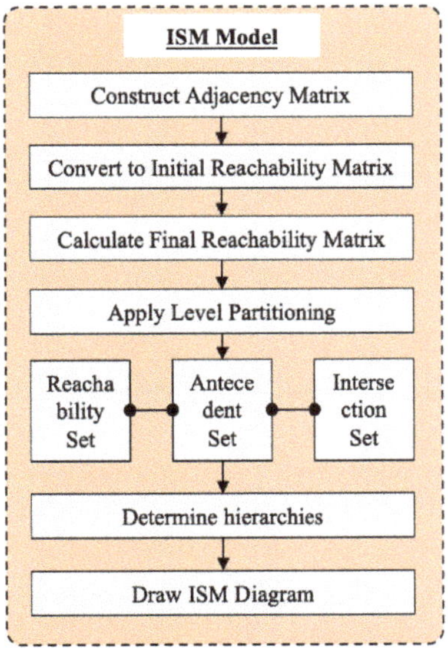

Figure 6. ISM steps (Source: drawn by the author).

Step 1: According to the four influence relationships of V, A, X and O given, a Structural Self Interaction Matrix (SSIM) is made, namely the Adjacency Matrix. The Adjacency Matrix in ISM is basically the same as the direct influence matrix in DEMATEL. The main difference is that in ISM, the adjacency matrix determines whether there is any influence relationship between factors, while in DEMATEL, the direct influence matrix indicates the degree of influence between influencing factors according to the scale given in Table 4. Equation (20) shows an example of adjacency matrix.

$$A(n_i \times n_j) = \begin{bmatrix} a_{11} & a_{12} & \cdots & a_{1j} \\ - & a_{22} & \cdots & a_{2j} \\ \cdots & \cdots & \cdots & \cdots \\ - & - & \cdots & a_{ij} \end{bmatrix} \tag{20}$$

In Equation (20), the diagonal element of SSIM $a_{11}, a_{22}, a_{33}, \ldots$ is set to be 1, and the upper triangular elements are replaced by four letters, V, A, X and O.

Step 2: The SSIM is converted into an Initial Reachability Matrix by replacing the letters on the upper triangle with binary digits 0 or 1. Similarly, the binary digits in the lower triangle element can be determined according to the four letters determined by the upper triangle edge. The value of each cell in the Reachability Matrix is 1 or 0, indicating that there is a connection between two node pairs. It means that one node can be reached from another node in the binary relationship of the graph.

Step 3: The final Reachability Matrix is generated by the application of the transformation laws shown in Equation (21). The conversion principle is that if any factor A relates to or influences factor B, and factor B relates to factor C, factor A will automatically relate to or influence factor C according to the Boolean algebra algorithm. The Transitivity Elements are marked as 1*.

$$A_{final}(n_i \times n_j) = \begin{bmatrix} a_{11}^f & a_{12}^f & \cdots & a_{1j}^f \\ a_{21}^f & a_{22}^f & \cdots & a_{2j}^f \\ \cdots & \cdots & \cdots & \cdots \\ a_{i1}^f & a_{i2}^f & \cdots & a_{ij}^f \end{bmatrix} \tag{21}$$

In Equation (21), the diagonal element of the final Reachability Matrix $a_{11}^f, a_{22}^f, a_{33}^f, \ldots$ is set to be 1, and the other elements are assigned to be 1 or 0 accordingly.

Step 4: After that, the Level Partitioning method is used to construct the hierarchy partitions and assign a hierarchy to each variable in the hierarchical structure. The Reachability Matrix needs to be decomposed to divide the areas of influencing factors. Based on the Reachability Matrix A_{final}, the Reachability Set, Antecedent Set and Intersection Set are calculated. Reachability Set represents the set of all factors in which the factor can be reached in A_{final}; Antecedent Set implies the set of all factors in which the factor can be reached in A_{final}; and Intersection Set means the intersection of Reachability Set and Antecedent Set. The Reachability Set represents a factor set composed of the enabling factor itself and other parameter sets that contribute to the realization of other factors. All parameter sets with binary digit 1 in the corresponding row in the final Reachability Matrix are considered. In addition, Antecedent Set is a factor set composed of contributing factor itself and other parameter sets that may be influenced by other factors. All parameter sets with binary digit 1 in the final Reachability Matrix are considered. The Intersection Set consists of all the common elements of the Reachability Set and the Antecedent Set. With the Reachability Matrix as the cardinal number, one factor is selected from each possibility set, which has the same elements as the Intersection Set. When the Intersection Set and the Reachability Set are perfectly matched, the corresponding factors will be assigned to their respective hierarchies, and these factors will be eliminated in subsequent iterations. After the stratified factors are removed, this operation will be repeated for the remaining factors, and all the first-hierarchy factors are ignored until all the factors are classified into different hierarchies. The iterative process continues until all factors are assigned to a certain hierarchy in the ISM, and the complete stratification result is finally obtained.

Step 5: The diagram described in Figure 6 shows the different hierarchies in the ISM structure, with the top factors mainly influenced by the bottom factors. The directed arrows show the direct and indirect influences between the considered factors.

4.3.4. The Construction Process of Cross-Impact Matrix Multiplication Applied to Classification (MICMAC)

Cross-Impact Matrix Multiplication Applied to Classification (MICMAC) means the principle of multiplication of influence matrix is applied to make the influence matrix reach a stable state. In the first part, the hierarchy and logical relationship between influencing factors are understood through the ISM. Based on the ISM Reachability Matrix, the influencing factors can be classified by using MICMAC analysis method, so as to further clarify the role of each factor in the system and the relationship between the factors, and finally calculate the dependence and driving force of the influencing factors. The MICMAC method can be used to identify the driving force and dependence of the influencing factors, so as to make recommendations in a more targeted manner. The analytical structure and classification equations are based on Godet [105], Figure 7 shows the flow chart of MICMAC analysis, and the result of this section is the analysis chart of driving force-dependence classification, with the following steps:

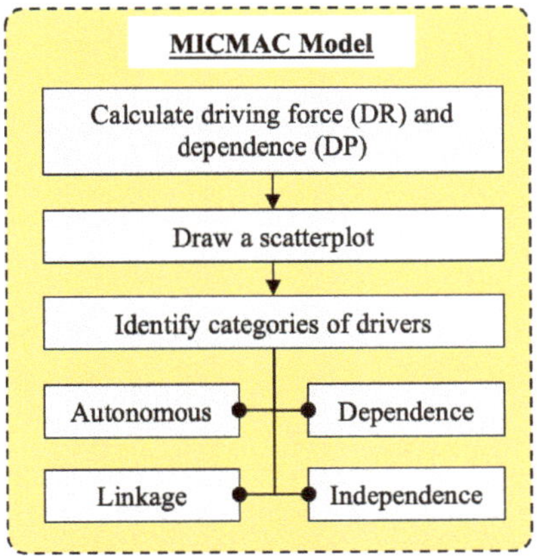

Figure 7. MICMAC analysis process (Source: drawn by the author).

Step 1: The driving force (DR_i) and dependence (DP_j) in the Reachability Matrix are calculated according to Equation (22). The driving force of influencing factors represents the sum of all binary digits-1 in the rows, while dependence is the sum of all binary digits 1 in the columns. Driving force indicates the degree to which one influencing factor drives other influencing factors. As the Reachability Set of each variable, it indicates the number of variables it can reach. The driving force indicates the degree to which the solution to this factor can help solve other factors. A greater driving force means more other factors can be solved. Dependence indicates the degree of dependence of other factors on one influencing factor, as well as the number of variables reaching it. The dependence represents the dependence of the solution to this factor on the solutions to other factors. A greater dependence means a greater dependence on the solutions to other factors. The influencing factors are classified according to driving force and dependence. Those ranking high in the list of driving forces have a strong ability to drive other factors, signifying that they have a greater influence on other factors. Those ranking high in the list of dependences are factors mainly depending on or slightly driven by other factors, meaning that the influencing factor is more dependent on other influencing factors.

$$\begin{cases} DR_i = \sum_{j=1}^{n} a_{ij}^{f} \\ DP_j = \sum_{i=1}^{n} a_{ij}^{f} \end{cases} \tag{22}$$

Step 2: The calculation result data of driving force and dependence are visualized in the form of scatter diagram in Figure 8. The coordinate system is divided into four quadrants, corresponding to autonomous cluster, dependence cluster, linkage cluster and independent cluster, respectively. With the driving force as the ordinate and the dependence as the abscissa, the driving-dependence power coordinate diagram based on the influencing factors of AI-based architectural design is drawn as followed:

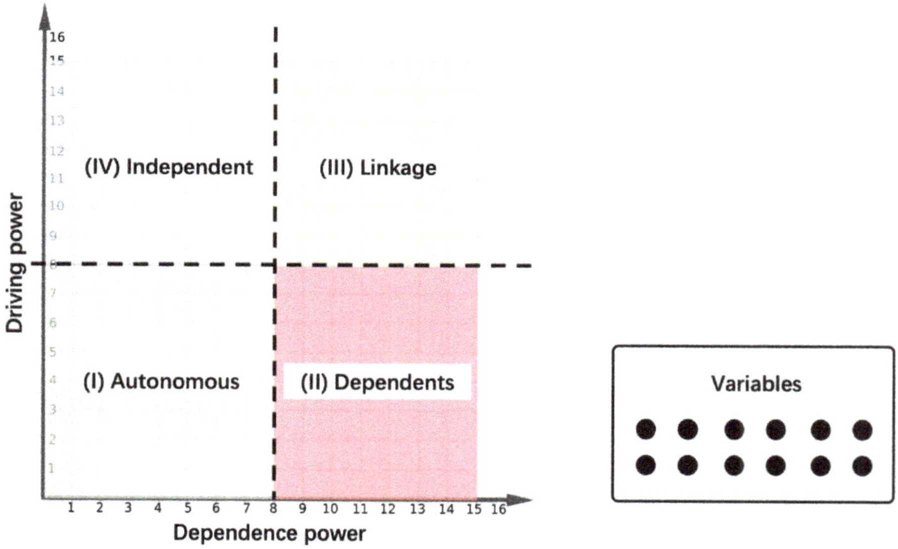

Figure 8. Coordinate system of driving force-dependence power (Source: drawn by the author).

5. Results and Data Analysis

Based on the definition and identification of 18 influencing factors, this study invited a panel of 15 experts to participate in the survey and evaluate the factors in order to analyze the impact mechanisms of AI-based architectural design. According to their professional fields and career backgrounds, the 15 experts were divided into three groups, each comprising five members. All participating experts have over 20 years of experience in their respective fields. The first group consisted of members from the architectural design industry, including architecture, design, engineering, and rendering professionals who have had exposure to AI technologies. The second group consisted of faculty and researchers from universities and research institutions, associated with architectural disciplines. The third group comprised professionals from the computer and internet industries, with extensive experience in software development and commercial applications of AI.

To ensure internal consistency, reliability testing was conducted using Cronbach's α. The coefficient for the combined expert questionnaire was 0.892, indicating strong reliability and consistency among expert evaluations. Prior to distribution, the questionnaire was reviewed by three external experts to assess content validity, ensuring that each influencing factor and corresponding linguistic scale accurately represented the intended conceptual dimension.

In the AHP and DEMATEL sections, each pairwise comparison matrix and direct-influence matrix was evaluated three times. Figure 9 illustrates the membership functions and bounded values for triangular and trapezoidal fuzzy numbers. To capture the fuzziness inherent in expert decision-making, all crisp numeric values were further converted into Triangular Fuzzy Numbers (TFNs) according to Figure 9. The figure also presents all linguistic assessment phrases along with their corresponding quantitative values and the converted fuzzy values. Beyond prioritizing each decision-maker's evaluation results, unclear or ambiguous situations were also accounted for using fuzzy logic, thereby enhancing the accuracy and reliability of the results.

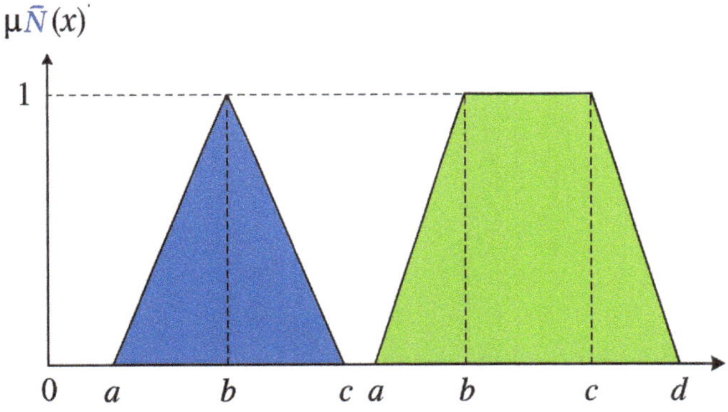

Figure 9. Conversion Method of Triangular Fuzzy Numbers (TFNs) (Source: Drawn by the author).

The abscissa in Figure 10 represents a normalized linguistic scale used in the fuzzy conversion process. It is dimensionless, corresponding to the expert-assigned influence levels ranging from 0 (no influence) to 5 (extreme influence). The ordinate $\mu\tilde{N}(x)$ indicates the membership degree of each linguistic term, ranging from 0 to 1, (a,b,c) denotes a triangular fuzzy number, and (a,b,c,d) denotes a trapezoidal fuzzy number. For the triangular fuzzy number $\tilde{N} = (a,b,c)$, a represents the lower bound value, b represents the intermediate value, and c represents the upper bound value. In the case of the trapezoidal fuzzy number $\tilde{N} = (a,b,c,d)$, a and d represent the lower and upper bound values, respectively. In Figure 10, the trapezoidal fuzzy number has two intermediate bounds, denoted as b and c. Equations (23) and (24) describe the triangular fuzzy number and trapezoidal fuzzy number, respectively.

$$\mu_{\tilde{N}}(x) = \begin{cases} 0 & x < a \\ \frac{x-a}{b-a} & a \leq x \leq b \\ \frac{c-x}{c-b} & b \leq x \leq c \\ 0 & x \geq c \end{cases} \tag{23}$$

$$\mu_{\tilde{N}}(x) = \begin{cases} 0 & x < a \\ \frac{x-a}{b-a} & a \leq x \leq b \\ 1 & b \leq x \leq c \\ \frac{d-x}{d-c} & c \leq x \leq d \\ 0 & x \geq d \end{cases} \tag{24}$$

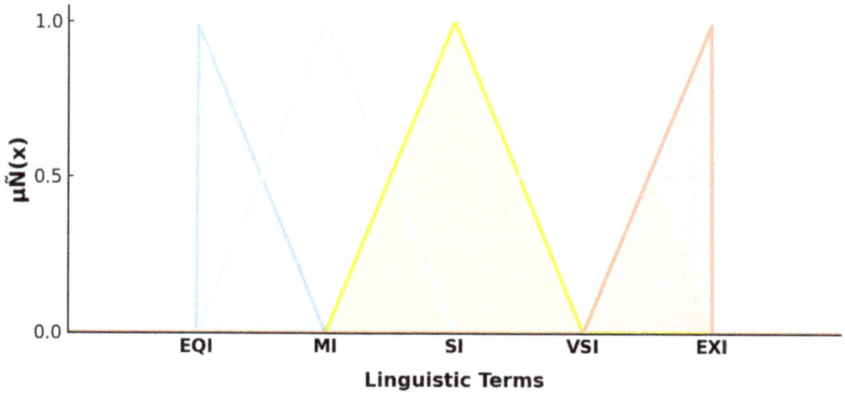

Figure 10. Conversion of Linguistic Terms and Triangular Fuzzy Numbers (Source: Drawn by the author).

If there are two triangular fuzzy numbers, such as $\tilde{N}_1 = (a_1, b_1, c_1)$ and $\tilde{N}_2 = (a_2, b_2, c_2)$, the calculation method between these two TFNs is as follows:

$$\begin{cases} \tilde{N}_1 + \tilde{N}_2 = (a_1, b_1, c_1) + (a_2, b_2, c_2) = (a_1 + a_2, b_1 + b_2, c_1 + c_2) \\ \tilde{N}_1 + \lambda = (a_1 + \lambda, b_1 + \lambda, c_1 + \lambda) \end{cases} \quad (25)$$

$$\begin{cases} \tilde{N}_1 - \tilde{N}_2 = (a_1, b_1, c_1) - (a_2, b_2, c_2) = (a_1 - c_2, b_1 - b_2, c_1 - a_2) \\ \tilde{N}_1 - \lambda = (a_1 - \lambda, b_1 - \lambda, c_1 - \lambda) \end{cases} \quad (26)$$

$$\begin{cases} \tilde{N}_1 \times \tilde{N}_2 = (a_1, b_1, c_1) \times (a_2, b_2, c_2) = (a_1 \times a_2, b_1 \times b_2, c_1 \times c_2) \\ \tilde{N}_1 \times \lambda = (a_1 \times \lambda, b_1 \times \lambda, c_1 \times \lambda) \end{cases} \quad (27)$$

$$\begin{cases} \tilde{N}_1 \div \tilde{N}_2 = (a_1, b_1, c_1) \div (a_2, b_2, c_2) = \left(\frac{a_1}{c_2}, \frac{b_1}{b_2}, \frac{c_1}{a_2}\right) \\ \tilde{N}_1 \div \lambda = \left(\frac{a_1}{\lambda}, \frac{b_1}{\lambda}, \frac{c_1}{\lambda}\right) \end{cases} \quad (28)$$

$$\left\{ \frac{1}{\tilde{N}_1} = \frac{1}{(a_1, b_1, c_1)} = \left(\frac{1}{c_1}, \frac{1}{b_1}, \frac{1}{a_1}\right) \right. \quad (29)$$

$$\tilde{N}_1 = (a_1,\ b_1,\ c_1),\ (\tilde{N}_1) = \frac{a_1,\ b_1,\ c_1}{3} \quad (30)$$

Among them, Equations (25)–(30) represent the addition, subtraction, multiplication, division, reciprocal operations between triangular fuzzy numbers, and the defuzzification calculation of fuzzy numbers, respectively. The resulting value $(\tilde{N}_1)$ is the defuzzified value. If there are k decision-makers expressing their opinions, the fuzzy numbers $\tilde{N}_1 = (a_1,\ b_1,\ c_1)$, $\tilde{N}_2 = (a_2,\ b_2,\ c_2)$, ..., $\tilde{N}_k = (a_k,\ b_k,\ c_k)$ can be aggregated as follows:

$$\overline{A}(\tilde{N}_1, \tilde{N}_2, \cdots, \tilde{N}_k) = \left(\frac{1}{k}\sum_{i=1}^{k} a_i, \frac{1}{k}\sum_{i=1}^{k} b_i, \frac{1}{k}\sum_{i=1}^{k} c_i\right) \quad (31)$$

5.1. Weighting and Hierarchical Ranking of Influencing Factors

In the AHP, a paired comparison matrix is used to describe the relative importance of each assessed indicator based on the scale provided in Table 4. In the analysis of this part, the local and global weights of all the influencing factors are derived through the AHP. The weights of the 6 primary influencing factors and the weights of 3 secondary influencing factors within each primary influencing factor are determined first. In addition, the global weights of all 18 secondary influencing factors are also calculated, resulting in an overall ranking. Table 5 demonstrates the final results of the AHP analysis and describes the weight and corresponding ranking of the primary influencing factors and shows the data visually in Figure 11.

Table 5. Total-relation Matrix (Source: drawn by the author).

	B01	B02	B03	Degree of Influence G	Centrality $G+R$	Causality $G-R$	Causal Relationship
B01	4.47365	5.19996	5.34733	15.02094	28.38925	1.652626	Cause
B02	4.10523	4.19996	4.61049	12.91569	27.51556	−1.68419	Result
B03	4.78943	5.19996	4.97890	14.96829	29.90502	0.031567	Cause
Influenced Degree R	13.36831	14.59988	14.93673	Threshold value (α)			4.76721

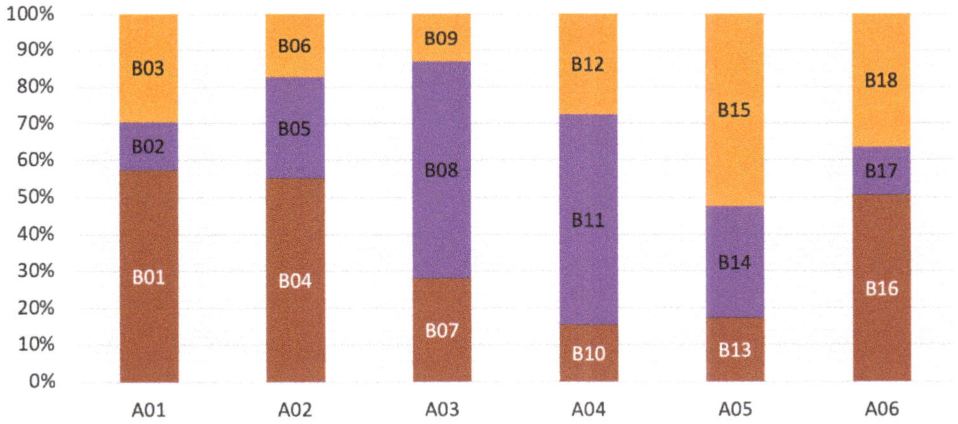

Figure 11. 18 Local weight distribution of secondary influencing factors in primary influencing factors (Source: drawn by the author).

According to the previous steps of calculating primary influencing factors of AHP, the triangular fuzzy numbers in the paired comparison matrix are standardized according to the matrix structure of "Expert decision-making panel 1". In addition, the weights of related secondary influencing factors are calculated, and whether the consistency is within the allowable range is checked. According to the analysis results, the consistency ratio of the pairing matrix of all secondary influencing factors is within the limit of 0.1 or 10%. The global weights of the influencing factors are evaluated based on Equation (9), and Table 5 shows the weights and rankings of all primary and secondary influencing factors, as well as the local and global weights. Figures 11 and 12 depict the local and global rankings and weight distributions of each influencing factor.

Figure 12. Global weight distribution of secondary influencing factors among primary influencing factors (Source: drawn by the author).

5.2. Causal Relationship of Influencing Factors

In DEMATEL, the degree of influence of each influencing factor on other factors is evaluated via the comparative scale in Table 4. Three expert panels express their own opinions in language and text and then convert these opinions into quantitative numerical values and triangular fuzzy numbers.

DEMATEL is used to determine the causal relationship of the selected influencing factors. With the primary influencing factor A01 as an example, the calculation process of DEMATEL is as follows: The opinions about influence of a single influencing factor evaluated by three expert panels on another factor are quantified into numerical values, and then fuzzy transformation is performed based on the scale described in Table 4.

The final step of DEMATEL is to calculate the Total-relation Matrix-T based on Equation (14), as shown in Table 5. The Total-relation Matrix (T) can be used to determine the influencing and influenced parties of each factor, thus ultimately helping to find the causal relationship between the influencing factors. Equation (17) is used to calculate the Influenced Degree (G) and the Influenced Degree (R) for each influencing factor. Then Equation (18) is adopted to calculate the Centrality Degree (CE) and Cause Degree (CA), and all the calculated values are shown in Table 5.

Table 5 shows the causal relationship between the three secondary influencing factors in the primary influencing factors A01. $G + R$ indicates the importance of each parameter and also, represents the degree of association of a particular influencing factor with other secondary influencing factors A higher $G + R$ value indicates that the influencing factor has a stronger or more significant relationship with other influencing factors, while a lower $G + R$ value indicates that the influencing factor has a weaker or less significant relationship with other influencing factors. In this case, B03 has the largest $G + R$ value, making it the most important secondary influencing factor among the primary influencing factor A01, and it also has a stronger relationship with the other influencing factors B01 and B02.

On the other hand, $G - R$ indicates the type of relationship between an influencing factor and other influencing factors. When the $G - R$ number is positive, it shows the cause group; when it is negative, it represents the result group. Table 6 shows that the influencing factors B01 and B03 belong to the cause group, implying that these two factors influence the factor B02. Similarly, B02 belongs to the result group, indicating that it is influenced by the other two factors B01 and B03.

Table 6. Final results of DEMATEL (Source: drawn by the author).

Primary Influencing Factors	Symbol	Secondary Influencing Factors	Influence Degree G	Influenced Degree R	Centrality Degree $G+R$	Cause Degree $G-R$	Causal Relationship	Threshold α
Technological factor	A01	B01	15.02094	13.36831	28.38925	1.65263	Cause	4.76721
		B02	12.91569	14.59988	27.51556	−1.68419	Result	
		B03	14.96829	14.93673	29.90502	0.03157	Cause	
Organizational factors	A02	B04	2.85864	3.21791	6.07656	−0.35927	Result	1.04999
		B05	3.81554	2.64792	6.46346	1.16761	Cause	
		B06	2.77574	3.58408	6.35983	−0.80834	Result	
Industrial environment factors	A03	B07	5.30708	4.96543	10.27252	0.34165	Cause	1.69524
		B08	5.75238	4.68137	10.43375	1.07102	Cause	
		B09	4.19768	5.61034	9.80803	−1.41266	Result	
Project factors	A04	B10	4.44132	4.17664	8.61796	0.26467	Cause	1.41168
		B11	3.62006	4.91617	8.53623	−1.29611	Result	
		B12	4.64371	3.61228	8.25599	1.03144	Cause	
Education factors	A05	B13	4.10804	4.43648	8.54452	−0.32844	Result	1.46586
		B14	5.06310	3.70182	8.76491	1.36128	Cause	
		B15	4.02161	5.05445	9.07606	−1.03284	Result	
Economy factors	A06	B16	4.75473	4.41511	9.16983	0.33962	Cause	1.49476
		B17	5.16605	4.15095	9.31700	1.01509	Cause	
		B18	3.53209	4.88680	8.41889	−1.35471	Result	

The threshold value (α) is similarly obtained by averaging all values of the Total-relation Matrix via the use of Equation (19). In Table 6, values greater than the threshold value are marked in bold font. Based on these values greater than (α), a "Factor-Causal Relationship Diagram" can be created for all 6 primary influencing factors, as shown in Figure 13. The same method and calculation process can be used to calculate the remaining five primary influencing factors separately. Table 5 shows the final DEMATEL results for all 6 primary influencing factors. Figure 14 depicts the scatter plots of $G + R$ and $G - R$ for the 6 primary influencing factors to indicate the degree of influence and effect. The results presented in Table 6 are based on deterministic MCDM computations. Traditional statistical significance tests and confidence intervals are not applicable. However, consistency ratio validation (CR $\leq$ 0.1) and cross-model verification among AHP, DEMATEL, ISM, and MICMAC ensure the robustness and reliability of these results.

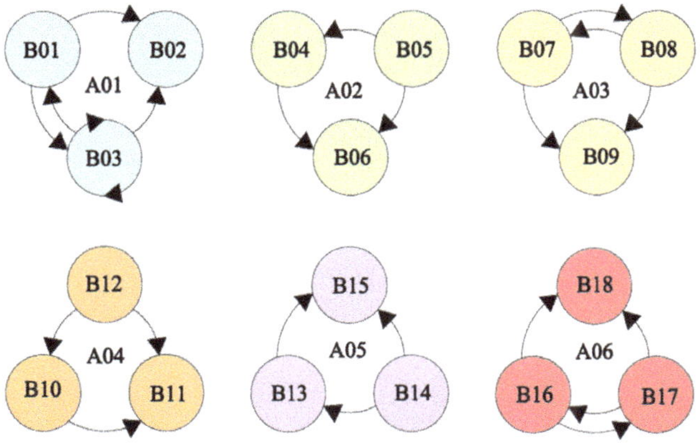

Figure 13. Factor-Causal Relationship Diagram of DEMATEL model (Source: drawn by the author).

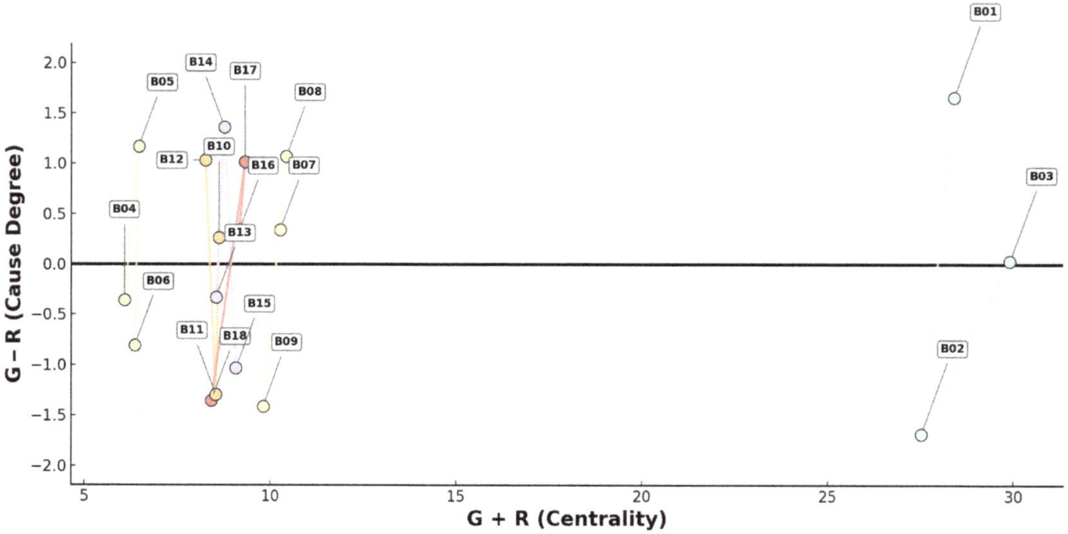

Figure 14. DEMATEL centrality, causality and causal analysis (Source: drawn by the author).

5.3. Hierarchy Diagram of Influencing Factors

The ISM is used to analyze the hierarchical linkages among the influencing factors. First, the interviewed panelists expressed their assessments with the letters V, A, X, and O. Table 7 explains the meaning of these letters in detail. On this basis, a Structural Self Interaction Matrix (SSIM) is developed to determine the types of interrelationships between the parameters. After the results of the SSIM questionnaire are obtained, the Plurality Rule is used to construct the final SSIM pairwise comparison matrix. The Plurality Rule is different from the Simple Majority Method. According to it, the occurring frequency of each element in the original SSIM pairwise comparison matrix is used as the statistical index, and the symbol with the highest number of occurrences is used as the corresponding element in the final SSIM pairwise comparison matrix. The basis for the SSIM procedure is the 18 secondary influencing factors that have been defined, and the relationship between them is shown in Figure 15.

Table 7. Symbols and their meanings in the ISM model (Source: drawn by the author).

Symbol	Meaning
V	i will lead to the realization of j
A	j will lead to the realization of i
X	Both i and j will contribute to the realization of each other's purposes
O	i and j have no relationship with each other

After the relationship of 18 secondary influencing factors of the ISM has been identified, the next step is to replace the letters with numerical values 1 and 0 to convert the SSIM into a binary matrix (Figures 16 and 17). Binary digits can be placed according to the following rules.

- V' means that the entry for the cell (i, j) at the upper triangular edge is 1, and the entry for the opposite cell (j, i) at the lower triangular edge is 0.

- A′ means the entry for the cell (i, j) at the upper triangle edge is 0, and the entry for opposite cell (j, i) at the lower triangle edge is 1.
- X′ indicates that the entry for the cell (i, j) at the upper triangular edge is 1, and the entry for the cell (j, i) at the lower triangle edge is also 1.
- O′ implies the entry for the cell (i, j) at the upper triangular edge is 0, and the entry for the cell (j, i) at the lower triangular edge is also 0.

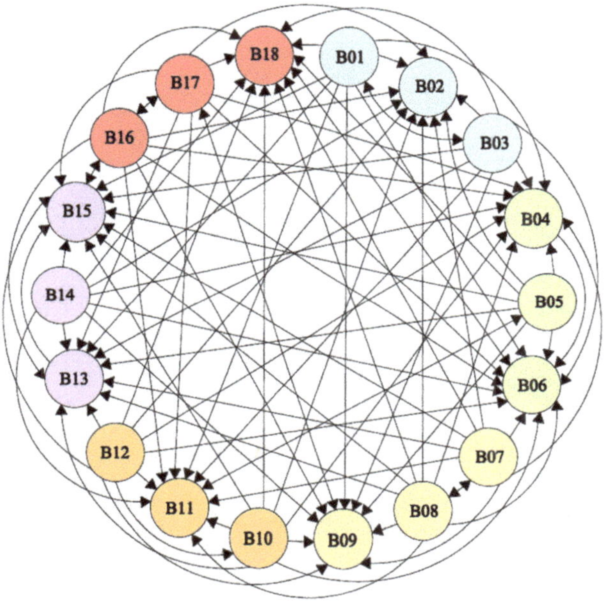

Figure 15. Relationship between the 18 secondary influencing factors of the ISM (Source: drawn by the author).

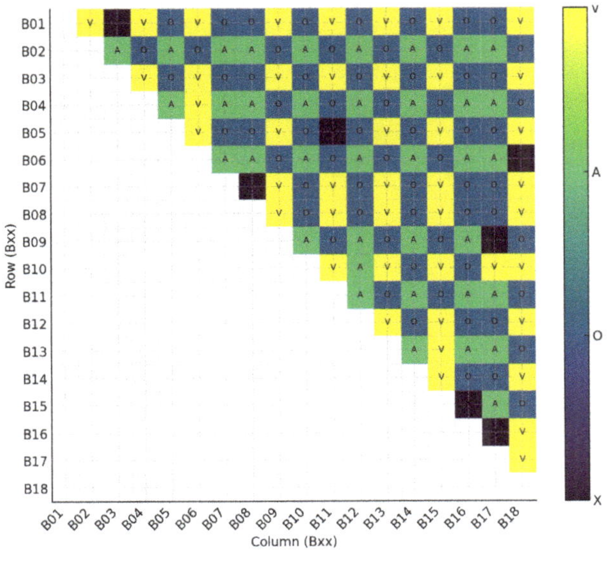

Figure 16. 8 Final SSIM pairwise comparison matrix (Source: drawn by the author).

	B01	B02	B03	B04	B05	B06	B07	B08	B09	B10	B11	B12	B13	B14	B15	B16	B17	B18
B01	1	1	1	1	0	1	0	0	1	0	1	0	1	0	1	0	0	1
B02	0	1	0	0	0	0	0	0	0	0	0	0	0	0	0	0	0	0
B03	1	1	1	1	0	1	0	0	1	0	1	0	1	0	1	0	0	1
B04	0	0	0	1	0	1	0	0	0	0	0	0	0	0	0	0	0	0
B05	0	1	0	1	1	1	0	0	1	0	1	0	1	0	1	0	0	1
B06	0	0	0	0	0	1	0	0	0	0	0	0	0	0	0	0	0	1
B07	0	1	0	1	0	1	1	1	1	0	1	0	1	0	1	0	0	1
B08	0	1	0	1	0	1	1	1	1	0	1	0	1	0	1	0	0	1
B09	0	0	0	0	0	0	0	0	1	0	0	0	0	0	0	0	1	0
B10	0	1	0	1	0	1	0	0	1	1	1	0	1	0	1	0	0	1
B11	0	0	0	0	1	0	0	0	0	0	1	0	0	0	0	0	0	0
B12	0	1	0	1	0	1	0	0	1	1	1	1	1	0	1	0	0	1
B13	0	0	0	0	0	0	0	0	0	0	0	0	1	0	1	0	0	0
B14	0	1	0	1	0	1	0	0	1	0	1	0	1	1	1	0	0	1
B15	0	0	0	0	0	0	0	0	0	0	0	0	0	0	1	1	0	0
B16	0	1	0	1	0	1	0	0	1	0	1	0	1	0	1	1	1	1
B17	0	1	0	1	0	1	0	0	1	0	1	0	1	0	1	1	1	1
B18	0	0	0	0	0	1	0	0	0	0	0	0	0	0	0	0	0	1

Figure 17. Initial Reachability Matrix (Source: drawn by the author).

According to this rule, all letters in Figure 16 are replaced by binary digits to obtain the initial Reachability Matrix depicted in Figure 17.

The transformation principles discussed in the previous theoretical analysis section should be applied to calculate the final Reachability Matrix described in Figure 18. Among them, 0 is replaced by 1 *, which means that if A influences B and B influences C, A will automatically influence C.

	B01	B02	B03	B04	B05	B06	B07	B08	B09	B10	B11	B12	B13	B14	B15	B16	B17	B18	Driving force	Ranking
B01	1	1	1	1	1*	1	0	0	1	0	1	0	1	0	1	1*	1*	1	13	1
B02	0	1	0	0	0	0	0	0	0	0	0	0	0	0	0	0	0	0	0	0
B03	1	1	1	1	1*	1	0	0	1	0	1	0	1	0	1	1*	1*	1	13	1
B04	0	0	0	1	0	1	0	0	0	0	0	0	0	0	0	0	0	1*	3	14
B05	0	1	0	1	1	1	0	0	1	0	1	0	1	0	1	1*	1*	1	11	8
B06	0	0	0	0	0	1	0	0	0	0	0	0	0	0	0	0	0	1	2	16
B07	0	1	0	1	1*	1	1	1	1	0	1	0	1	0	1	1*	1*	1	13	1
B08	0	1	0	1	1*	1	1	1	1	0	1	0	1	0	1	1*	1*	1	13	1
B09	0	1*	0	1*	0	1*	0	0	1	0	1*	0	1*	0	1*	1*	1	1*	10	11
B10	0	1	0	1	1*	1	0	0	1	1	1	0	1	0	1	1*	1*	1	12	6
B11	0	1*	0	1*	1	1*	0	0	1*	0	1	0	1*	0	1*	0	0	1*	9	13
B12	0	1	0	1	1*	1	0	0	1	1	1	1	1	0	1	1*	1*	1	13	1
B13	0	0	0	0	0	0	0	0	0	0	0	0	1	0	1	1*	0	0	3	14
B14	0	1	0	1	1*	1	0	0	1	0	1	0	1	1	1	1*	1*	1	12	6
B15	0	1*	0	1*	0	1*	0	0	1*	0	1*	0	1*	0	1	1	1*	1*	10	11
B16	0	1	0	1	1*	1	0	0	1	0	1	0	1	0	1	1	1	1	11	8
B17	0	1	0	1	1*	1	0	0	1	0	1	0	1	0	1	1	1	1	11	8
B18	0	0	0	0	0	1	0	0	0	0	0	0	0	0	0	0	0	1	2	16
Dependence	2	14	2	14	11	16	2	2	13	2	13	1	14	1	14	13	12	16	162	
Ranking	12	3	12	3	11	1	12	12	7	12	7	17	3	17	3	7	10	1		

Figure 18. Final Reachability Matrix (Source: drawn by the author).

The hierarchy operation is performed to determine the level of each factor. In this step, the Reachability Set and the Antecedent Set are determined. The Reachability Set includes the factors it may influence and itself, while the Antecedent Set involves all factors that can reach the factor and itself. Tables 5–8 depicts the division about the first hierarchy and the first iteration. Afterwards, an ISM hierarchical structure diagram is established based on all iteration results and hierarchical division, as shown in Figure 19. B02, B06, B13, and B18 are at the top of the hierarchy, and these four factors do not influence or promote other factors but are influenced by lower-hierarchy factors. In addition, the low-hierarchy factor B12 is the most critical factor among all factors that directly or indirectly influence other parameters above it.

Table 8. Calculation results of combined AHP-DEMATEL-ISM-MICMAC model (Source: drawn by the author).

MICMAC		ISM		AHP		DEMATEL		Accumulated Horizontal Weights	Accumulated Cluster Weights
Quadrant	**Quadrant Name**	**Secondary IF**	**ISM Hierarchy**	**Global Weight Values**	**Global Rankings**	**Centrality $G+R$**	**Cause Degree $G-R$**		
Quadrant I	Autonomous cluster	There are no influencing factors in the first quadrant							
Quadrant II	Dependence cluster (Top hierarchy)	B02	Layer 1	0.04553	9	27.51556	−1.68419	0.13458	0.20151
		B06		0.02113	14	6.35983	−0.80834		
		B13		0.00949	18	8.54452	−0.32844		
		B18		0.05843	7	8.41889	−1.35471		
		B04	Layer 2	0.06693	5	6.07656	−0.35927	0.06693	
Quadrant III	Linkage cluster (Intermediate hierarchy)	B09	Layer 3	0.01067	17	9.80803	−1.41266	0.14747	0.31189
		B11		0.13680	2	8.53623	−1.29611		
		B15	Layer 4	0.02877	12	9.07606	−1.03284	0.13084	
		B16		0.08100	4	9.16983	0.33962		
		B17		0.02107	15	9.31700	1.01509		
		B05	Layer 5	0.03358	11	6.46346	1.16761	0.03358	
Quadrant IV	Independence cluster (Bottom hierarchy)	B01	Layer 6	0.19653	1	28.38925	1.65263	0.42076	0.48659
		B03		0.10132	3	29.90502	0.03157		
		B07		0.02243	13	10.27252	0.34165		
		B08		0.04707	8	10.43375	1.07102		
		B10		0.03687	10	8.61796	0.26467		
		B14		0.01654	16	8.76491	1.36128		
		B12	Layer 7	0.06583	6	8.25599	1.03144	0.06583	

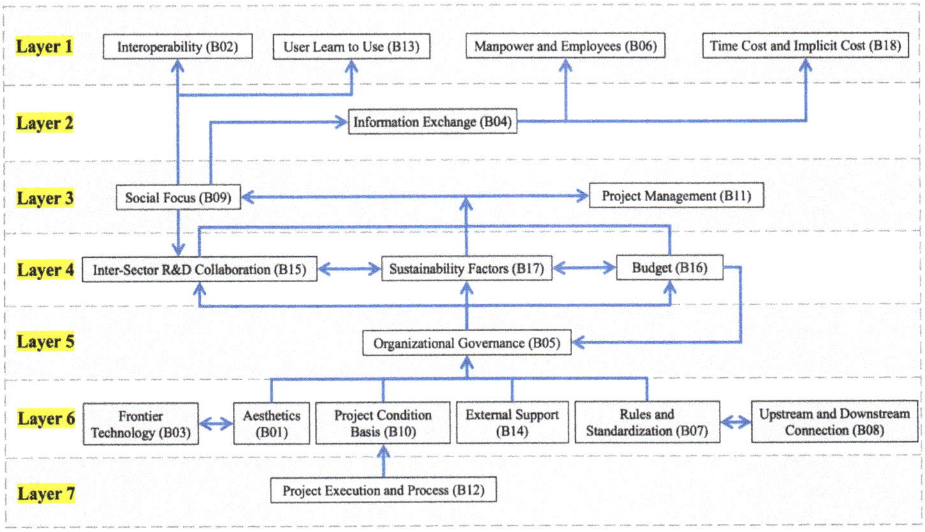

Figure 19. ISM hierarchical structure (Source: drawn by the author).

5.4. Analysis of Driving Force-Dependence of Influencing Factors

MICMAC analysis helps to classify and identify factors based on their driving force and dependence. Figure 17 calculates the driving force and dependence of all 18 factors via Equation (22). Driving force determines the potential of a factor to influence or promote other factors, while dependence determines the dependence of a factor on other factors. Figure 17 shows the scatter plot of MICMAC analysis based on driving force and dependence, with the horizontal axis representing dependence and the vertical axis representing driving force.

The horizontal and vertical axis boundaries separating the four quadrants shown in Figure 20 are determined based on the driving force and dependence values of the influencing factors. In this research, the boundary is set at the midpoint between the maximum driving force and the dependent force value. According to the calculation of the ISM step, the maximum driving force is 13, so the horizontal axis of the coordinate remains at the midpoint 6.5. Similarly, the maximum dependent force is 16, so the vertical axis of the coordinate remains at the midpoint 8.

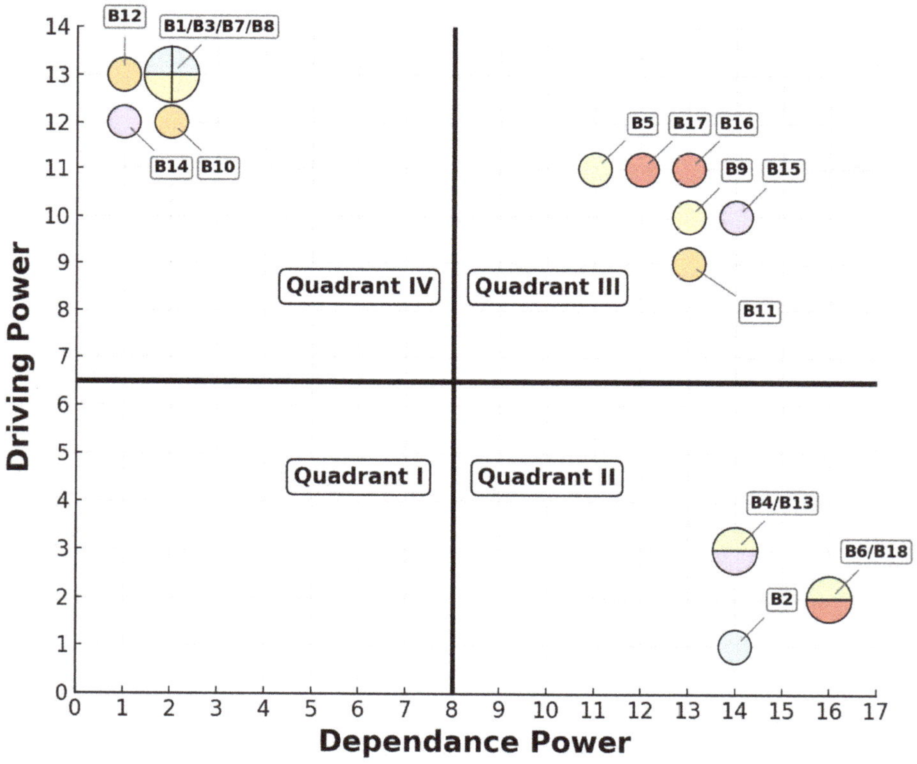

Figure 20. Scatter plot of MICMAC analysis results (Source: drawn by the author).

The scatter plot in Figure 20 is divided into four quadrants, indicating the properties of each selected factor. The first quadrant represents an autonomous cluster of influencing factors, and no factor fits this group, indicating that all selected factors have contributed to the influencing mechanism of research on AI-based architectural design. The elements in the dependent cluster (second quadrant) have high dependence, but the driving force there is low. In this case, B02, B04, B06, B13, and B18 are easily influenced by other parameters.

Similarly, B05, B09, B11, B15, B16, and B17 are factors of linkage cluster with the high driving force and high dependence (third quadrant). Finally, B01, B03, B07, B08, B10, B12, and B14 are in independent cluster (fourth quadrant), indicating that these elements are independent and have high driving force, but low dependence.

The outcomes from AHP, DEMATEL, ISM, and MICMAC assessments are interconnected and jointly display the multi-dimensional processes of AI adoption in architectural design. The AHP assessments deliver quantitative weightings and relative importance of influencing factors to build the base for causal assessment. The DEMATEL analysis identifies the directionality of these factors, identifying the cause-and-effect groups. The ISM model converts the relationships into a hierarchy that makes it clear the multi-level dependencies in the system. Finally, the MICMAC confirms and refines these relationships by clustering the factors into four groups based on their driving and dependence power. Together, these sequential approaches create a cohesive causal–hierarchical framework that both quantifies and interprets the interdependencies of the technological, organizational, human, and economic agents of AI-based architectural design.

6. Discussion

The research in this section starts with the construction of the combined AHP-DEMATEL-ISM-MICMAC model to determine the influencing mechanism of AI-based architectural design. The four multi-standard decision-making methods applied serve different objectives, and the interrelationships between various influencing factors are analyzed from different perspectives. Finally, the conclusions are drawn. Through the integration of AHP, DEMATEL, ISM, and MICMAC, a unified hybrid MCDM framework was established to quantify both the hierarchical importance and causal dynamics among influencing factors of AI-based architectural design. The AHP results provided clear quantitative weighting and ranking; DEMATEL identified cause-and-effect relationships and clarified the driving mechanisms; ISM constructed a hierarchical structural model linking multi-level factors; and MICMAC classified factors by driving power and dependence. Together, these methodological results validate the framework proposed in the Introduction and demonstrate that the combined model can reveal interrelationships and dependencies that single analytical methods fail to capture. This integration thus confirms the robustness, interpretability, and empirical potential of the AIAD influence mechanism framework (Figures 21 and 22).

The AHP method is used to determine the importance of influencing factors. According to Table 5, the technological factor (A01) has the highest weight of 34.338%, followed by the project factor (A04) with a weight of 23.951%, indicating that the technological factor is the most relevant parameter among the 6 primary influencing factors. Education factor (A05) is the least important factor among the primary influencing factors, with a weight of 5.48%. Similarly, AHP analysis is also used to determine the most basic secondary influencing factors among each major factor. The local rankings shown in Table 5 and Figure 20 illustrate the most important and least important secondary influencing factors among each primary influencing factor. According to the global weight ranking shown in Table 5, aesthetics (B01) and user learning (B13) are, respectively, the most important indicator and least important indicator overall among the 18 secondary influencing factors. In addition, based on the local weights calculated by AHP in Table 5, the influencing factors are divided into three groups, namely high priority factors, intermediate priority factors, and low priority factors. The influencing factors with weights between 0.45 and 0.6 belong to the top priority group; those with weights between 0.25 and 0.40 belong to the intermediate priority group, while those with weights between 0.1 and 0.2 belong to the low priority group. Figure 23 describes the graphic representation of factors, which are divided into three local weight groups and specifically shown in Figure 24.

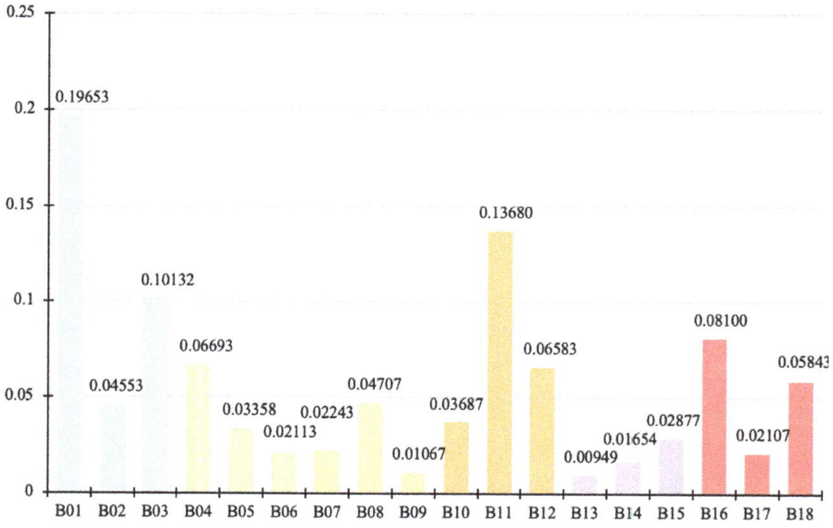

Figure 21. Global weight data visualization (Source: drawn by the author).

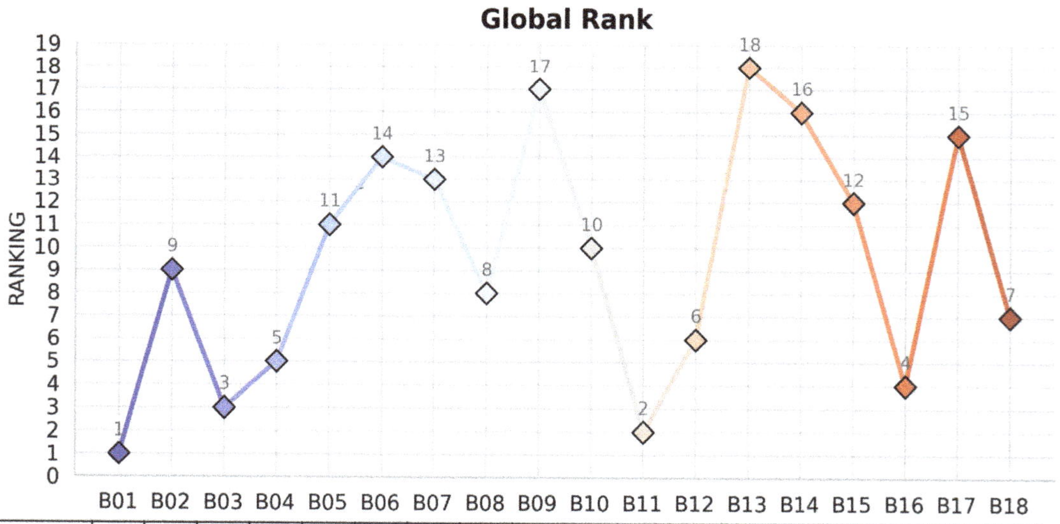

Global Rank	1	9	3	5	11	14	13	8	17	10	2	6	18	16	12	4	15	7

Figure 22. Global ranking data visualization (Source: drawn by the author).

The DEMATEL method is used to determine the causal relationship between the features shown in Table 5. The influence degree is determined via the calculation of the Influence Degree (G) and the Influenced Degree (R). Centrality (G – R) *is* used to identify the correlation between influencing factors, while causality ($G - R$) is used to determine the type of influence. If an influencing factor has a high G value and a high R value, it indicates that the factor has a strong potential to influence other factors and also a strong tendency to be influenced by other factors. Similarly, when the values of Influence Degree (G) and

Influenced Degree (R) decrease, the ability to influence other factors and the likelihood of being influenced by other factors also decrease. A positive Cause Degree ($G - R$) value means that the ability to influence other factors is greater than the tendency to be influenced by other factors, so it belongs to the cause group. A negative Cause Degree ($G - R$) value indicates that the tendency to be influenced by other factors is greater than the ability to influence other factors, and therefore it belongs to the result group. Table 5 shows that cutting-edge technology (B03) has the highest centrality ($G + R$) value of 29.90502, followed by aesthetics (B01), with the second highest centrality ($G + R$) value of 28.38925. Thus, aesthetics (B01) and cutting-edge technology (B03) are of substantial importance in the field of architectural design, and these two factors also influence other factors. From the calculation results of the Cause Degree $G - R$ value, project management (B11) has the smallest Cause Degree $G - R$ value, so it has the greatest tendency to be influenced by other factors, followed by interoperability (B02), whose Cause Degree $G - R$ value is the second lowest. On the other hand, project execution and process optimization (B12) are the most robust influencing factors in this group, with the highest Cause Degree ($G - R$) value, making it the least influenced by other factors, followed by aesthetics (B01), with a Cause Degree ($G - R$) value of 1.65263, ranking second. The Cause Degree ($G - R$) values are displayed in descending order, as shown in Figure 17. The influencing factors on the positive side of the coordinates in Figure 17 belong to the cause group, while the influencing factors on the negative side belong to the result group.

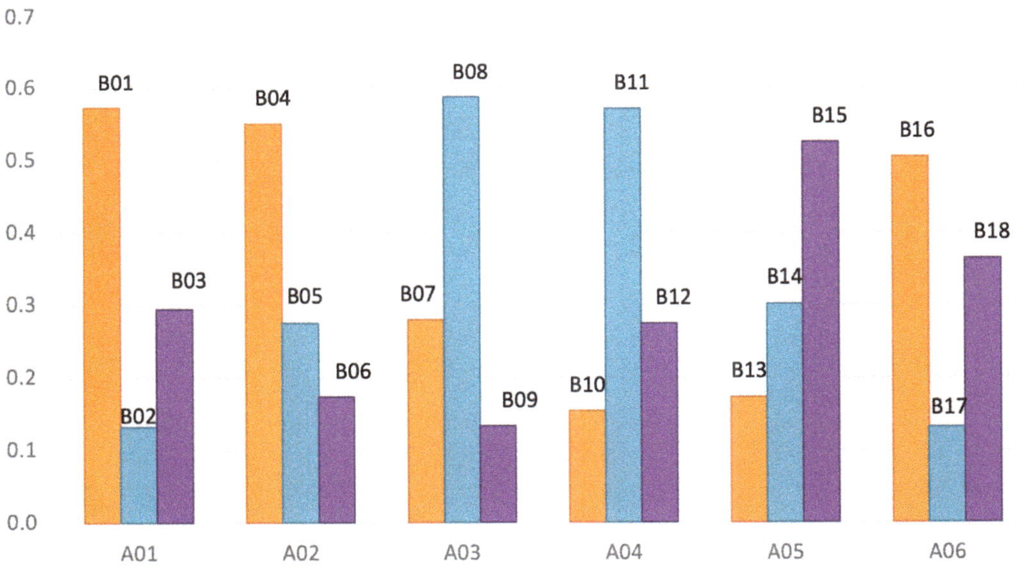

Figure 23. Local ranking of secondary influencing factors among primary influencing factors (Source: drawn by the author).

The ISM method is used to establish the relationship between the influencing factors at each hierarchy described in Figure 16. The results show that project execution and process optimization (B12) are at the bottom of the hierarchy, while interoperability (B02), manpower and employees (B06), user learning (B13), as well as time costs and hidden costs (B18) are at the top. The arrows in Figure 16 indicate that the factors of project execution and process optimization (B12) have a direct or indirect influence on all other factors above its hierarchy, making it one of the basic influencing factors that must be addressed in AI-based architectural design in order to optimize other indicators. Moreover, the influencing factors included in the sixth hierarchy have the same characteristics as project execution and process optimization (B12), and most elements starting from the fifth hierarchy are directly or indirectly controlled by the 6 parameters in the sixth hierarchy. On the other hand, the elements in the first and second hierarchies are the most sensitive, and they are seriously influenced by the factors below their hierarchy in the hierarchical structure. The parameters at the intermediate hierarchies, namely the third, fourth, and fifth hierarchies, have the characteristics of influencing others and are also influenced by other influencing factors.

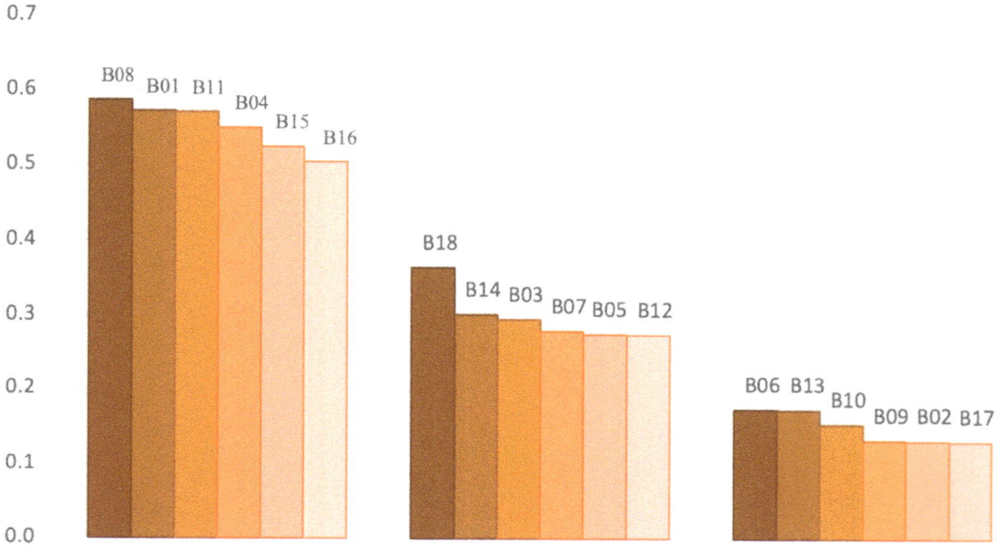

Figure 24. Local Weight Categories in AHP Analysis (High Priority Group–Intermediate Group–Low Priority Group) (Source: drawn by the author).

MICMAC analysis is closely related to ISM analysis. It is used to determine the driving force and dependence of influencing factors. The ability to influence or drive other factors is represented by driving force, while dependence represents the tendency to be influenced or dependent on other parameters. The scatter plot in Figure 17 shows that none of the influencing factors belong to autonomous cluster, as there are no factors in the first quadrant. It means that there are no parameters with weak driving force and dependence. Similarly, the dependence clusters in the second quadrant are variable interoperability (B02), information exchange (B04), manpower and employees (B06), user learning (B13), and time costs and hidden costs (B18), indicating low driving force and high dependence of these five parameters. The organizational governance (B05), social attention (B09), project management (B11), inter-departmental R&D cooperation (B15), budget (B16) and sustainability and intensification factors (B17) in the third quadrant are the linkage clusters with strong driving force and strong dependence, while aesthetics (B01), cutting-edge technology (B03) and industrial laws and regulations (B17), connection between industrial upstream and downstream enterprises (B08), project condition basis (B10), project execution and process optimization (B12), and external support (14) in the fourth quadrant in independent clusters with high potential of being driven and low dependence. Figure 25 visualizes the flow of influence from MICMAC quadrants to ISM hierarchical layers and down to secondary factors (B01–B18). Link widths correspond to

AHP global weights, providing an integrated view that connects classification (MICMAC), structure (ISM), and importance (AHP). The visualized relationship for the MICMAC-ISM distribution of secondary factors is shown in Figure 26 by a form of Sankey Diagram.

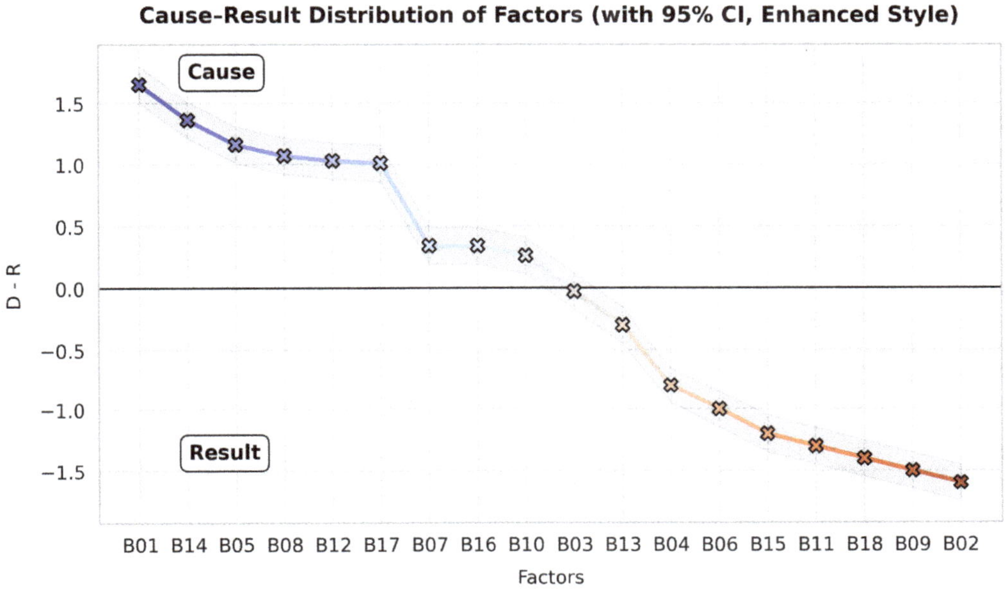

Figure 25. Factors divided into Cause Zone and Result Zone (with 95% CI) (Source: drawn by the author).

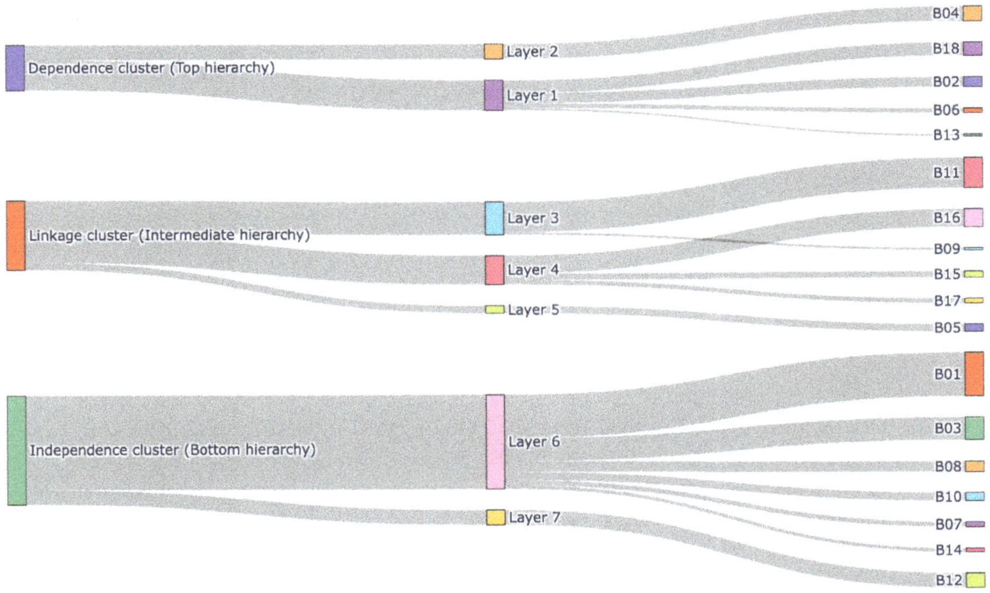

Figure 26. Sankey Diagram of MICMAC Quadrants → ISM Layers → Secondary Influencing Factors (Source: drawn by the author).

From the combination of the four models as a whole, it can be seen that according to AHP analysis, the most important influencing factor is aesthetics (B01) based on global weights, while aesthetics (B01) also has the second highest centrality ($G + R$) value in DEMATEL analysis. In addition, the cutting-edge technology (B03) obtained the largest centrality ($G + R$) value in the DEMATEL analysis, although it ranked third in the AHP priority list. Project execution and process optimization (B12) occupies the lowest hierarchy in the ISM and is used to drive other factors above its hierarchy. Therefore, in DEMATEL, the D-R value of the project execution and process optimization (B12) factor is the highest, indicating its potential of strong driving force and low dependence. In MICMAC analysis, the factors of project execution and process optimization (B12) are also described in a similar manner, as they belong to the fourth quadrant and imply the same results. The 6 influencing factors located at the sixth hierarchy in the ISM have a positive Cause Degree ($G - R$) value in DEMATEL and occupy the fourth quadrant in MICMAC analysis, indicating that these factors are independent clusters with excellent driving potential. When the ISM hierarchy rises to the fifth hierarchy, it can be seen that the influential factor of organizational governance (B05) is moved to the third quadrant, indicating that it has a high driving force and dependence, and also has a positive Cause Degree ($G - R$) value in DEMATEL analysis. As the ISM hierarchy continues to rise, the driving power of influencing factors decreases with the increase in dependence trend. Therefore, the parameters at the top hierarchy of the ISM hierarchical structure are dependent and occupy the second quadrant of the MICMAC graph. On the other hand, the types at the lowest hierarchy of the ISM hierarchical structure are independent and occupy the fourth quadrant in MICMAC analysis.

For the first two ISM hierarchies, all 5 influencing factors are dependent on other factors below their hierarchy, so these factors occupy the second quadrant and have a negative Cause Degree ($G - R$) value, indicating that they have strong dependence and poor driving potential. The two factors in the third hierarchy, social attention (B09) and project management (B11), are located in the third quadrant, indicating that these two factors are highly dependent on other factors and have excellent driving force. The intermediate four hierarchies of the ISM have three parameters: cross departmental R&D cooperation (B15), budget (B16), and sustainability and intensification factors (B17), all of which have significant driving force and dependence. Therefore, the third quadrant is suitable for them in the MICMAC analysis chart. Thus, the final results of the applied methods are relatively close, demonstrating the high accuracy and precision of the research conclusions. Table 8 provides an overview of the entire analysis results.

7. Conclusions

This study primarily analyzes the factors and mechanisms influencing artificial intelligence (AI) technology in the architectural design industry, exploring the inherent relationships between these factors. Based on the influencing factors identified in the quantitative literature review, this part constructed a hybrid AHP-DEMATEL-ISM-MICMAC model and applied it to the collected data. First, the AHP method was used to implement global weighting and ranking to identify the most relevant factors and their contributions to the analysis. Next, DEMATEL was used to determine the causal relationships among the influencing factors. Based on this, the ISM was used to construct a hierarchical structure diagram. Finally, MICMAC was used to identify the driving forces and dependencies of the considered factors. The results of this study will help architectural design firms better explore and analyze the mechanisms influencing AI technology and serve as a foundation for subsequent research.

From a theoretical perspective, this study enriches the theoretical framework for the interdisciplinary integration of architectural design theory and computer artificial intelligence technology and furthers the empirical research and dynamic simulation of AI adoption intentions in the architectural design field. Using bibliometric and qualitative analysis methods, this study further develops the theoretical framework for the influencing mechanisms of AI technology in architectural design, including relationships among influencing factors, hierarchical structure diagrams, causal relationships, impact strength, importance ranking, and factor attributes. These findings can serve as a theoretical foundation for this research direction and drive further research.

From a practical perspective, the research is not only instructive to the architectural design industry in understanding drivers and barriers to the adoption of artificial intelligence, but also useful for understanding the integration of AI in areas of cultural tourism and regional spatial innovation. Using AI driven integrated design intelligence, firms can maximise creativity, optimise resource use, and balance technical efficiency with cultural historicity. This research presents informed strategic and educational references for sustainable experience environments and exemplifies an economic and social application of AI in future-oriented tourism-based architectural space design.

Although this research provides a systematic and integrated understanding of the influential mechanisms of AI adoption within the architectural design domain, the study does have some limitations that should be acknowledged. First, although the expert participant sample size was reasonably small, it was sufficient to conduct the AHP and the DEMATEL analysis, which may limit the generalizability of the findings. Future research may expand the sample base to incorporate a variety of stakeholders, including policymakers, practitioners, and researchers in various locations. Second, the hybrid MCDM framework used in this study is all-inclusive, but utilizing MCDMs is still a subjective assessment procedure, as pairwise comparisons and expert scores provide a basis for personal bias despite the reports of consistency ratios and cross-method validation. Finally, the study is mostly cross-sectional in design, and longitudinal or dynamic modeling methods such as System Dynamics (SD) and Structural Equation Modeling (SEM) are proposed for use in future studies to validate and model the temporal evolution of AI adoption mechanisms.

Author Contributions: Conceptualization, X.W. and Y.Z.; methodology, Y.Z.; software, X.S. and Y.Z.; validation, Y.Z.; formal analysis, X.X. and Y.Z.; investigation, W.Z. and Y.L.; resources, R.X.; data curation, X.X., Y.S. and X.L.; writing—original draft preparation, Y.Z.; writing—review and editing, X.W. and Y.Z.; visualization, X.X.; supervision, Y.Z.; project administration, X.W. All authors have read and agreed to the published version of the manuscript.

Funding: This research received no external funding.

Data Availability Statement: The data that support the findings of this study are available from the corresponding author upon reasonable request.

Acknowledgments: We thank all the support from the research team members, as well as the intangible help from their affiliations. The authors have reviewed and edited the output and take full responsibility for the content of this publication. The authors wish to express their thanks to the editors and reviewers for their contributional comments. This research was inspired by the transformative power of Artificial Intelligence and its profound impact on the field of architectural design. Over the past years, and even now, AI has reshaped the boundaries of this industry. The designers, even the tourism planners have been rethinking the new relationship with the computational logic.

Conflicts of Interest: The authors declare no conflicts of interest.

Abbreviations

The following abbreviations are used in this manuscript:

AIAD	Artificial Intelligence-based Architectural Design e
AI	Artificial Intelligence
AHP	Analytic Hierarchy Process
DEMATEL	Decision-Making Trial and Evaluation Laboratory
ISM	Interpretive Structural Modeling
MICMAC	Cross-Impact Matrix Multiplication Applied to Classification

References

1. Hartl, A.; Peterka, J. Germany's Human-Centred Approach to AI is Inclusive, Evidence-Based and Capacity-Building. Available online: https://oecd.ai/en/wonk/germany-takes-an-inclusive-and-evidence-based-approach-for-capacity-building-and-a-human-centred-use-of-ai (accessed on 18 May 2021).
2. Manzoor, B.; Othman, I.; Durdyev, S.; Ismail, S.; Wahab, M.H. Influence of artificial intelligence in Civil engineering toward sustainable development—A systematic literature review. *Appl. Syst. Innov.* **2021**, *4*, 52. [CrossRef]
3. Alexander, C. *A Pattern Language: Towns, Buildings, Construction*; Oxford University Press: Oxford, UK, 1977.
4. Sutherland, I.E. Sketchpad a man-machine graphical communication system. *Simulation* **1964**, *2*, R-3–R-20. [CrossRef]
5. Gero, J.S. Chapter 9—An overview of knowledge engineering and its relevance to CAAD. In *Computer-Aided Architectural Design Futures*; Pipes, A., Ed.; Butterworth-Heinemann: Oxford, UK, 1986; pp. 107–119. [CrossRef]
6. Haugeland, J. *Mind Design II: Philosophy, Psychology, and Artificial Intelligence*; MIT Press: Cambridge, UK, 1997.
7. Mehmood, M.U.; Chun, D.; Han, H.; Jeon, G.; Chen, K. A review of the applications of artificial intelligence and big data to buildings for energy-efficiency and a comfortable indoor living environment. *Energy Build.* **2019**, *202*, 109383. [CrossRef]
8. Harapan, A.; Indriani, D.; Rizkiya, N.F.; Azbi, R.M. Artificial Intelligence in Architectural Design. *Int. J. Des. (INJUDES)* **2021**, *1*, 1–6. [CrossRef]
9. Kusters, R.; Misevic, D.; Berry, H.; Cully, A.; Le Cunff, Y.; Dandoy, L.; Díaz-Rodríguez, N.; Ficher, M.; Grizou, J.; Othmani, A.; et al. Interdisciplinary Research in Artificial Intelligence: Challenges and Opportunities. *Front. Big Data* **2020**, *3*, 577974. [CrossRef] [PubMed]
10. Bostrom, N. How long before superintelligence? *Int. J. Futures Stud.* **1998**, *2*, 1–9.
11. Gottfredson, L.S. Mainstream science on intelligence: An editorial with 52 signatories, history, and bibliography. *Intelligence* **1997**, *24*, 13–23. [CrossRef]
12. Strelkova, O. Three Types of Artificial Intelligence. Ph.D. Thesis, Khmelnitsky National University, Khmelnytsky, Ukraine, 2017.
13. Cichocka, J.M.; Browne, W.N.; Rodriguez, E. Optimization in the architectural practice. In Proceedings of the 22nd International Conference of the Association for Computer-Aided Architectural Design Research in Asia (CAADRIA), Suzhou, China, 5–8 April 2017; pp. 387–396.
14. Simon, H.A. The science of design: Creating the artificial. *Des. Issues* **1988**, *4*, 67–82. [CrossRef]
15. Gidel, T.; Gautier, R.; Duchamp, R. Decision-making framework methodology: An original approach to project risk management in new product design. *J. Eng. Des.* **2005**, *16*, 1–23. [CrossRef]
16. Hatchuel, A. Towards design theory and expandable rationality: The unfinished program of Herbert Simon. *J. Manag. Gov.* **2001**, *5*, 260–273. [CrossRef]
17. Simon, H.A. The logic of heuristic decision making. In *Models of Discovery*; Springer: Cham, Switzerland, 1977; pp. 154–175.
18. Pan, Y.; Zhang, L. Roles of artificial intelligence in construction engineering and management: A critical review and future trends. *Autom. Constr.* **2021**, *122*, 103517. [CrossRef]
19. Darko, A.; Chan, A.P.C.; Adabre, M.A.; Edwards, D.J.; Hosseini, M.R.; Ameyaw, E.E. Artificial Intelligence in the AEC Industry: Scientometric Analysis and Visualization of Research Activities. *Autom. Constr.* **2020**, *112*, 103081. [CrossRef]
20. Casey, R.M. Other Experts: Disciplinary and Aesthetic Impacts of Artificial Intelligence. *Archit. Des.* **2020**, *90*, 14–21.
21. Ekici, B.; Kazanasmaz, Z.T.; Turrin, M.; Taşgetiren, M.F.; Sariyildiz, I.S. Multi-Zone Optimisation of High-Rise Buildings Using Artificial Intelligence for Sustainable Metropolises. Part 2: Optimisation Problems, Algorithms, Results, and Method Validation. *Sol. Energy* **2021**, *224*, 309–326. [CrossRef]
22. Li, Y.; Chen, H.; Yu, P.; Yang, L. A review of artificial intelligence in enhancing architectural design efficiency. *Appl. Sci.* **2025**, *15*, 1476. [CrossRef]
23. Liu, F.; Deng, K. AI knows Aesthetics: AI-Generated Interior design Identification using Deep Learning Algorithms. *IEEE Access* **2025**, *13*, 87621–87639. [CrossRef]

24. Ullah, Z.; Al-Turjman, F.; Mostarda, N.; Gagliardi, R. Applications of Artificial Intelligence and Machine Learning in Smart Cities. *Comput. Commun.* **2020**, *154*, 313–323. [CrossRef]
25. ADIO-MOSES, D.A.; Sunday, O. Artificial Intelligence for Sustainable Development of Intelligent Buildings. In Proceedings of the 9th CIDB Postgraduate Conference, Cape Town, South Africa, 2–4 February 2016; pp. 1–4.
26. Tamke, M.; Nicholas, P.; Zwierzycki, M. Machine Learning for Architectural Design: Practices and Infrastructure. *Int. J. Archit. Comput.* **2018**, *16*, 123–143. [CrossRef]
27. Vardhan, R. Machine Learning (Artificial Intelligence) in Architecture Design Process. *Int. J. Archit. Des. Manag.* **2020**, *3*, 45–56.
28. Monlezun, D.J.; Sotomayor, C.; Girault, M.I.; Garcia, A.; Gallagher, C. From data interoperability to 'moral interoperability'in the global health data architecture: Integrated use case of AI-driven computational ethical analysis with Bayesian-propensity score and cost-benefit analyses optimizing efficiency and equity in colorectal cancer. *Med. Ética* **2024**, *35*, 990–1054.
29. El-Khouly, T.; Abdelhalim, O. Preserving conceptual design integrity: Strategies for enhancing interoperability in architectural digital design workflows. *Sci. Rep.* **2024**, *14*, 30595. [CrossRef] [PubMed]
30. Kindratenko, V. A Comparison of the Accuracy of an Electromagnetic and a Hybrid Ultrasound-Inertia Position Tracking System. *Presence* **2001**, *10*, 657–663. [CrossRef]
31. Oxman, R.E. Expert System for Generation and Evaluation in Architectural Design. Ph.D. Thesis, Technion—Israel Institute of Technology, Haifa, Israel, 1988. Available online: http://papers.cumincad.org/cgi-bin/works/paper/45b7 (accessed on 1 October 2025).
32. Currie, K.; Tate, A. O-Plan: The Open Planning Architecture. *Artif. Intell.* **1991**, *52*, 49–86. [CrossRef]
33. Wang, K.; Zhao, Y.; Gangadhari, R.K.; Li, Z. Analyzing the adoption challenges of the Internet of things (Iot) and artificial intelligence (ai) for smart cities in china. *Sustainability* **2021**, *13*, 10983. [CrossRef]
34. Karadağ, D.; Ozar, B. A new frontier in design studio: AI and human collaboration in conceptual design. *Front. Archit. Res.* 2025, *in press*. [CrossRef]
35. Scotta, P.J.; Lawson, B.R.; Ryu, J. An Intelligent Tutorial System for Computer Aided Architectural Design. In *Artificial Intelligence in Design '91*; Gero, S., Ed.; Butterworth-Heinemann: Oxford, UK, 1991. [CrossRef]
36. Rane, N.; Choudhary, S.; Rane, J. Integrating Building Information Modelling (BIM) with ChatGPT, Bard, and similar generative artificial intelligence in the architecture, engineering, and construction industry: Applications, a novel framework, challenges, and future scope. *SSRN Electron. J.* **2023**. [CrossRef]
37. Merhej, J.; Harb, H.; Abouaissa, A.; Idoumghar, L. Toward a new era of smart and secure healthcare information exchange systems: Combining blockchain and artificial intelligence. *Appl. Sci.* **2024**, *14*, 8808. [CrossRef]
38. Wang, S.; Du, G.; Dai, S.; Miao, M.; Zhang, M. Efficient information exchange approach for medical IoT based on AI and DAG-enabled blockchain. *Heliyon* **2025**, *11*, e41617. [CrossRef]
39. Balachandran, M.; Rosenman, M.A.; Gero, J.S. A Knowledge-Based Approach to the Automatic Verification of Designs from CAD Databases. In *Artificial Intelligence in Design '91*; Gero, J.S., Ed.; Butterworth-Heinemann: Oxford, UK, 1991. [CrossRef]
40. Igor, S. DDS-Distributed Design System: A Paradigm for Modeling Conceptual Architectural Design. In Proceedings of the InterSymp '94, Advances in Computer-Based Design Systems, Baden-Baden, Germany, 8 August 1994; The International Institute for Advanced Studies in Systems Research and Cybernetics: Baden-Baden, Germany, 1994; pp. 79–88. Available online: https://www.researchgate.net/profile/Igor-Svetel/publication/324113817_DDS-Distributed_Design_System_A_Paradigm_for_Modeling_Conceptual_Architectural_Design/links/5abe6c7e0f7e9bfc0459a2d1/DDS-Distributed-Design-System-A-Paradigm-for-Modeling-Conceptual-Architectural-Design.pdf (accessed on 1 October 2025).
41. Hakimi, M.; Zarinkhail, M.S.; Musawi, S.Z. Exploring the fusion of enterprise architecture, Blockchain, and AI in digital governance: A systematic review. *Int. J. Softw. Eng. Comput. Sci. (IJSECS)* **2024**, *4*, 497–511. [CrossRef]
42. Fahlevi, M.; Moeljadi; Aisjah, S.; Djazuli, A. Corporate Governance in the Digital Age: A Comprehensive Review of Blockchain, AI, and Big Data Impacts, Opportunities, and Challenges. In Proceedings of the 8th International Conference on Energy, Environment, Epidemiology and Information System (ICENIS 2023), Semarang City, Indonesia, 8–9 August 2023; EDP Sciences: Les Ulis, France, 2023; Volume 448.
43. Dhar, R.; Vaidhyanathan, K.; Varma, V. Leveraging generative AI for architecture knowledge management. In Proceedings of the 2024 IEEE 21st International Conference on Software Architecture Companion (ICSA-C), Hyderabad, India, 4–8 June 2024; IEEE: Piscataway, NJ, USA, 2024.
44. Kolbjørnsrud, V. Designing the Intelligent Organization: Six principles for Human-AI collaboration. *Calif. Manag. Rev.* **2024**, *66*, 44–64. [CrossRef]
45. Jin, S.; Tu, H.; Li, J.; Fang, Y.; Qu, Z.; Xu, F.; Liu, K.; Lin, Y. Enhancing architectural education through artificial intelligence: A case study of an AI-assisted architectural programming and design course. *Buildings* **2024**, *14*, 1613. [CrossRef]

46. Pallavi, J.; Tripathi, V.; Malladi, R.; Khang, A. *Data-Driven Artificial Intelligence (AI) Models in the Workforce Development Planning. Designing Workforce Management Systems for Industry 4.0;* CRC Press: Boca Raton, FL, USA, 2023; pp. 159–176.
47. Krishnan, P. An integrated strategic architectural framework for AI-augmented HRM. *Int. J. Sci. Res. (IJSR)* **2024**, *13*, 183–192. [CrossRef]
48. Morandini, S.; Fraboni, F.; De Angelis, M.; Puzzo, G.; Giusino, D.; Pietrantoni, L. The impact of artificial intelligence on workers' skills: Upskilling and reskilling in organisations. *Informing Sci.* **2023**, *26*, 39–68. [CrossRef] [PubMed]
49. Torricelli, M.C. Architectural design and regulation: A troubled but necessary relationship. *TECHNE—J. Technol. Archit. Environ.* **2024**, *27*, 21–26. [CrossRef]
50. Li, Z.; Zhao, Y.; Suman, S.K.; Bardhan, A. Stochastic simulation of microenvironment comfort and greenhouse gas emission of residential building using Monte-Carlo and hybrid intelligence paradigms. *Environ. Dev. Sustain.* **2025**, 1–43. [CrossRef]
51. Mehta, P. Intelligence Workflow for Architectural Design Process. In *Advancements in Architectural, Engineering, and Construction Research and Practice: Integrating Disruptive Technologies and Innovation for Future Excellence;* Springer International Publishing AG: Cham, Switzerland, 2024; p. 53.
52. Oveisi, S.; Gholamrezaei, F.; Qajari, N.; Goodarzi, M.; Moin, M.-S. Review of artificial intelligence-based systems: Evaluation, standards, and methods. *Adv. Stand. Appl. Sci.* **2024**, *2*, 4–29.
53. Kafle, V.P.; Hirayama, T.; Miyazawa, T.; Jibiki, M.; Harai, H. Network control and management automation: Architecture standardization perspective. *IEEE Commun. Stand. Mag.* **2021**, *5*, 106–114. [CrossRef]
54. Cihon, P. *Standards for AI Governance: International Standards to Enable Global Coordination in AI Research & Development;* Future of Humanity Institute, University of Oxford: Oxford, UK, 2019; Volume 40, pp. 340–342.
55. Lund, B.; Orhan, Z.; Mannuru, N.R.; Bevara, R.V.K.; Porter, B.; Vinaih, M.K.; Bhaskara, P. Standards, frameworks, and legislation for artificial intelligence (AI) transparency. *AI Ethics* **2025**, *5*, 3639–3655. [CrossRef]
56. Fischer, G.; Nakakoji, K. Empowering Designers with Integrated Design Environments. In *Artificial Intelligence in Design '91;* Gero, J.S., Ed.; Butterworth-Heinemann: Oxford, UK, 1991. [CrossRef]
57. Płoszaj-Mazurek, M.; Ryńska, E.; Grochulska-Salak, M. Methods to Optimize Carbon Footprint of Buildings in Regenerative Architectural Design with the Use of Machine Learning, Convolutional Neural Network, and Parametric Design. *Energies* **2020**, *13*, 5289. [CrossRef]
58. Fang, C.; Lai, Y.; Wen, Z. Research on Key Technologies of Intelligent Integrated System for Architectural Design Enterprises. In Proceedings of the 6th International Conference on Environmental Science and Civil Engineering, Nanchang, China, 4–5 January 2020; Volume 455, p. 012209.
59. McDermid, J.; Jia, Y.; Habli, I. Upstream and Downstream AI Safety: Both on the Same River? *arXiv* **2024**, arXiv:2501.05455.
60. Zandi-Nia, A. TOPGENE: An Artificial Intelligence Approach to a Design Process. 1993. Available online: https://repository.tudelft.nl/record/uuid:b89db6aa-6ace-4f01-a663-9aeeed26537a (accessed on 1 October 2025).
61. Kurcjusz, M.; Stefańska, A. Transformative integration of Artificial Intelligence in architectural design. *Architectus* **2025**, *1*, 89–99. [CrossRef]
62. Kurmann, D. Sculptor—A Tool for Intuitive Architectural Design. In *The Global Design Studio, Proceedings of the Sixth International Conference on Computer-Aided Architectural Design Futures, Singapore, 24–26 September 1995;* Centre for Advanced Studies in Architecture, National University of Singapore: Singapore, 1995; pp. 323–330, ISBN 9971-62-423-0. Available online: http://papers.cumincad.org/cgi-bin/works/Show_id=caadria2010_003/paper/fa87 (accessed on 1 October 2025).
63. Zheng, H.; Yuan, P.F. A Generative Architectural and Urban Design Method through Artificial Neural Networks. *Build. Environ.* **2021**, *205*, 108178. [CrossRef]
64. Banz, G. An Iterative Approach to Computer-Aided Architectural Design. *J. Archit. Plan. Res.* **1985**, *2*, 187–200.
65. Wang, K.; Ying, Z.; Goswami, S.S.; Yin, Y.; Zhao, Y. Investigating the role of artificial intelligence technologies in the construction industry using a Delphi-ANP-TOPSIS hybrid MCDM concept under a fuzzy environment. *Sustainability* **2023**, *15*, 11848. [CrossRef]
66. Zabala-Vargas, S.; Jaimes-Quintanilla, M.; Jimenez-Barrera, M.H. Big data, data science, and artificial intelligence for project management in the architecture, engineering, and construction industry: A systematic review. *Buildings* **2023**, *13*, 2944. [CrossRef]
67. Rafsanjani, H.N.; Nabizadeh, A.H. Towards human-centered artificial intelligence (AI) in architecture, engineering, and construction (AEC) industry. *Comput. Hum. Behav. Rep.* **2023**, *11*, 100319. [CrossRef]
68. Rane, N.; Choudhary, S.; Rane, J. Artificial Intelligence (Ai) and Internet of Things (Iot)–based sensors for monitoring and controlling in architecture, engineering, and construction: Applications, challenges, and opportunities. Engineering, and Construction: Applications, Challenges, and Opportunities (November 20, 2023). *SSRN Electron. J.* 2023.
69. Hanafy, N.O. RETRACTED: Artificial intelligence's effects on design process creativity: A study on used AI Text-to-Image in architecture. *J. Build. Eng.* **2023**, *80*, 107999. [CrossRef]

70. Cortiços, N.D.; Zheng, X.; Duarte, C.C. The Impact of Artificial Intelligence on Architecture: A Comprehensive Analysis of AI Software Tools and Their Global Adoption. In Proceedings of the International Conference on Building Materials and Construction, Okinawa, Japan, 21–24 February 2025; Springer Nature: Singapore, 2025.
71. Mulesa, O.; Horvat, P.; Radivilova, T.; Sabadosh, V.; Baranovskyi, O.; Duran, S. Design of mechanisms for ensuring the execution of tasks in project planning. *arXiv* **2025**, arXiv:2501.01255. [CrossRef]
72. Bhatt, M.; Suchan, J.; Schultz, C.; Kondyli, V.; Goyal, S. Artificial Intelligence for Predictive and Evidence Based Architecture Design. In Proceedings of the Thirtieth AAAI Conference on Artificial Intelligence, Phoenix, AZ, USA, 12–17 February 2016.
73. Zeytin, E.; Kösenciğ, K.Ö.; Öner, D. The role of AI design assistance on the architectural design process: An empirical research with novice designers. *J. Comput. Des.* **2024**, *5*, 1–30. [CrossRef]
74. Amer, N.A. Architectural design in the light of AI concepts and applications. *MSA Eng. J.* **2023**, *2*, 628–646. [CrossRef]
75. Dall'Asta, J.C.; Marco, G.D. *AI Machine Learning in Creative Architectural Design Processes. xArch–Creativity in the Age of Digital Reproduction Symposium*; Springer Nature: Singapore, 2023.
76. Ho, Y.-F.; Wang, H.-L.; Liu, C.-C. System Dynamics and Genetic Artificial Neural Network Models for the Monitoring and Early Warning of Urban Housing Market. Retrieved from System Dynamics Society Website. 2012. Available online: https://proceedings.systemdynamics.org/2012/proceed/papers/P1234.pdf (accessed on 1 October 2025).
77. Reffat, R. Utilization of artificial intelligence concepts and techniques for enriching the quality of architectural design artifacts. In Proceedings of the 1st International Conference in Information Systems, Philadelphia, PA, USA, 8–10 December 1981; pp. 1–13.
78. Yeh, I.-C.; Hsu, T.-K. Building Real Estate Valuation Models with Comparative Approach through Case-Based Reasoning. *Appl. Soft Comput.* **2018**, *65*, 260–271. [CrossRef]
79. Yu, J.-B.; Yu, Y.; Wang, L.-N.; Yuan, Z.; Ji, X. The Knowledge Modeling System of Ready-Mixed Concrete Enterprise and Artificial Intelligence with ANN-GA for Manufacturing Production. *J. Intell. Manuf.* **2016**, *27*, 905–914. [CrossRef]
80. Allison James, T.; Cardin, M.-A.; McComb, C.; Ren, Y.; Selva, D.; Tucker, C.; Witherell, P.; Zhao, Y. Artificial Intelligence and Engineering Design. *J. Mech. Des.* **2022**, *144*, 1–6. [CrossRef]
81. Hafner, M.; Rajšter, D.; Žibert, M.; Tušar, T.; Ženko, B.; Žnidaršič, M.; Fuart, F.; Vladušič, D. Artificial Intelligence Support for Tunnel Design in Urban Areas. In *Tunnels and Underground Cities: Engineering and Innovation Meet Archaeology, Architecture and Art*; CRC Press: Boca Raton, FL, USA, 2019.
82. Idi, D.B.; Khaidzir, K.A.M. Critical Perspective of Design Collaboration: A Review. *Front. Archit. Res.* **2018**, *7*, 544–560. [CrossRef]
83. Januszkiewicz, K.; Paszkowska, N. Climate Change Adopted Building Envelope for the Urban Environment. In A New Approach to Architectural Design, Proceedings of the International Multidisciplinary Scientific GeoConference: SGEM 3, Albena, Bulgaria, 28 June–7 July 2016; ProQuest: Ann Arbor, MI, USA, 2016; pp. 515–522.
84. Özel, G. Interdisciplinary AI: A Machine Learning System for Streamlining External Aesthetic and Cultural Influences in Architecture. In *Architectural Intelligence*; Springer: Berlin/Heidelberg, Germany, 2020.
85. Özel, G.; Ennemoser, B. Interdisciplinary AI. In *ACADIA 2019: Ubiquity and Autonomy*; Acadia Publishing Company: Mount Pleasant, SC, USA, 2019.
86. Zielińska-Dąbkowska, K.; Barbara, B. Creating a More Conscious Built Environment for Day-and Night-Time Setting through Interdisciplinary Collaboration. In Proceedings of the PLDC 6th Global Lighting Design Convention in Paris/FR, Paris, France, 1–4 November 2017.
87. Ali, A.K.; Lee, O.J. Facade Style Mixing Using Artificial Intelligence for Urban Infill. *Architecture* **2023**, *3*, 258–269. [CrossRef]
88. Steenson, M.W. Why architecture and artificial intelligence? In *XRDS: Crossroads, The ACM Magazine for Students*; ACM Digital Library: London, UK, 2018; Volume 24, pp. 16–19.
89. Hu, H.; Jiang, S.; Goswami, S.S.; Zhao, Y. Fuzzy integrated Delphi-ISM-MICMAC hybrid multi-criteria approach to optimize the artificial intelligence (AI) factors influencing cost management in civil engineering. *Information* **2024**, *15*, 280. [CrossRef]
90. Wang, Y.; Chen, L. Architectural and Landscape Garden Planning Integrated with Artificial Intelligence Parametric Analysis. *Secur. Commun. Netw.* **2022**, *2022*, 8577269. [CrossRef]
91. Wei, L. AI Concepts in Architectural Design. *IOP Conf. Ser. Mater. Sci. Eng.* **2018**, *392*, 062016. [CrossRef]
92. Zhao, Y.; Genovese, P.V.; Li, Z. Intelligent thermal comfort controlling system for buildings based on IoT and AI. *Future Internet* **2020**, *12*, 30. [CrossRef]
93. Bikulčiūtė, G. Timber Upward Extension: Exploration of the Use of Parametric Modelling and Machine Learning for Initial Building Extension Design. Master Thesis, Delft University of Technology, Delft, The Netherlands, 2021.
94. Arora Jasbir, S.; Baenziger, G. Uses of Artificial Intelligence in Design Optimization. *Comput. Methods Appl. Mech. Eng.* **1986**, *54*, 303–323. [CrossRef]

95. Dan, R.; Ghantous, K.; Otani, R.K. Performance Measures from Architectural Massing Using Machine Learning. In Proceedings of the IASS Annual Symposia, Amsterdam, The Netherlands, 17–20 August 2015; pp. 1–12.
96. Tang, B.; Chen, Z.; Hefferman, G.; Pei, S. Incorporating Intelligence in Fog Computing for Big Data Analysis in Smart Cities. *IEEE Trans. Ind. Inform.* **2017**, *13*, 2140–2150. [CrossRef]
97. Jiang, P.; Wang, T.; Han, B.; Gao, X.; Zhang, J.; Wen, C.-K.; Jin, S.; Li, G. Artificial Intelligence-Aided OFDM Receiver: Design and Experimental Results. *arXiv* **2018**, arXiv:1812.06638.
98. Mohammadpour, A.; Karan, E.; Asadi, S. Artificial Intelligence Techniques to Support Design and Construction. ISARC. *Proc. Int. Symp. Autom. Robot. Constr.* **2019**, *36*, 1282–1289.
99. Saaty, T.L. Decision making with the analytic hierarchy process. *Int. J. Serv. Sci.* **2008**, *1*, 83–98. [CrossRef]
100. Wind, Y.; Saaty, T.L. Marketing applications of the analytic hierarchy process. *Manag. Sci.* **1980**, *26*, 641–658. [CrossRef]
101. Chen, J.-K.; Chen, I.-S. Using a novel conjunctive MCDM approach based on DEMATEL, fuzzy ANP, and TOPSIS as an innovation support system for Taiwanese higher education. *Expert Syst. Appl.* **2010**, *37*, 1981–1990. [CrossRef]
102. Gabus, A.; Fontela, E.; Gabus, S. *World Problems, An Invitation to Further Thought Within the Framework of DEMATEL*; Battelle Geneva Research Center: Geneva, Switzerland, 1972; Volume 1, pp. 12–14.
103. Ocampo, L.A.; Himang, C.M.; Kumar, A.; Brezocnik, M. A novel multiple criteria decision-making approach based on fuzzy DEMATEL, fuzzy ANP and fuzzy AHP for mapping collection and distribution centers in reverse logistics. *Adv. Prod. Eng. Manag.* **2019**, *14*, 297–322. [CrossRef]
104. Warfield, J.N. Developing interconnection matrices in structural modeling. *IEEE Trans. Syst. Man Cybern.* **2010**, *1*, 81–87. [CrossRef]
105. Godet, M. *From Anticipation to Action: A Handbook of Strategic Prospective*; Unesco Publishing: Paris, France, 1994.

buildings

MDPI

Article

Screen Façade Pattern Design Driven by Generative Adversarial Networks and Machine Learning Classification for the Evaluation of a Daylight Environment

Hyunjae Nam [1] and Dong Yoon Park [2,*]

[1] Department of Architecture, Kwangwoon University, Seoul 01897, Republic of Korea; hyunjae_nam@kw.ac.kr
[2] Department of Refrigeration and Air-Conditioning Engineering, Chonnam National University, Yeosu 59626, Republic of Korea
* Correspondence: dypark@jnu.ac.kr

Abstract: This research seeks to identify optimised screen façade patterns and ratios for the effective management of daylight ingress and glare effects. It employs generative adversarial networks (GANs) to generate pattern variations and further evaluates the resultant variations through daylight simulations for application in screen façades. The generated pattern data were classified by hierarchical clustering to distinguish distinct feature groups, and they were subsequently utilised as façade configurations. The pattern data were assessed through daylight performance metrics: spatial daylight autonomy (sDA), annual sunlight exposure (ASE), and daylight glare probability (DGP). The results of the annual-based simulations indicate that façade patterns with frame ratios in the range of 50–65% are useful in reducing the areas exposed to intensive glare on the façade side while maintaining the minimum required lighting conditions. The overall influence of screen façades on interior daylighting in a large space (e.g., 10 m $\times$ 10 m) was found to be limited. Their performance is notable in reducing glare discomfort areas within approximately 2.5 m of south-facing façades. This study supports an application strategy in which screen façades are used to manage the extent of areas exposed to daylight ingress within an interior space.

Keywords: screen façade; generative pattern; artificial intelligence in architecture; daylight simulation

1. Introduction

The façade of a building serves as its 'face' or 'frontage', which combines exterior features with essential functions for building performance [1]. As façades act as filters and complex systems connecting interior and exterior environments, the early design stage involves multi-disciplinary processes that require the integration of human comfort, structural safety, durability, material efficiency, and cost effectiveness [2]. To meet the indoor occupants' needs, one of the major building design criteria is human comfort. This includes the sub-categories of visual comfort, daylight control, acoustics, and heating/cooling [3]. The aesthetic perception of building façades is determined by a blend of visual, cultural and psychological factors, depending on how people identify the outward appearance of buildings [4,5]. Façade design often entails challenges in achieving a balance between practical performance and visual qualities.

To achieve the dual purpose of combining environmental responsiveness with aesthetics, screen façades (often referred to as perforated façades) can be employed as a façade design type [6]. They are designed with geometric patterns, and play a crucial role in solar shading. The perforated portions allow controlled daylight penetration, to reduce heat gain and enhance building performance, while maintaining visual connections with the exterior environment [7]. With increasing interest in the aspect of sustainability-related building performance, contemporary versions of screen façades have focused on building envelopes that distribute daylight in indoor spaces [8]. Recent research has addressed the assessment of visual comfort, glare reduction, and outside views for occupants, and the geometric aspects of façade design [8]. For instance, the performance-oriented design approach combines architectural designs with environmental technologies to enhance building performance. Advancements in computational design methods have fostered new pathways using building data in this design process [9].

Artificial intelligence (AI) technologies, coupled with high-performance computing capacity, have supported designers' decision-making methods for generating and evaluating architectural designs. This allows architects to assess both design variations and functional properties [10,11]. While visual qualities in architectural design are generally based on aesthetic considerations, data-driven metrics enable the use of measurable outcomes to support design alternatives [12]. In the research domain of building façades integrated with AI techniques, key trending data metrics include energy performance, thermal comfort assessment, and daylight optimisation [13]. The process of decision-making for generating design options is based on building contexts such as geometry, geography and typology, and follows a systematic methodology. This involves the preparation and configuring of relevant data; the application of generative models; performance evaluations; assessment of compliance with predefined requirements; and the development of final design solutions [14].

For this research, generative adversarial networks (GANs) and machine learning (ML) classification based on convolutional neural networks (CNNs) are employed to explore a data-driven design methodology, which concentrates on generative screen façade patterns and the clustering of their features. Furthermore, the features' effects on indoor environmental quality are evaluated. Previous design automation methods in architecture have included evolutionary computation, artificial neural networks, fractals, swarm intelligence, and cellular automata [15]. Given a remarkable increase in studies employing AI methods, GANs have emerged as a transformative technique in architectural research. GAN models are primarily applied in computer vision, as they enable image synthesis, translation and enhancement, for generating images or two-dimensional representations [16]. To address the relationship between image generative techniques and three-dimensional model simulations that are suitable for practical applications, this study investigates the generative method of designing screen façade features using GANs, and their integration with daylight simulation analyses.

1.1. GANs in the Architectural Context

Proposed by Goodfellow et al. in 2014 [17], the adversarial nets framework has been widely applied across various industries. The learning process is formalised to train the Generator and Discriminator simultaneously, in order to optimise the final Generator to produce increasingly improved data outputs. Following this model, the applications of deep convolutional generative adversarial networks (DCGAN) illustrated the potential of black-and-white feature generation, but this depended on large volumes of data, and required addressing the challenge of blurry images [18–20]. As early GANs suffered from drawbacks such as mode collapse and training instability, Wasserstein GAN (WGAN) improved the issue by proposing the Wasserstein loss function [21]. StyleGAN advanced the modelling framework by enabling fine-grained control over image synthesis, while it required fewer datasets compared to previous approaches [22].

The GAN model has been increasingly integrated into architectural and urban studies, supported by deep neural networks that enable image translation, text-to-image synthesis, and graph-based generation. For instance, Pix2Pix, a conditional GAN model, performs image-to-image translation tasks utilising segmentation mapping, in order to generate façade or urban street representations [23]. CycleGAN facilitates the synthesis of paired datasets, such as perspective street images or urban aerial views with corresponding labels [24]. In addition, text-to-image synthesis techniques, such as AttnGAN, enable the generation of building images from textual descriptions by utilising attention mechanisms, for detailed visual outputs [25]. Furthermore, GraphGAN has extended GAN's ability to handle textual and graph-structured data [26].

For spatial and volumetric studies, the GAN model has been employed across a range of applications, from 2D layout composition to 3D object modelling. For example, House-GAN is a graph-constrained house layout generator designed to provide multiple options for compatible room compositions, by employing bubble diagrams [27]. GTGAN and Roof-GAN produce roof geometry that fits into the building footprint, incorporating a graph-transformer-based generator [28,29]. Moreover, there has been a growing trend towards advancing the technique to incorporate 3D models. Building-GAN presents a volumetric design approach to generate buildings' rough 3D geometry, defined by programmes and a 2D layout based on node networks [30]. In addition, 3DGAN has developed 3D volume generation, represented in voxel grids, by training on 3D data to create 3D objects [31]. Studies on GANs related to architectural and urban contexts have involved the subject of generating room layout, building envelope and volumetric shape [32].

1.2. Façade Design Integrated with AI and Daylight Simulation

A wide range of design strategies for façade shading devices have been developed to enhance indoor daylight quality. These strategies involve two-dimensional patterned screens that provide shading, airflow, privacy, ornamentation (e.g., Mashrabiya, Kumiko, Jali) and configurable architectural elements (e.g., membranes, shutters, kinetic devices) [33]. Research on façade systems can be generally categorised into static and dynamic devices [34]. Façade systems manage changing environmental conditions and are responsive to environmental data, subject to temporal variation. Optimally responsive static devices and spontaneously adaptive dynamic systems have been examined.

In studies on adaptable façade materials, shading devices have been investigated using glass with varying light transmittance that reacts to specific solar incidence angles [33]. For fabric-based devices, openness and angular configuration are crucial factors in determining effective daylight infiltration [35]. The research domain investigating the design optimisation of static devices has focused on identifying effective solutions for balancing daylight controls with reducing dependence on artificial lighting.

Louvres represent one of the most widely used strategies for daylight control. The examination of geometrical configurations has increasingly been applied to achieve optimised performance. Supported by computational methods, these investigations significantly reduce the time required, compared to conventional evaluation processes, and they enable testing beyond a limited set of design options [34,36]. Furthermore, ML techniques for daylight prediction, combined with genetic algorithms for optimisation, have emerged as contemporary approaches in façade design.

Ongoing research has emphasised the optimisation of façade systems to enhance daylight performance and occupant comfort. The deployment of double-skin façades, integrated with perforated screen layers, has demonstrated notable capacity in enhancing luminance distribution and reducing visual discomfort from glare [37]. Building orientations influence the optimal perforation ratios for screen façades that require customised solutions for sunlight exposure [38,39]. Façade performance simulations have adopted an integrative framework combining daylighting metrics with site-specific environmental data to enable rigorous performance assessment [40,41]. AI techniques allow the efficient evaluation of daylight metrics through data-driven methodologies.

When combining the CNN and GAN methods for building performance estimations related to façade design, this involves the challenge of translating the ML techniques into design decision-making solutions. CNN models are effective for data classification, detection and segmentation, while GAN models are useful for data prediction, synthesis and transformation [42]. To evaluate façade performance, commonly used daylight metrics include illuminance calculations, spatial daylight autonomy (sDA), annual sunlight exposure (ASE), daylight glare probability (DGP), useful daylight illuminance (UDI), and daylight factor (DF). Studies on façade design have mainly centred on developing daylight prediction models driven by deep learning to estimate performance metrics [43].

Regarding building façade design, the GAN model has facilitated the technique of manipulating building exterior images, such as reproducing traditional features, restoring partial façade images, modifying window details, and synthesising textures for 3D models. Combined with segmentation mapping and text-to-image techniques, the model could be trained with a collection of historical building façade image data, to reproduce varied traditional styles of building exterior features [44–46]. For image in-painting, its application fills in missing parts of façade images, or removes elements arranged in front of buildings, such as trees, cars and pedestrians [47]. GAN further automates the modelling of window frames images, including the details of width, subdivision and profile, by combining CNN-based recognition of architectural features [48]. For texture 3D mapping, FrankenGAN enables the integration of façade and roof image textures into volumetric virtual environments [49,50].

Although generative AI models have been primarily utilised for architectural image manipulation, their potential has been increasingly recognised for the rapid exploration of design alternatives. While image manipulation of building visuals has been widely investigated, relatively few studies have focused on using generative AI to create or newly produce forms for architectural element designs, based on training data.

2. Methods

2.1. Research Process and Objective

The aim of this study is to utilise GAN to generate façade pattern designs, which are then evaluated using daylight performance simulation. This research contributes to the investigation of AI-driven generative design approaches that facilitate the exploration of performance-based strategies and support the evaluation of façade design effectiveness. This study focuses on employing a trained generative model to produce form alternatives for façade element design. The application of generative AI was not limited to two-dimensional image manipulations of architectural representations, but aimed to utilise AI-generated patterns applied to architectural elements. This enabled their simulation within three-dimensional environments that incorporate daylight evaluations.

The daylight simulations were conducted with the environmental data specified by a south-oriented test space in South Korea. The research consisted of three main processes:

pattern-making, variation-categorising, and daylight performance evaluation (see Figure 1). In Step 1, the StyleGAN model produced variations in screen façade patterns, in order to allow the exploration of design features. In Step 2, a hierarchical classification approach was employed using the Orange tool integrated with the SqueezeNet CNN model, to identify pattern features. In Step 3, the daylight effects of selected patterns were measured through performance simulations. The simulations were conducted using Rhino and Grasshopper plugins, including the Climate Studio tool.

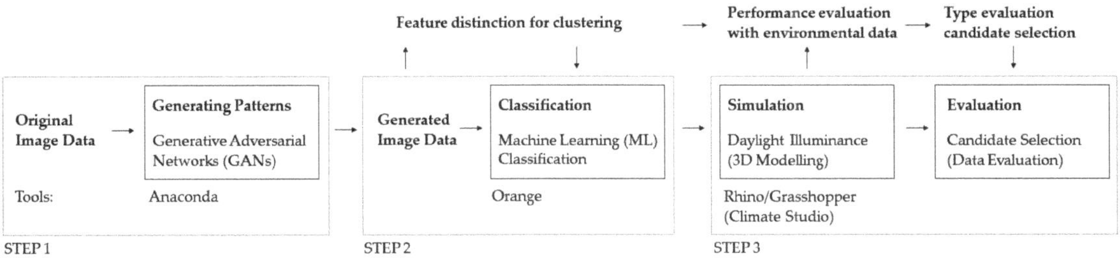

Figure 1. Workflow of the research process.

For pattern making, 664 black-and-white images were collected. These were resized to 256 × 256 pixels for training. The StyleGAN3 model was utilised, as it can generate fine details and variations with limited datasets; this facilitates the manipulation of features through unsupervised training processes. The output of 5000 newly generated image data produced by the StyleGAN model were classified by resembling features though CNN classification processes. The augmented pattern data provided more available variations, and a wider range of proportions of frame (black part) and void (white part) in the pattern images. After the phase of clustering the data, the percentages of frame and void parts in similar patterns were assessed. The categorised pattern images were placed on a south-side building façade with 3D modelling. They were used as varied options to measure illuminance calculations—specifically, sDA, ASE, and DGP, which are key metrics for a building's daylight performance. The simulation-based approach evaluated the daylight performance of screen façade designs in a regularly occupied space.

ML techniques were employed as a supporting method for the design of an architectural component. Recent GAN models have enabled high-resolution image feature generation. Previously, training early GAN models required over 100,000 images. In this study, a relatively small dataset of black-and-white binary frame feature images was used to train façade frame design models. In addition, the Climate Studio tool excels in delivering highly accurate daylight simulations for passive solar strategies, glare control, and sustainable building compliance. The simulations with this tool verified the detailed measurement of daylight effects for occupant comfort and the climate-specific analysis.

2.2. Framework of the CNN and GAN Model

As a deep learning model, CNNs are composed of multiple layers of processing, and all the weights in the CNNs are learned using the back-propagation technique [51]. For computer vision, starting with the input image whose pixels are building blocks, CNN models process four stages: a convolutional layer, a normalisation layer, a pooling layer, and a fully connected layer. First, the convolutional layer applies filters. It multiplies its values with overlapping values, and adds them all together to form a single output value. In the normalisation layer, the feature maps, produced via the filters, can be inserted into a non-linear function, such as ReLU activation. From the feature maps, the pooling (sub-sampling) layer calculates a summary statistic of the neighbouring outputs and shrinks the feature's spatial size. The fully connected layer receives its input from the final outputs of the pooling or convolutional layer, and its flattening process involves converting all the values into a one-dimensional vector [52].

The output is compared using a loss function for classification tasks. In ML, loss refers to the difference between a model's predicted value and the actual value for a single sample: the loss function calculates this difference. A lower loss indicates better model performance, as it signifies a closer match between predictions and actual values. The error is propagated back through the network using back-propagation, which computes gradients for weight updates. The activation functions can adaptively adjust the parameters of the correction unit, thereby enhancing recognition accuracy during training [53]. The process is repeated across multiple training processes, to refine the model's ability to classify images. The final feature map is passed through fully connected layers to produce a probability distribution over possible classes, with the class having the highest probability as the output.

In the model for generating GANs, CNNs are employed in both the generator and the discriminator networks, where classification processes are manipulated by training the discriminator to output probabilities that guide the generator to produce more accurate images (see Figure 2). As training progresses, the generator increasingly produces data that closely resemble authentic images, while the discriminator improves its ability to distinguish between genuine and synthesised samples.

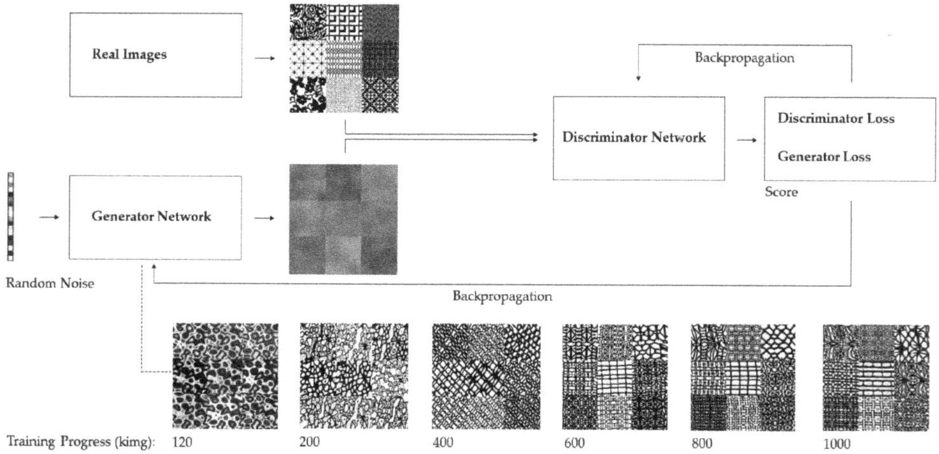

Figure 2. Framework of GAN process.

The basic formula underlying the StyleGAN model is derived from the standard GAN framework, expressed as follows [17]:

$$\min_{G}\max_{D} V(D,G) = E_{x\sim P_{data}(x)}[\log D(x)] + E_{z\sim P_z(z)}[\log(1 - D(G(z)))] \quad (1)$$

In this formula, the generator (*G*) and discriminator (*D*) are engaged in a two-player min-max game with value function *V*(*D*,*G*). The discriminator aims to distinguish real data (*x*) from generated ones by maximising the former's score (*D*(*x*)) while minimising that of the latter (*D*(*G*(*z*))). The generator tries to deceive the discriminator by producing data that resemble real data, to minimise their likelihood of being identified as fake. The goal is to train *G* to produce realistic images that *D* cannot distinguish from real ones.

The StyleGAN model amends the traditional GAN generator, so that random noise is mapped to intermediate latent spaces in order to control specific visual features. Noise injection at each layer further adds fine details. Random noise is added at each generator layer to introduce stochastic variations, thus creating fine-grained and confirming diversity in the generated outputs. Instead of feeding noise directly into the generator, StyleGAN maps into an intermediate latent space using a fully connected mapping network.

In the StyleGAN model, the convolutional layers refine and transform features progressively as the image resolution increases. In progressive growing, the image resolution is increased step-by-step by adding convolutional blocks. Adaptive Instance Normalisation (AdaIN) replaces the need for traditional transposed convolution by allowing the latent vector to control the activations in the generator. The latent vector is transformed into styles at different layers, thus modulating the convolutional layers' output through AdaIN. This provides precise control over various aspects of the generated image. Hence, StyleGAN enables the control of details such as shape, composition, texture, and sharpness in images, and is useful for generating high-contrast images with clear feature separation.

2.3. Daylight Assessment

Screen façades use patterned designs to enhance visual appeal and indoor privacy, control daylight, and adapt to environmental conditions for improved thermal efficiency. Regarding these objectives, regulating the ratio between solid frames and voids is essential for retaining a connection between interior and exterior spaces and filtering natural light. The standards of building sustainability provide guidelines for daylight maintenance, in order to effectively regulate sunlight, reduce electrical lighting usage, and minimise glare.

Design strategies for achieving daylighting management indicate the use of annual computer simulations to analyse two key metrics: sufficient daylight (sDA) and extent of excessive sunlight exposure (ASE) [54]. sDA is a widely utilised metric in daylighting analysis: it quantifies the percentage of floor area receiving adequate daylight illuminance within an interior space, and is typically defined as achieving at least 300 lux for a minimum of 50% of annual occupied hours. This metric evaluates how natural light sufficiently illuminates the space during periods of occupancy. In addition, ASE measures the percentage of floor area receiving sunlight above a specified threshold for more than a specified number of hours per year. The thresholds in the ASE standards are generally 1000 lux and 250 h. This metric identifies areas at risk of excessive solar exposure, which can lead to visual discomfort from glare. sDA and ASE calculations assess daylight performance from an occupant's perspective. The analysis grids need to be no more than 0.6 m^2, and positioned at a height of 0.76 m above the finished floor.

The approved daylight metrics method, IES LM-83-12 (2012) [55], introduced by the Illuminating Engineering Society, defines spatiotemporal metrics through sDA300/50% and ASE1000/250h [56]. These metrics represent the percentage of a space that receives sDA and the ASE, respectively. The sDA metric evaluates the sufficiency of natural daylight in an indoor space. The formula measures the percentage of a space that meets or exceeds a specified illuminance level (e.g., 300 lux) for a given fraction (e.g., 50%) of occupied time annually. It is defined as follows:

$$sDA_{300/50\%} = \frac{\sum_i S(i)}{\sum_i P_i} \in [0,\ 1],\ S(i) = \begin{cases} 1 & if\ s_i \geq \tau t_y \\ 0 & if\ s_i < \tau t_y \end{cases} \tag{2}$$

The function $S(i)$ estimates whether the illuminance target at points (P_i) meets daylight requirements, where s_i counts illuminance exceedances of the target, τ is the required time fraction, and t_y represents annual occupied timesteps. ASE measures annual glare risk from excessive sunlight exposure, calculated as follows:

$$ASE_{1000/250h} = \frac{\sum_i A(i)}{\sum_i P_i} \in [0,\ 1],\ A(i) = \begin{cases} 1 & if\ a_i \geq T_y \\ 0 & if\ a_i < T_y \end{cases} \tag{3}$$

The function $A(i)$ evaluates whether the illuminance target the points (P_i) exceeds annual glare limits, where a_i counts illuminance surpasses a threshold (e.g., 1000 lux) and T_y is the annual hour threshold (e.g., 250).

DGP measures daylight glare by evaluating the likelihood of uncomfortable glare caused by direct sunlight through windows. sDA and ASE evaluate annual daylight availability and usability, while illuminance calculations and DGP assess specific lighting levels and glare conditions at a given moment. In the method of illuminance calculation, daylight can be measured by illuminance levels at two key times of the year (21 September and 21 March) at 9 a.m. and 3 p.m. under clear sky conditions [54]. These times are designated as representative of the equinoxes, when day and night are of equal length. The recommended daylight illuminance range for the regularly occupied floor area spans from 300 lux to 3000 lux, to provide sufficient natural lighting to support occupant comfort and optimal visual performance [54].

The DGP formula predicts visual discomfort caused by daylight glare in indoor environments. The formula is defined by the following [57]:

$$DGP = 5.87 \times 10^{-5} E_v + 9.18 \times 10^{-2} \log\left(1 + \sum_i \frac{L_{s,i}^2 \omega_{s,i}}{E_v^{1.87} P_i^2}\right) + 0.16 \tag{4}$$

E_v represents the vertical illuminance at eye level, indicating the surrounding brightness at the observer's position. $L_{s,i}$ refers to the luminance of glare source, and $\omega_{s,i}$ is the solid angle of the glare source. P_i is the position index, which accounts for how centrally a glare source appears within the viewer's field of vision. The relative contribution of each glare source increases with its brightness, size in the field of view, and proximity to the centre of vision, while it decreases as the surrounding vertical illuminance becomes higher due to visual adaptation. DGP combines the global brightness and contrast-based glare effects from individual bright sources [57,58].

According to the relationship between glare rating and DGP range, a DGP $\leq$ 0.35 indicates no glare, values between 0.35 and 0.40 represent acceptable glare, and values above 0.40 correspond to uncomfortable glare [59]. Lower DGP values indicate less glare, leading to a more comfortable visual environment. Thus, a well-balanced daylighting design maximises natural light, while minimising glare and excessive sunlight exposure.

For glare measurement, spatial disturbing glare (sDG) indicates the percentage of views across the regularly occupied floor area that experience discomfort glare for at least 5% of the working time in a year. The calculation method is based on spatial temporal DGP values for different view directions in a simulation space [60].

The EN 17037:2018 'Daylight of Buildings' Standard [61] provides the minimum target daylight factor and the recommended lux values. It specifies that the daylighting condition should maintain 300 lux for 50% of the space and 100 lux minimum over 95% of the space. It also states that the range of 500–750 lux is the average level for daylight [62]. In the IES LM-83-12 (2012) standard, sDA uses a minimum threshold of 300 lux to indicate sufficient daylight conditions, whereas ASE applies a 1000 lux threshold to identify potential glare exposure.

The abovementioned measurement methods are recommended in the standards of sustainable building design for aspects of daylight management. In the LEED Daylight Credit options (EQ Credit), the measurement methods involve sDA and ASE. The lux levels ranging from 300 to 3000 are specified for either simulation-based modelling or on-site measurement, conducted at a specific time. The 3000 lux threshold serves as an upper limit for ASE, to prevent visual discomfort.

2.4. Screen Façade Design and Daylight Simulation

Daylight simulations were conducted using façade patterns generated by GAN models. The test space for this study was an open-plan office type space, located in Seoul, South Korea (37.56° N, 126.97° E). The simulations employed the Seoul EPW weather file (KOR_SO_Seoul.WS.471080_TMYx.2004–2018) under an 8 a.m.–6 p.m. occupancy schedule with Daylight Saving Time (DST). The space has a south-facing window and an external façade system. It is composed of a floor area of 10 m × 10 m with a ceiling height of 4 m; each façade panel is 2 m × 2 m and made of grey aluminium (see Figure 3, left).

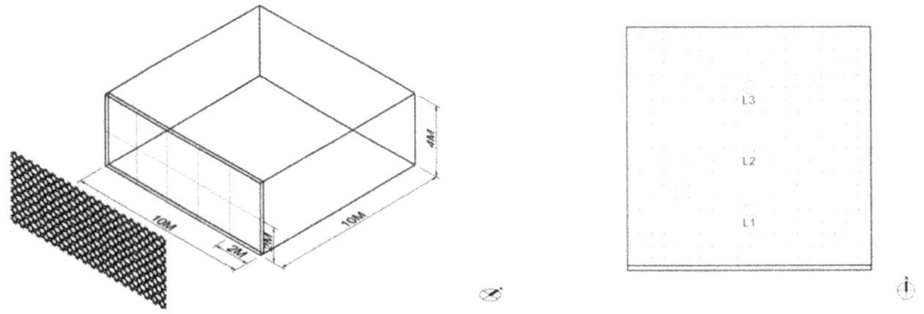

Figure 3. Simulation space dimension (**left**) and DGP sensor locations (**right**).

The interior materials followed the LM83 standards, which were developed by the Illuminating Engineering Society (IES); these define the metrics for evaluating daylight performance in buildings, with reflectance values of 70% for the ceiling, 50% for the walls, and 20% for the floor. The window glazing was Clear—Solarban 90 (3), with a visible light transmittance (VLT) of 50%, a visible light reflectance (VLR) of 19%, a U-value of 1.63, and a solar heat gain coefficient (SHGC) of 0.33. Daylight simulations were performed using the Climate Studio plug-in for Rhino, to calculate daylight metrics with the grid setting, as shown in Figure 3 right, and Table 1.

Table 1. Simulation space input parameters.

Simulation Conditions	Input Parameters
Location Data	Seoul, South Korea (latitude 37.56° N, longitude 126.97° E) KOR_SO_Seoul.WS.471080_TMYx.2004–2018
Occupancy Schedule	8 a.m.–6 p.m. with DST
Space Dimensions (m)	Floor: 10 m × 10 m, Height: 4 m
Interior Materials	Ceiling: LM83 (VLR: 70%), Wall: LM83 (VLR: 50%), Floor: LM83 (VLR: 20%)
Window Glass Type	Clear—Solarban 90 (3) (VLT: 50%, VLR: 19%, UVal: 1.63, SHGC: 0.33)
Window Orientation	South Side
Total Window Area	40 m^2
Façade Panel Dimensions	2 m × 2 m
Façade Panel Material	Grey Aluminium Façade (VLR: 37%)
Daylight Availability Grid	Sensor Spacing: 0.5 m, Work-plane Offset: 0.76 m
Point-in-time Illuminance Grid	Sensor Spacing: 0.5 m, Work-plane Offset: 0.76 m
Annual Glare Grid	Sensor Spacing: 0.5 m, View-plane Offset: 1.2 m

3. Results

3.1. Classification of Pattern Features

Hierarchical clustering was applied to assess the similarity between pattern images. In the resulting groupings (Figures 4 and 5), the *X*-axis represents the images arranged according to clusters, while the *Y*-axis shows the Euclidean distance between clusters. A cut-off line defines the threshold used to group the data into clusters. Below the dendrograms in Figures 4 and 5, example images corresponding to clusters are displayed.

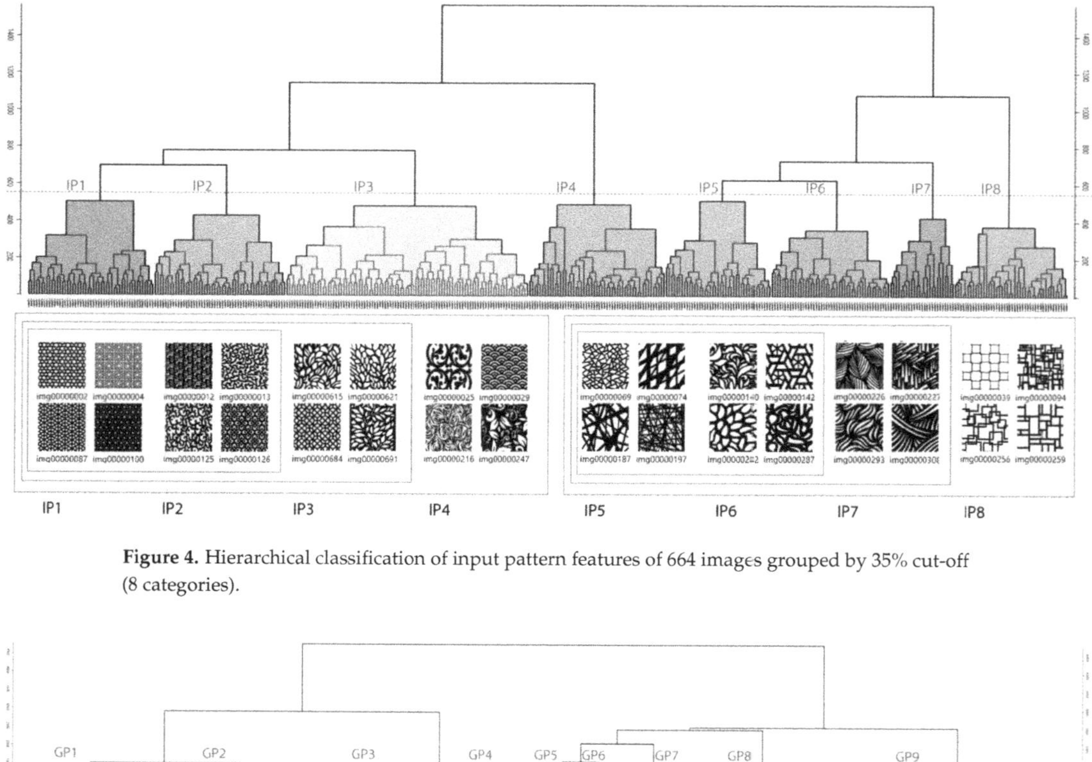

Figure 4. Hierarchical classification of input pattern features of 664 images grouped by 35% cut-off (8 categories).

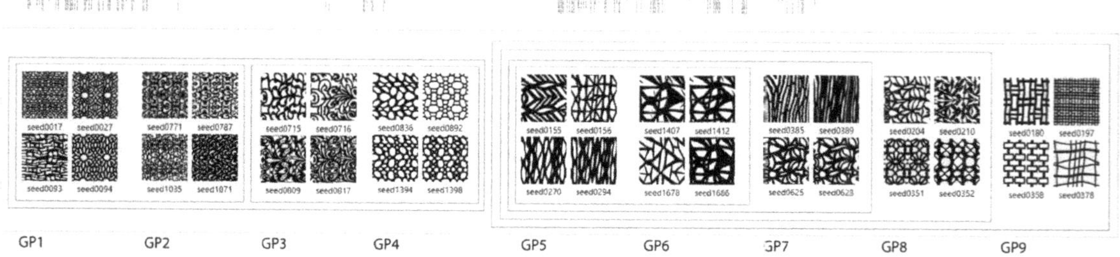

Figure 5. Hierarchical classification of generated pattern features of 5000 images grouped by 28% cut-off (9 categories).

By applying hierarchical classification, the CNN model grouped the collection of input pattern (IP) image data into distinct classes. For clustering the 664 input training data images, a 35% cut-off threshold was applied. The classification tree was trimmed to preserve 35% of its structure, while grouping similar patterns accordingly. This process resulted in eight distinct categories, organising the images based on their pattern characteristics. As illustrated in Figure 4, which presents the clustering groups and corresponding samples (IP1 to IP8), the input images form two main branches: tightly structured regular patterns (IP1 to IP4) and large irregular patterns (IP5 to IP8). IP4 and IP8 deviate from the main grouping, and it is noticed that the patterns in these groups are less similar in their subdivisions.

The CNN classification of the 5000 images which are the generated pattern (GP) images from StyleGAN3, treated with a 28% cut-off, represents nine categories (see Figure 5). Similar to the abovementioned input data classification case, the clustering of the GP images is divided into two main groups that show regular patterns (GP1 to GP4) and relatively irregular patterns (GP5 to GP9). Figure 6 depicts one of the groupings of subdivisions in the GP7 cluster, which contains similar patterns. The output results, based on training with input data that include available pattern designs, show a varied mix of patterns.

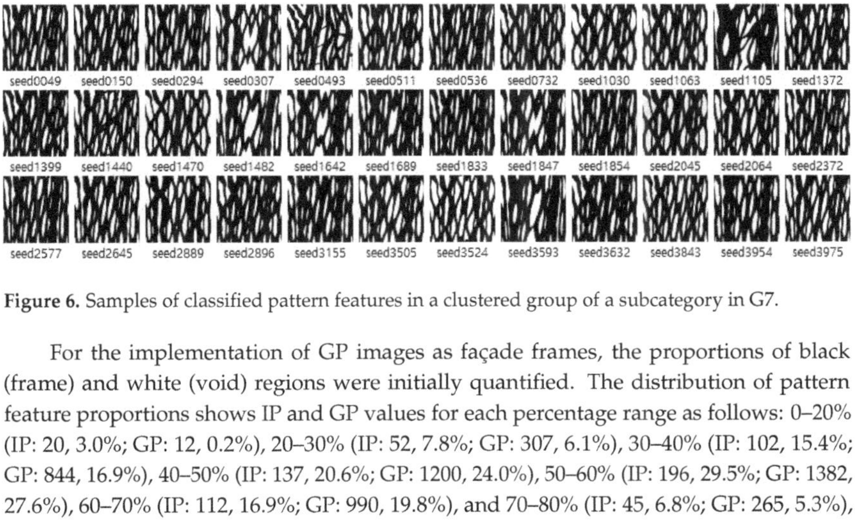

Figure 6. Samples of classified pattern features in a clustered group of a subcategory in G7.

For the implementation of GP images as façade frames, the proportions of black (frame) and white (void) regions were initially quantified. The distribution of pattern feature proportions shows IP and GP values for each percentage range as follows: 0–20% (IP: 20, 3.0%; GP: 12, 0.2%), 20–30% (IP: 52, 7.8%; GP: 307, 6.1%), 30–40% (IP: 102, 15.4%; GP: 844, 16.9%), 40–50% (IP: 137, 20.6%; GP: 1200, 24.0%), 50–60% (IP: 196, 29.5%; GP: 1382, 27.6%), 60–70% (IP: 112, 16.9%; GP: 990, 19.8%), and 70–80% (IP: 45, 6.8%; GP: 265, 5.3%), thus demonstrating that the output GPs closely match the proportional distribution of the input IPs across all ranges. The percentage differences between IP and GP distributions vary between 1.5% and 3.4% throughout the ranges. This shows that, through training, new images were generated that closely correspond to the ratio of the input image numbers.

3.2. Assessment of ASE and sDA Results

To determine the optimal screen façade frame ratio for daylight performance, ASE and sDA simulations were conducted under the conditions specified in Table 1. The percentages of frames corresponding to each pattern were verified. Some of the clustered patterns presenting similar form characteristics, as classified by the aforementioned CNN categorisation, were selected to compare ASE and sDA outcomes. The simulation results demonstrate that both metrics were influenced more significantly by the frame density than by the frame shape. Table 2 provides the simulation visual data, showing two samples selected from clustered patterns for frame ratios ranging from 40% to 80%, at 5% intervals. According to Table 2, the two different features present similar values that differ by less than 2%. In the tables, the simulation visualisations are presented as plan views, with south positioned at the bottom and north at the top.

Table 2. ASE and sDA Simulation by 40 to 80 percentage of pattern features.

	No Frame	**40**	**45**	**50**	**55**	**60**	**65**	**70**	**75**	**80**
Frame		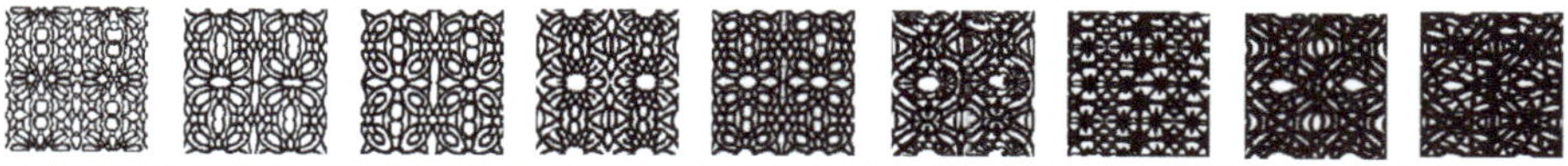								
sDA	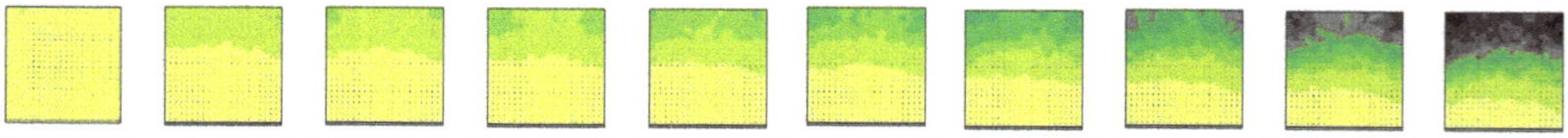									
sDA (%)	100	100	100	100	100	100	99.5	94.8	77.8	64.5
ASE	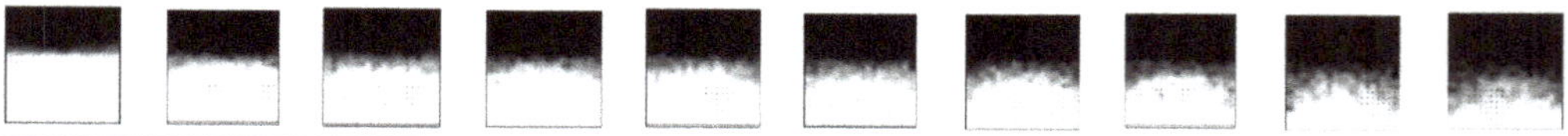									
ASE (%)	56.3	49.5	45.3	43.3	42.3	37.8	36.5	33.5	24.8	19.0
Avg. Lux	5173	3184	2939	2663	2401	2160	1877	1629	1353	1088
Frame										
sDA	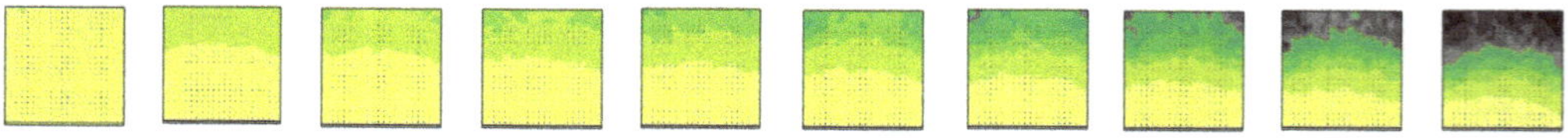									
sDA (%)	100	100	100	100	100	100	99.3	95.0	78.8	65.3
ASE	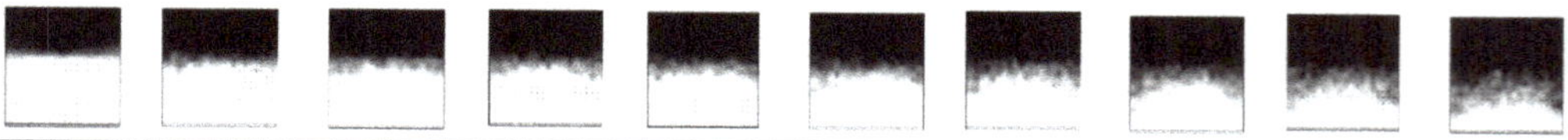									
ASE (%)	56.3	50.3	45.5	45.8	43.3	39.8	35.8	31.5	25.3	19.0
Avg. Lux	5173	3186	2930	2676	2410	2166	1884	1623	1368	1081

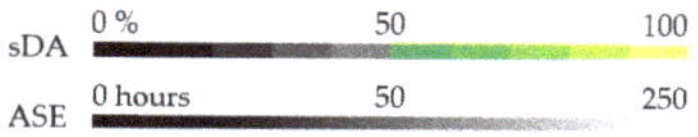

The results illustrate that, when the simulated frame density exceeds 70%, sDA values significantly decline, and the graphically represented sunlight distribution further indicates that the annual sunlight exposure fails to reach the rear of the room. For the frames above 70% density, the ASE value's rate of decline nearly doubles, compared to those below this threshold. With respect to the unit of illuminance, the 45% frame exhibits average lux values near 3000, and the values above this percentage remain below 3000.

For more detailed simulations using glare effective frame density, the analysis examined the limited percentage of frame densities ranging from 50% to 65%, with clustered similar frame features. Percentages of 40% and 45% were excluded, as they were close to the average lux level of 3000, while 75% and 80% were also excluded, for being near the 70% threshold. Thus, the analysis focused on transmission percentages with detailed comparisons at 50%, 55%, 60%, and 65%. These percentages were tested across five different types of frame features: geometrical, floral, random, circular, and linear patterns, which provide a total of 20 samples (see Figure 7). Precedent studies and design applications frequently reference these patterns as commonly used typologies in screen façade design, which establishes their relevance and validity for architectural analysis and daylight simulation. The specified comparisons focused on glare effects, to ensure the evaluation of visual comfort under differing light transmission conditions.

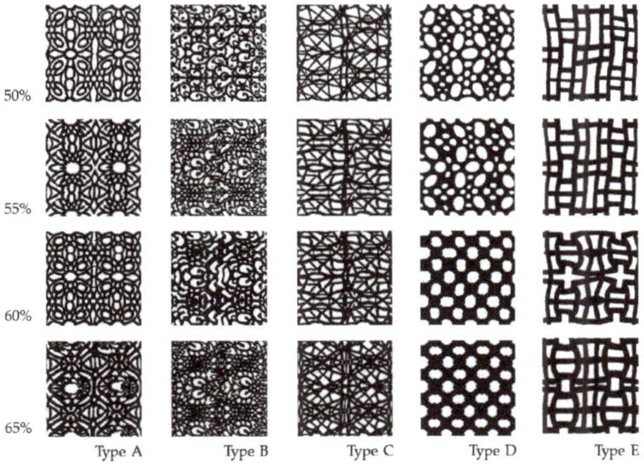

Figure 7. Classified variations in pattern for the simulation of daylight. Five types: geometrical (A), floral (B), random (C), circular (D), linear patterns (E).

3.3. Comparison of DGP Effects Simulated Using Five Pattern Types

The DGP simulations were conducted using five distinct pattern features. The annual glare effects were measured at the sensor locations illustrated in Figure 3 (right), and each point includes four directional pie slices. Table 3 presents the measurement data for Type A frames, which show an example of DGP simulation results. In the DGP visualisation (Table 3), the south side is positioned at the bottom. For a comparison of DGP results for all frame types, Figure 8 shows detailed data, including the different levels of glare effects measured at three sensor points.

Table 3. Glare simulation results for Type A frames with 50% to 65% density.

	No Frame	A50	A55	A60	A65
DGP Visualisation		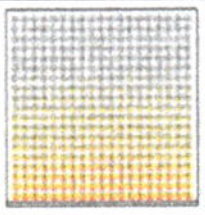	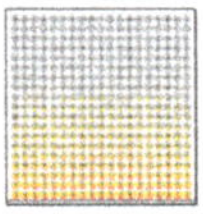	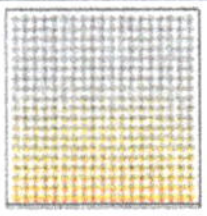	
Imperceptible (%)	69	86	88	90	92
Perceptible (%)	6	4	3	3	2
Disturbing (%)	7	3	3	2	2
Intolerable (%)	18	7	6	5	4
sDG-5 (%)	56.09	35.60	32.55	29.5	26.45

DGP 

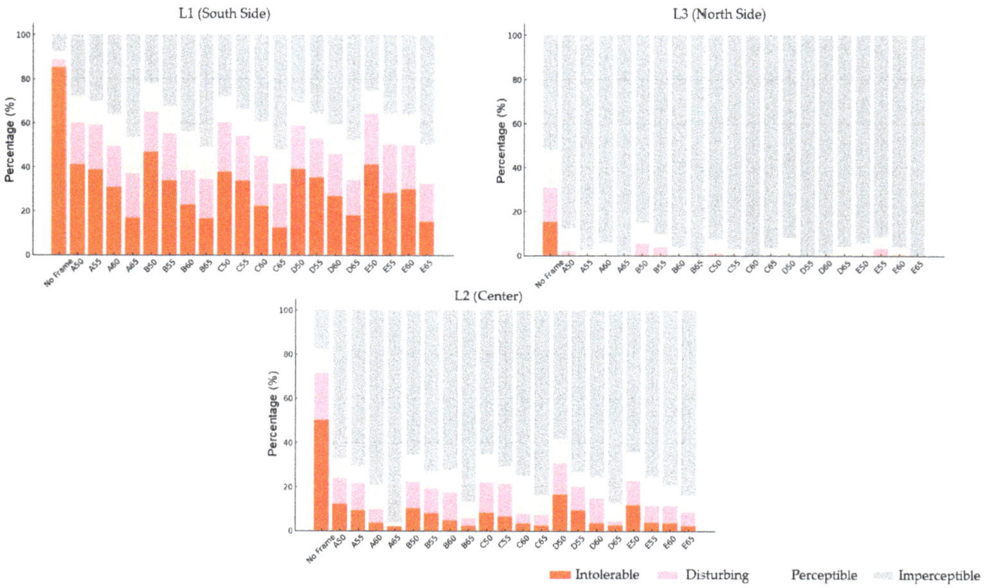

Figure 8. Comparison of glare effects for five screen façade types: results for south (L1), centre (L2), and north (L3) zones, showing Intolerable, Disturbing, Perceptible, and Imperceptible glare categories.

As presented in Table 3, the total discomfort glare incidence (intolerable and disturbing) without a frame is 25%. When a frame of 50% density is installed, it decreases to 10%. The simulation results for every 5% reduction in frame density result in a corresponding 1% decrease in the uncomfortable glare effects. Additionally, the sDG-5 (spatial daylight glare) metric evaluated discomfort glare potential by analysing the worst 5% of lighting conditions across the entire space. The results demonstrate a reduction from 56% (unframed condition) to 35% (with 50% frame density), with each 5% increase in frame density resulting in approximately a 3% reduction in sDG-5.

Figure 8 presents stacked column charts comparing five different façade types and their frame densities. In the charts, the letters represent the façade type, and the number indicates the frame density percentage (e.g., A50 refers to Type A with 50% frame density). The DGP metric was assessed at the evaluation points L1, L2, and L3 (as defined in Figure 3), to assess the likelihood of visual discomfort caused by glare. This metric was used to compare glare levels across the three points.

The effectiveness of screen façade frames in reducing visual discomfort is obvious across all three observation points. This effect is more noticeable towards the back of the room, which is probably due to the decreased reach of light reflections. At point L1 (located on the south side, about 2.5 m from the frontage), the intolerable rate is reduced by nearly half when any of the 50% screen façade frames are used, compared to no frame. At this point, the intolerable rate without any screen frame is 85.3%, whereas with 50% framing, it drops to between 37.9% and 46.8%. At point L2, the intolerable rate without a frame is 50.2%, and with 50% frames, it decreases significantly, to between 8.2% and 16.7%. At point L3 (about 2.5 m from the back side), the intolerable rate is 15.4% with no frame, while all 20 types of frames reduce the intolerable rate to 0%. At L3, the imperceptible rate (no detectable glare) is 51.9% without a frame, whereas with the frames, the results range from 85.2% to 100%.

Among the five types tested, there are only minor differences in terms of decreasing the glare effects. At L1, Type B is slightly less effective in reducing glare effects. At L2, Type D is also not very effective, but at L3, Type D shows almost no detectable glare. Although numerical comparisons reveal these variations, the overall rate of glare reduction is not dramatically different across types. However, when comparing 50% and 65% frame density, all types show noticeable reductions in glare effects. In fact, increasing the frame density from 50% to 65% results in more than double the rate of glare reduction.

3.4. Evaluation of Measured Daylight Intensity Levels on March 21 and September 21

To assess glare discomfort across frame variations, the percentages of areas exceeding the two lux thresholds of 1000 and 3000 were assessed, measured on specified dates in March and September. Two specific dates (21 March and 21 September) offer a moderate condition for evaluating typical daylight performance, without seasonal extremes. Whereas lux levels above 1000 indicate the minimum daylight requirements for typical indoor lighting conditions, those exceeding 3000 specify areas exposed to strong direct sunlight, where glare controls may be necessary to maintain visual comfort. Table 4 shows one of samples using Type A; this includes simulated area illustrations and measured values, categorised at the specific time points. It illustrates the distribution of areas gaining intensive daylight, and the percentage of areas that exceed the two lux thresholds.

Table 4. Lux measurements at specific time points (50% to 65% of Type A).

	No Frame	A50	A55	A60	A65
21 March 9:00	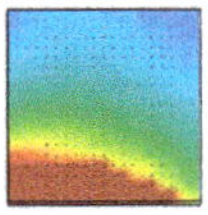	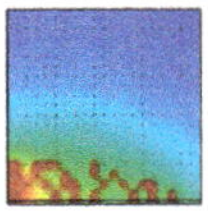	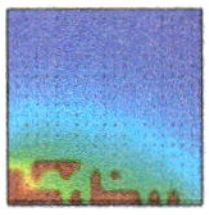		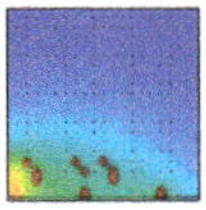
Above 1000 lux (%)	46.5	20.2	16.3	13.0	7.4
Above 3000 lux (%)	14.9	6.9	6.9	4.4	2.7
21 March 15:00					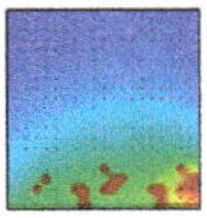
Above 1000 lux (%)	67.3	34.0	29.6	25.4	20.4
Above 3000 lux (%)	19.1	9.9	9.9	9.4	4.7
21 September 9:00				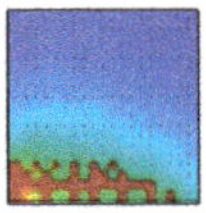	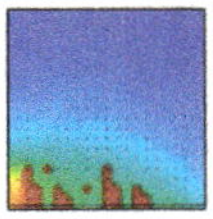
Above 1000 lux (%)	50.6	22.1	19.1	15.5	10.2
Above 3000 lux (%)	15.5	8.0	6.3	9.6	5.5
21 September 15:00				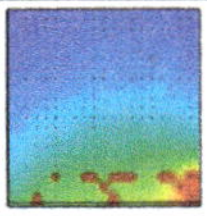	
Above 1000 lux (%)	63.9	31.5	27.7	24.0	18.8
Above 3000 lux (%)	18.2	5.5	8.3	3.8	5.8

As shown in Figure 9, describing the comparison of all variations, the overall result indicates that the percentage of areas above 1000 lux consistently decreases with increasing frame ratios. In contrast, for areas exceeding 3000 lux, some of the values are irregular and not apt to regularly decreasing. The steady decrease in values above 1000 lux is mirrored by a consistent increase in values below 1000 lux, corresponding to the proportional changes in frame ratio. Thus, the front side areas may receive filtered direct sunlight, which affects glare depending on the frame shape, whereas the back areas are relatively less influenced by the differences in frame ratios and features. Variations in frame ratio and shape have trivial impacts on daylight effects in areas to the back of the space. Despite minor differences in values above the 3000 lux level, the measurements recorded on 21 September at 09:00 and 15:00 demonstrate that lower values are mostly associated with Types A and D. Similarly, data from March reveal a tendency of lower values in these types; however, the differences compared to other types are not notable.

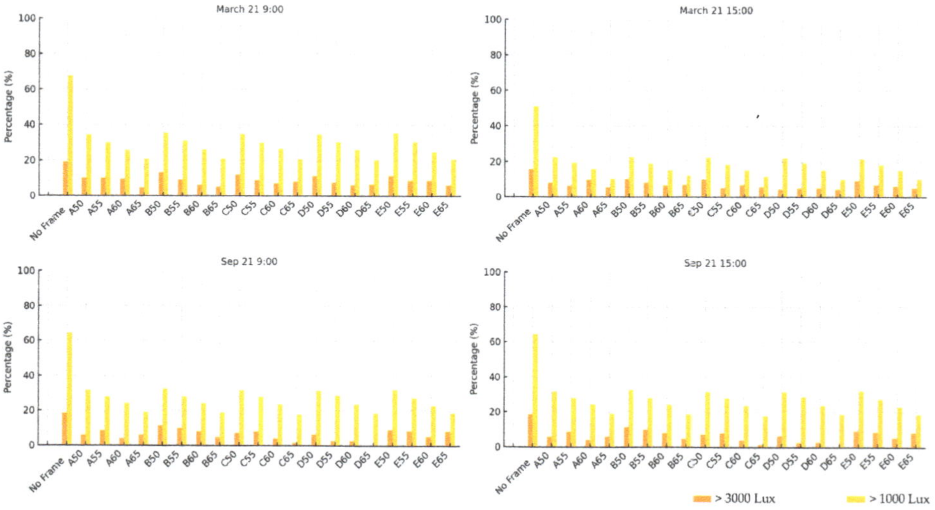

Figure 9. Comparison of area percentages exceeding 1000 lux and 3000 lux thresholds on 21 March and 21 September, according to frame variations.

By grouping the same ratio of frames, the compared evaluation of mean values of the types accessed the distribution of intense daylight lux that causes extreme glare discomfort levels (see Figure 10). The comparison of mean values of this daylight simulation may indicate how the dissimilar ranges of min and max values are arranged. The abovementioned simulations illustrate that the lux values in the back side of the room are less influenced than in the front side. High lux values, including some extreme levels, are mostly recorded in the front side. Regarding the mean value measurement, the more extreme high values there are, the higher the mean value results. This can help to evaluate the uniformity of daylight scattering. According to this assessment, some of the Type A and D values are slightly lower, but not noticeably different. However, the mean values of Type B and E are mostly high, which suggests that more high daylight intensities are gained in the front side when projecting some frame figures and ratios in the two types.

For the 21 September, 15:00 dataset, Type E exhibits notably higher values compared to the other types. This may be caused by the frame features, which are linear-based figures with large voids or open portions, and may lead to elevated lux measurements, thus directly influencing the mean value in the graph. Moreover, Type A (a geometrically repeated shape with a very dense frame) and Type D (a circular-based shape with relatively large voids) show only minimal impact on the mean values. Thus, the differences in those mean values are too marginal to be considered practically significant. Type E demonstrates high mean lux values, which represent more glare discomfort areas, and it requires higher effectiveness for sunlight filtering control. This performance is attributable to the generated design of relatively large open parts, which allow more intense light transmission.

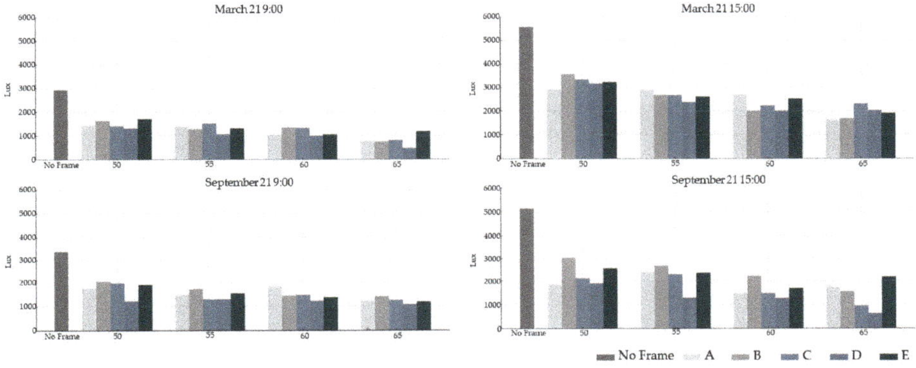

Figure 10. Assessment of mean lux values on 21 March and 21 September, arranged by the same proportions of frame variations.

As shown in Figure 11, which compares the mean and median values, the latter consistently decrease with the frame ratio. Estimation of median values provides a measure of central tendency that is less influenced by extreme values, compared to the mean values. The tendency of consistently decreasing median values, and the irregular variations in mean values corresponding to decreasing frame ratios, indicate that certain front areas experience extreme lux values depending on frame configurations. A comparison of the mean and median values demonstrates that the areas exposed to daylight ingress are still affected by direct sunlight. Nevertheless, the research shows that frames can help to reduce the extent of interior areas exposed to intensive daylight ingress.

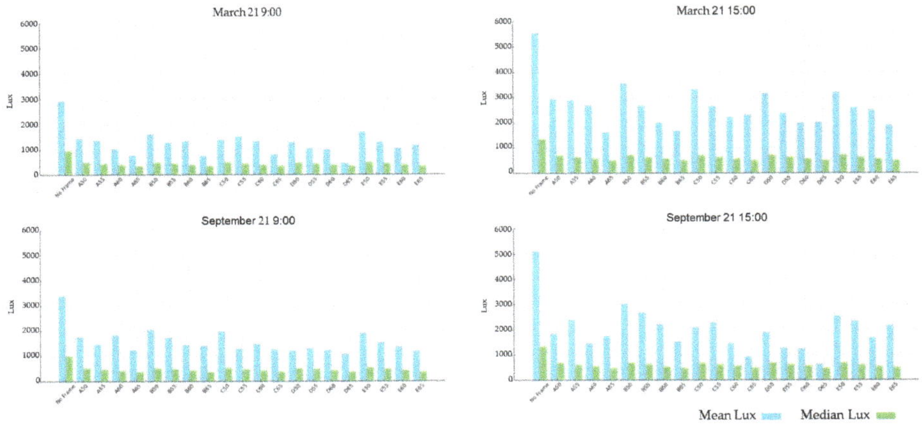

Figure 11. Comparison of the mean and median values on 21 March and 21 September for different frame configurations.

4. Conclusions

The generated outputs, produced by blending input images containing typical pattern examples, provided an increased variety of variations for testing simulations of similar configurations with different frame ratios. It was noticed that the generated results were highly dependent on the diversity of the training dataset. The CNN-based classification of IP and GP images confirmed that the classes and volume of the augmented output data closely corresponded to the types and similar patterns present in the original inputs. The learning processes in the StyleGAN3 model enabled new images to be generated, even with a small number of training datasets. However, the unsupervised processes used in generating the output features pose challenges for their direct application in façade design.

On the basis of the augmented pattern feature set, this investigation identified effective patterns for a south-facing test space under environmental conditions in South Korea. The evaluation of frame ratios, ranging from 40% to 80%, showed that frame shapes had little significant effect on the ASE and sDA metrics. The annual sunlight analyses of sDA demonstrated that at frame ratios above 70%, daylight ingress reaching to the rear areas was measurably reduced, and for frame ratios below 45%, the filtering effect maintained average light levels at below 3000 lux. The annual daylight simulation results showed that screen façade patterns with frame ratios of 50–65% managed daylight ingress to reduce the extent of areas exposed to intensive glare while maintaining the minimum required lighting conditions. Within the range of 50–65%, illuminance level tests for DGP with five different patterns demonstrated that regularly repeated pattern designs produced a slight improvement in glare comfort. The rear area in the 10 m × 10 m space was minimally affected by daylight in the simulation. Screen façade systems remain effective in reducing the extent of glare discomfort areas adjacent to the façade.

The annual-based simulations indicate that the tendency of decreasing daylight effects with decreasing frame ratios is consistent. However, simulations conducted at specific times show that different frame shapes can irregularly influence the mean values depending on their configurations. Through the comparison of numerical results, this study demonstrates the daylight-control effectiveness of both frame ratios and types. While the research focuses on a single factor, pattern density, in relation to visual comfort, multiple factors, such as material properties and spatial layout, contribute to further details of screen façade performance. Incorporating these additional factors in future studies is expected to provide a comprehensive evaluation of the effectiveness of screen façades.

Author Contributions: Conceptualization, H.N.; methodology, H.N. and D.Y.P.; software, H.N.; validation, H.N. and D.Y.P.; formal analysis, H.N.; investigation, H.N.; resources, H.N. and D.Y.P.; data curation, H.N.; writing—original draft preparation, H.N.; writing—review and editing, H.N. and D.Y.P.; visualisation, H.N. All authors have read and agreed to the published version of the manuscript.

Funding: This research received no external funding.

Data Availability Statement: The original contributions presented in this study are included in the article. Further inquiries can be directed to the corresponding author.

Conflicts of Interest: The authors declare no conflicts of interest.

Abbreviations

The following abbreviations are used in this manuscript:

AI	Artificial intelligence
GANs	Generative adversarial networks
ML	Machine learning
CNNs	Convolutional neural networks
sDA	Spatial daylight autonomy
ASE	Annual sunlight exposure
DGP	Daylight glare probability
sDG	Spatial daylight glare
IP	Input pattern
GP	Generated pattern

References

1. Simpson, J.A. *Oxford English Dictionary*, 2nd ed.; Oxford University Press: Oxford, UK, 1989; p. 728.
2. Moghtadernejad, S.; Mirza, M.S.; Chouinard, L.E. Façade design stages: Issues and considerations. *J. Archit. Eng.* **2018**, *25*, 04018033. [CrossRef]
3. Bianchi, S.; Andriotis, C.; Klein, T.; Overend, M. Multi-criteria design methods in façade engineering: State-of-the-art and future trends. *Build. Environ.* **2024**, *250*, 111184. [CrossRef]
4. Hoces, A.P.; Oldenhave, M. What makes a façade beautiful? *J. Facade Des. Eng.* **2021**, *9*, 21–46. [CrossRef]
5. Moscoso, C.; Chamilothori, K.; Wienold, J.; Andersen, M.; Matusiak, B. Regional differences in the perception of daylit scenes across Europe using virtual reality. Part I: Effects of window size. *LEUKOS* **2021**, *18*, 294–315. [CrossRef]
6. Emami, N.; Giles, H. Geometric patterns, light and shade: Quantifying aperture ratio and pattern resolution in the performance of shading screens. *Nexus Netw. J.* **2016**, *18*, 197–222. [CrossRef]
7. Chi, D.A.; Moreno, D.; Navarro, J. Design optimisation of perforated solar façades in order to balance daylighting with thermal performance. *Build. Environ.* **2017**, *125*, 383–400. [CrossRef]
8. Dastoum, M.; Guevara, C.S.; Arranz, B. Efficient daylighting and thermal performance through tessellation of geometric patterns in building façade: A systematic review. *Energy Sustain. Dev.* **2024**, *83*, 101563. [CrossRef]
9. Li, S.; Liu, L.; Peng, C. A review of performance-oriented architectural design and optimization in the context of sustainability: Dividends and challenges. *Sustainability* **2020**, *12*, 1427. [CrossRef]
10. Zheng, H.; Yuan, P.F. A generative architectural and urban design method through artificial neural networks. *Build. Environ.* **2021**, *205*, 108178. [CrossRef]
11. Özerol, G.; Selçuk, S.A. Machine learning in the discipline of architecture: A review on the research trends between 2014 and 2020. *Int. J. Archit. Comput.* **2022**, *21*, 23–41. [CrossRef]
12. Demir, G.; Çekmiş, A.; Yeşilkaynak, V.B.; Unal, G. Detecting visual design principles in art and architecture through deep convolutional neural networks. *Autom. Constr.* **2021**, *130*, 103826. [CrossRef]
13. Shan, R.; Junghans, L. Multi-objective optimization for high-performance building façade design: A systematic literature review. *Sustainability* **2023**, *15*, 15596. [CrossRef]
14. Jiang, F.; Ma, J.; Webster, C.J.; Chiaradia, A.J.; Zhou, Y.; Zhao, Z.; Zhang, X. Generative urban design: A systematic review on problem formulation, design generation, and decision-making. *Prog. Plann.* **2023**, *180*, 100795. [CrossRef]
15. Pena, M.L.C.; Carballal, A.; Rodríguez-Fernández, N.; Santos, I.; Romero, J. Artificial intelligence applied to conceptual design: A review of its use in architecture. *Autom. Constr.* **2021**, *124*, 103550. [CrossRef]
16. Wu, A.N.; Stouffs, R.; Biljecki, F. Generative adversarial networks in the built environment: A comprehensive review of the application of GANs across data types and scales. *Build. Environ.* **2022**, *223*, 109477. [CrossRef]
17. Goodfellow, I.; Pouget-Abadie, J.; Mirza, M.; Xu, B.; Warde-Farley, D.; Ozair, S.; Courville, A.; Bengio, Y. Generative adversarial nets. *arXiv* **2014**, arXiv:1406.2661. [CrossRef]
18. Oh, S.; Jung, Y.; Kim, S.; Lee, I.; Kang, N. Deep generative design: Integration of topology optimization and generative models. *J. Mech. Des.* **2019**, *141*, 111405. [CrossRef]
19. Zhang, T.; Tilke, P.; Dupont, E.; Zhu, L.; Liang, L.; Bailey, W. Generating geologically realistic 3D reservoir facies models using deep learning of sedimentary architecture with generative adversarial networks. *Pet. Sci.* **2019**, *16*, 541–549. [CrossRef]
20. Radford, A.; Metz, L.; Chintala, S. Unsupervised representation learning with deep convolutional generative adversarial networks. *arXiv* **2015**, arXiv:1511.06434. [CrossRef]

21. Arjovsky, M.; Chintala, S.; Bottou, L. Wasserstein GAN. *arXiv* **2017**, arXiv:1701.07875. [CrossRef]
22. Karras, T.; Laine, S.; Aila, T. A style-based generator architecture for generative adversarial networks. *arXiv* **2018**, arXiv:1812.04948. [CrossRef]
23. Isola, P.; Zhu, J.; Zhou, T.; Efros, A.A. Image-to-image translation with conditional adversarial networks. *arXiv* **2016**, arXiv:1611.07004. [CrossRef]
24. Zhu, J.; Park, T.; Isola, P.; Efros, A.A. Unpaired image-to-image translation using cycle-consistent adversarial networks. *arXiv* **2017**, arXiv:1703.10593. [CrossRef]
25. Xu, T.; Zhang, P.; Huang, Q.; Zhang, H.; Gan, Z.; Huang, X.; He, X. AttnGAN: Fine-grained text to image generation with attentional generative adversarial networks. *arXiv* **2017**, arXiv:1711.10485. [CrossRef]
26. Wang, H.; Wang, J.; Wang, J.; Zhao, M.; Zhang, W.; Zhang, F.; Xie, X.; Guo, M. GraphGAN: Graph representation learning with generative adversarial nets. *arXiv* **2017**, arXiv:1711.08267. [CrossRef]
27. Nauata, N.; Chang, K.; Cheng, C.; Mori, G.; Furukawa, Y. House-GAN: Relational generative adversarial networks for graph-constrained house layout generation. *arXiv* **2020**, arXiv:2003.06988. [CrossRef]
28. Tang, H.; Zhang, Z.; Shi, H.; Li, B.; Shao, L.; Sebe, N.; Timofte, R.; Luc, V.G. Graph transformer GANs for graph-constrained house generation. *arXiv* **2023**, arXiv:2303.08225. [CrossRef]
29. Qian, Y.; Zhang, H.; Furukawa, Y. Roof-GAN: Learning to generate roof geometry and relations for residential houses. *arXiv* **2020**, arXiv:2012.09340. [CrossRef]
30. Chang, K.; Cheng, C.; Luo, J.; Murata, S.; Nourbakhsh, M.; Tsuji, Y. Building-GAN: Graph-conditioned architectural volumetric design generation. *arXiv* **2021**, arXiv:2104.13316. [CrossRef]
31. Wu, J.; Zhang, C.; Xue, T.; Freeman, W.T.; Tenenbaum, J.B. Learning a probabilistic latent space of object shapes via 3D generative-adversarial modeling. *arXiv* **2016**, arXiv:1610.07584. [CrossRef]
32. Parente, J.; Rodrigues, E.; Rangel, B.; Martins, J.P. Integration of convolutional and adversarial networks into building design: A review. *J. Build. Eng.* **2023**, *76*, 107155. [CrossRef]
33. Premier, A. Solar shading devices integrating smart materials: An overview of projects, prototypes and products for advanced façade design. *Archit. Sci. Rev.* **2019**, *62*, 455–465. [CrossRef]
34. Hazbei, M.; Rafati, N.; Kharma, N.; Eicker, U. Optimizing architectural multi-dimensional forms; a hybrid approach integrating approximate evolutionary search, clustering and local optimization. *Energy Build.* **2024**, *318*, 114460. [CrossRef]
35. Wienold, J.; Kuhn, T.E.; Christoffersen, J.; Andersen, M. Annual glare evaluation for fabrics. In Proceedings of the PLEA 2017 Conference, Edinburgh, UK, 3–5 July 2017; Available online: https://www.researchgate.net/publication/329538959 (accessed on 8 November 2025).
36. Rafati, N.; Hazbei, M.; Eicker, U. Louver configuration comparison in three Canadian cities utilizing NSGA-II. *Build. Environ.* **2023**, *229*, 109939. [CrossRef]
37. Srisamranrungruang, T.; Hiyama, K. Balancing of natural ventilation, daylight, thermal effect for a building with double-skin perforated facade (DSPF). *Energy Build.* **2020**, *210*, 109765. [CrossRef]
38. Srisamranrungruang, T.; Hiyama, K. Correlations between building performances and design parameters of double-skin facade utilizing perforated screen. *Jpn. Archit. Rev.* **2021**, *4*, 537–550. [CrossRef]
39. Abdelhamid, Y.M.S.; Wahba, S.M.; ElHusseiny, M. The Effect of Parametric Patterned Façade Variations on Daylight Quality, Visual Comfort, and Daylight Performance in Architecture Studio-Based Tutoring. *J. Daylighting* **2023**, *10*, 173–191. [CrossRef]
40. Lin, C.-H.; Tsay, Y.-S. A metamodel based on intermediary features for daylight performance prediction of façade design. *Build. Environ.* **2021**, *206*, 108371. [CrossRef]
41. Nourkojouri, H.; Zomorodian, Z.S.; Tahsildoost, M.; Shaghaghian, Z. A machine-learning framework for daylight and visual comfort assessment in early design stages. In Proceedings of the Building Simulation 2021: 17th Conference of IBPSA, Bruges, Belgium, 1–3 September 2021; pp. 1268–1275. [CrossRef]
42. Li, X.; Yuan, Y.; Liu, G.; Han, Z.; Stouffs, R. A predictive model for daylight performance based on multimodal generative adversarial networks at the early design stage. *Energy Build.* **2024**, *305*, 113876. [CrossRef]
43. Lu, Y.; Wu, W.; Geng, X.; Liu, Y.; Zheng, H.; Hou, M. Multi-Objective Optimization of Building Environmental Performance: An Integrated Parametric Design Method Based on Machine Learning Approaches. *Energies* **2022**, *15*, 7031. [CrossRef]
44. Yu, Q.; Malaeb, J.; Ma, W. Architectural facade recognition and generation through generative adversarial networks. In Proceedings of the 2020 International Conference on Big Data & Artificial Intelligence & Software Engineering (ICBASE), Chengdu, China, 23–25 October 2020; IEEE: New York, NY, USA, 2020; pp. 310–316. [CrossRef]
45. Chen, F.; Mai, M.; Huang, X.; Li, Y. Enhancing the sustainability of AI technology in architectural design: Improving the matching accuracy of Chinese-style buildings. *Sustainability* **2024**, *16*, 8414. [CrossRef]

46. Sun, C.; Zhou, Y.; Han, Y. Automatic generation of architecture facade for historical urban renovation using generative adversarial network. *Build. Environ.* **2022**, *212*, 108781. [CrossRef]
47. Zhang, J.; Fukuda, T.; Yabuki, N. Automatic object removal with obstructed façades completion using semantic segmentation and generative adversarial inpainting. *IEEE Access* **2021**, *9*, 117486–117495. [CrossRef]
48. Hu, H.; Liang, X.; Ding, Y.; Yuan, X.; Shang, Q.; Xu, B.; Ge, X.; Chen, M.; Zhong, R.; Zhu, Q. Semi-supervised adversarial recognition of refined window structures for inverse procedural façade modelling. *ISPRS J. Photogramm. Remote Sens.* **2022**, *192*, 215–231. [CrossRef]
49. Kelly, T.; Guerrero, P.; Steed, A.; Wonka, P.; Mitra, N.J. FrankenGAN. *ACM Trans. Graph.* **2018**, *37*, 1–14. [CrossRef]
50. Du, Z.; Shen, H.; Li, X.; Wang, M. 3D building fabrication with geometry and texture coordination via hybrid GAN. *J. Ambient Intell. Humaniz. Comput.* **2020**, *13*, 5177–5188. [CrossRef]
51. Alhichri, H.; Bazi, Y.; Alajlan, N.; Bin Jdira, B. Helping the Visually Impaired See via Image Multi-labeling Based on SqueezeNet CNN. *Appl. Sci.* **2019**, *9*, 4656. [CrossRef]
52. Bhatt, D.; Patel, C.; Talsania, H.; Patel, J.; Vaghela, R.; Pandya, S.; Modi, K.; Ghayvat, H. CNN Variants for Computer Vision: History, Architecture, Application, Challenges and Future Scope. *Electronics* **2021**, *10*, 2470. [CrossRef]
53. Al-Saffar, A.A.M.; Tao, H.; Talab, M.A. Review of Deep Convolution Neural Network in Image Classification. In Proceedings of the 2017 International Conference on Radar, Antenna, Microwave, Electronics, and Telecommunications (ICRAMET), Kuala Lumpur, Malaysia, 3–5 July 2017; IEEE: Piscataway, NJ, USA, 2017; pp. 1–5. [CrossRef]
54. U.S. Green Building Council. *LEED v4 for Building Design and Construction (BD+C)*; Updated 2 July 2018; U.S. Green Building Council: Washington, DC, USA, 2018; Available online: https://www.usgbc.org/resources/leed-v4-building-design-and-construction-current-version (accessed on 8 November 2025).
55. Illuminating Engineering Society (IES). *IES Spatial Daylight Autonomy (sDA) and Annual Sunlight Exposure (ASE)—Approved Method*; IES: New York, NY, USA, 2012; Available online: https://www.ies.org/standards (accessed on 8 November 2025).
56. Ayoub, M. A Review on Machine Learning Algorithms to Predict Daylighting inside Buildings. *Sol. Energy* **2020**, *202*, 249–275. [CrossRef]
57. Wienold, J.; Christoffersen, J. Evaluation methods and development of a new glare prediction model for daylight environments with the use of CCD cameras. *Energy Build.* **2006**, *38*, 743–757. [CrossRef]
58. Reinhart, C.F.; Wienold, J. The daylighting dashboard: A simulation-based design analysis for daylit spaces. *Build. Environ.* **2011**, *46*, 386–396. [CrossRef]
59. McNeil, A.; Burrell, G. Applicability of DGP and DGI for Evaluating Glare in a Brightly Daylit Space. In Proceedings of the ASHRAE & IBPSA-USA SimBuild 2016: Building Performance Modeling Conference, Salt Lake City, UT, USA, 10–12 August 2016; pp. 57–64. Available online: https://publications.ibpsa.org/conference/paper/?id=simbuild2016_C008 (accessed on 8 November 2025).
60. Lu, S.; Tzempelikos, A. Comparison of Simulation Methods for Glare Risk Assessment with Roller Shades. *Buildings* **2024**, *14*, 1773. [CrossRef]
61. *EN 17037:2018*; Daylight in Buildings. European Committee for Standardization (CEN): Brussels, Belgium, 2018.
62. Hraška, J.; Čurpek, J. The practical implications of the EN 17037 minimum target daylight factor for building design and urban daylight in several European countries. *Heliyon* **2023**, *10*, e23297. [CrossRef] [PubMed]

buildings

MDPI

Article

Automated Image-to-BIM Using Neural Radiance Fields and Vision-Language Semantic Modeling

Mohammad H. Mehraban [1,*], Shayan Mirzabeigi [2,3,*], Mudan Wang [4], Rui Liu [5] and Samad M. E. Sepasgozar [6]

[1] School of Construction, Property and Surveying, College of Technology and Environment, London South Bank University, London SE1 0AA, UK
[2] Department of Sustainable Resources Management, State University of New York College of Environmental Science and Forestry, Syracuse, NY 13210, USA
[3] Department of Mechanical and Aerospace Engineering, Syracuse University, Syracuse, NY 13244, USA
[4] Department of Engineering, University of Cambridge, Cambridge CB3 0FA, UK; mw923@cam.ac.uk
[5] M.E. Rinker, Sr. School of Construction Management, University of Florida, Gainesville, FL 32611, USA; liurui@ufl.edu
[6] School of Built Environment, University of New South Wales, Sydney, NSW 2052, Australia; sepas@unsw.edu.au
* Correspondence: s4131120@lsbu.ac.uk (M.H.M.); smirzabeigi@esf.edu (S.M.)

Abstract: This study introduces a novel, automated image-to-BIM (Building Information Modeling) workflow designed to generate semantically rich and geometrically useful BIM models directly from RGB images. Conventional scan-to-BIM often relies on specialized, costly, and time-intensive equipment, specifically if LiDAR is used to generate point clouds (PCs). Typical workflows are followed by a separate post-processing step for semantic segmentation recently performed by deep learning models on the generated PCs. Instead, the proposed method integrates vision language object detection (YOLOv8x-World v2) and vision based segmentation (SAM 2.1) with Neural Radiance Fields (NeRF) 3D reconstruction to generate segmented, color-labeled PCs directly from images. The key novelty lies in bypassing post-processing on PCs by embedding semantic information at the pixel level in images, preserving it through reconstruction, and encoding it into the resulting color labeled PC, which allows building elements to be directly identified and geometrically extracted based on color labels. Extracted geometry is serialized into a JSON format and imported into Revit to automate BIM creation for walls, windows, and doors. Experimental validation on BIM models generated from Unmanned Aerial Vehicle (UAV)-based exterior datasets and standard camera-based interior datasets demonstrated high accuracy in detecting windows and doors. Spatial evaluations yielded up to 0.994 precision and 0.992 Intersection over Union (IoU). NeRF and Gaussian Splatting models, Nerfacto, Instant-NGP, and Splatfacto, were assessed. Nerfacto produced the most structured PCs suitable for geometry extraction and Splatfacto achieved the highest image reconstruction quality. The proposed method removes dependency on terrestrial surveying tools and separate segmentation processes on PCs. It provides a low-cost and scalable solution for generating BIM models in aging or undocumented buildings and supports practical applications such as renovation, digital twin, and facility management.

Keywords: facility management; architecture; artificial intelligence; as-built; reconstruction; drawing; modeling; digital twin; image to BIM; scan to BIM

1. Introduction

Aging buildings represent a major challenge in the global construction landscape, with a substantial share urgently requiring retrofitting and upgrades to comply with current performance and safety standards [1]. A significant portion of the built environment lacks reliable as-built documentation, a problem especially prevalent in aging residential and commercial buildings where original design drawings are often missing, inaccurate, or outdated [2]. The absence of precise as-built information could create serious challenges in carrying out building simulations, cost estimations, and renovation planning. To address this, more accurate and up-to-date digital models can be created. Overall, the practical applications of these models are energy retrofitting, facility management, post-disaster reconstruction, façade renovation, solar panel placement, and interior redesign, all of which rely on sufficiently detailed digital representations of existing buildings. These models not only enhance operational efficiency in facility management but also play a vital role in improving energy performance and supporting sustainability goals [3]. Without them, these processes become time-consuming, error-prone, and costly, often requiring extensive on-site measurements and manual reconstruction of building geometry.

In addition, the construction sector accounts for nearly 40% of global energy use and carbon emissions, and retrofitting the existing building stock is essential to achieve decarbonization and sustainability targets [4]. However, many aging buildings remain undocumented or poorly represented in digital form, limiting the ability of owners and facility managers to plan retrofits, monitor performance, and implement data-driven maintenance. Automating the generation of building models from imagery offers a practical pathway to accelerate digital transformation across the industry. It enables small firms and public agencies, often constrained by cost and technical expertise, to access up-to-date spatial data for energy analysis, facility management, retrofit and renovation planning. This shows the importance of application of digital workflows, especially when integrated with Artificial Intelligence (AI) techniques, which contribute not only to technical innovation but also to societal goals of reducing emissions, extending building life cycles, and improving safety and occupant comfort through better-informed decision-making [5].

To address these challenges and enhance the accessibility of digital modeling solutions, Scan-to-BIM has emerged as a workflow for capturing the geometry of physical structures using 3D scanning technologies and creating intelligent models within BIM software [6,7]. This approach is valuable for generating as-built BIM models of aging or repurposed buildings that lack original design documents [8]. The conventional Scan-to-BIM workflow consists of acquiring 3D PC data, analyzing and classifying building elements, and manually converting the segmented data into as-built BIM models [9–11]. However, despite its widespread adoption, this process remains labor-intensive and difficult to standardize [12]. As a result, recent research has increasingly focused on automating the segmentation and classification of PCs using Deep Neural Networks (DNN) algorithms to extract semantically segmented features along with their corresponding geometry to achieve a fully automated Scan-to-BIM workflow [12].

Although these approaches have advanced the scan-to-BIM reconstruction process, several challenges remain. Firstly, the degree of automation remains constrained, as the generation of high-quality 3D semantic and BIM models still depends on manual or semi-automated tasks in existing approaches [10,11,13]. Secondly, current modeling techniques do not fully utilize the semantic information embedded in PCs, as segmentation is performed after PC generation, missing valuable priors that could improve integration and geometric consistency [14,15]. Third, PCs, which are an essential data source for developing BIM models [16], are typically obtained through range-based techniques such as laser scanning (LiDAR) or image-based methods such as digital photogrammetry [17]. Despite their effectiveness, these methods present challenges in terms of cost, efficiency, and the need for post-processing [18,19]. At their current stage, both methods require post-processing of the generated point cloud to perform semantic segmentation of building elements and extract geometric information necessary for BIM modeling.

With the advancement of AI techniques, post-processing on PCs has improved classification and segmentation accuracy; however, it continues to pose challenges to automation in both range-based and image-based methods. Common issues include noise in raw data, structural incompleteness due to occlusions in scans [20], and difficulties detecting components on reflective or textureless surfaces [21]. In image-based methods, projection-based label transfer might lead to misalignment errors [22]. Moreover, both approaches involve high computational effort and manual intervention. A further limitation lies in the strong dependency on the quality and domain relevance of training data. Widely used 3D segmentation datasets such as S3DIS [23] exhibit non-uniform sampling, noise, and missing regions, which, despite enabling high point-wise semantic accuracy, can degrade object-level reconstruction fidelity [24]. Likewise, 2D datasets like ADE20K [25] and NYU Depth V2 [26] lack the architectural specificity and spatial coherence necessary for reliable BIM modeling, although they could be popular for general segmentation tasks [27].

For this reason and to maximize the potential of PCs, this study introduces a novel method that integrates NeRF and computer vision-language models to generate structured, segmented, and color-labeled PCs directly from images, after which the geometry of building elements is extracted and the BIM model is generated automatically. The proposed method addresses identified challenges by (1) automating the workflow, (2) embedding semantic labels during reconstruction to eliminate misalignment, avoid post-processing, reduce computational overhead, and mitigate scan-related issues, (3) removing dependence on LiDAR or photogrammetry to reduce cost and setup complexity, and (4) bypassing limitations of domain-specific 3D and 2D datasets by leveraging direct image-based labeling through large pretrained models. The proposed method is also experimentally evaluated using metrics that assess spatial precision, geometric consistency, and reconstruction performance across both interior and exterior datasets to validate its effectiveness for automated BIM generation.

This paper is organized as follows. Section 2 reviews existing studies and identifies the research gaps. Section 3, Methodology, outlines the integrated workflow for combining image segmentation, NeRF-based 3D reconstruction, and automated BIM modeling. Section 4, Results, provides quantitative evaluations of segmentation accuracy, spatial alignment, and reconstruction quality using multiple NeRF models. Section 5, Discussion, reflects on the implications of the findings, highlights the methodological contributions, and identifies remaining challenges and future directions. Finally, Section 6, Conclusion, summarizes the key outcomes and practical advantages of the proposed method.

2. Literature Review

The automated Scan-to-BIM process has significantly evolved through the integration of DNN-based methods over the past decade. This evolution has been driven by the need to process large-scale PCs efficiently, enhance semantic segmentation, and improve topological consistency in as-built BIM reconstruction. The following sections review the existing studies and identify research gaps, as well as key contributions that have advanced the Scan-to-BIM workflow through improvements in geometry-based, hybrid, and deep learning approaches.

2.1. Traditional Geometry-Based Approaches

Early Scan-to-BIM automation research focused on geometry-based techniques, using planar segmentation, topology rules, and shape detection to extract structural elements from PCs. Tang et al. [28] provided an early comprehensive review by classifying methods into geometric modeling, object recognition, and relationship modeling, while also identifying challenges such as manual intervention, noise, and occlusions. Xiong et al. [29] extended these efforts with a two-phase methodology that combined planar segmentation and voxelization to detect walls, floors, and ceilings, with visibility reasoning and shape estimation for semantic enrichment of detections.

As BIM adoption increased, semi-automated approaches emerged to reduce manual effort by combining rule-based methods with user intervention. Jung et al. [8] introduced a hybrid approach that integrated Random Sample Consensus (RANSAC)-based segmentation, grid-based filtering, and boundary tracing to extract architectural elements with subsequent human refinement. Volk et al. [10] reviewed BIM adoption technological limitations and highlighted that while laser scanning, photogrammetry, and automated object recognition have improved PCs processing, the conversion of unstructured PCs data into semantically rich BIM models remains a challenge.

Subsequent methods have integrated into machine learning or optimization algorithms to improve segmentation and topology in automated Scan-to-BIM workflows. For example, Croce et al. [30] proposed a semi-automatic approach that combines Machine Learning techniques, specifically the Random Forest, for semantic segmentation and classification of architectural elements in 3D point clouds. They utilized Rhino and Grasshopper, to reconstruct parametric models for H-BIM applications. Ochmann et al. [31] proposed a volumetric multi-story reconstruction method formulated as an integer linear programming problem, using RANSAC-based plane detection to identify structural surfaces and Markov clustering to group spatially related elements to enforce geometric and topological constraints. Bassier and Vergauwen [32] proposed an unsupervised method that detects different wall axis types (straight, curved, and polyline-based) and reconstructs wall connections using clustering, geometric feature extraction, and topology reconstruction to generate IFC-compliant BIM models. Rausch and Haas [33] proposed an automated parametric approach for updating the shape and pose of BIM elements using PCs. Their dyna-BIM method applies genetic algorithms and simulated annealing to align as-designed BIMs with as-built data. Additionally, Perez-Perez et al. [34] enhanced segmentation in complex environments by integrating Support Vector Machines for semantic classification with AdaBoost for geometric labeling and probabilistic graphical models. Their method refined the detection of planar and non-planar features while preserving semantic consistency throughout the automated reconstruction.

2.2. *Deep Learning-Based Approaches*

Recent advancements in PC processing have greatly improved the accuracy and efficiency of 3D reconstruction and segmentation, which benefits Scan-to-BIM applications. Large-scale annotated datasets like ScanNet [35] have enabled better deep learning models for scene understanding. Methods such as PointNet [36], PointCNN [37], and PointNeXt [38] have refined feature extraction and classification. SEGCloud [39] improved segmentation accuracy, and PointNetLK [40] advanced PCs registration. These developments laid the foundation for deep learning in Scan-to-BIM workflows to reduce manual effort and increase automation in as-built modeling.

Huan et al. [41] proposed GeoRec, a DNN for geometry-enhanced semantic 3D reconstruction. The model integrates a geometry extractor with deep learning to improve layout estimation, camera pose recovery, and object detection via three modules: room layout, object detection, and object reconstruction. Tang et al. [42] developed a hybrid approach combining deep learning with morphological operations and RANSAC-based plane detection. Their method classifies PCs into thirteen semantic categories, refines spatial relationships through Markov Random Field optimization, and uses grammar-based modeling to generate IFC-compliant BIM models.

Recent studies have further advanced Scan-to-BIM automation by enhancing DNN models, segmentation, and connectivity detection. Campagnolo et al. [43] developed a fully automated pipeline using DNN-based instance segmentation with BIM-Net++, a lightweight voxel-based Convolutional Neural Networks (CNN) designed for semantic segmentation that identifies architectural elements such as walls, floors, and roofs. Their method refines segmentation via RANSAC for planar and Density-Based Spatial Clustering of Applications with Noise (DBSCAN) for non-planar elements before BIM reconstruction. Wu et al. [44] presented FLKPP, a prototype that integrates neural networks with architectonic grammar for improved segmentation and reconstruction. Their method uses KPConv for 3D semantic segmentation, floor-layer preprocessing, and DNN-based line detection to generate 2D floor plan grids before reconstructing BIM elements like walls, doors, and columns. Drobnyi et al. [45] proposed a deep geometric neural network for connectivity detection, modeling spatial relationships through planar segmentation, region growing, and proximity-based clustering with a PointNeXt-based model for edge classification to automate digital twin construction. Mahmoud et al. [46] introduced a framework that first applies a deep learning model for PC segmentation, followed by room clustering using DBSCAN. Line detection via RANSAC extracts walls and major structural elements, while a Dynamo-based algorithm automates the parametric reconstruction of structured components like walls and floors. The framework achieved high accuracy in semantic segmentation and geometric reconstruction, which enhances the automation of Scan-to-BIM workflows.

2.3. Image-Based Approaches

In addition to the range-based Scan-to-BIM methods previously discussed, recent studies have investigated image-based workflows as cost-effective and accessible alternatives to LiDAR-based approaches. These methods typically utilize 2D RGB images captured through handheld devices or UAV. Semantic segmentation is performed using DNNs, after which 3D PCs are generated using photogrammetric techniques such as Structure-from-Motion (SfM) or Multi-View Stereo (MVS).

Han et al. [47] developed an indoor reconstruction method using LiDAR sensors and image-based MVS data. They applied DeepLabv3 for semantic segmentation, trained on the Cityscapes dataset and their own annotations. Their system reconstructed walls, floors, and ceilings. Similarly, Pantoja-Rosero et al. [20] aimed to automate the generation of Level of Detail (LOD3) building models, focusing on masonry structures, using SfM and DNN-based semantic segmentation. Their method combined SfM to generate sparse PCs and camera poses with TernausNet deep learning models to segment façade openings. Polyfit is used to create LOD2 models, which were upgraded to LOD3 by triangulating segmented openings into 3D space. The findings demonstrate that the pipeline effectively reconstructs LOD3 models.

In infrastructure-focused work, Saovana et al. [48] introduced a method called Point cloud Classification based on image-based Instance Segmentation (PCIS). This approach utilizes digital images processed through CNN to generate 2D masks, which are transformed into 3D masks using camera parameters from SfM. These masks classify PCs by projecting rays from camera positions through the masks to the PCs. The findings demonstrate that PCIS achieves high accuracy, with an F1-score of 0.96 for one-class classification and 0.83 for six-class classification. Puliti et al. [49] introduced a method combining infrared thermography and SfM to detect subsurface defects in building envelopes. They applied a segmentation algorithm using temperature-based sliding windows and edge detection to identify thermal anomalies. The method achieved IoU of 78% for the handheld IR camera test and 83% for the UAV-based IR camera test, along with an F1-score of 0.87 for both tests, demonstrating high accuracy in automated damage detection.

Studies have also paid attention to exterior and interior BIM reconstruction. For example, Yang et al. [50] proposed an image-based approach for automatic as-built BIM generation by reconstructing 3D facades and identifying surface materials. Using images from uncalibrated cameras, PCs are created via SfM, segmented with RANSAC, and analyzed through semantic reasoning to detect elements like walls and windows. Wong et al. [22] proposed an image-based Scan-to-BIM method for interior building reconstruction using handheld phone imagery. Their method integrates photogrammetry, semantic segmentation, projection, and geometry-based refinement. Frames were processed using SfM and MVS to create dense PCs, followed by RANSAC and DBSCAN for structural surface detection. YOLOv8, trained on the HBD dataset, was used to segment building components for 2D images. These semantic masks were projected onto the 3D PC using a pinhole camera model. Weighted voting improved label consistency, and boundary refinements addressed windows and doors. The final data was exported to Revit for automated BIM generation, achieving 100% recognition accuracy and a geometric error of 0.056 m.

2.4. Neural Radiance Field 3D Reconstruction

While existing image-based Scan-to-BIM methods have shown promising results, they typically depend on photogrammetry to reconstruct point clouds and then apply semantic labels through projection or manual mapping. This two-step process is often vulnerable to issues such as occlusions, noisy or incomplete geometry, and inaccurate label alignment, especially in complex indoor scenes with clutter, reflective surfaces, or textureless regions. To address these limitations, NeRF is explored in this research, which eliminates the need for intermediate point clouds and projection by directly learning a continuous volumetric representation from posed 2D images. NeRF enables a more integrated and robust workflow for view synthesis and geometry reconstruction and offers higher fidelity and resilience in challenging environments common to indoor BIM applications.

NeRF, introduced by Mildenhall et al. [51], marked a significant breakthrough in photorealistic view synthesis and 3D scene reconstruction. NeRF represents a static scene as a continuous volumetric function that maps five-dimensional inputs, comprising a 3D spatial location and a 2D viewing direction, to a color and volume density. This function is learned through a fully connected Multilayer Perceptron (MLP), which estimates view-dependent radiance and differential opacity at each sampled coordinate. By casting rays from virtual cameras through the scene and integrating predicted values using differentiable volume rendering, NeRF can generate novel views with remarkable visual fidelity from a sparse set of posed RGB images. It is capable of reconstructing fine geometry and complex lighting effects more efficiently than traditional mesh-based or voxel-based techniques. Unlike prior approaches that rely on discretized representations or require ground-truth 3D geometry, NeRF can be trained using only 2D images and camera intrinsics, which makes it a versatile tool for image-based scene reconstruction.

Building upon this foundation, advancements have been made to adapt NeRF for practical applications. Instant-NGP, proposed by Müller et al. [52], reduces training time and memory usage through multi-resolution hash encoding and a compact, fully fused MLP. This model enables near-real-time reconstruction. To improve robustness in real-world scenes with camera pose noise and variable lighting conditions, Nerfacto was introduced as part of the Nerfstudio framework by Tancik et al. [53]. It combines pose refinement, proposal sampling, and hash-based density fields to achieve stable reconstructions even in noisy or incomplete datasets conditions. Based on the 3D Gaussian Splatting technique introduced by Kerbl et al. [54], Splatfacto replaces volumetric grids and MLPs with differentiable 3D Gaussians. This representation supports direct optimization over Gaussian attributes such as position, opacity, and anisotropy. It achieves competitive visual quality and supports real-time rendering through tile-based rasterization.

These advancements highlight NeRF's emerging potential as a foundation for the next generation of Scan-to-BIM methods, offering an alternative to conventional workflows that rely on physical scanning devices for geometric data acquisition. With recent improvements in speed, robustness, and output quality, NeRF models such as Instant-NGP, Nerfacto, and Splatfacto may facilitate BIM generation based on image-derived information. However, despite its technical potential, the integration of NeRF into Scan-to-BIM workflows remains largely unexplored.

Despite ongoing advancements, current Scan-to-BIM studies still follow a two-stage process: first generating PCs using scanning devices such as LiDAR or photogrammetry, then applying semantic segmentation in a separate post-processing step using deep learning models on the PCs. This can also be a fragmented process due to multiple tasks, increasing processing time, adding complexity, and constraining the level of automation achievable. This study aims to offer a workflow to avoid or minimize limitations through an automated image-to-BIM method presented in the following sections.

3. Methodology

This study introduces a four-phase method that converts 2D images into a BIM model by combining DNN, computer vision, and geometric processing techniques. As illustrated in Figure 1, the workflow includes: (1) multi-view image acquisition followed by object detection and segmentation, (2) 3D scene reconstruction, PCs generation, and feature extraction, (3) automated BIM modeling in Autodesk Revit, (4.1) evaluation of NeRF models (4.2) and validation of the proposed method through semantic, spatial, and geometric performance metrics using case studies.

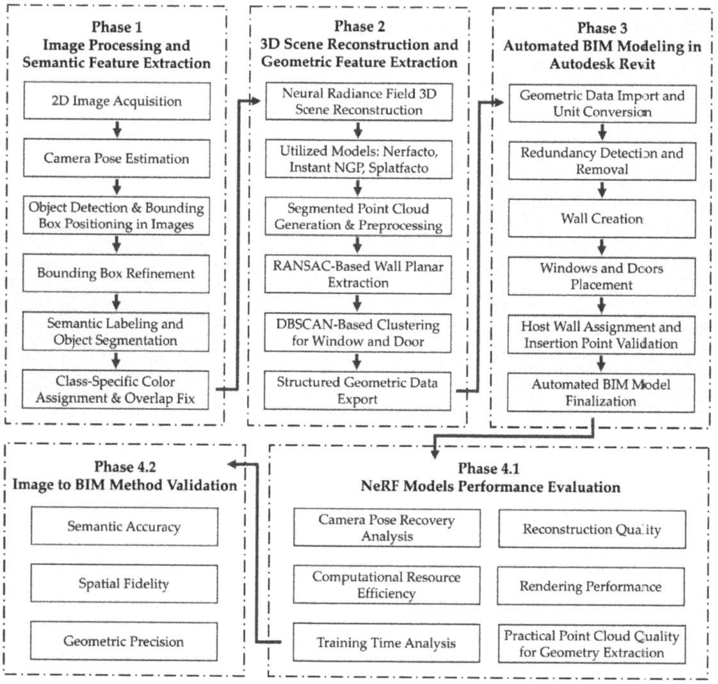

Figure 1. Proposed image-to-BIM method workflow from image input to automated BIM modeling.

3.1. *Image Processing and Semantic Feature Extraction*

3.1.1. Image Acquisition and Camera Pose Estimation

To reconstruct the scene accurately, images of the building from multiple angles are needed. The wider the coverage, the higher the quality of the NeRF reconstruction. In this study, two distinct real-world experimental case study datasets were used to evaluate the proposed method. One dataset consists of exterior images captured around the building, and the other consists of interior images captured from within the building to assess its performance in reconstructing both outdoor and indoor scenes.

Dataset 1 was collected from the exterior facades of an educational building in Turin, Italy. A UAV, the DJI Mini 4 Pro drone, capable of recording 4K video at 60 frames per second, captured the entire building exterior. The aerial survey generated high-resolution image frames with an effective resolution of 3840 × 2160 pixels, extracted from the recorded video stream. As shown in Figure 2, the UAV followed six flight paths at different altitude levels. Five rectilinear passes at heights of 2 m, 8 m, 14 m, 20 m, and 28 m, to have a complete façade coverage, while a final circular path at 38 m captured the upper structure and roof geometry. This structured survey provided a comprehensive dataset for the proposed image-to-BIM automation workflow.

Figure 2. Aerial survey paths used for Dataset 1 image acquisition.

Dataset 2 was collected from the interior space of a room located in London. Unlike the UAV-based exterior survey, this dataset was acquired using a standard smartphone camera. A 60 s 4K video at a resolution of 3840 × 2160 pixels was recorded while walking through the room to capture the interior scene from multiple viewpoints.

Image frames were then extracted from the recorded video streams to construct the input datasets. To prepare the data for NeRF-based reconstruction, COLMAP was used to estimate camera poses and to output both the 3D coordinates of the camera positions and their corresponding viewing directions, which are essential for accurate NeRF training. As shown in Figure 3, the top-down view generated by COLMAP visualizes the confined indoor space, including the estimated camera poses and walking path.

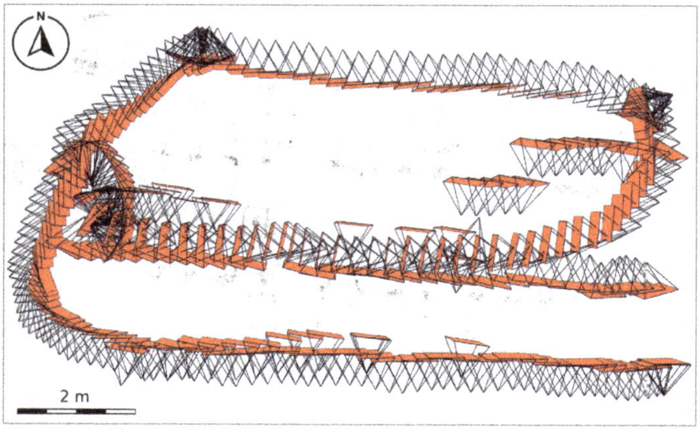

Figure 3. Top-down view of camera poses and walking path for Dataset 2.

3.1.2. Object Detection and Semantic Segmentation

After image acquisition, architectural elements were extracted through a process consisting of object detection, bounding box refinement, class-specific segmentation, and overlap resolution to first isolate only the building objects of interest (walls, windows, and doors in this study), and then apply color-labeled masks to those detected objects to prepare them for NeRF-based scene reconstruction. The embedded semantic information in the segmented images enabled the NeRF model to generate PCs in which each point inherits a class-specific color and preserves the identity of architectural elements throughout the reconstruction process.

The process began with object detection using YOLOv8x-worldv2 model, an open-vocabulary object detection model that uses CNN-based processing and vision-language pre-training [55]. The vision–language pre-training in YOLO-World enhances the model's ability to detect objects by connecting image features and text embeddings. It performs open-vocabulary object detection using its pre-trained weights and enables recognition of new categories based on text prompts such as wall, window, or door [55]. This allows the model to detect architectural elements directly without additional retraining or fine-tuning on building-specific datasets. The model was employed to identify walls, windows, and doors within the input images and to generate bounding boxes annotated with class labels and confidence scores. Detection was performed using class-specific confidence thresholds to optimize accuracy for each object type. A lower threshold was applied for wall detection to maximize recall and broaden coverage, while higher thresholds were used for windows and doors to reduce false positives and improve precision. The model produced bounding boxes annotated with class labels and confidence scores. Following initial detection, redundant bounding boxes were filtered using a geometric merging strategy based on IoU calculations. Bounding boxes with IoU values exceeding 0.5 were merged to eliminate duplicates and to consolidate overlapping predictions into a single, unique representation per object.

The refined bounding boxes were then processed by an instance of the Segment Anything Model (SAM) 2.1, which is a computer vision model that employs a unified, prompt-based architecture to generate pixel-level segmentation masks in images [56]. Each bounding box served as a prompt for SAM to delineate the spatial extent of walls, windows, and doors. To visually encode semantic identity for subsequent NeRF-based reconstruction, predefined class-specific RGB values were applied. For Dataset 1, the segmentation masks used the following color scheme: walls in soft yellow (RGB: [220, 230, 50]), windows in green (RGB: [0, 255, 0]), and doors in blue (RGB: [0, 0, 255]). For Dataset 2, a distinct set of color codes was used: walls in red (RGB: [150, 50, 50]), windows in dark green (RGB: [0, 100, 0]), and doors in blue (RGB: [0, 0, 255]). In cases where objects overlapped in the 2D view, such as windows embedded in walls or doors positioned along edge boundaries, a hierarchical priority rule was applied. This rule resolved conflicts by assigning precedence to windows and doors over walls, to make sure that smaller embedded components were preserved and correctly labeled without being overridden by larger elements. Algorithm 1 outlines the full detection and segmentation workflow in pseudocode. Figure 4 shows an example transformation from a raw image to a segmented output, with each element clearly color-coded.

Algorithm 1: Object Detection and Segmentation

Input:

- Input image: I
- Object detection model (YOLOv8x-worldv2): M_{YOLO}
- YOLO confidence thresholds: τ_o, τ_w
- Bounding box merging IoU threshold: τ_{IoU}
- Predefined class labels and corresponding RGB colors: L, C_{RGB}
- Segmentation model (SAM 2.1): M_{SAM}

Output:

- Segmented image: I_{seg}

---

1. **Initialize**: Load I, M_{YOLO}, M_{SAM}, L, and C_{RGB}
2. **Define function** DetectObjects(I, τ_o, τ_w, M_{YOLO}):
    - Apply M_{YOLO} with confidence threshold τ_w for walls and τ_o for windows and doors objects detection.
    - Extract bounding boxes and class labels $\{B, C\}$.
    - **Return**: Detected objects $\{B, C\}$.
3. **End function**
4. Call DetectObjects (I, τ_o, τ_w, M_{YOLO}): obtain detected elements $\{B, C\}$.
5. **Define function** MergeBoundingBoxes ($\{B, C\}$, τ_{IoU}):
    - For each pair of overlapping bounding boxes, compute IoU.
    - Merge boxes where IoU exceeds τ_{IoU}.
    - **Return**: Refined bounding boxes $\{B', C'\}$.
6. **End function**
7. Call MergeBoundingBoxes ($\{B, C\}$, τ_{IoU}): refine detected elements $\{B', C'\}$.
8. **Define function** SegmentObjects $\left(I, \{B', C'\}, M_{SAM}, L, C_{RGB}\right)$:
    - For each bounding box in $\left\{B', C'\right\}$, apply M_{SAM}.
    - Assign predefined colors from C_{RGB} to segmented elements based on L.
    - Apply hierarchical rules to resolve overlaps.
    - **Return**: Segmented image I_{seg}.
9. **End function**
10. Call SegmentObjects $\left(I, \{B', C'\}, M_{SAM}, L, C_{RGB}\right)$: obtain I_{seg}.
11. **Return**: Segmented image I_{seg}.

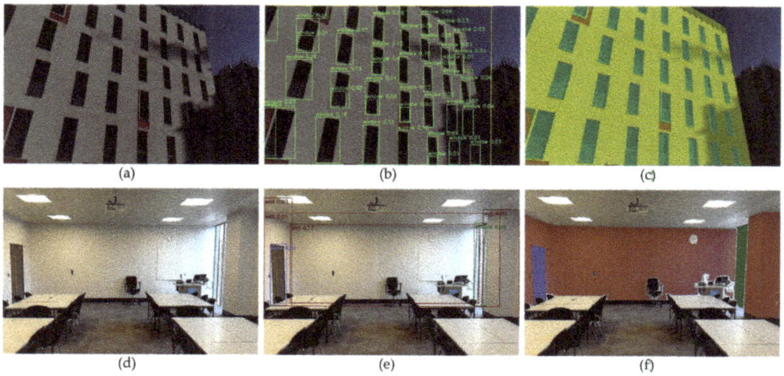

Figure 4. Transformation workflow illustrated using Dataset 1 (**top**) and Dataset 2 (**bottom**): (**a**,**d**) original images, (**b**,**e**) YOLO object detection results, and (**c**,**f**) SAM-generated segmentation masks.

3.2. Three-Dimensional Scene Reconstruction and Geometric Feature Extraction

3.2.1. Three-Dimensional Reconstruction Using Neural Radiance Fields

3D reconstruction models of Instant-NGP, Nerfacto, and Splatfacto were employed within the Nerfstudio framework to reconstruct the scenes from segmented images. Figure 5 illustrates NeRF reconstruction workflow applied on Dataset 1. In Figure 5a, semantically segmented images are used as multi-view inputs. These images are processed by COLMAP to estimate camera poses, shown in Figure 5b, where each triangle represents a viewpoint distributed around the building. Using the estimated poses and labeled RGB frames, NeRF constructs a scene-specific volumetric representation by casting rays from each camera location into the 3D scene, as depicted in Figure 5c. Along each ray, spatial samples are evaluated by a neural network to predict color and density. These predictions are integrated through differentiable volume rendering to reproduce the appearance of the input views. This process enables NeRF to learn a continuous function that maps 3D coordinates and viewing directions to radiance values, resulting in a high-fidelity, color-labeled 3D reconstruction of the building.

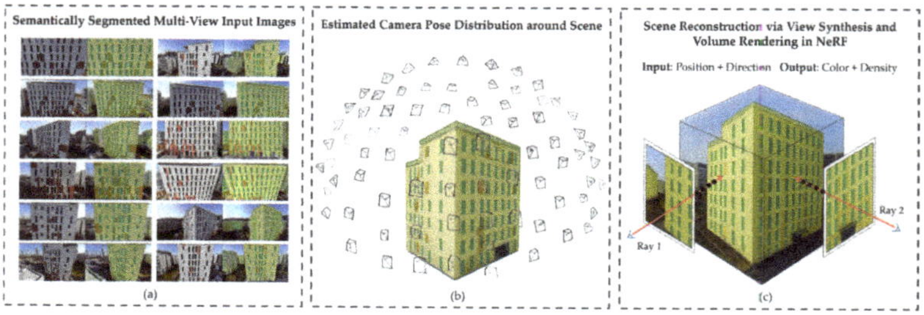

Figure 5. Illustration of the NeRF-based reconstruction workflow: (**a**) segmented image inputs, (**b**) estimated camera poses, and (**c**) volumetric rendering of the reconstructed 3D scene.

A distinguishing characteristic of NeRF methods is their optimization strategy. Unlike other DNN that aim to generalize across large datasets and avoid overfitting, NeRF models are intentionally overfitted to a single scene-specific dataset. This scene-specific optimization enables the model to learn fine-grained spatial and photometric details, resulting in high-fidelity volumetric representations tailored to the input scene.

To evaluate the impact of input data size on NeRF performance, a series of controlled experiments were conducted using subsets of the image dataset with increasing numbers of input frames. Specifically, NeRF models were trained on datasets comprising 50, 100, 150, 200, 250, 300, 350, 400, 500, and 550 images. This incremental sampling strategy allowed for a systematic assessment of how image quantity influences reconstruction quality, training stability, and PC quality. By varying the number of input views, the study aimed to identify thresholds beyond which additional data yield diminishing returns in terms of spatial completeness and semantic consistency in the reconstructed 3D scene. The results provide insights into optimal data requirements for different NeRF variants, particularly in the context of semantically segmented architectural environments.

In the proposed method, the segmentation labels embedded in the 2D images assist each NeRF model in aligning images from different viewpoints, leading to the generation of dense and color-encoded 3D PCs. The color information of each point corresponds directly to the segmentation labels, thereby preserving the identity of architectural elements in the reconstructed scene. Figure 6 demonstrates sample results of NeRF-based reconstruction using Nerfacto and segmented images produced by the proposed method.

Figure 6. Nerfacto reconstruction outputs with embedded semantic information derived from 2D image segmentation for (**a**,**b**) Dataset 1 and (**c**,**d**) Dataset 2.

3.2.2. Point Clouds Preprocessing

The PCs generated from the NeRF reconstruction were preprocessed using Open3D 0.19.0 to optimize computational efficiency. Statistical outlier removal was applied to eliminate noise by discarding points that exhibited significant deviation from their local neighborhoods, thereby improving the overall quality and consistency of the data.

A voxel grid down-sampling algorithm with a 0.01 m voxel size is applied to reduce the point density and computational overhead while preserving structural details. The voxelization technique partitions the 3D space into discrete volumetric elements (voxels) and groups spatially adjacent points based on a fixed distance threshold. Seed points are iteratively selected, and neighboring points within the specified threshold are aggregated into clusters until the entire PC is organized into compact spatial groupings [57,58]. This method reduces the number of points in large-scale 3D scenes and maintains spatial detail and geometric continuity. It enables faster processing, reduces memory usage, and preserves the architectural integrity necessary for subsequent feature extraction. Figure 7 demonstrates PCs exported from the Nerfacto model for both exterior and interior datasets.

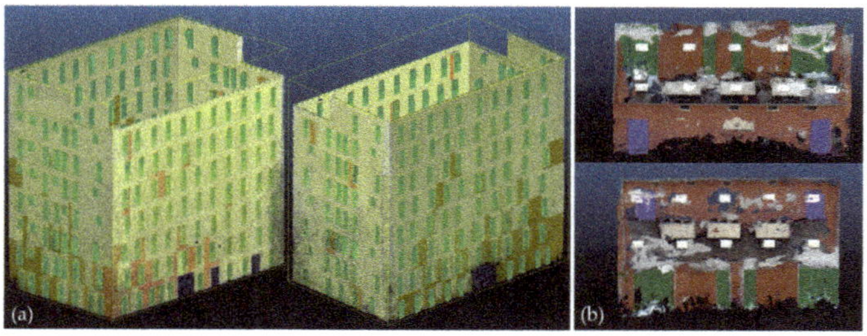

Figure 7. Extracted PCs from Nerfacto showing front and rear views for (**a**) Dataset 1, (**b**) Dataset 2.

3.2.3. RANSAC-Based Wall Planar Extraction

To extract wall features from the segmented PCs, a color-based filtering method is first applied. Since walls were pre-segmented with a yellow label in Dataset 1, a threshold-based filtering operation is used to isolate points where the red and green channels exceed 0.45, while the blue channel remains below 0.1. This selection method is utilized to retain only the wall regions and to reduce the influence of unwanted objects in the dataset. Following this, statistical outlier removal is performed using a neighborhood-based filtering approach, where points with fewer than 20 neighbors within a radius defined by a standard deviation ratio of 3.0 are discarded, to remove noise and isolate points.

To delineate wall geometries, RANSAC algorithm is employed for planar segmentation. RANSAC iteratively selects a random subset of points to fit a plane model, and classifies inliers that conform within a 0.3 m distance threshold while rejecting outliers. A maximum of 1000 iterations ensures that the model converges to an optimal planar representation of the walls. This iterative approach allows the detection of multiple wall planes and continues until either a predefined maximum number of walls is extracted or the remaining point count becomes insufficient for reliable plane fitting. Once planar segmentation is complete, a 2D line estimation is applied using Principal Component Analysis (PCA) on the XY coordinates of the inlier points. PCA is used to estimate the dominant direction of the wall segment, and the inlier points are projected onto this direction vector. The extreme projected points are designated as the start and end points of the wall. The wall height is determined from the minimum and maximum z-values of the inliers. Each wall is stored with its 2D direction vector, start and end points, base z-value, and height.

3.2.4. DBSCAN-Based Clustering for Window and Door Extraction

Following wall extraction, windows and doors are identified and isolated from the PCs using a color-based thresholding approach. The green channel is used to extract window points, where pixels with green intensity above 0.4 and low red and blue values are retained. Similarly, door points are extracted using a blue intensity threshold above 0.4, with low values in the other channels. This ensures that only the pre-segmented architectural elements are selected while unrelated objects are discarded.

To group these points into distinct architectural components, DBSCAN algorithm was employed. DBSCAN is suited for PCs clustering as it efficiently detects clusters of varying density and identifies outliers. The clustering parameters include eps = 0.32 and min_points = 60 for windows, and eps = 0.85 and min_points = 25 for doors. These values define the search radius and minimum cluster size and ensures that only significant and continuous structures are retained while filtering out noise. Figure 8 shows the PCs processing results, with walls extracted using RANSAC and windows and doors clustered using DBSCAN, represented by axis-aligned bounding boxes.

(a)  (b)

Figure 8. Point cloud processing results showing walls extracted using RANSAC and windows and doors clustered using DBSCAN with bounding boxes for (**a**) Dataset 1 and (**b**) Dataset 2.

Once clustering is complete, each detected window and door cluster is enclosed in an axis-aligned bounding box, which encapsulates the spatial extent of the object. Each bounding box stores key geometric attributes, including the center coordinates which represent the midpoint of the detected object, and the extent, which defines its width, height, and depth. Geometric attributes of each bounding box are used to assign window and door families and types, based on their correspondence to predefined Revit profiles.

To establish spatial relationships within the BIM model, each bounding box is assigned a host wall ID by computing the nearest wall based on the Euclidean distance between the bounding box center and detected wall planes. This ensures correct associations between extracted elements and their structural counterparts. Algorithm 2 illustrates the PCs Processing and Feature Extraction workflow in pseudocode.

3.2.5. Geometric Data Serialization in JSON Format

To facilitate BIM integration, the extracted geometric parameters from the PCs segmentation and clustering process are structured and serialized into a JSON file. This file serves as an intermediate data representation that preserves critical architectural information in a format that ensures compatibility with downstream automation workflows.

The JSON file is organized into three primary sections: "walls", "windows", and "doors". Each wall entry includes a unique identifier, the 2D direction vector, the calculated start and end points, the base elevation, the measured wall height, and its orientation (horizontal or vertical). Similarly, each window and door entry contains a unique identifier, a reference to the host wall, and the bounding box parameters (center and extent), along with the object type label. By structuring the extracted data into a standardized JSON format, this approach enables automated data exchange between PCs, processing tools, and BIM platforms such as Autodesk Revit. Figure 9 illustrates the structure of the generated JSON file, showcasing how architectural features are serialized to enable seamless integration with the BIM model.

```
{
  "walls": [
    {
      "id": "wall_id",
      "2d_equation": [
        "plane_coefficient_a",
        "plane_coefficient_b"
      ],
      "start_point": [
        "start_x",
        "start_y"
      ],
      "end_point": [
        "end_x",
        "end_y"
      ],
      "height": "wall_height"
    }
```

```
  "windows": [
    {
      "id": "window_id",
      "host_wall": "host_wall_id",
      "center": [
        "center_x",
        "center_y",
        "center_z"
      ],
      "extent": [
        "width",
        "depth",
        "height"
      ]
    }
  ],
```

```
  "doors": [
    {
      "id": "door_id",
      "host_wall": "host_wall_id",
      "center": [
        "center_x",
        "center_y",
        "center_z"
      ],
      "extent": [
        "width",
        "depth",
        "height"
      ]
    }
  ]
}
```

Figure 9. JSON file structure showing extracted features of walls, windows and doors.

Algorithm 2: PCs Processing and Feature Extraction

Input:

- Segmented PCs and voxel size for down sampling: $\boldsymbol{P}, \boldsymbol{v}$
- RANSAC distance threshold and maximum iterations for RANSAC: τ_d, n_{max}
- Maximum number of planes to detect: m_{max}
- Color thresholds for walls (τ_y), windows (τ_g), and doors (τ_b)
- DBSCAN parameters for clustering: $\boldsymbol{eps}, \boldsymbol{min\_points}$

Output:

- Extracted walls, windows, and doors with geometric attributes: D_{BIM}

1. **Initialize**: Load $\boldsymbol{P}$.
2. Downsample $\boldsymbol{P}$ using v.
3. Extract $\{\boldsymbol{X}, \boldsymbol{Y}, \boldsymbol{Z}\}$ coordinates and RGB values from $\boldsymbol{P}$.
4. **Define function** DetectWalls$(\boldsymbol{P}, \tau_y)$,
    - ○ Filter points where Red channel > τ_y, Green channel > τ_y, Blue channel < 0.1.
    - ○ **Return**: Wall points P_W.
5. **End function**
6. Call DetectWalls($\boldsymbol{P}$, τ_y): obtain P_W.
7. Remove noise and outliers from P_W.
8. **For** $i = \mathbf{1}$ to m_{max}:
    - ○ **If** remaining points < 100, break.
    - ○ Apply RANSAC (τ_d, n_{max}), to segment a plane {**A,B,C,D**}. Extract inlier points $P_{inliers}$.
    - ○ Compute best-fit line, start/end points $\{P_1, P_2\}$. Compute height from Z-coordinates of $P_{inliers}$.
    - ○ Save $\{\mathbf{A}, \mathbf{B}, \mathbf{C}, \mathbf{D},\ P_1, P_2, \boldsymbol{height}\}$ to wall attributes D_{walls}.
    - ○ Remove $P_{inliers}$ from remaining points P_W.
9. **End for**
10. **Define function** DetectWindowsAndDoors($\boldsymbol{P}$, τ_g, τ_b):
    - ○ Extract window points P_{win}: Green channel > τ_g, Red/Blue channels < 0.4.
    - ○ Extract window points P_{door}: Blue channel > τ_b, Red/Green channels < 0.1.
    - ○ **Return**: P_{win}, P_{door}.
11. **End function**
12. Call DetectWindowsAndDoors($\boldsymbol{P}$, τ_g, τ_b): obtain P_{win}, P_{door}.
13. **Define function** ClusterPoints($\boldsymbol{P}, \boldsymbol{eps}, \boldsymbol{min\_points}$):
    - ○ Apply DBSCAN clustering. Extract bounding boxes $B_{clusters}$.
14. **Return**: $B_{clusters}$.
15. **End function**
16. Call ClusterPoints(P_{win}, $\boldsymbol{eps} = 0.32$, $\boldsymbol{min}_{points} = 60$) to cluster windows.
17. Call ClusterPoints(P_{door}, $\boldsymbol{eps} = 0.85$, $\boldsymbol{min}_{points} = 25$) to cluster doors.
18. **Define function** AssignHostWall($\boldsymbol{B}$, D_{walls}):
    - ○ For bounding box $\boldsymbol{b}$ in $\boldsymbol{B}$: Compute perpendicular distance to D_{walls}, assign closest wall.
    - ○ **Return**: Updated $\boldsymbol{B}$ with host wall assignments.
19. **End function**
20. Call AssignHostWall(B_{win}, D_{walls}), and AssignHostWall(B_{door}, D_{walls}).
21. **Define function** ExportBIMData(D_{walls}, B_{win}, B_{door}, $output\_file$):
    - ○ Serialize D_{walls},B_{win}, B_{door} to JSON file.
    - ○ **Return**: Success message.
22. **End function**
23. Call ExportBIMData(D_{walls}, B_{win}, B_{door}, $bim\_data.json$).
24. **Return**: Extracted BIM data D_{BIM}

3.3. *Automated BIM Generation in Autodesk Revit*

3.3.1. Geometric Data Import and Unit Conversion

The final stage of the workflow involves the automated generation of a BIM model within Autodesk Revit using RevitPythonShell 2023 and the Revit API. The JSON file containing geometric data is first imported, and all coordinates and dimensions are converted from meters to feet using a conversion factor of 3.28084.

Before wall creation, a duplicate removal algorithm is applied to the JSON wall entries to eliminate repeated geometries. This is performed using a custom distance-based filter with a 0.1 m tolerance and an angular similarity threshold of 5 degrees. The filtering process removes geometrically redundant wall entries, such as identical or reversed start and end points, to make sure walls representing the same physical structure are not created multiple times due to minor geometric variation or noise. This leads to a clean and minimal wall layout suitable for BIM integration.

3.3.2. Wall Creation, Door and Window Placement, and Host Assignment

Walls are created by constructing line elements between the start and end coordinates obtained from the JSON file and assigning the corresponding wall heights. A predefined wall type is selected from the available project elements, and each wall is instantiated using the Wall. Create a method by passing a Line object defined between the start and end points. This is performed within a Revit transaction. The created wall elements are indexed using their custom IDs to allow subsequent steps such as window and door placement, to correctly reference and attach elements to the appropriate host walls.

Following the generation of wall geometry, door and window family instances are created. For each door and window, an insertion point is calculated directly from the center coordinates provided in the JSON file. The host wall is determined by matching the custom wall identifier. However, if a direct match fails due to duplicate removal, a fallback mechanism is employed. This mechanism computes the minimum distance between the element's insertion point and all wall segments using 2D point-to-line proximity. The nearest wall is then assigned as the host to make sure that every door and window is correctly embedded within a wall geometry.

A door family symbol is then retrieved and activated from the project, and a new door instance is placed at the computed insertion point. Similarly, for each window, the corresponding family symbol is retrieved and activated before instantiation at the specified coordinates. All modifications are performed within the same Revit transaction, and upon completion, the transaction is committed to finalizing the BIM model. Algorithm 3 illustrates the BIM modeling in Revit workflow using RevitPythonShell in pseudocode. Figure 10 shows the BIM model generated from the JSON file.

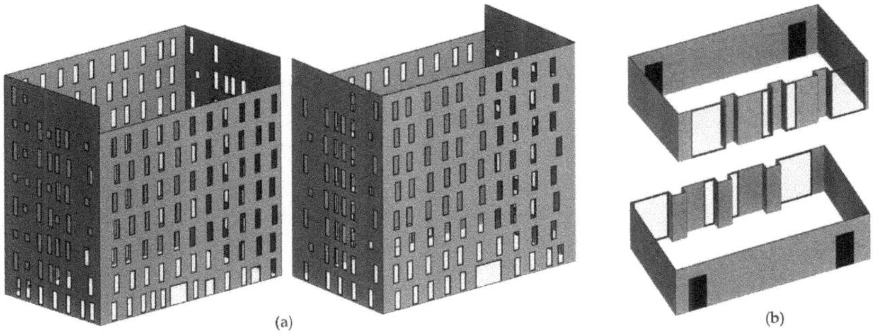

Figure 10. Automated BIM models generated from JSON data in Revit using RevitPythonShell for (**a**) Dataset 1 and (**b**) Dataset 2.

Algorithm 3: Automated BIM Generation in Autodesk Revit

Input:

- BIM data in JSON format: D_{BIM}
- Revit wall type, window type, and door type: $T_{wall}, T_{win}, T_{door}$
- Tolerance for duplicate walls: τ_{dup}
- Angular similarity threshold: φ_{sim}
- Conversion factor: meters_to_feet

Output:

- Walls, doors, and windows placed in the Revit project.

1. **Initialize:**
    - Load D_{BIM} from the JSON file.
    - Convert all dimensions from meters to feet using meters_tc_feet.
2. **Define function** RemoveDuplicateWalls($D_{BIM}, \tau_{dup}, \varphi_{sim}$):
    - For each pair of walls in D_{BIM}
        - Compare start and end points of both walls.
        - Compute direction vectors of the wall segments.
    - If the distance between endpoints < τ_{dup} and angular difference between direction vectors < φ_{sim}.
        - Mark one wall as duplicate.
    - Remove marked duplicates from D_{BIM}.
    - **Return**: Filtered wall data.
3. **End function**
4. Call RemoveDuplicateWalls($D_{BIM}, \tau_{dup}, \varphi_{sim}$)
5. **Start a transaction** in Revit.
6. **Define function** CreateWalls(D_{BIM}, T_{wall}):
    - Find T_{wall} in the Revit project.
    - Get the level in the project.
    - For each wall in D_{BIM}:
        - Extract start point, end point, and height.
        - Create a wall using Revit API and Store the created wall.
    - **Return**: Created walls and their heights.
7. **End function**
8. Call CreateWalls(D_{BIM}, T_{wall}) to create walls.
9. **Define function** CreateDoors(D_{BIM}, $walls$, T_{door}):
    - For each door in D_{BIM}:
        - Find T_{door} in the Revit project.
        - Find the host wall using the wall ID or the duplicate mapping if necessary.
        - Place door in Revit at the specified insertion point.
10. **End function**
11. Call CreateDoors(D_{BIM}, $walls$, T_{door}).
12. **Define function** CreateWindows(D_{BIM}, $walls$, T_{win}):
    - For each window in D_{BIM}:
        - Find T_{win} in the Revit project.
        - Find the host wall using the wall ID or the duplicate mapping if necessary.
        - Place window in Revit at the specified insertion point.
13. **End function**
14. Call CreateWindows(D_{BIM}, $walls$, T_{win}).
15. Commit the transaction.
16. **Return**: Successfully created walls, doors, and windows in Revit.

3.4. Evaluation Metrics

This section presents the evaluation framework used to assess the effectiveness of the proposed image-to-BIM method. The assessment is organized into two parts: (1) benchmarking the performance of the three NeRF models utilized in the reconstruction stage, and (2) evaluating the semantic, spatial, and geometric quality of the final generated BIM.

3.4.1. NeRF Model Performance Analysis

To comprehensively assess the suitability of each NeRF model for integration into the automated image-to-BIM workflow, a multi-criteria evaluation was conducted to examine critical aspects of model performance, including pose estimation accuracy, computational efficiency, training time, reconstruction and rendering quality, and the practical PC quality for geometry extraction.

Camera Pose Recovery Analysis examined the relationship between dataset size and successful camera pose estimation. COLMAP, integrated within the Nerfstudio framework, was used to evaluate the percentage of recovered poses across varying input sizes. This analysis is important, as the accuracy of pose estimation directly affects the completeness and reliability of NeRF-based 3D reconstruction. Controlled experiments were conducted using image subsets ranging from 50 to 550 frames to determine the minimum data volume required for stable and accurate pose registration.

Computational Resource Efficiency was evaluated by monitoring system resource usage, including Central Processing Unit (CPU), Graphics Processing Unit (GPU), and Random Access Memory (RAM) consumption, throughout the training process for each NeRF model. All measurements were recorded under consistent experimental conditions. A high-performance system equipped with an Intel Core Ultra 9 185H CPU and an NVIDIA RTX 4090 GPU was used to ensure a fair comparison and to eliminate hardware-related bottlenecks.

Training Time Analysis was conducted to evaluate the training efficiency of each NeRF model under varying data conditions. Each model was benchmarked using datasets containing 150 to 550 input frames to assess how both the volume of input data and the underlying model architecture influence total training time.

Reconstruction Quality and Rendering Performance were evaluated across the NeRF models using multiple standard metrics applied to datasets of increasing input size. Peak Signal-to-Noise Ratio (PSNR) was used to quantify image reconstruction fidelity, where higher values indicate better visual accuracy. SSI measured the preservation of structural details in the reconstructed scene. Learned Perceptual Image Patch Similarity (LPIPS), which captures perceptual differences between images based on deep feature representations, was also analyzed, with lower values reflecting better perceptual similarity. In addition to visual quality, rendering performance was assessed by calculating the average number of Rays Processed Per Second (RPS), which reflects computational throughput, and the average number of Frames Per Second (FPS), which indicates overall rendering speed.

PC Quality for Geometry Extraction was analyzed to determine each NeRF model's effectiveness in producing structured and usable spatial data for downstream processing. In this workflow, the PC reconstructed by each NeRF model serves as the input for geometric reasoning tasks, including element detection and spatial representation of architectural components. The process incorporates color-coded segmentation, plane fitting, clustering, and axis-aligned geometry extraction to identify walls, windows, and doors. Consequently, the spatial accuracy, structural clarity, and noise level of the generated PCs directly influence the automatic geometry extraction. Models that generate clean, high-fidelity PCs result in more accurate segmentation, fewer false positives, and better alignment of extracted geometry within the final BIM model.

3.4.2. Automated BIM Creation Performance Evaluation

This subsection outlines the quantitative criteria used to evaluate the performance of the proposed image-to-BIM method in generating semantically accurate and geometrically reliable BIM models. The evaluation focuses on three critical dimensions: semantic accuracy, spatial fidelity, and geometric precision of the generated BIM elements.

Semantic Accuracy was assessed by comparing the automatically detected windows and doors in the final BIM output against ground-truth annotations. This criterion evaluates the method's ability to accurately identify and classify building elements within the reconstructed scene. Spatial Fidelity was measured through area-based overlap analysis between the predicted and ground-truth footprints. Metrics such as precision, recall, F1 score, and IoU were used to quantify the degree of alignment between predicted and actual spatial layouts. Geometric Precision focused on the dimensional consistency of extracted elements. Specifically, the perimeter measurements of detected objects were compared against ground-truth references to assess scale accuracy and geometric conformity.

To evaluate the spatial accuracy of the extracted building elements, this study employed widely adopted metrics including Precision (Correctness), Recall (Completeness), F1 Score, and IoU. Precision is defined as the ratio of the intersection area to the predicted area, while Recall measures the ratio of the intersection area to the actual area. The F1 Score, as the harmonic mean of Precision and Recall, provides a balanced indication of model performance. These metrics are commonly used in BIM evaluation benchmarks, as shown by Khoshelham et al. [59]. IoU, defined as the intersection area divided by the union of predicted and actual areas, is widely used in segmentation evaluations, as described by Yang et al. [50].

The specific formulas used to compute these spatial metrics are as follows:

- Intersection Area: Region shared between predicted and actual areas.
- Precision (Correctness): Intersection Area/Predicted Area
- Recall (Completeness): Intersection Area/Actual Area
- F1 Score: 2 × (Precision × Recall)/(Precision + Recall)
- IoU: Intersection Area/(Actual Area + Predicted Area—Intersection Area)

This evaluation supports assessment of the method's ability to convert 2D imagery into accurate, semantically rich, and geometrically aligned BIM models.

4. Results

This section presents the simulation results of the proposed image-to-BIM method, and covers both the performance of the NeRF models and the accuracy of BIM generation. Subsections highlight key findings on camera pose recovery, computational efficiency, training time, and rendering performance. The final stages focus on PC quality for geometry extraction and the precision of the generated BIM models. Results are structured to reflect technical performance and practical utility across interior and exterior datasets.

4.1. Camera Pose Recovery Analysis

The impact of image data size on camera pose estimation was examined to determine the minimum data volume required for stable NeRF initialization. As shown in Figure 11, the percentage of successfully recovered poses increases significantly with an increasing number of input frames. With 50 frames, COLMAP recovered just 4% of camera poses. The recovery rate gradually improves, reaching 36% at 100 frames and 55.5% at 200. A sharp increase occurs between 200 and 250 frames, where pose recovery exceeds 92%. Beyond this point, the performance plateaus, with recovery stabilizing between 94% and 98% from 250 to 550 frames. Notably, Nerfstudio's default setting for frame extraction from video datasets is approximately 300 frames, which, based on these results, offers sufficiently high pose coverage for reliable NeRF reconstruction in many cases. In this study, 550 frames were used to ensure near-complete pose recovery for the exterior scene and to support the generation of dense and accurate 3D models.

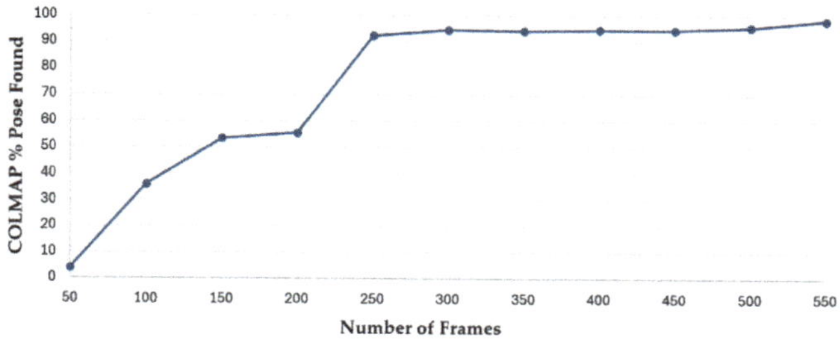

Figure 11. The relationship between the number of input frames and the percentage of successfully recovered poses using COLMAP in Nerfstudio.

This trend emphasizes the importance of spatial image overlap in achieving robust matching features. Visual gaps between consecutive views at lower frame counts limit COLMAP's ability to identify consistent key points and reduce pose estimation success. As the number of frames increases, the likelihood of overlapping content improves. The observed jump in performance beyond 250 frames suggests that spatial coverage became sufficient for this particular case. However, the optimal threshold may vary depending on scene complexity, camera motion, and lighting conditions.

4.2. Computational Resource Efficiency

System resource usage was analyzed to compare the computational demands of the evaluated NeRF models during training. Figure 12 shows that CPU usage was highest for Nerfacto, which utilized an average of 52.9% of the CPU. Instant-NGP showed moderate usage at 31.4%, while Splatfacto maintained the lowest CPU load with an average of 5.3%. This highlights that Nerfacto's volumetric pipeline and scene encoding require more CPU resources, whereas Splatfacto, driven primarily by GPU-based rasterization, places minimal demand on the CPU.

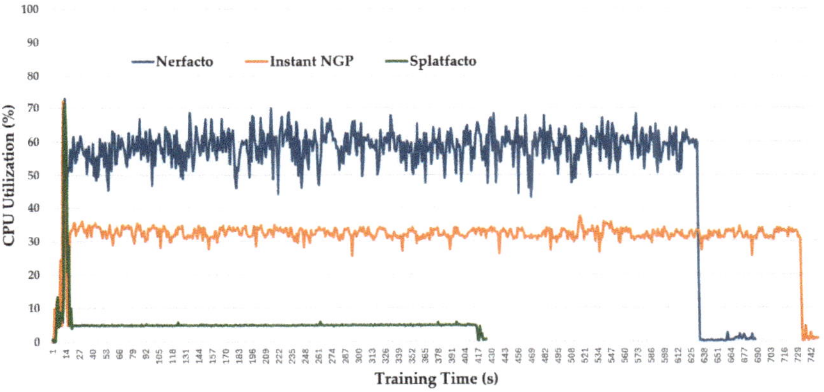

Figure 12. CPU usage percentage over training time across NeRF models.

GPU utilization patterns, shown in Figure 13, paint a different picture. Splatfacto demonstrated the highest average GPU usage at 81.7%, maintaining a high level of utilization throughout training. Instant-NGP followed with 66.9%, while Nerfacto averaged 45.8%. These values reflect the models' varying reliance on GPU-intensive operations, with Splatfacto showing strong dependence on GPU rendering via Gaussian Splatting.

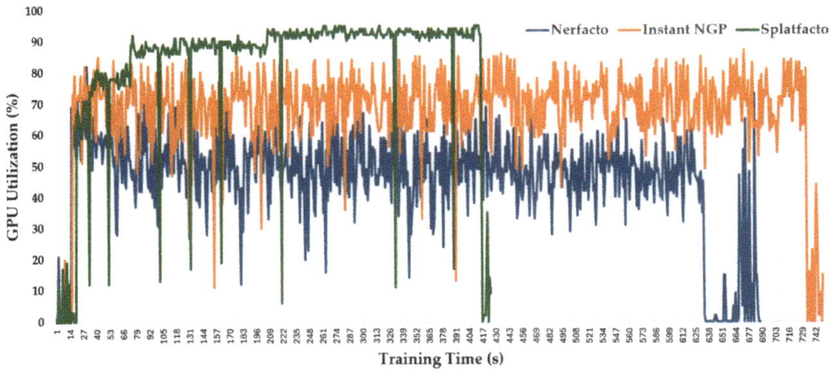

Figure 13. GPU usage percentage over training time across NeRF models.

Figure 14 combines both RAM and GPU memory usage across the training period. GPU memory consumption was lowest for Splatfacto, averaging 2.5 GB, followed by Instant-NGP at

3.3 GB and Nerfacto at 5.6 GB. In terms of RAM usage, Splatfacto again showed the smallest footprint with an average of 3.7 GB. Instant-NGP used approximately 6.7 GB, while Nerfacto maintained the highest RAM usage at around 11 GB throughout the training process. These observations highlight Splatfacto's system and GPU memory efficiency, making it well-suited for resource-constrained environments.

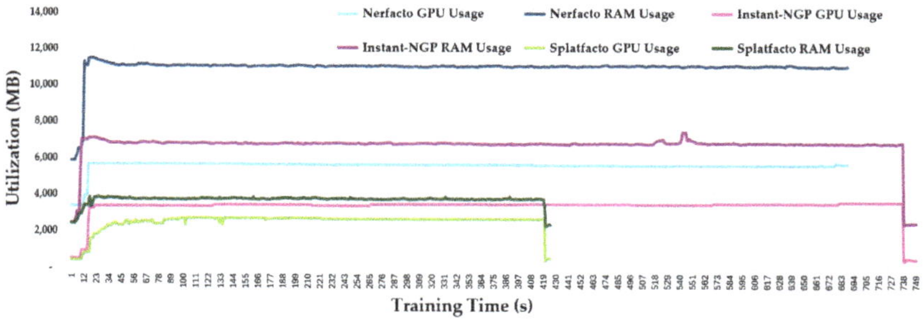

Figure 14. RAM and GPU memory usage over training time across NeRF models.

The results show that Splatfacto is the most efficient model, consistently combining high GPU utilization with the lowest CPU, system RAM, and GPU memory demands. Its high GPU load reflects efficient exploitation of modern hardware optimized for parallel processing and real-time rendering. This efficiency stems from its GPU-based Gaussian splatting approach, which offloads the bulk of computation to the GPU and minimizes CPU and memory overhead. In contrast, Nerfacto delivers high-quality volumetric reconstructions but places the most significant strain on CPU and system memory, consistent with the complexity of its architecture. Instant-NGP offers a balanced profile, achieving faster training with moderate usage of all system resources. These findings inform the selection of a NeRF model, considering hardware availability, training efficiency, and application-specific objectives. A deeper exploration of how these computational trade-offs relate to reconstruction accuracy and practical deployment is presented in Section 4.4.

4.3. Training Time Analysis

Training duration was benchmarked across NeRF models to assess time efficiency under consistent hardware and data conditions. As illustrated in Figure 15, Splatfacto consistently achieved the fastest training times across all tested configurations. Its training duration ranged from 410 to 439 s, averaging 425.8 s overall. This performance is directly attributed to its reliance on GPU-accelerated Gaussian splatting, which optimizes the rendering process. In contrast, Nerfacto required longer to complete training, with times ranging from 682 to 694 s and an average of 688.8 s. The higher training time reflects the complexity of Nerfacto's volumetric rendering pipeline and its greater reliance on CPU and memory resources, as previously discussed in Section 4.2. Instant-NGP, while recognized for its fast convergence and efficiency in NeRF literature, showed the longest training times in this evaluation. With durations ranging from 736 to 762 s and an average of 749.4 s, it lagged behind Splatfacto and Nerfacto under identical hardware.

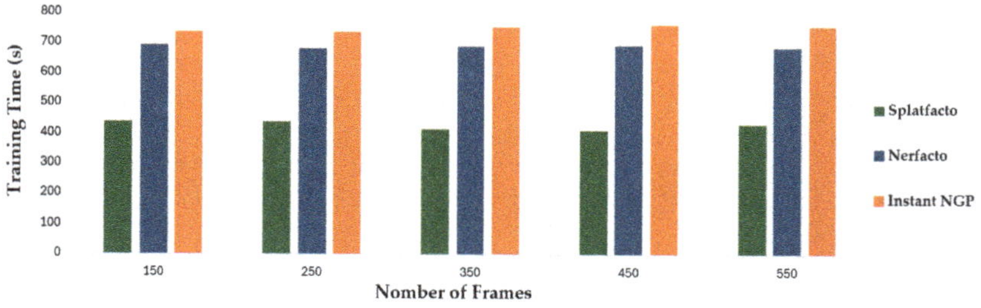

Figure 15. Training time comparison across evaluated NeRF models.

Overall, the comparison highlights Splatfacto as the most time-efficient model in this setup, offering rapid training regardless of input size. Interestingly, the number of input frames had a minimal impact on the overall training time for any evaluated models. Each model maintained a consistent training duration despite varying the dataset size.

4.4. Reconstruction Quality and Rendering Performance

Reconstruction fidelity and rendering speed were evaluated to compare the visual quality and throughput efficiency of the NeRF models. As shown in Figure 16, Splatfacto consistently achieves the highest PSNR values across all frame counts, ranging from 17.79 at 150 to 22.88 at 550 frames. Instant-NGP follows with values between 17.16 and 18.95, while Nerfacto performs the weakest, improving gradually from 15.63 to 18.52. This indicates that Splatfacto produces sharper and less noisy reconstructions, especially as scene coverage increases.

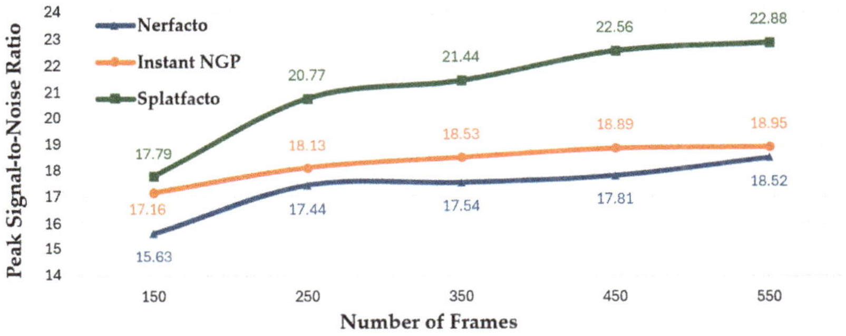

Figure 16. PNSR comparison across evaluated NeRF models.

Similarly, Figure 17 shows that Splatfacto leads in SSI, progressing from 0.69 to 0.86 as the number of frames increases. Instant-NGP improves steadily from 0.65 to 0.73, while Nerfacto again lags behind, rising from 0.62 to 0.68. Results highlight Splatfacto's stronger ability to preserve structural fidelity and perceptual quality in the rendered outputs.

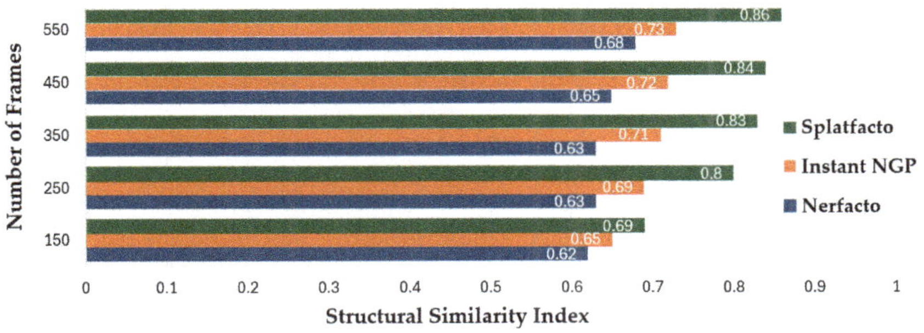

Figure 17. SSI comparison across evaluated NeRF models.

The LPIPS evaluation, presented in Figure 18, shows that Splatfacto achieves the lowest perceptual error across all input sizes. As frames increase from 150 to 550, LPIPS values for Splatfacto consistently decrease from 0.31 to 0.15, reflecting a closer perceptual match between the reconstructed and reference images. Instant-NGP shows moderate performance, with values decreasing from 0.44 to 0.34. Nerfacto shows relatively higher LPIPS values, starting at 0.47 and decreasing to 0.35 as the number of frames increases, ultimately approaching the performance of Instant-NGP at higher input sizes. These results indicate that Splatfacto produces more visually faithful reconstructions, especially in scenarios with richer input data.

Beyond visual quality, rendering performance results in Table 1 show a clear computational advantage for Splatfacto. It processes approximately 71,295,630 rays per second and generates

137.924 frames per second, significantly outperforming Nerfacto, which reaches 838,423 rays and 1.616 frames per second, and Instant-NGP, which handles 341,203 rays and 0.654 frames per second. This high efficiency comes from Splatfacto's Gaussian splatting architecture that avoids volumetric sampling and neural field queries, allowing much faster rendering.

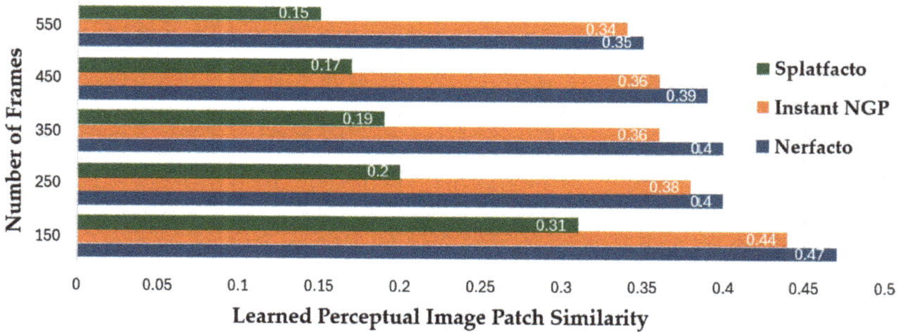

Figure 18. LPIPS comparison across evaluated NeRF models.

Table 1. Rendering speed comparison of NeRF models based on rays and frames per second.

Metrics	Instant NGP	Nerfacto	Splatfacto
Num Rays Per Sec	341,203	838,423	71,295,630
Num Frames per Sec	0.654	1.616	137.924

The results highlight the trade-offs among the evaluated models. Splatfacto delivers the highest reconstruction quality and rendering speed, making it a strong choice for scenarios that prioritize both fidelity and efficiency. Nerfacto produces reasonably good visual quality but requires more CPU and memory resources and renders more slowly due to its volumetric processing pipeline. Instant-NGP shows moderate visual quality and computational demand performance, but it falls short of Splatfacto in rendering speed and output precision.

4.5. Practical PC Quality for Geometry Extraction

To evaluate each model's suitability for geometric feature extraction, the structural clarity and consistency of the reconstructed PC were analyzed. Figure 19 presents the extracted PCs from the reconstructed interior scene using each NeRF model, illustrating both front and rear views of the classroom. These color-labeled outputs visually demonstrate each reconstruction's structural completeness and spatial clarity. Among the three models, the PC generated by Nerfacto exhibits the most consistent geometry and clean surface representation. Wall boundaries, furniture contours, and door/window regions appear sharp and continuous, providing a stable foundation for geometric segmentation and facilitating accurate alignment in downstream processing. The Instant-NGP output retains recognizable scene layout but introduces soft edges and localized noise, particularly near object boundaries. While core architectural features remain identifiable, the reduced edge sharpness may introduce spatial ambiguity during plane fitting or clustering, affecting the precision of wall, window, and door extraction.

Although Splatfacto excels in reconstruction quality, training speed, and rendering efficiency, its integration into geometry extraction workflows presents practical limitations. Since Splatfacto reconstructs scenes using 3D Gaussian splats and lacks native PC export in Nerfstudio, this study employed the 3DGS-to-PC framework by Stuart and Pound [60] to convert splats into PCs. This framework samples points from Gaussians based on their volume, filters outliers using Mahalanobis distance, and recalculates colors from rendered images to improve visual accuracy. However, the converted outputs are shown in Figure 19 contain structural noise, such as floating clusters, blurred edges, and irregular densities that obscure object boundaries and disrupt spatial consistency. Although Splatfacto achieves high PSNR and SSI scores, these irregularities in the PCs hinder accurate wall, window, and door classification and extraction within the Image to BIM workflow.

(a)
(b)
(c)

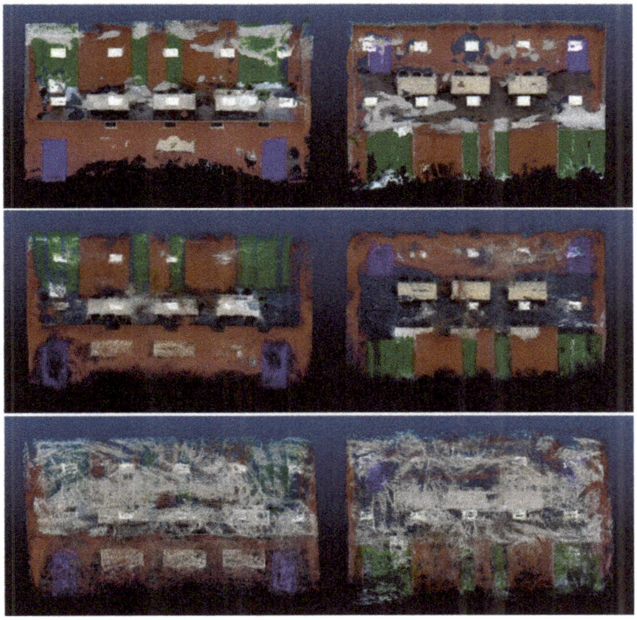

Figure 19. Generated color-labeled point clouds showing front and back of the classroom (Dataset 2) extracted from (**a**) Nerfacto, (**b**) Instant NGP, and (**c**) Splatfacto model.

4.6. Automated BIM Creation Results and Evaluation

The final phase of the proposed method was assessed through the generation of BIM models from reconstructed scenes. This subsection presents the results on semantic accuracy, spatial alignment, and geometric precision, based on comparisons between the generated output and ground-truth annotations. As shown in Figure 6, the reconstruction process using segmented images enables precise label transfer and results in a successful reconstructed 3D scene where building elements such as walls, windows, and doors are preserved across the scene with their predefined colors. Building on this labeled reconstruction, Figure 7 displays the exported color-labeled PCs, which serve as the input for subsequent processing. Geometric features are then extracted through wall plane fitting and object clustering, as illustrated in Figure 8. These extracted elements are automatically serialized and imported into Autodesk Revit to generate the final BIM model, shown in Figure 10. Together, these stages demonstrate the method's ability to maintain semantic integrity, capture accurate geometry, and produce a structured and automation-ready BIM output directly from 2D imagery.

The workflow's performance is evaluated using three critical criteria: (1) semantic accuracy in detecting windows and doors, (2) geometric precision evaluated using perimeter comparisons, and (3) spatial fidelity assessed through area-based overlap metrics.

Table 2 presents the number of doors and windows in the analysis of the semantic feature extraction results in both datasets. The proposed method correctly identified all architectural elements: 248 windows and four doors in Dataset 1, and 4 windows and two doors in Dataset 2. This perfect match with the ground truth highlights the reliability of the element detection process and confirms the method's ability to maintain semantic precision across different scene types.

To contextualize these results, Table 3 compares door and window extraction performance against previous Scan-to-BIM studies that employed PC-based and image-based approaches. Across references [22,46,61,62], reported accuracies for door and window instance detection range between 96 and 100 percent. Due to various types and meanings for accuracy, the clarification is needed that the successful identification of an element is assumed as accuracy in detection. The proposed image-to-BIM method achieves results consistent with these benchmarks, which match the highest reported accuracies in detecting an element without reliance on laser scanning or PC input. In these benchmark studies, the number of detected windows and doors ranged from 0 to 28, whereas the proposed method successfully detected up to 248 windows without any error.

Table 2. Doors and windows identified in the datasets using the proposed method.

Building Dataset	No. of Actual Windows	No. of Predicted Windows	No. of Actual Doors	No. of Predicted Doors	Window Accuracy	Door Accuracy
Dataset 1	248	248	4	4	100%	100%
Dataset 2	4	4	2	2	100%	100%

Table 3. Selected studies comparing the accuracy of successfully detecting doors and windows in their chosen case studies.

Method/Dataset	No. of Actual Windows	No. of Predicted Windows	No. of Actual Doors	No. of Predicted Doors	Window Accuracy	Door Accuracy
[46]/Collected 1,2	21	21	25	24	100%	96%
[61]/Dataset 1, 2, 3	7	7	6	6	100%	100%
[62]/Data 1,2	4	4	4	4	100%	100%
[22]/Average	28	28	11	11	100%	100%

Further geometric evaluation was conducted using perimeter accuracy. As shown in Table 4. The proposed method demonstrated a strong ability to maintain geometric consistency between the reconstructed models and ground-truth buildings. For Dataset 1, the predicted perimeter was 100.38 m, compared to the actual perimeter of 100.32 m, resulting in a minimal deviation of 0.06 m and an accuracy of 99.94%. For Dataset 2, the predicted perimeter was 37.83 m versus an actual value of 37.27 m, with an error of 0.56 m and an accuracy of 98.49%.

Table 4. Evaluation of the reconstructed BIM model based on predicted perimeters.

Building Dataset	Actual Perimeter (m)	Predicted Perimeter (m)	Error (m)	Accuracy (%)
Dataset 1	100.32	100.38	0.06	99.94
Dataset 2	37.27	37.83	0.56	98.49

Table 5 compares the proposed method's perimeter accuracy with previously published results. In the benchmark study [46], perimeter deviations ranged from 0.019 to 0.929 m, corresponding to accuracies between 99.30 and 99.90 percent. The proposed image-to-BIM approach achieves comparable geometric precision.

Table 5. Quantitative comparison of reconstructed BIM model based on predicted perimeters.

Method/Dataset	Actual Perimeter (m)	Predicted Perimeter (m)	Error (m)	Accuracy (%)
[46]/Collected 1	149.734	150.663	−0.929	99.30
[46]/Collected 2	27.492	27.473	0.019	99.90

Table 6 presents the spatial accuracy evaluation based on area comparisons. For Dataset 1, the predicted building footprint aligns closely with the reference geometry, achieving a precision of 0.994, a recall of 0.997, an F1 score of 0.996, and an IoU of 0.992. Dataset 2 reconstruction yields a predicted area of 83.06 m^2 and an intersection of 80.88 m^2, resulting in a precision of 0.974, a recall of 0.995, an F1 score of 0.984, and an IoU of 0.969. These metrics confirm the pipeline's ability to preserve spatial accuracy and generate BIM models that consistently reflect real-world dimensions.

Table 6. Evaluation of the reconstructed BIM model based on predicted area.

Building Dataset	Actual Area (m^2)	Predicted Area (m^2)	Intersection Area (m^2)	Precision	Recall	F1 Score	IoU
Dataset 1	583.17	585.20	581.71	0.994	0.997	0.996	0.992
Dataset 2	81.26	83.06	80.88	0.974	0.995	0.984	0.969

4.7. Comparative Analysis with Scan-to-BIM Literature

To contextualize the performance of the proposed method, a comparative analysis was conducted against several recent AI enhanced Scan-to-BIM approaches, as summarized in Table 7. The comparison demonstrates that the proposed method achieves state-of-the-art performance on both Dataset 1 and Dataset 2. Across the selected benchmark studies, evaluated metric values fall within the range of 0.93–0.999, and the proposed method performs at a comparable or higher level of spatial accuracy than traditional Scan-to-BIM. The slightly higher accuracy observed on Dataset 1 can be attributed to the superior input quality provided by the UAV's stabilized 4K camera and structured flight path.

Table 7. Comparative evaluation of recent BIM reconstruction techniques based on predicted area.

Method	Dataset	Precision	Recall	F1 Score	IoU
The present study, Dataset 1: DJI Mini 4 Pro drone for image acquisition YOLO and SAM2 for image detection and segmentation NeRF for 3D reconstruction and PC generation		0.994	0.997	0.996	0.992
The present study, Dataset 2: Standard smartphone camera for image acquisition YOLO and SAM2 for image detection and segmentation NeRF for 3D reconstruction and PC generation		0.974	0.995	0.984	0.969
Mahmoud, Zhao [61]: Leica RTC360 3D laser scanner for PC acquisition RandLA-Net for PC semantic segmentation		0.994	0.996	0.995	0.990
Mahmoud, Chen [63]: NavVis M6 mobile laser scanner for PC acquisition RandLA-Net for semantic segmentation		0.991	0.993	0.992	0.984
Mahmoud, Li [62]: Faro Focus 3D laser range scanner for PC acquisition RandLA-Net for semantic segmentation		0.989	0.990	0.989	0.978
Mahmoud, Chen [46]: NavVis M6 indoor mobile mapping 3D scanner RandLA-Net for semantic segmentation		0.999	0.997	0.998	0.998
Gao et al. [64]: Mobile Laser Scanning for PC acquisition Mask R-CNN for semantic segmentation		0.930	0.970	0.950	-

Unlike conventional Scan-to-BIM studies the present method provides a more efficient and less expensive solution. For example, the conventional approach relies on costly LiDAR or laser-scanning hardware as well as PC processing and CNN-based PC segmentation networks such as

RandLA-Net or Mask R-CNN. However, the proposed method performed detection and segmentation directly on RGB imagery using open-source vision–language models (YOLO and SAM) combined with NeRF or Gaussian Splatting for 3D reconstruction which is cost-free and removes the need for PC segmentation.

4.8. Comparative Analysis with NeRF-Based Methods

Recent NeRF-based reconstruction studies have introduced varying levels of automation; however, their workflow remains distinct from the method presented in this study. NeRF-to-BIM [65] demonstrated an initial attempt to couple NeRF reconstruction with BIM creation, where Instant-NeRF produced PCs later segmented by PointNeXt to classify structural elements such as beams and columns. Although this work verified the potential of NeRF-generated data for BIM applications, it required intensive post-processing and manual refinement. Harbingers of NeRF-to-BIM [66] extended this to a three-stage process combining NeRF reconstruction, fine-tuned PointNeXt segmentation on synthetic BIM-derived datasets, and BIM generation; however, it still relied on labeled PCs and separate training steps. Similarly, Li et al. [67] applied Nerfacto to reconstruct building façades from UAV imagery, followed by PointNet++ segmentation of the NeRF-derived PCs. Montas-Laracuente et al. [68] adopted Gaussian Splatting to generate high-fidelity meshes for heritage documentation but without semantic or BIM automation. In contrast, the proposed method explicitly advances this line of research by bypassing PC post-processing, embedding semantic information directly at the image level before NeRF training. This early-stage semantic integration allows class labels to propagate throughout the 3D reconstruction, resulting in PCs that are already color-segmented and labeled during generation. Consequently, precise geometry extraction can be performed without additional segmentation or manual refinement, thereby achieving a higher degree of automation and practical efficiency than previous NeRF-based approaches.

4.9. Comparative Analysis of Evaluated NeRF Models

Since the proposed method relies on NeRF-based reconstruction, selecting an appropriate model is important. Table 8 presents a detailed comparison of three NeRF models, evaluating them across visual fidelity, computational performance, and PC suitability for BIM extraction. Among them, Splatfacto delivers the highest reconstruction quality and speed, far surpassing the performance of Instant-NGP and Nerfacto. Despite its speed and visual quality, Splatfacto has practical limitations for Scan-to-BIM workflows. It does not natively export PCs, requiring an external conversion step that introduces structural noise and blurs object boundaries. As a result, the generated PC lacks the consistency needed for object extraction.

Table 8. Comparative evaluation of examined NeRF models.

Metrics	Instant NGP	Nerfacto	Splatfacto
Average Training Time	749.4	688.8	425.8
PSNR	18.95	18.52	22.88
SSI	0.73	0.68	0.86
LPIPS	0.34	0.35	0.15
Average CPU Utilization (%)	31.4	52.9	5.3
Average GPU Utilization (%)	66.9	45.8	81.7
Average RAM Utilization (GB)	6.7	11	3.7
Average GPU Utilization (GB)	3.3	5.6	2.5
Num RPS	341,203	838,423	71,295,630
Num FPS	0.654	1.616	137.924
Native PC Generation	Yes	Yes	No
PC quality for Geometry Extraction	Medium	High	Low

In contrast, while Nerfacto's visual metrics are slightly lower than those of Splatfacto, it produces the most structured and spatially coherent PC outputs, making it more suitable for geometry extraction. Instant-NGP, while known for its speed in NeRF literature, shows longer training times in this evaluation and delivers moderate reconstruction quality. Its PCs exhibit soft edges and localized noise, which may hinder precise segmentation and alignment in BIM generation tasks. Nonetheless, it offers a balanced computational profile, with moderate resource efficiency. Overall, these findings suggest that Nerfacto is the most suitable model for geometry-aware applications, such as Scan-to-BIM, where spatial consistency is crucial.

5. Discussion

5.1. Key Contributions and Implications

The primary contribution of this work lies in offering a method for automated BIM generation from images using accessible hardware and open-source tools. It bridges critical gaps in the Scan-to-BIM literature by (1) demonstrating that BIM models can be generated from image data alone, eliminating reliance on scanning equipment by producing PCs directly from RGB images using NeRF volumetric rendering. This is achieved by integrating object-level semantic segmentation with NeRF-based 3D reconstruction in a unified method, allowing the system to learn spatial structure directly from labeled RGB inputs rather than relying on traditional photogrammetry or LiDAR-based scans; (2) demonstrating, for the first time, how semantic identity can be embedded into NeRF-based volumetric reconstruction and subsequently extracted as structured geometric data for BIM modeling. This removes the need for post-reconstruction segmentation by embedding semantic labels at the pixel level during preprocessing using computer vision-language techniques. These labels are preserved throughout the rendering process, eliminating projection-based mapping that might lead to misalignment and inconsistency, and ensuring that each building element retains its identity from image input to final BIM output; and (3) developing the workflow from image acquisition to BIM output without requiring domain-specific training data. The extracted geometry is serialized in a structured JSON format and directly imported into Revit, enabling automation of BIM model creation based on the building elements embedded semantic and geometric attributes.

Additionally, this study performs a comparative evaluation of three reconstruction methods, namely Instant-NGP, Nerfacto, and Splatfacto, in the context of Scan-to-BIM automation. It establishes criteria for selecting suitable models based on PC quality, rendering efficiency, and spatial fidelity, identifying Nerfacto as the most effective for geometry extraction. This may advance the application of NeRF models using the criteria beyond view synthesis and introduces them as viable tools for geometry-aware BIM modeling.

In practical terms, the proposed method transforms how existing buildings are digitized by eliminating the need for terrestrial scanning devices, or the tedious manual on-site surveying. Tasks that were once labor-intensive, equipment-dependent, and costly such as site surveying and digital modeling, can benefit from using widely accessible camera devices, expanding the practicality and scalability of BIM-based planning across the construction and facilities sector.

The framework is especially impactful for aging, undocumented, or under-maintained buildings, where original drawings are often unavailable. It facilitates rapid creation of digital twins for a wide range of practical applications, including renovation planning, space optimization, and exterior façade restoration. The resulting BIM model is generated directly within Revit using native building elements, which enables compatibility with existing BIM workflows. It functions not only as a geometric record but also it can be useful as an operational asset for facility management tasks such as quantity take-offs, material tracking, and renovation cost estimation performed directly within the Revit environment. Furthermore, the model can be exported from Revit to open formats such as IFC, supporting interoperability with facility management and asset information systems commonly used in practice. In energy retrofit scenarios, the method provides reliable building geometry for tasks such as insulation upgrades, envelope improvements, and solar panel placement, where models can be used directly within Revit for energy analyses or exported to IDF or gbXML formats for integration with tools like EnergyPlus and OpenStudio. However, all these applications need to be tested and evaluated as future studies. The accessibility and speed of this approach could make it a compelling solution for practitioners seeking to modernize building data acquisition workflows without the burden of costly hardware or extensive manual effort.

5.2. Limitations and Future Research Direction

Despite its strengths, the study identified limitations as well. First, NeRF reconstruction quality remains sensitive to image completeness and clarity, and occlusions or inadequate image coverage can compromise model accuracy and completeness. Moreover, lighting variation, textureless or reflective surfaces, and the presence of dynamic objects during image capture may further reduce reconstruction fidelity by introducing inconsistencies in color, depth, and surface definition, which can ultimately lead to reconstruction failure. Second, the performance of the proposed Image-to-BIM workflow was validated on two scenes, one exterior and one interior, as a proof of concept. However, broader validation on buildings featuring intricate or unconventional architectural styles remains untested, which may affect its generalizability. Future research should extend the evaluation to a wider range of typologies, including heritage buildings and complex geometries, to assess the scalability and robustness of the method across diverse architectural conditions.

Third, the present system focuses exclusively on core building elements such as walls, doors, and windows. To enhance the versatility and completeness of this method, future investigations should expand semantic classification and geometric reconstruction capabilities to other building components, including floors, ceilings, columns, stairs, and complex internal spatial layouts. Fourth, While this study successfully automates several fragmented components of the image-to-BIM workflow, including segmentation, reconstruction, element extraction, and BIM creation, future work should focus on developing an end-to-end unified framework that seamlessly integrates all stages into a single automated pipeline. Fifth, while Gaussian splatting methods such as Splatfacto showed the highest potential in reconstruction quality, the lack of native PC export in current implementations remains a limitation. Future work should address this gap to unlock the full utility of Gaussian-based reconstructions in geometry-driven BIM applications. Sixth, incorporating adaptive parameter adjustments within geometric algorithms could improve performance and flexibility across architectural typologies and conditions.

Seventh, a comprehensive ablation study should be conducted to evaluate the contribution of each component, including YOLO for detection, SAM for segmentation, NeRF and Gaussian Splatting for reconstruction, and to optimize their interaction within the framework. This will clarify each module's impact on accuracy and efficiency and guide future improvements in the image-to-BIM workflow. Eighth, all experiments were conducted on a high-end RTX 4090 GPU, which significantly reduced training time. Future research should evaluate the framework's scalability on mid-range GPUs and cloud-based computing platforms to ensure broader accessibility and assess performance trade-offs under different hardware configurations. Lastly, while the proposed method effectively creates BIM models for undocumented buildings, future research should focus on extending the framework to enable continuous maintenance and digital twin updates by allowing new image inputs to be reprocessed to detect and integrate physical changes within the existing building model.

6. Conclusions

This study introduced an automated image-to-BIM method that integrates vision-language segmentation, NeRF-based 3D reconstruction, and structured geometric modeling to generate semantically rich and spatially accurate BIM models from ordinary 2D images. Experimental validation demonstrates that the proposed method achieves strong semantic, spatial, and geometric performance while eliminating the need for traditional scanning tools such as LiDAR or photogrammetry. Its key novelty lies in unifying semantic segmentation and 3D reconstruction in the chosen context, by embedding object labels during NeRF processing, thereby removing the need for post-processing on PCs and enabling a more efficient method to automatically generate BIM model.

Experimental validation confirms the method's high performance across both semantic and geometric dimensions considering its limitations. The system successfully detected windows and doors across two distinct datasets: an exterior scene captured via UAV and an interior scene recorded with a handheld smartphone. In area-based evaluations, the method achieved a precision of 0.994, an IoU of 0.992 for the exterior case, and 0.974 precision with 0.969 IoU for the interior case. Perimeter comparisons confirmed geometric consistency, with deviations of just 0.05 m and 0.56 m for the exterior and interior datasets, yielding accuracies of 99.94% and 98.49%, respectively. The proposed method consistently achieved superior performance in comparative evaluations against recent deep learning-based reconstruction methods. It recorded higher precision (up to 0.994), F1 scores (up to 0.996), and IoU values (up to 0.992), outperforming existing approaches.

In evaluating three NeRF variants, Splatfacto demonstrated the highest image-based reconstruction quality, with PSNR of 22.88, SSI of 0.86, and LPIPS of 0.15, alongside industry-leading rendering speeds of 137.9 FPS and 71M rays per second. However, due to structural artifacts and density inconsistencies introduced during PC conversion, Splatfacto proved less effective for downstream geometric extraction. In contrast, Nerfacto, while slightly lower in visual quality, generated cleaner, more structured PCs that enabled more reliable element detection, making it a more suitable choice for geometry-aware BIM modeling within the proposed method.

By removing reliance on expensive scanning hardware and minimizing technical barriers, this method presents a scalable and accessible alternative for automated BIM generation. Its applicability spans a wide range of real-world use cases, including architectural documentation, renovation planning, energy retrofitting, facility management, and digital twin development. This work not only demonstrates a practical, low-cost pathway for digitizing existing buildings but also contributes to the theoretical advancement of image-driven reconstruction by establishing a new benchmark for semantic-aware NeRF-based Scan-to-BIM automation.

Author Contributions: Conceptualization, M.H.M. and S.M.E.S.; methodology, M.H.M., S.M., M.W., R.L. and S.M.E.S.; software, M.H.M.; validation, M.H.M.; formal analysis, M.H.M.; investigation, M.H.M.; data curation, M.H.M.; writing—original draft preparation, M.H.M., S.M., M.W., R.L. and S.M.E.S.; writing—review and editing M.H.M., S.M., M.W., R.L. and S.M.E.S.; visualization, M.H.M.; supervision, S.M.E.S.; funding acquisition, S.M. All authors have read and agreed to the published version of the manuscript.

Funding: This research received no external funding.

Data Availability Statement: The original contribution presented in the study is included in the article. Further inquiries can be directed to the corresponding authors.

Acknowledgments: The authors express their gratitude to Alireza Ghomimoghadam for his support in data collection.

Conflicts of Interest: The authors declare no conflicts of interest.

Abbreviations

The following abbreviations are used in this manuscript:

AI	Artificial Intelligence
BIM	Building Information Modeling
PC	Point Cloud
CPU	Central Processing Unit
CNNs	Convolutional Neural Networks
DNN	Deep Neural Networks
DBSCAN	Density-Based Spatial Clustering of Applications with Noise
FPS	Frames Per Second
GPU	Graphics Processing Unit
IoU	Intersection over Union
JSON	JavaScript Object Notation
LPIPS	Learned Perceptual Image Patch Similarity
LOD	Level of Detail
MLP	Multilayer Perceptron
MVS	Multi-View Stereo
NeRF	Neural Radiance Fields
PSNR	Peak Signal-to-Noise Ratio
PCIS	Point cloud Classification based on image-based Instance Segmentation
PCA	Principal Component Analysis
RAM	Random Access Memory

RANSAC	Random Sample Consensus
RPS	Rays Processed Per Second
SSI	Structural Similarity Index
SfM	Structure-from-Motion
UAV	Unmanned Aerial Vehicle

References

1. Kaashi, S.; Vilventhan, A. Development of a building information modelling based decision-making framework for green retrofitting of existing buildings. *J. Build. Eng.* **2023**, *80*, 108128. [CrossRef]
2. Wang, D.; Jiang, Q.; Liu, J. Deep-Learning-Based Automated Building Information Modeling Reconstruction Using Orthophotos with Digital Surface Models. *Buildings* **2024**, *14*, 808. [CrossRef]
3. Mehraban, M.H.; Alnaser, A.A.; Sepasgozar, S.M.E. Building Information Modeling and AI Algorithms for Optimizing Energy Performance in Hot Climates: A Comparative Study of Riyadh and Dubai. *Buildings* **2024**, *14*, 2748. [CrossRef]
4. Mehraban, M.H.; Sepasgozar, S.M.; Ghomimoghadam, A.; Zafari, B. AI-Enhanced Automation of Building Energy Optimization Using a Hybrid Stacked Model and Genetic Algorithms: Experiments with Seven Machine Learning Techniques and a Deep Neural Network. *Results Eng.* **2025**, *26*, 104994. [CrossRef]
5. Mehraban, M.H.; Mirzabeigi, S.; Faraji, S.; Soltanian-Zadeh, S.; Sepasgozar, S.M.E. AI-Driven Prediction of Building Energy Performance and Thermal Resilience During Power Outages: A BIM-Simulation Machine Learning Workflow. *Buildings* **2025**, *15*, 3950. [CrossRef]
6. Rocha, G.; Mateus, L.; Fernández, J.; Ferreira, V. A Scan-to-BIM Methodology Applied to Heritage Buildings. *Heritage* **2020**, *3*, 47–67. [CrossRef]
7. Badenko, V.; Fedotov, A.; Zotov, D.; Lytkin, S.; Volgin, D.; Garg, R.; Liu, M. Scan-to-Bim Methodology Adapted for Different Application. *ISPRS Int. Arch. Photogramm. Remote Sens. Spat. Inf. Sci.* **2019**, *42*, 1–7. [CrossRef]
8. Jung, J.; Hong, S.; Jeong, S.; Kim, S.; Cho, H.; Hong, S.; Heo, J. Productive modeling for development of as-built BIM of existing indoor structures. *Autom. Constr.* **2014**, *42*, 68–77. [CrossRef]
9. Hong, S.; Jung, J.; Kim, S.; Cho, H.; Lee, J.; Heo, J. Semi-automated approach to indoor mapping for 3D as-built building information modeling. *Comput. Environ. Urban Syst.* **2015**, *51*, 34–46. [CrossRef]
10. Volk, R.; Stengel, J.; Schultmann, F. Building Information Modeling (BIM) for existing buildings—Literature review and future needs. *Autom. Constr.* **2014**, *38*, 109–127. [CrossRef]
11. Macher, H.; Landes, T.; Grussenmeyer, P. From Point Clouds to Building Information Models: 3D Semi-Automatic Reconstruction of Indoors of Existing Buildings. *Appl. Sci.* **2017**, *7*, 1030. [CrossRef]
12. Cotella, V.A. From 3D point clouds to HBIM: Application of Artificial Intelligence in Cultural Heritage. *Autom. Constr.* **2023**, *152*, 104936. [CrossRef]
13. Hübner, P.; Weinmann, M.; Wursthorn, S.; Hinz, S. Automatic voxel-based 3D indoor reconstruction and room partitioning from triangle meshes. *ISPRS J. Photogramm. Remote Sens.* **2021**, *181*, 254–278. [CrossRef]
14. Bello, S.A.; Yu, S.; Wang, C.; Adam, J.M.; Li, J. Review: Deep Learning on 3D Point Clouds. *Remote Sens.* **2020**, *12*, 1729. [CrossRef]
15. Tran, H.; Khoshelham, K. Procedural Reconstruction of 3D Indoor Models from Lidar Data Using Reversible Jump Markov Chain Monte Carlo. *Remote Sens.* **2020**, *12*, 838. [CrossRef]
16. Borkowski, A.S.; Kubrat, A. Integration of Laser Scanning, Digital Photogrammetry and BIM Technology: A Review and Case Studies. *Eng* **2024**, *5*, 2395–2409. [CrossRef]
17. Lichti, D.; Gordon, S.; Stewart, M.; Franke, J.; Tsakiri, M. Comparison of Digital Photogrammetry and Laser Scanning. In Proceedings of the ISPRS Commission II Symposium 2002: Integrated System for Spatial Data Production, Custodian and Decision Support, Xi'an, China, 20–23 August 2002.
18. Rashdi, R.; Martínez-Sánchez, J.; Arias, P.; Qiu, Z. Scanning Technologies to Building Information Modelling: A Review. *Infrastructures* **2022**, *7*, 49. [CrossRef]
19. Lato, M.; Kemeny, J.; Harrap, R.M.; Bevan, G. Rock bench: Establishing a common repository and standards for assessing rockmass characteristics using LiDAR and photogrammetry. *Comput. Geosci.* **2013**, *50*, 106–114. [CrossRef]
20. Pantoja-Rosero, B.G.; Achanta, R.; Kozinski, M.; Fua, P.; Perez-Cruz, F.; Beyer, K. Generating LOD3 building models from structure-from-motion and semantic segmentation. *Autom. Constr.* **2022**, *141*, 104430. [CrossRef]
21. Kim, H.; Remaggi, L.; Jackson, P.J.; Fazi, F.M.; Hilton, A. 3D Room Geometry Reconstruction Using Audio-Visual Sensors. In Proceedings of the 2017 International Conference on 3D Vision (3DV), Qingdao, China, 10–12 October 2017; pp. 621–629.
22. Wong, M.O.; Sun, Y.; Ying, H.; Yin, M.; Zhou, H.; Brilakis, I.; Kelly, T.; Lam, C.C. Image-based scan-to-BIM for interior building component reconstruction. *Autom. Constr.* **2025**, *173*, 106091. [CrossRef]

23. Armeni, I.; Sener, O.; Zamir, A.R.; Jiang, H.; Brilakis, I.; Fischer, M.; Savarese, S. 3D Semantic Parsing of Large-Scale Indoor Spaces. In Proceedings of the 2016 IEEE Conference on Computer Vision and Pattern Recognition (CVPR), Las Vegas, NA, USA, 27–30 June 2016; pp. 1534–1543.
24. Cai, G.; Pan, Y. Understanding the Imperfection of 3D point Cloud and Semantic Segmentation algorithms for 3D Models of Indoor Environment. *AGILE GISci. Ser.* **2022**, *3*, 2. [CrossRef]
25. Zhou, B.; Zhao, H.; Puig, X.; Fidler, S.; Barriuso, A.; Torralba, A. Scene Parsing through ADE20K Dataset. In Proceedings of the 2017 IEEE Conference on Computer Vision and Pattern Recognition (CVPR), Honolulu, HI, USA, 21–26 July 2017; pp. 5122–5130.
26. Silberman, N.; Hoiem, D.; Kohli, P.; Fergus, R. Indoor Segmentation and Support Inference from RGBD Images. In Proceedings of the Computer Vision—ECCV 2012, Berlin/Heidelberg, Germany, 7–13 October 2012; pp. 746–760.
27. Wong, M.O.; Ying, H.; Yin, M.; Yi, X.; Xiao, L.; Duan, W.; He, C.; Tang, L. Semantic 3D reconstruction-oriented image dataset for building component segmentation. *Autom. Constr.* **2024**, *165*, 105558. [CrossRef]
28. Tang, P.; Huber, D.; Akinci, B.; Lipman, R.; Lytle, A. Automatic reconstruction of as-built building information models from laser-scanned point clouds: A review of related techniques. *Autom. Constr.* **2010**, *19*, 829–843. [CrossRef]
29. Xiong, X.; Adan, A.; Akinci, B.; Huber, D. Automatic creation of semantically rich 3D building models from laser scanner data. *Autom. Constr.* **2013**, *31*, 325–337. [CrossRef]
30. Croce, V.; Bevilacqua, M.G.; Caroti, G.; Piemonte, A. Connecting Geometry and Semantics Via Artificial Intelligence: From 3D Classification of Heritage Data to H-Bim Representations. *Int. Arch. Photogramm. Remote Sens. Spat. Inf. Sci.* **2021**, *43*, 145–152. [CrossRef]
31. Ochmann, S.; Vock, R.; Klein, R. Automatic reconstruction of fully volumetric 3D building models from oriented point clouds. *ISPRS J. Photogramm. Remote Sens.* **2019**, *151*, 251–262. [CrossRef]
32. Bassier, M.; Vergauwen, M. Unsupervised reconstruction of Building Information Modeling wall objects from point cloud data. *Autom. Constr.* **2020**, *120*, 103338. [CrossRef]
33. Rausch, C.; Haas, C. Automated shape and pose updating of building information model elements from 3D point clouds. *Autom. Constr.* **2021**, *124*, 103561. [CrossRef]
34. Perez-Perez, Y.; Golparvar-Fard, M.; El-Rayes, K. Segmentation of point clouds via joint semantic and geometric features for 3D modeling of the built environment. *Autom. Constr.* **2021**, *125*, 103584. [CrossRef]
35. Dai, A.; Chang, A.X.; Savva, M.; Halber, M.; Funkhouser, T.; Nießner, M. ScanNet: Richly-Annotated 3D Reconstructions of Indoor Scenes. In Proceedings of the 2017 IEEE Conference on Computer Vision and Pattern Recognition (CVPR), Honolulu, HI, USA, 21–26 July 2017; pp. 2432–2443.
36. Qi, C.R.; Su, H.; Mo, K.; Guibas, L.J. Pointnet: Deep learning on point sets for 3D classification and segmentation. In Proceedings of the IEEE Conference on Computer Vision and Pattern Recognition, Honolulu, HI, USA, 21–26 July 2017; pp. 652–660.
37. Li, Y.; Bu, R.; Sun, M.; Wu, W.; Di, X.; Chen, B. Pointcnn: Convolution on x-transformed points. *Adv. Neural Inf. Process. Syst.* **2018**, *31*. [CrossRef]
38. Qian, G.; Li, Y.; Peng, H.; Mai, J.; Hammoud, H.; Elhoseiny, M.; Ghanem, B. Pointnext: Revisiting pointnet++ with improved training and scaling strategies. *Adv. Neural Inf. Process. Syst.* **2022**, *35*, 23192–23204. [CrossRef]
39. Tchapmi, L.; Choy, C.; Armeni, I.; Gwak, J.; Savarese, S. Segcloud: Semantic segmentation of 3D point clouds. In Proceedings of the 2017 International Conference on 3D Vision (3DV), Qingdao, China, 10–12 October 2017; pp. 537–547.
40. Aoki, Y.; Goforth, H.; Srivatsan, R.A.; Lucey, S. Pointnetlk: Robust & efficient point cloud registration using pointnet. In Proceedings of the IEEE/CVF Conference on Computer Vision and Pattern Recognition, Long Beach, CA, USA, 16–20 June 2019; pp. 7163–7172.
41. Huan, L.; Zheng, X.; Gong, J. GeoRec: Geometry-enhanced semantic 3D reconstruction of RGB-D indoor scenes. *ISPRS J. Photogramm. Remote Sens.* **2022**, *186*, 301–314. [CrossRef]
42. Tang, S.; Li, X.; Zheng, X.; Wu, B.; Wang, W.; Zhang, Y. BIM generation from 3D point clouds by combining 3D deep learning and improved morphological approach. *Autom. Constr.* **2022**, *141*, 104422. [CrossRef]
43. Campagnolo, D.; Camuffo, E.; Michieli, U.; Borin, P.; Milani, S.; Giordano, A. Fully Automated Scan-to-BIM Via Point Cloud Instance Segmentation. In Proceedings of the 2023 IEEE International Conference on Image Processing (ICIP), Kuala Lumpur, Malaysia, 8–11 October 2023.
44. Yijie, W.; Maosu, L.; Fan, X. Towards fully automatic Scan-to-BIM: A prototype method integrating deep neural networks and architectonic grammar. In Proceedings of the 2023 European Conference on Computing in Construction and the 40th International CIB W78 Conference, Heraklion, Greece, 10–12 July 2023.
45. Drobnyi, V.; Li, S.; Brilakis, I. Connectivity detection for automatic construction of building geometric digital twins. *Autom. Constr.* **2024**, *159*, 105281. [CrossRef]
46. Mahmoud, M.; Chen, W.; Yang, Y.; Yaxin, L. Automated BIM generation for large-scale indoor complex environments based on deep learning. *Autom. Constr.* **2024**, *162*, 105376. [CrossRef]

47. Han, J.; Rong, M.; Jiang, H.; Liu, H.; Shen, S. Vectorized indoor surface reconstruction from 3D point cloud with multistep 2D optimization. *ISPRS J. Photogramm. Remote Sens.* **2021**, *177*, 57–74. [CrossRef]
48. Saovana, N.; Yabuki, N.; Fukuda, T. Automated point cloud classification using an image-based instance segmentation for structure from motion. *Autom. Constr.* **2021**, *129*, 103804. [CrossRef]
49. Puliti, M.; Montaggioli, G.; Sabato, A. Automated subsurface defects' detection using point cloud reconstruction from infrared images. *Autom. Constr.* **2021**, *129*, 103829. [CrossRef]
50. Yang, J.; Shi, Z.-K.; Wu, Z.-Y. Towards automatic generation of as-built BIM: 3D building facade modeling and material recognition from images. *Int. J. Autom. Comput.* **2016**, *13*, 338–349. [CrossRef]
51. Mildenhall, B.; Srinivasan, P.P.; Tancik, M.; Barron, J.T.; Ramamoorthi, R.; Ng, R. Nerf: Representing scenes as neural radiance fields for view synthesis. *Commun. ACM* **2021**, *65*, 99–106. [CrossRef]
52. Müller, T.; Evans, A.; Schied, C.; Keller, A. Instant neural graphics primitives with a multiresolution hash encoding. *ACM Trans. Graph.* **2022**, *41*, 1–15. [CrossRef]
53. Tancik, M.; Weber, E.; Ng, E.; Li, R.; Yi, B.; Wang, T.; Kristoffersen, A.; Austin, J.; Salahi, K.; Ahuja, A. Nerfstudio: A modular framework for neural radiance field development. In Proceedings of the ACM SIGGRAPH 2023 Conference Proceedings, Los Angeles, CA, USA, 6–10 August 2023; pp. 1–12.
54. Kerbl, B.; Kopanas, G.; Leimkühler, T.; Drettakis, G. 3D gaussian splatting for real-time radiance field rendering. *ACM Trans. Graph.* **2023**, *42*, 139:1–139:14. [CrossRef]
55. Cheng, T.; Song, L.; Ge, Y.; Liu, W.; Wang, X.; Shan, Y. Yolo-world: Real-time open-vocabulary object detection. In Proceedings of the IEEE/CVF Conference on Computer Vision and Pattern Recognition, Long Beach, CA, USA, 16–20 June 2019; pp. 16901–16911.
56. Ravi, N.; Gabeur, V.; Hu, Y.-T.; Hu, R.; Ryali, C.; Ma, T.; Khedr, H.; Rädle, R.; Rolland, C.; Gustafson, L. Sam 2: Segment anything in images and videos. *arXiv* **2024**, arXiv:2408.00714.
57. Rusinkiewicz, S.; Levoy, M. Efficient variants of the ICP algorithm. In Proceedings of the Proceedings Third International Conference on 3D Digital Imaging and Modeling, Quebec City, QC, Canada, 28 May–1 June 2001; IEEE: New York, NY, USA, 2001.
58. Zhang, P.; Xiao, Y.; Wang, X.; Duan, B. Semantic segmentation of point clouds of field obstacle-crossing terrain for multi-legged rescue equipment based on random forest. In Proceedings of the 2020 International Conference on Artificial Intelligence and Electromechanical Automation (AIEA), Tianjin, China, 26–28 June 2020; IEEE: New York, NY, USA, 2020.
59. Khoshelham, K.; Tran, H.; Acharya, D.; Vilariño, L.D.; Kang, Z.; Dalyot, S. Results of the ISPRS benchmark on indoor modelling. *ISPRS Open J. Photogramm. Remote Sens.* **2021**, *2*, 100008. [CrossRef]
60. Stuart, L.A.; Pound, M.P. 3DGS-to-PC: Convert a 3D Gaussian Splatting Scene into a Dense Point Cloud or Mesh. *arXiv* **2025**, arXiv:2501.07478.
61. Mahmoud, M.; Zhao, Z.; Chen, W.; Adham, M.; Li, Y. Automated Scan-to-BIM: A deep learning-based framework for indoor environments with complex furniture elements. *J. Build. Eng.* **2025**, *106*, 112596. [CrossRef]
62. Mahmoud, M.; Li, Y.; Adham, M.; Chen, W. Automated material-aware BIM generation using deep learning for comprehensive indoor element reconstruction. *Autom. Constr.* **2025**, *175*, 106196. [CrossRef]
63. Mahmoud, M.; Chen, W.; Yang, Y.; Liu, T.; Li, Y. Leveraging Deep Learning for Automated Reconstruction of Indoor Unstructured Elements in Scan-to-BIM. *Int. Arch. Photogramm. Remote Sens. Spat. Inf. Sci.* **2024**, *48*, 479–486. [CrossRef]
64. Gao, X.; Yang, R.; Chen, X.; Tan, J.; Liu, Y.; Liu, S. Indoor scene reconstruction from LiDAR point cloud based on roof extraction. *J. Build. Eng.* **2024**, *97*, 110874. [CrossRef]
65. Hachisuka, S. *NeRF-to-BIM: Semantic Segmentation for Construction Project with Neural Radiance Fields*; Stanford University, Department of Civil and Environmental Engineering: Stanford, CA, USA, 2022.
66. Shun, H.; Alberto, T.; Martin, F. Harbingers of NeRF-to-BIM: A case study of semantic segmentation on building structure with neural radiance fields. In Proceedings of the 2023 European Conference on Computing in Construction and the 40th International CIB W78 Conference, Heraklion, Greece, 10–12 July 2023.
67. Li, Z.; Wang, Q.; Yue, H.; Nie, X. Toward Automatic 3D Model Reconstruction of Building Curtain Walls from UAV Images Based on NeRF and Deep Learning. *Remote Sens.* **2025**, *17*, 3368. [CrossRef]
68. Montas-Laracuente, N.; Delgado Martos, E.; Pesqueira-Calvo, C.; Intra Sidola, G.; Maitín, A.; Nogales, A.; García-Tejedor, Á.J. Automatic 3D Reconstruction: Mesh Extraction Based on Gaussian Splatting from Romanesque–Mudéjar Churches. *Appl. Sci.* **2025**, *15*, 8379. [CrossRef]

buildings

MDPI

Article

FP-MAE: A Self-Supervised Model for Floorplan Generation with Incomplete Inputs

Jing Zhong [1,†], Ran Luo [2,†], Peilin Li [3], Tianrui Li [1], Pengyu Zeng [1], Zhifeng Lei [1], Tianjing Feng [4,*] and Jun Yin [1,*]

1 Shenzhen International Graduate School, Tsinghua University, Shenzhen 518055, China; zhongj24@mails.tsinghua.edu.cn (J.Z.); ltr23@mails.tsinghua.edu.cn (T.L.); zeng-py24@mails.tsinghua.edu.cn (P.Z.); leizf24@mails.tsinghua.edu.cn (Z.L.)
2 School of Architecture, South China University of Technology, Guangzhou 510640, China; 201930093463@mail.scut.edu.cn
3 Department of Architecture, College of Design and Engineering, National University of Singapore, Singapore 117566, Singapore; e1351227@u.nus.edu
4 Institute for Environmental Design and Engineering, The Bartlett, University College London, London WC1H 0NN, UK
* Correspondence: ucbvtf1@ucl.ac.uk (T.F.); yinj24@mails.tsinghua.edu.cn (J.Y.)
† These authors contributed equally to this work.

Abstract

Floor plans are a central representational component of architectural design, operating in close relation to sections, elevations, and three-dimensional reasoning to support the production and understanding of architectural space. In this context, we address the bounded computational task of completing incomplete floor plan representations as a form of early-stage design assistance, rather than treating the floor plan as an isolated architectural object. Within this workflow, being able to automatically complete a floor plan from an unfinished draft is highly valuable because it allows architects to generate preliminary schemes more quickly, streamline early discussions, and reduce the repetitive workload involved in revisions. To meet this need, we present FP-MAE, a self-supervised learning framework designed for floor plan completion. This study proposes three core contributions: (1) We developed FloorplanNet, a dedicated dataset that includes 8000 floorplans consisting of both schematic line drawings and color-coded plans, providing diverse yet consistent examples of residential layouts. (2) On top of this dataset, FP-MAE applies the Masked Autoencoder (MAE) strategy. By deliberately masking sections of a plan and using a lightweight Vision Transformer (ViT) to reconstruct the missing regions, the model learns to capture the global structural patterns of floor plans from limited local information. (3) We evaluated FP-MAE across multiple masking scenarios and compared its performance with state-of-the-art baselines. Beyond controlled experiments, we also tested the model on real sketches produced during the early stages of design projects, which demonstrated its robustness under practical conditions. The results show that FP-MAE can produce complete plans that are both accurate and functionally coherent, even when starting from highly incomplete inputs. FP-MAE is a practical and scalable solution for automated floor plan generation. It can be integrated into design software as a supportive tool to speed up concept development and option exploration, and it also points toward broader opportunities for applying AI in architectural automation. While the current framework operates on two-dimensional plan representations, future extensions may integrate multi-view information such as sections or three-dimensional models to better reflect the relational nature of architectural design representations.

Keywords: architectural design; floor plan reconstruction; self-supervised learning; vision transformer; masked autoencoders

1. Introduction

1.1. Research Background

Architectural design is inherently an iterative and problem-solving process. Rather than producing complete solutions at once, architects typically begin with partial sketches or schematic floor plans and gradually refine them through repeated cycles of drawing, evaluation, and revision [1–6]. Design cognition research has long shown that sketching and diagramming are essential for externalizing thinking, supporting reflection, and fostering creativity in architectural practice [7,8]. In this sense, floor plans function not only as representational outputs but also as active cognitive tools throughout the design process. This iterative workflow is particularly evident in residential design, where the drafting and continuous modification of floor plans require significant expertise, time, and labor [3,9,10]. Early-stage designs often consist of incomplete or fragmented plans, yet transforming these drafts into coherent and viable layouts remains a labor-intensive task. Consequently, there is a growing demand for intelligent tools that can assist architects during the conceptual phase by accelerating iteration rather than replacing human judgment [11–15].

Within this context, automatic floor plan completion from partial sketches is not treated as an end in itself, but as a means to support architectural workflows. By inferring plausible spatial configurations from incomplete inputs, such systems can provide rapid visual feedback, generate alternative layouts, and reduce repetitive manual revisions. This early intervention of AI-based assistance has the potential to improve design efficiency, lower time and cost, and enrich design exploration, while keeping the architect's critical decision-making at the core of the process.

Modern computer vision techniques have advanced rapidly, but they typically require large amounts of data and extensive labeled images for supervised training [16]. In natural image domains, visual data often contain substantial redundancy, allowing missing regions to be inferred from surrounding context without requiring a deep understanding of high-level semantics [17,18]. Architectural floor plans, by contrast, are not generic visual images but domain-specific representations governed by design conventions, spatial typologies, and functional constraints. They are more structured, abstract, and semantically diverse than natural images [19–24]. As a result, models operating on floor plans must capture precise geometric relationships while also learning underlying design logic and functional zoning. This combination of geometric accuracy and semantic reasoning poses additional challenges for the generation and completion of architectural plans [25–29].

1.2. Contribution

To address these challenges, we first created a new architectural floor plan reconstruction dataset named FloorplanNet, which was designed to capture the complexity and diversity of residential architectural plans. This dataset contains a variety of residential building layouts and floor plan images (both line-drawing style and colored plans), providing rich resources for training and evaluating floor plan generation models.

Next, we propose a floor plan reconstruction method based on masked autoencoders, as illustrated in Figure 1. In this method, parts of the input floor plan are masked, and a lightweight Vision Transformer (ViT) model is trained to reconstruct the masked sections. In this way, the model learns to infer the complete floor plan structure from limited partial information. This approach employs a self-supervised learning paradigm, allowing the model's understanding of floor plan images to go beyond simple local features and instead capture global structural patterns.

https://doi.org/10.3390/buildings16030558

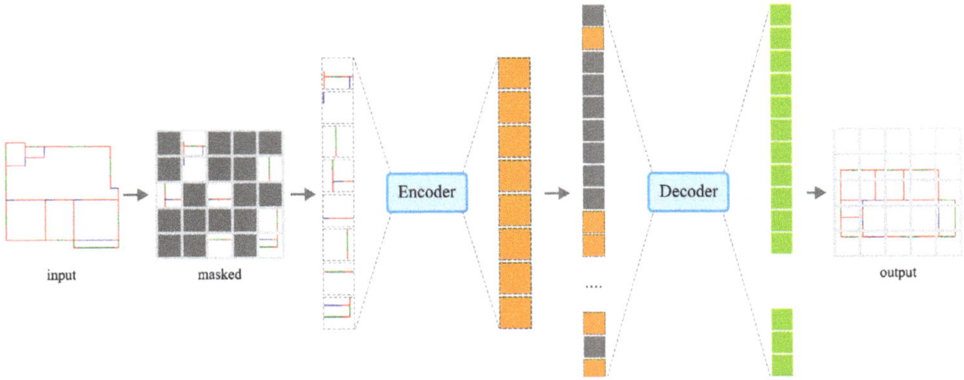

Figure 1. FP-MAE Architecture Diagram.

Moreover, we conducted extensive experiments to validate the effectiveness of our method. We evaluated the performance of FP-MAE in terms of reconstruction accuracy under various masking scenarios and compared it with current state-of-the-art models. Experimental results show that FP-MAE achieves outstanding performance in this kind of reconstruction task. Compared to existing models on automatic floor plan generation, our method directly addresses the critical task of floor plan completion from partial drawings, making a unique contribution to the field of computer-aided architectural design.

It is important to note that architectural sketches and partial drawings are, by nature, incomplete and open-ended. As a result, the completion of a partial floor plan should not be interpreted as a deterministic recovery of an author's original design intent, but rather as the generation of a plausible hypothesis under missing information. In practice, multiple valid completions may exist for the same partial input, and divergences between generated results and reference designs are therefore to be expected, especially in ambiguous cases.

Within this scope, FP-MAE is positioned not as a complete generative architectural design system, but as a representational and reconstructive baseline that learns strong plan-level priors from incomplete floor plan inputs through self-supervised learning. By enabling robust hypothesis generation under missing or degraded information, the proposed framework provides a foundational capability that can support future generative, constraint-aware, or context-integrated floor plan design workflows. Accordingly, the scope of this work is limited to building-scale floor plan representations, with a particular focus on residential layouts and early-stage plan completion or option exploration.

Rather than offering finalized designs, FP-MAE is positioned as an assistive tool that accelerates early phase iteration, where architects often explore multiple spatial configurations before refining structure, context, or program. The framework complements human design judgment by streamlining the generation of formal spatial proposals that can be further adapted to project specific needs.

2. Related Works

2.1. Application of Self-Supervised Learning

In the field of natural language processing (NLP) and computer vision (CV), self-supervised learning has become a highly influential pre-training method [30–36]. The core mechanism of this approach is masking certain parts of the input data and training the model to predict the missing parts, which can help the model to learn the inherent structure of the data [37–39]. In NLP, models like BERT [40] and GPT [41] use Masked Language Modeling (MLM) techniques, which involve randomly masking fragments of

https://doi.org/10.3390/buildings16030558

input text and training the model to predict the masked parts [42,43]. This approach has proven successful in capturing deep semantic features of language. In the field of computer vision, self-supervised learning has similarly shown great potential [44–46]. For instance, BEiT [47,48] introduced a form of masked image modeling by predicting masked discrete visual tokens within an image, analogous to the MLM method in NLP. Although BEiT demonstrated the promise of masked prediction in vision, its approach, which relied on a discrete VAE tokenizer, could be inefficient for high-resolution images and typically required a large amount of labeled data for fine-tuning to achieve strong performance [49,50]. These methods still face challenges when training on very large-scale datasets, and designing suitable pretext tasks often requires domain-specific knowledge.

In recent years, several masked modeling frameworks for images have further advanced self-supervised Vision Transformer (ViT) pre-training [51,52]. Masked Autoencoders (MAE) by He et al. [18] proposed a simple yet powerful approach: mask a high proportion of input image patches and train an asymmetric encoder–decoder to reconstruct the missing pixels, which showed that large ViT models can be effectively pre-trained without any labels by reconstructing masked images. Xie et al. introduced SimMIM [53], a simplified masked image modeling framework that forgoes complex tokenization or teacher networks, directly using pixel regression on masked patches as the pretext task. Another notable variant is iBOT [54], which uses a self-distillation approach where a teacher network provides target features for masked patches, allowing the model to learn high-level semantics beyond just pixel reconstruction. These self-supervised ViT variants have collectively established masked image modeling as an effective strategy for learning rich visual features without annotations. In parallel, recent architectural studies have shown that learning latent spatial representations from floor plan images can significantly improve generative and reconstruction tasks [55–57]. Our FP-MAE builds upon this line of work by adapting the masked autoencoding concept to the domain of architectural floor plans, which have unique structural characteristics compared to natural images.

2.2. Development of Autoencoders

Autoencoders (AEs) are a class of neural networks designed for learning compressed representations of data [58]. They consist of an encoder that maps input data to a lower-dimensional latent space and a decoder that reconstructs the original input from this latent code [59]. Denoising Autoencoders (DAEs) [60] is an extension of basic AEs, which introduce noise or corruptions into the input data to train the network to reconstruct the original, undamaged contents. This approach encourages the learned latent representation to capture features and enhances the model's robustness to input perturbations. The concept of autoencoders has further evolved into several variants, such as Variational Autoencoders (VAEs) [61], which impose a probabilistic structure on the latent space. VAEs learn not just a single deterministic code but a distribution over the latent space for each input, enabling generative sampling by decoding random latent vectors from the learned distribution. VAEs provide a powerful approach for generative modeling, though they may encounter issues like blurred outputs or mode collapse during training. Deepak Pathak et al. (2016) proposed a pioneering approach in the image inpainting domain by introducing a context encoder to generate missing image regions using surrounding context [62]. This demonstrated that meaningful visual features could be learned by predicting missing parts, marking a representative use of AE-like structures for image generation. Another notable development is Neural Discrete Representation Learning (2017), which introduced VQ-VAE [63], a variant of VAE that replaces continuous latent variables with discrete codes via a learnable codebook. This quantization mitigates posterior collapse, ensuring latent variables are not ignored by an overpowered decoder. Chen & Guo (2023) reviewed the

https://doi.org/10.3390/buildings16030558

applications and challenges of AEs in deep learning [64], pointing out that existing methods often face high computational costs when handling high-dimensional data.

With the rise of Vision Transformers and self-supervised learning, autoencoder-based frameworks have recently been revitalized in the form of masked autoencoders, which reconstruct missing image regions from sparsely observed inputs. In particular, masked image modeling methods explicitly remove a large portion of the input and train the network to recover the missing content, thereby encouraging the model to learn global structural and semantic information rather than relying on local texture cues. Recent studies further demonstrate that improvements in masking strategies and positional encoding can enhance reconstruction stability and spatial representation ability in masked autoencoder architectures [65].

In our work, the FP-MAE framework can be viewed as a form of masked autoencoder and we explicitly mask large portions of the input floor plan image and train the network to reconstruct the missing regions. This approach forces the model to capture the global floor plan structure and semantics, so that the decoder can regenerate missing parts. By doing so without needing ground-truth labels for what the missing part should contain, FP-MAE combines the strengths of autoencoder architectures with the masked prediction strategy from recent self-supervised ViT models.

2.3. Architectural Floor Plan Generation

In the field of architecture, the automatic generation of floor plans has emerged as a promising research direction aimed at improving design efficiency and quality through computational methods [66–72]. Early approaches to floor plan generation included rule-based algorithms or optimization techniques. For example, before the deep learning era, Merrell et al. (2010) [73] employed optimization to arrange rooms within a layout under given constraints, demonstrating the feasibility of automated layout synthesis. With the advent of deep learning, data-driven approaches have increasingly gained traction. Wu et al. (2019) [74] pioneered a large-scale data-driven technique for automatically generating residential floor plans given certain boundary constraints, such as a fixed external shape. They introduced the RPLAN dataset consisting of thousands of annotated floor plans and a model to generate interior layouts that fit a given building constraint. This work laid the data foundation for subsequent learning-based studies in floor plan generation.

More recently, graph-based deep learning methods have been proposed to address increasingly complex spatial relationships in floor plans. For instance, Lu et al. (2025) introduced a deep edge-aware graph neural network framework for large-scale floor plan generation, emphasizing non-local spatial dependencies and edge-specific relationships to better capture global layout structure, particularly for complex public buildings [67]. This line of work highlights the importance of explicitly modeling long-range spatial relations and architectural constraints when dealing with large and intricate layouts.

Several generative model frameworks have been explored for layout generation. Graph2Plan, proposed by Hu et al. (2020) [75], combines graph neural networks (GNNs) and CNN-based image generation to synthesize floor plan layouts from high-level graph specifications of room connectivity. In Graph2Plan, the input is a graph where nodes represent rooms and edges represent adjacency; the model learns to produce a floor plan that respects these topological constraints. Generative Adversarial Networks (GANs) have also been applied: HouseGAN [76] was one of the first GAN-based models to generate room layouts from scratch given a set of rooms and their relationships. It treats the floor plan as a graph-constrained generation problem and produces layouts that satisfy the input adjacency relationships. Nauata et al. (2021) later introduced House-GAN++ [77], a refined GAN-based layout generation method that improves diversity and precision of generated

 https://doi.org/10.3390/buildings16030558

layouts and even incorporates door placement into the generation process. House-GAN++ uses a more complex training setup and requires a rich database of design iterations to achieve good results, illustrating the challenge of applying GANs in this domain. More recently, diffusion models have shown superior capability in generative tasks. HouseDiffusion, proposed by Shabani et al. (2024) [78], is a diffusion-based method for generating vectorized floor plans under multiple conditioning constraints. It uses a diffusion process over floor plan representations (such as coordinates of walls and doors) to gradually produce realistic layouts. This approach improved the precision and diversity of generated plans and can incorporate conditions like user-specified room counts or functional zone locations. However, diffusion-based methods can struggle with highly complex layouts or strict constraints, as the multi-step generation may deviate from expectations without careful conditioning [79–81]. Other recent works have explored two-stage generation, which first generate a high-level bubble diagram or room adjacency graph, and then generate a consistent floor plan. For instance, Rahbar et al. (2022) [82] use a coarse-to-fine approach with a conditional GAN to refine a bubble diagram into a detailed plan. Transformer-based models have also been applied. Tang et al. (2023) [83] introduce a graph transformer to handle topological constraints, and Sun et al. (2022) [84] developed WallPlan, which uses a graph generation network for walls combined with a semantics network for room types. Upadhyay et al. (2023) [85] proposed an end-to-end layout generation method with minimal post-processing, further simplifying the pipeline. In parallel, recent studies have begun to explore progressive and interactive generation paradigms that better align with real-world architectural workflows. FloorPlan-DeepSeek (FPDS) proposes a vector-based, autoregressive "next room prediction" framework inspired by large language models, enabling incremental floor plan construction rather than one-shot generation [86]. By representing floor plans as sequences of room vectors and supporting conditional generation from partial layouts or textual prompts, FPDS emphasizes controllability, interpretability, and integration with human-in-the-loop design processes. In recent research, there have also been methods that combine natural language processing technology with building floor plan generation to improve user friendliness, such as Tell2Design [87], HouseLLM [88] and ChatHouseDiffusion [89].

Compared to the above-mentioned works that generate floor plans largely from scratch, given some input constraints like graphs or textual descriptions, our method focuses on the reconstruction or completion of architectural floor plans from partial inputs. This is a relatively under-explored scenario. One related recent study by Gueze et al. (2023) [90] addresses floor plan reconstruction from sparse views, using a graph neural network combined with a constrained diffusion model to infer a complete plan from a sparsely observed subset of rooms or walls. Their approach incorporates explicit architectural knowledge by using GNNs on partial graph data and then refining with diffusion. In contrast, our FP-MAE works directly on images of floor plans and does not require an explicit graph or constraint input. Partial floor plan representations, such as partially masked floor plan images or incomplete drawings that are consistent with the data distribution and masking strategies used in this study, can serve as input to the model. By leveraging a self-supervised masked autoencoder framework, FP-MAE learns to inpaint missing regions in floor plan images in a way that preserves global consistency and functional zoning. FP-MAE is one of the first self-supervised vision transformer approaches applied to architectural floor plan completion, which provides a novel perspective on floor plan generation. Rather than synthesizing designs from abstract specifications, we enable interactive design refinement, where an initial sketch drawn by an architect can be automatically completed into a reasonable full layout. This complementary direction has broad applications in computer-aided designs.

 https://doi.org/10.3390/buildings16030558

3. Methodology

In this section, we provide a detailed description of the FP-MAE architectural design, dataset construction, and training procedure. The FP-MAE model consists of two primary components: a lightweight Vision Transformer encoder and an asymmetric decoder, which together form a masked autoencoder tailored for floor plan reconstruction. We also discuss the key design decisions, including patch size, masking strategy, loss function, dataset and sampling settings.

The model was implemented in PyTorch 2.0 (Meta AI, Menlo Park, CA, USA) using Python 3.10 (Python Software Foundation, Wilmington, DE, USA), and trained with CUDA 11.8 (NVIDIA Corporation, Santa Clara, CA, USA) on NVIDIA RTX 4090 GPUs (NVIDIA Corporation, Santa Clara, CA, USA).

3.1. FP-MAE Encoder

Our encoder is based on a ViT architecture and operates only on the visible, unmasked image patches from the input floor plan. First, an input floor plan image of a fixed size is divided into regular, non-overlapping patches. Each visible patch is embedded by a linear projection to a latent vector, and positional embeddings are added to encode each patch's location within the floor plan. We then feed the set of embedded visible patch tokens through a series of Transformer encoder blocks. These Transformer blocks use self-attention to allow global information exchange among the visible tokens, enabling the model to capture relationships between distant parts of the floor plan. Notably, the encoder does not see or process the masked regions at all, which means no placeholder tokens for masked patches are input to the encoder. Through the encoding process, the model learns a latent representation encapsulating the layout structure present in the partial input.

3.2. FP-MAE Decoder

The decoder's role is to take the encoded representation of the visible patches and predict the content of the masked patches, thereby reconstructing the complete floor plan. The input to the decoder is the union of encoded visible patch tokens from the encoder and a set of mask tokens that serve as placeholders for each missing patch. Each mask token is a learned vector that indicates a placeholder where the model needs to fill in missing content. Before feeding into decoder Transformer blocks, we add positional embeddings to all tokens in this full token set, both encoded visible tokens and mask tokens. This step is important; without positional information, the decoder would not know where each mask token belongs, spatially in the floor plan image. After adding positional embeddings, we append the mask tokens to the sequence of encoder outputs, maintaining the correct order corresponding to original patch position, and feed the combined sequence into the decoder. The decoder then processes this full sequence through its own Transformer blocks. Essentially, the decoder learns to inpaint the masked areas based on the encoded context provided by the visible patches. Because the decoder has access to the mask tokens and the encodings of visible context, it can attend to both known and unknown regions and attempt to hallucinate plausible content for the unknown parts. We keep the decoder relatively shallow to ensure the overall model remains efficient; most of the model's capacity is concentrated in the encoder for feature learning, while the decoder is mainly tasked with reconstruction. This asymmetric encoder–decoder design has proven effective for floor plan reconstruction, particularly because large portions of the input may be missing, and a heavier decoder would risk overfitting to specific masking patterns seen during training.

 https://doi.org/10.3390/buildings16030558

3.3. Loss Function

The core goal of FP-MAE is to restore complete floor plans from partial ones, simplifying the frequent task of modifying floor plans during the architectural design process and intuitively inspiring architects in a fast manner. The FP-MAE framework for architectural floor plan reconstruction adopts a straightforward autoencoding method, reconstructing new image signals from partially obtained ones. We define the loss function as the Mean Squared Error (MSE) between the reconstructed and original images over the masked regions:

$$L_{\text{MAE}} = \frac{1}{N_{\text{mask}}} \sum_{i \in \text{mask}} (x_i - \hat{x}_i)^2$$

where x_i represents the i-th masked input data, $\hat{x}_i$ denotes the model's prediction for the i-th data point and N_{mask} indicates the number of masked input points. This loss function measures the average reconstruction error on the missing portions of the image. By minimizing this loss function, we can effectively update the model parameters, allowing the model to gradually learn how to reconstruct the masked portions of the images, thereby generating more accurate complete architectural floor plans. We found that a simple MSE loss was sufficient and effective, likely because floor plans are structurally constrained and relatively low-texture, so using MSE keeps the training objective straightforward and stable.

3.4. Dataset

The FloorplanNet dataset we utilized pertains to residential architectural floor plans, consisting of 300 collected Real-plan floor plans and 7700 standardized R-plan floor plans, which include colored plans and line drawings. In the line drawing subset, where standardized layouts are generated by the RPLAN toolbox, different colors represent various architectural components, as illustrated in Figure 2.

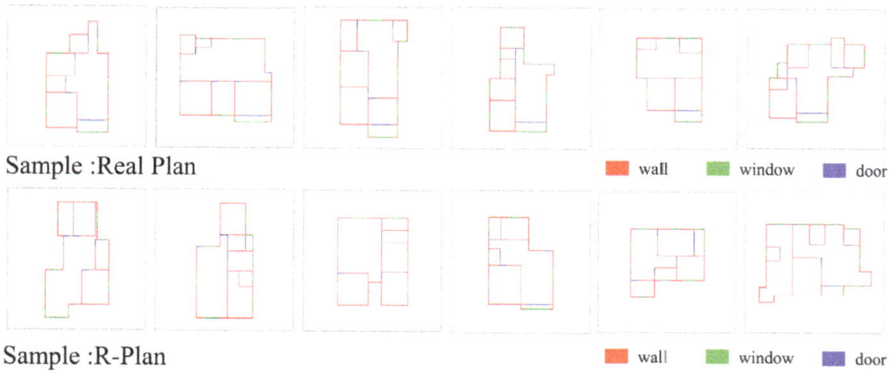

Figure 2. Illustration of the line drawing floor plan subset.

The colored floor plans subset, as shown in Figure 3, depict different residential layouts, with various colors and shapes denoting different room types or functional area (bedrooms, bathrooms, kitchen, living room, and balcony), providing semantic cues.

Both subsets are accompanied by detailed labels and metadata, which not only enrich the dataset but also ensure the robustness and broad applicability of the experimental results. Although our FP-MAE training uses only the raw images, the diversity and scale of FloorplanNet make it well-suited for training our self-supervised model and evaluating its generalization. Taken together, these components make FloorplanNet a comprehensive dataset for the evaluation of architectural floor plan reconstruction methods.

https://doi.org/10.3390/buildings16030558

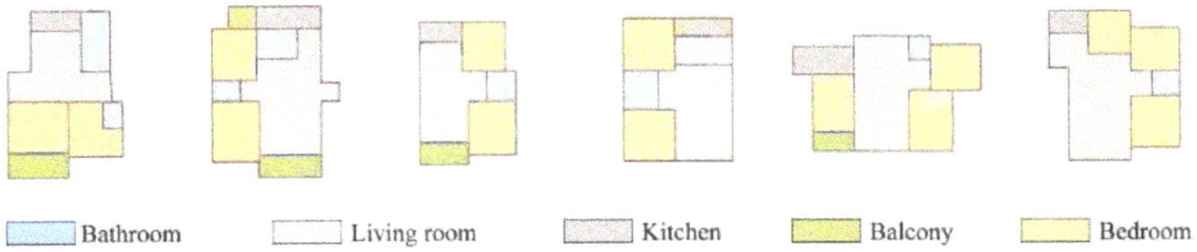

Figure 3. Illustration of the colored drawing floor plan subset.

It is worth noting that FloorplanNet is intentionally constructed with a focus on residential layouts, providing a controlled and well-defined domain for studying floor plan completion. This design choice allows the model to learn stable spatial priors under consistent functional and regulatory conditions. At the same time, it establishes a clear baseline from which future research can expand toward more complex building typologies, such as office buildings, public facilities, and mixed-use developments, each of which introduces distinct spatial organizations and design constraints. In this sense, FloorplanNet serves as a targeted and extensible dataset rather than a fixed representation of architectural form.

3.5. Sampling Strategies

We divide architectural floor plans into regular, non-overlapping image patches. We then sample a portion of these patches and mask the remaining ones. As shown in Figure 4, our sampling strategy starts with random sampling: small patches are randomly selected without replacement, following a uniform distribution. The advantages of using random sampling are as follows:

(1) High random sampling and masking reduce redundancy, turning patch reconstruction into extrapolation from masked neighbors.
(2) Uniform distribution avoids central bias, but diverse sampling strategies are used due to uneven information distribution in floor plans.
(3) We apply large-scale masking to provide the encoder with ample room to operate efficiently, using sparse input image patches to predict an entire architectural floor plan from limited information.

Figure 4. Random Masking Method.

4. Experiments

4.1. Self-Supervised Pretraining

We train FP-MAE in a self-supervised manner, using only incomplete floor plan images and their original complete versions without external labels. To generate training data, we take images from our FloorplanNet dataset and randomly mask out portions of each image

https://doi.org/10.3390/buildings16030558

(details on masking strategies follow in Section 4.2). The model is then trained to predict the missing parts. We divided the FloorplanNet dataset into training, validation, and test sets, containing 7000, 500, and 500 floor plan images, respectively. During training, only the training set images are used for learning. We monitor performance on the validation set, which is also with masks applied, to tune hyperparameters and decide when to stop training.

We also experimented with data augmentation to improve generalization. We found that heavy augmentations were not necessary for FP-MAE. The model performed very well even with only basic geometric augmentations like random cropping and horizontal flipping. In fact, we observed that augmentations which alter the color or brightness of the floor plans tended to hurt performance. This is likely because in our dataset, different room types or architectural elements are color-coded, so altering colors confuses the model. Therefore, we avoided color-based augmentations and mainly used random crops, random resized crops and flips during training to inject some variation. The training procedure thus largely teaches the model to reconstruct missing parts under a distribution of partial observations that include random spatial variations but preserves the inherent structural and color patterns of floor plans.

4.2. Masking and Sampling Strategies

A key aspect of our methodology is the strategy used to mask parts of the floor plan during training. As shown in Figure 5, we employed multiple masking strategies to diversify the training scenarios and simulate practical use cases. We began with a random sampling masking strategy, randomly selecting a portion of the floor plan patches for masking. By doing so, the model is forced to infer the complete floor plan structure from limited information. We found that, unlike natural images where relatively lower masking ratios are typically adopted, architectural floor plans benefit from a higher masking ratio (e.g., 75%). In our experiments, such high masking not only proved feasible but also encouraged the model to learn the global structure and semantic information of the entire plan. This is because floor plans inherently exhibit more repetitive and constrained spatial patterns, such as wall continuity and room arrangements, which allow the model to infer missing regions effectively even with fewer visible clues.

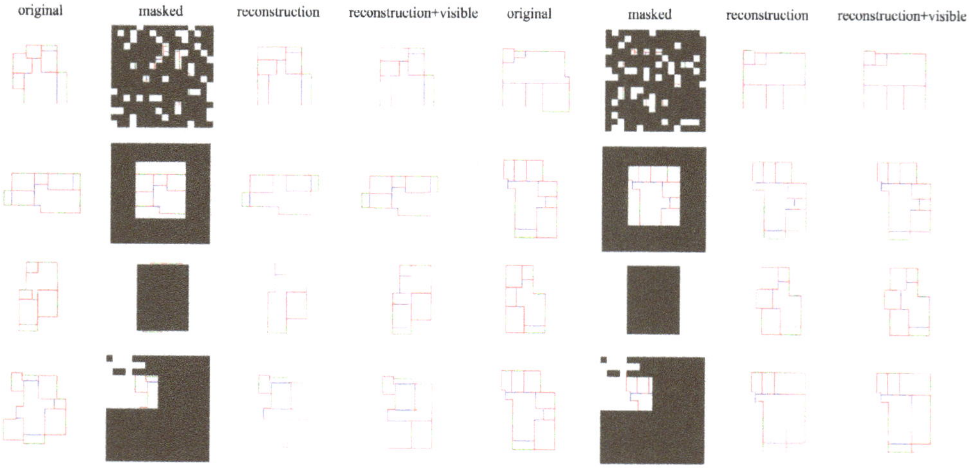

Figure 5. Example Results Comparison of Different Masking Strategies.

https://doi.org/10.3390/buildings16030558

If the model is trained exclusively with purely random masks, it may fail to generalize to the types of structured missing regions that frequently occur in real design practice. For instance, when an architect deliberately leaves an entire portion of the drawing blank for later refinement. To approximate such scenarios, we introduced several alternative masking strategies, including center sampling, edge sampling, one-sided sampling and so on. These strategies mask larger, contiguous regions of the floor plan, requiring FP-MAE to reconstruct missing content from broader contextual cues rather than evenly scattered fragments. It should be noted that these geometric masking patterns are introduced as a controlled abstraction to systematically study missing regions during training and evaluation, rather than as a faithful representation of real architectural sketch incompleteness.

Our experiments reveal that reconstruction quality is not only determined by the amount of visible information, but also closely tied to the spatial distribution of patches. With a fixed patch size, more uniform distributions tend to yield clearer and more coherent results, while irregular arrangements often produce degraded outputs. Furthermore, we observed an intriguing phenomenon: as the distance between masked and visible patches increases, the reconstructed regions become visually blurrier and less precise, yet the reconstruction task paradoxically becomes easier. In these cases, the model can rely on structural regularities in floor plans (such as wall continuity or typical room arrangements) to generate plausible completions without being constrained by fine-grained details.

These findings underscore the importance of tailoring masking strategies to the unique characteristics of architectural drawings, rather than relying solely on approaches developed for natural images. By employing a variety of masking and sampling strategies, we ensure that FP-MAE is robust to diverse partial input scenarios. Whether the missing data is randomly distributed or concentrated in a specific region, the model has encountered similar situations during training and learned to handle them effectively.

4.3. Qualitative Experimental Results

In this section, we present the reconstruction results of FP-MAE under different masking strategies and compare its performance under varying conditions. Below is an analysis of the experimental results for each strategy:

(1) Random Masking (80% masked): Figures 6 and 7 show examples of FP-MAE reconstructions where the input patches were randomly masked (Figure 6 for a line-drawing plan, Figure 7 for a colored plan). Despite the extremely large amount of missing information, the model is still able to restore a reasonable architectural floor plan structure and make local adjustments that align with the visible content. In the line drawing case, the input might have only sparse wall segments and a few visible corners. FP-MAE completes the structure by drawing walls that enclose spaces, effectively guessing the presence of rooms. One can see that the primary functional zoning remains clear in the output. Some small details are understandably imperfect, for example, the exact positions of doors and windows in the reconstructed portion may not match the original and room dimensions might be slightly off, since multiple configurations could satisfy the limited cues. In the colored plan case, FP-MAE not only reconstructs the walls but also fills the correct color in many areas, indicating it inferred the room types. However, those differences do not detract from the overall feasibility of the layout, and an architect could take the output for a valid design. It should be noted that FP-MAE operates at the level of two-dimensional plan configuration and does not model experiential or inhabitation-related aspects of space symbolized by the walls. These results highlight FP-MAE's ability to perform extrapolation: given disjoint glimpses of a layout, it extrapolates the likely connecting structure.

https://doi.org/10.3390/buildings16030558

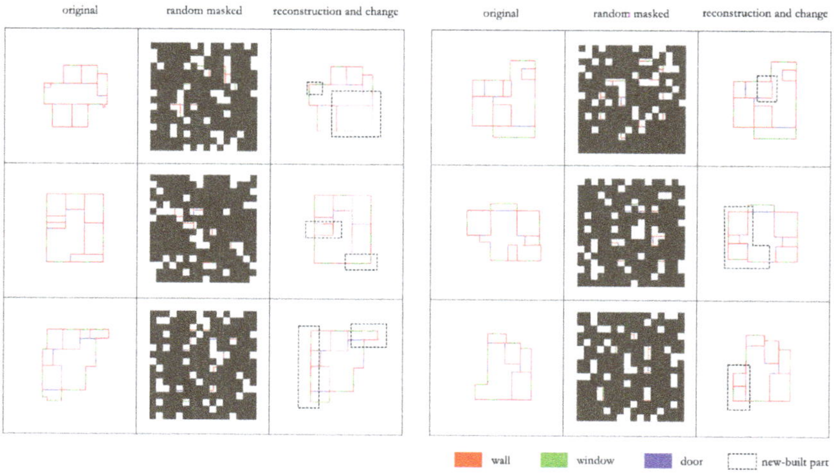

Figure 6. Detailed Diagram of Random Masking—Line Drawing.

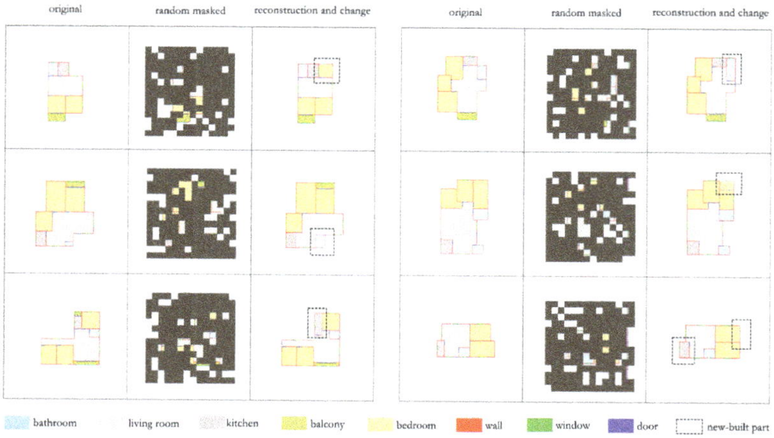

Figure 7. Detailed Diagram of Random Masking—Colored Floor Plan.

(2) Center Masking (30% masked in center): Figure 8 provides examples where the entire center of the floor plan was missing, and the input had only the outer frame, like an empty house outline with some peripheral rooms drawn. FP-MAE's output in this case successfully reconstructs the main internal layout. We do notice in such cases that while the structure is usually dead-on, with walls aligning perfectly with existing ones at the boundary of the masked area, the content of the central reconstructed area can have more variability. For instance, the model might place two small rooms where the original had one large room. This reflects the model's training to minimize MSE loss, and in ambiguous situations it might produce an "average" solution or select one plausible option among many. Despite this, crucial architectural elements like continuity of walls and maintaining accessible pathways were satisfied. These cases show that FP-MAE has a good understanding of how rooms typically connect in a residential layout even if the middle portion is unseen.

https://doi.org/10.3390/buildings16030558

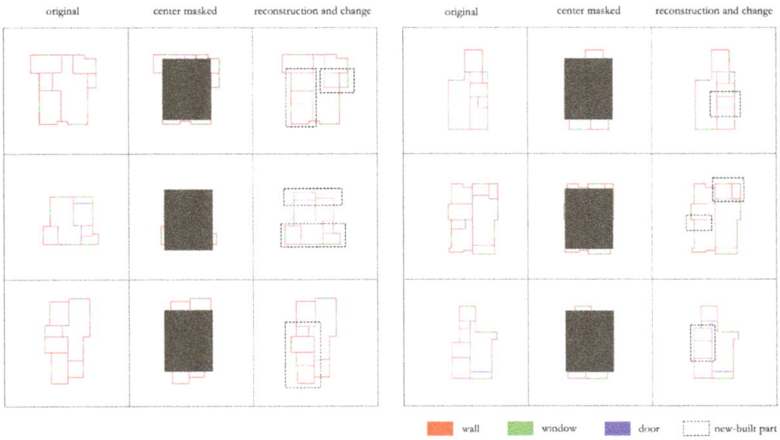

Figure 8. Detailed Diagram of Center Masking.

(3) Perimeter (Edge) Masking (70% edges masked): Figure 9 shows an example input where the border of the floor plan is missing, and only some interior rooms are visible, along with FP-MAE's reconstruction of the perimeter. The model effectively restores the outline of the house, adding exterior walls that close off the layout. If the visible interior suggested a rectangular overall shape, the output reflected that shape at the edges. In the illustrated output, edge rooms that were entirely masked are reconstructed; for instance, an edge might show a balcony connecting to the interior. These reconstructed edge rooms display slight variations: sometimes the model may not perfectly recover their exact shape or may confuse a balcony with a room due to limited evidence. Nonetheless, FP-MAE consistently generates plausible completions in masked edge regions, rather than leaving gaps. In practical applications, this ability enables the model to suggest extensions for a partially drawn interior plan.

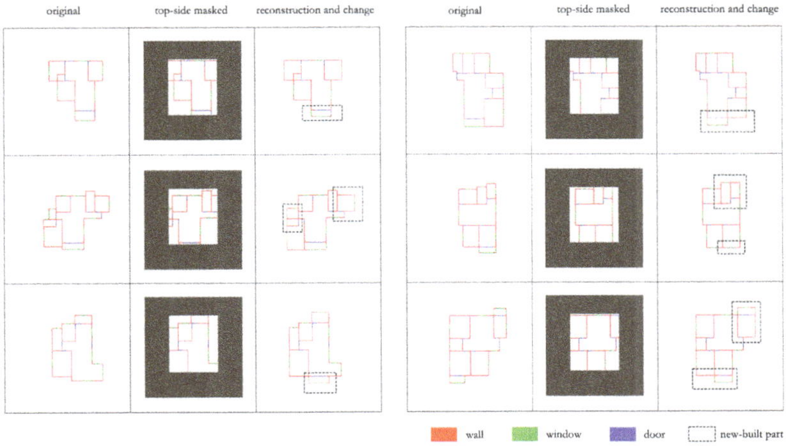

Figure 9. Detailed Diagram of Perimeter Masking.

(4) Spotted-perimeter Masking (75% masked): Figure 10 presents an example input where the outer boundary and some central patches of the floor plan are masked, leaving only discontinuous central fragments visible. Unlike edge masking, which only removes the entire outline, spotted-perimeter masking adds intermittent gaps in the center, forcing FP-MAE to reconstruct the overall outline and simultaneously fill

 https://doi.org/10.3390/buildings16030558

in missing central details. In this scenario, the model attempts to close the layout by extrapolating exterior walls and reconstructing rooms attached to the edge. Because as much as 75% of the plan is missing, the reconstructed results often appear simplified or slightly blurred. Certain details, such as window placement or exact room proportions, may be inaccurately inferred, and in some cases the model may misalign confuse a balcony or a small room. Nevertheless, FP-MAE consistently produces a coherent and plausible boundary rather than leaving large gaps. This shows that even under extremely sparse input conditions, the model retains sufficient prior knowledge to imagine reasonable edge structures. In practical applications, this means that spotted-perimeter masking could support early-stage design tasks in which only a small portion of the layout is provided, offering plausible completions of the entire plan.

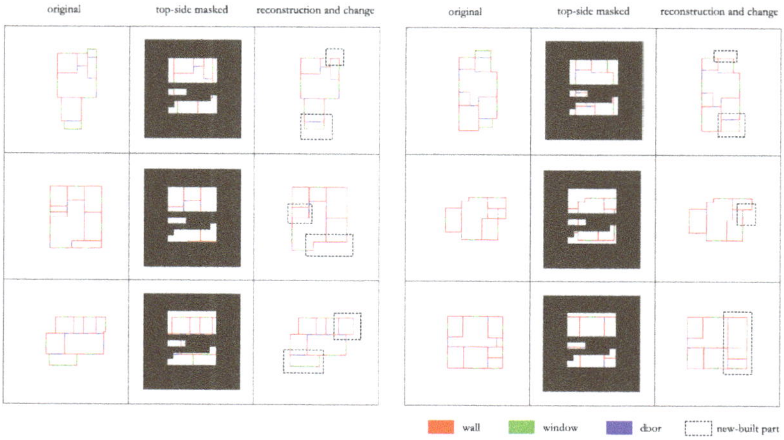

Figure 10. Detailed Diagram of Spotted-perimeter Masking.

(5) Biased-keyhole Masking (90% masked): Figure 11 shows an extreme case in which only a very small "keyhole-shaped" region of the floor plan is left visible, while the remaining 90% of the layout is masked. This setting emulates a scenario where only a limited fragment of the design is available, for instance a small corner or partial core, while the remainder of the plan is left unspecified. FP-MAE must therefore extrapolate nearly the entire structure from this narrow clue. In the reconstructed outputs, the model attempts to extend the visible fragment into a complete house layout. For example, if the revealed patch suggests part of a corridor or a wall junction, FP-MAE generates surrounding rooms and boundaries consistent with that structure. However, given the extreme sparsity of information, the results tend to be simplified and blurred. Fine elements such as windows, doors, or exact proportions are often missing or roughly approximated. Some reconstructed walls also exhibit lower contrast and slight misalignment, reflecting the uncertainty of inferring large-scale structure from minimal evidence. Despite these challenges, FP-MAE still produces layouts that are structurally coherent rather than chaotic, filling masked regions with plausible room divisions and exterior walls. This demonstrates the model's ability to rely on strong prior knowledge of floor plan regularities, even when trained under very sparse conditions.

https://doi.org/10.3390/buildings16030558

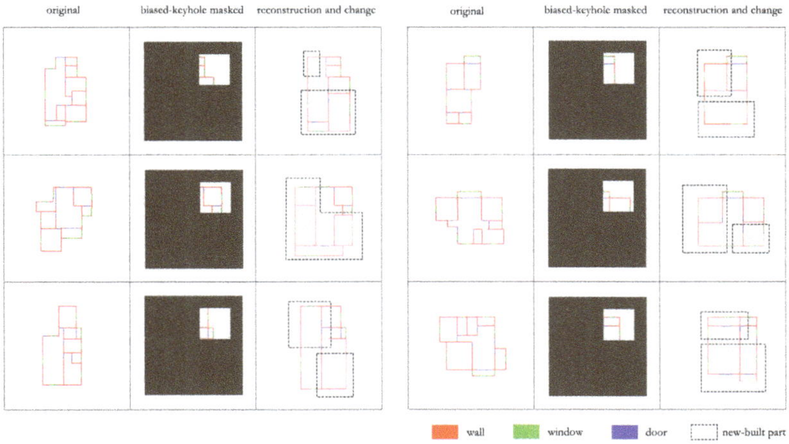

Figure 11. Detailed Diagram of Biased-keyhole Masking.

(6) One-Sided Masking (30% missing one side): It refers to a strategy in which only a single boundary of the floor plan image is masked. This setting emulates realistic design scenarios where architects extend or modify a specific edge of a layout, such as adding new rooms to one wing of a house or expanding a facade. In our implementation, we systematically masked either the top, bottom, or right side of the plan in separate experiments, thereby creating diverse but structured missing regions. A masking ratio of approximately 30% was applied to these boundary regions, indicated as gray blocks in Figure 12. This level of masking was carefully selected to preserve most of the original spatial organization while still introducing a meaningful reconstruction challenge. Because the essential layout remains visible, FP-MAE can effectively leverage the intact structural cues to infer the missing parts. The model not only restores the broader spatial configuration but also accurately reconstructs fine-grained elements such as walls, doors, and room boundaries. The results demonstrate that one-sided masking allows FP-MAE to excel at producing reconstructions that are both structurally coherent and visually convincing, highlighting its ability to generalize even when large continuous areas are absent.

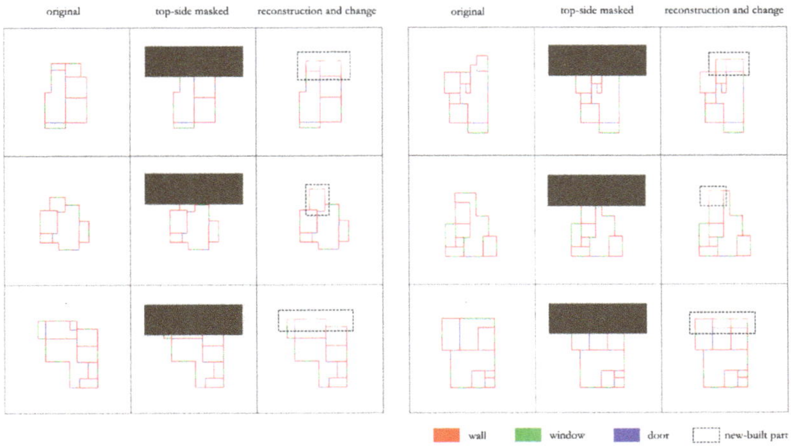

Figure 12. *Cont.*

https://doi.org/10.3390/buildings16030558

Figure 12. Detailed Diagram of One-Sided Masking.

(7) Corner Masking (75% masked, only a corner visible): Figure 13 provides an example with only a small top-left corner of the floor plan given and everything else masked. The output in this case shows the model's attempt to imagine the rest of the house. In the example, the visible corner might contain a bedroom. FP-MAE then conjectured a layout that extends from that bedroom—it might add a living room adjacent to it, bedrooms on the other end, etc. The reconstructed areas are a bit more generic: walls are correctly placed to form rooms, but one can see they are somewhat simplified or blurred in drawing quality. For instance, windows might be missing or roughly placed since the model is less certain where they should go. Some walls may also appear with lower contrast or slight misalignment as the model balances many possibilities. Still, the output is a valid floor plan. It is impressive that with a tiny fraction of input, the model does not produce chaotic lines; instead, it outputs a structured set of spaces. This demonstrates strong prior knowledge learned by FP-MAE about what constitutes a plausible floor plan.

https://doi.org/10.3390/buildings16030558

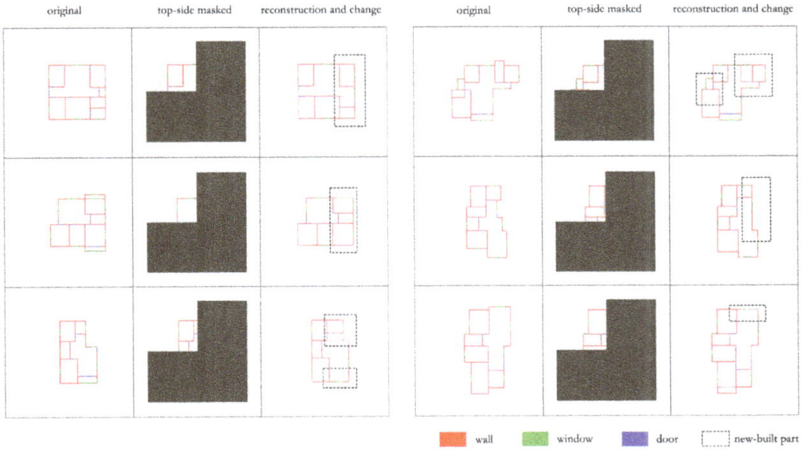

Figure 13. Detailed Diagram of Corner Masking.

(8) Spotted-corner Masking (80% masked): Figure 14 illustrates an input where most of the floor plan is obscured, leaving only a fragmented corner region partially visible. Unlike standard corner masking, where a single continuous corner is revealed, spotted-corner masking introduces discontinuous patches in the top-left corner area. This makes the reconstruction task even more challenging, as FP-MAE must infer the overall layout from scattered local clues rather than a single coherent boundary. In the outputs, the model extends the incomplete fragments into a full residential layout. For instance, if a visible fragment suggests part of a balcony or corridor, FP-MAE extrapolates plausible adjacent spaces, adding living areas or bedrooms in reasonable positions. However, due to the high masking ratio (80% of the plan missing) and the fragmented nature of the input, the reconstructions often appear blurred or simplified. Windows and doors may be roughly placed or omitted, and some walls show reduced contrast or slight misalignment. Nevertheless, FP-MAE consistently produces structured and coherent layouts rather than chaotic lines. Even with such limited and discontinuous input, the model leverages strong architectural priors to fill in plausible spaces, demonstrating its robustness in handling highly sparse and irregular masking scenarios.

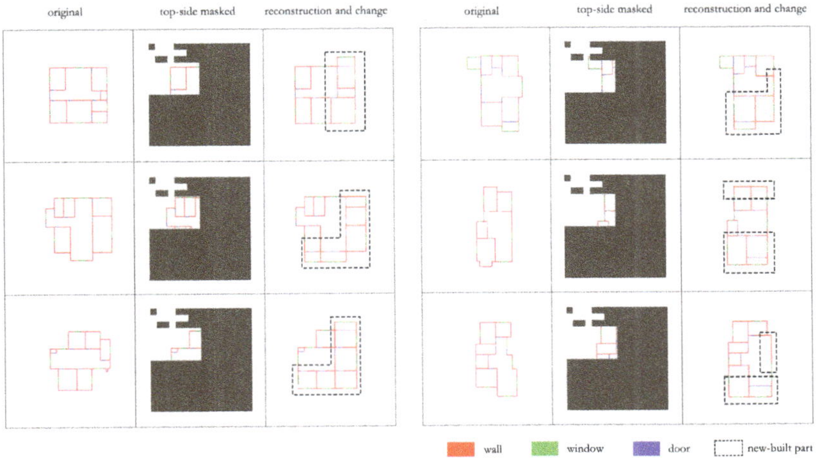

Figure 14. Detailed Diagram of Spotted-corner Masking.

https://doi.org/10.3390/buildings16030558

Overall, the qualitative experiments confirm that FP-MAE successfully learns to complete floor plan drawings in a variety of scenarios. It respects architectural conventions (e.g., aligning walls, preserving room adjacencies, not blocking circulation paths) even when guessing large parts of the layout. The model effectively generalizes from common patterns in the training data, which means it can serve as a smart assistant for architects given a sketch or partial plan, it produces a reasonable complete plan that can then be further refined.

4.4. Quantitative Experimental Results

To quantitatively evaluate FP-MAE, we computed several image-based metrics that are commonly used to assess image reconstruction quality: FID (Fréchet Inception Distance), PSNR (Peak Signal-to-Noise Ratio), and SSIM (Structural Similarity Index). We evaluated these metrics on the test set of FloorplanNet under various masking strategies, and we also compare FP-MAE with two baseline methods: Pix2Pix and CycleGAN, which were trained or tuned for the floor plan completion task.

Table 1 summarizes the results. We report metrics for FP-MAE under eight representative masking scenarios on the line drawing floor plan images. We also include FP-MAE's performance on the colored floor plan images under the random masking scenario to show its effectiveness on colored inputs. Finally, we list the performance of Pix2Pix and CycleGAN on the line drawing task with random masking for comparison. In each column, higher PSNR/SSIM and lower FID indicate better reconstruction quality, and the best result for each metric is bold.

Table 1. Results on FloorPlanNet. The best results are indicated in bold.

Method	DATA	FID	PSNR	SSIM
Random Masking	Line Drawing	12.6053	79.7688	0.9757
Random Masking	Colored Drawing	17.2192	79.7638	0.9724
Center Masking	Line Drawing	22.0109	77.7863	0.9738
Perimeter Masking	Line Drawing	12.4044	78.6158	0.9609
Spotted-perimeter Masking	Line Drawing	16.8733	79.3059	0.9637
Biased-keyhole Masking	Line Drawing	17.4593	79.3542	0.9632
One-sided Masking	Line Drawing	**8.84111**	**80.1424**	**0.9794**
Corner Masking	Line Drawing	27.3668	76.0285	0.9247
Spotted-corner Masking	Line Drawing	19.3524	81.3495	0.9423
Pix2Pix	Line Drawing	76.3275	68.3546	0.9334
CycleGan	Line Drawing	90.3235	64.3487	0.9468

5. Discussion and Conclusions

Our experimental results clearly demonstrate that FP-MAE achieves outstanding performance in the task of floor plan reconstruction, providing strong evidence for the promise of self-supervised learning methods in architectural design automation. Unlike traditional supervised approaches that depend on large volumes of carefully annotated data, FP-MAE leverages the intrinsic structure of floor plans through a self-supervised masking strategy. By reconstructing missing regions of an image, the model is encouraged to learn rich structural and semantic representations without explicit labels. This learning paradigm not only reduces the cost of data preparation but also offers a scalable solution that can be generalized to diverse architectural contexts.

5.1. Contribution to Architectural Image Completion

One of the core contributions of FP-MAE lies in the introduction of a novel architecture for architectural image completion. While masked autoencoders have been extensively

 https://doi.org/10.3390/buildings16030558

studied in natural image domains, their adaptation to architectural drawings presents distinct challenges. Architectural floor plans are abstract representations that encode geometric relationships, circulation patterns, and functional zoning. Unlike natural images, where local texture redundancy often allows simple patch-based inference, floor plans require strong global structural coherence. Even minor geometric deviations, such as a misplaced wall segment, can fundamentally alter circulation, adjacency, and usability. To address these characteristics, FP-MAE adopts a Vision Transformer–based architecture, which is particularly well suited to capturing long-range spatial dependencies across an entire plan that are difficult to model with conventional convolutional networks. This design enables the model to reason about architectural structure beyond local neighborhoods, prioritizing representational capacity and global consistency. Our experimental results demonstrate that FP-MAE preserves structural integrity in reconstructed plans, maintaining both local detail and overall spatial logic even under severe masking conditions. At the same time, the transformer-based formulation establishes a flexible foundation for future efficiency-oriented extensions. Promising directions include exploring lighter transformer variants, reducing model depth or attention heads, and applying model compression or knowledge distillation techniques to transfer learned spatial priors into more compact architectures. Moreover, the self-supervised pretraining stage can be performed offline or centrally, allowing downstream fine-tuning or inference with substantially reduced computational requirements. Together, these directions outline a clear pathway toward improving the accessibility and scalability of FP-MAE for broader architectural practice contexts without compromising its core architectural capabilities.

Alongside the model, we also introduced a new dataset, FloorplanNet, specifically tailored to the architectural domain. This dataset encompasses a wide range of residential layouts represented in both line drawings and colored semantic floorplans. Such diversity allows FP-MAE to learn not only geometric continuity but also semantic regularities, such as the placement of bedrooms adjacent to bathrooms or kitchens connected to living rooms. The combination of model and dataset forms a unified framework that pushes the boundary of how self-supervised learning can be applied in architecture.

A particularly noteworthy outcome of our study is the model's ability to capture pixel-level details while simultaneously demonstrating a deeper understanding of architectural semantics. In many experiments, FP-MAE successfully reconstructed fine features such as door openings, room boundaries, and circulation corridors, even when these regions were completely masked. More importantly, the reconstructions were functionally coherent, preserving adjacent relationships that align with architectural norms. This suggests that the model is not simply memorizing patterns but is internalizing design logic that governs spatial organization. Such a capability is significant because it points toward the possibility of using self-supervised learning not just for visual restoration but for capturing design knowledge embedded in floor plans. This knowledge could later be leveraged for tasks such as automated space evaluation, circulation optimization, or even the generation of entirely new layouts conditioned on specific requirements.

5.2. Implications for Architectural Practice

Beyond technical performance, FP-MAE has important implications for architectural practice. Rather than replacing architectural authorship, the framework can be used as an optional digital assistant to support the exploration of alternative plan configurations and to reduce repetitive redrawing during early design iterations. In early-stage design, where rapid iteration is essential, FP-MAE can provide immediate feedback by completing partially sketched ideas into coherent layouts. This capability may support iterative

https://doi.org/10.3390/buildings16030558

comparison and discussion of design alternatives, while preserving the central role of the architect in evaluating, refining, and validating spatial decisions.

In architectural education, FP-MAE-like tools can facilitate learning by making spatial organization more explicit. Students often struggle to translate abstract concepts into coherent floor plans and to understand the implications of partial design decisions. A system that completes incomplete sketches offers immediate visual feedback, helping students grasp spatial relationships, circulation patterns, and programmatic logic. Recent research indicates that generative AI can support design pedagogy by acting as an active collaborator in exploratory learning processes [91]. Within studio teaching, FP-MAE can encourage iterative experimentation by lowering the cost of revision and allowing students to quickly test and refine design ideas.

FP-MAE also has potential applications in historical building preservation and digital reconstruction. Many historical floor plans are incomplete, damaged, or fragmentary, limiting their usability for architectural analysis and conservation. Recent machine learning research has demonstrated the feasibility of reconstructing missing architectural elements from partial historical drawings [92,93]. In this context, FP-MAE can assist in inferring plausible completions of missing plan segments that are consistent with the spatial logic and conventions of a given historical period. Such reconstructions can support restoration analysis, comparative studies, and the digital documentation of architectural heritage.

5.3. Limitations and Future Research Directions

Although FP-MAE demonstrates clear advantages, it is important to acknowledge the limitations of the current study. First, while the reconstructions are structurally sound, there remain cases where finer details such as window placement or exact dimensions deviate from the ground truth. These deviations highlight the challenge of aligning pixel-level fidelity with semantic accuracy. Future work could address this by incorporating geometric constraints into the reconstruction process, ensuring that generated walls remain orthogonal or that circulation paths remain accessible. Beyond plan-internal geometry, real-world architectural applications are also shaped by external constraints such as climatic conditions, geographical context, and regulatory or environmental requirements, which are not considered in the current framework but could be integrated in future extensions. However, real architectural sketches often exhibit heterogeneous incompleteness, where partial lines, local continuities, and corrections coexist within the same drawing, introducing levels of ambiguity that are not captured by the current masking schemes. Extending the framework to account for such sketch-level uncertainty, for example through stroke-based, vectorized, or graph-based representations, represents an important direction for future research. It should be emphasized that the outputs of FP-MAE are speculative reconstructions intended to support human interpretation, rather than authoritative or definitive design decisions. Under highly ambiguous or underspecified inputs, the model may generate plausible but incorrect or undesired configurations, and human oversight remains essential.

Second, the current study establishes a foundation for several promising research directions. While the present experiments focus on residential floor plans, this setting provides a stable testbed for developing and validating self-supervised reconstruction strategies. However, architectural practice spans a much broader range of building typologies, including offices, educational facilities, healthcare buildings, and large public spaces, each characterized by distinct spatial logics and regulatory constraints. Extending FP-MAE to these typologies would significantly broaden its applicability and offer a rigorous evaluation of the model's robustness under more complex functional conditions. In parallel, expanding the dataset in scale and geographic diversity would enable the model to capture cross-regional and cross-cultural variations in architectural conventions and spatial norms,

https://doi.org/10.3390/buildings16030558

leading to more generalized and transferable representations. Beyond individual buildings, future work may also explore extensions to the urban scale, where predictive and assistive modeling can support scenario-based analysis of land use and long-term development, serving as a suggestive tool for planning and policy rather than a deterministic solution.

Third, while our self-supervised approach eliminates the need for labeled data, it may benefit from multimodal integration. For instance, combining floor plan images with textual descriptions of programmatic requirements could allow the model to generate reconstructions that are not only structurally plausible but also aligned with user intent. Similarly, extending FP-MAE to operate on 3D building layouts or multi-level floor plans would open new avenues for real-world application.

Another important direction for future research concerns robustness and generalization under more heterogeneous input conditions. In the present study, FP-MAE is evaluated using controlled masking strategies that provide a systematic and reproducible way to analyze reconstruction behavior under varying degrees of incompleteness. These settings establish a clear baseline for understanding how the model extrapolates global structure from partial observations. Building on this foundation, future work will extend evaluation to more sketch-like inputs that better reflect real design practice, including freehand drawings with irregular proportions, uneven line quality, and localized noise. In addition, more complex and unstructured occlusion patterns, such as irregular gaps, fragmented strokes, or non-contiguous missing regions, will be explored to approximate real-world sketching and revision scenarios. These extensions will enable a more comprehensive assessment of FP-MAE's robustness while further strengthening its applicability to early-stage architectural workflows.

An additional avenue for future research concerns the qualitative assessment and functional usability of reconstructed floor plans. While the present study focuses on image-based reconstruction metrics to establish a clear and reproducible baseline, future extensions can incorporate architecture-aware evaluation criteria that reflect functional and spatial performance. Recent studies have proposed dedicated spatial and graph-based metrics to quantify aspects such as room accessibility, adjacency logic, and proportional consistency, offering a promising complement to visual similarity measures [26]. In addition, rule-based checks or lightweight constraint validation modules could be integrated to flag implausible proportions, missing circulation paths, or violations of basic architectural conventions. Such evaluation layers would enable FP-MAE to operate more effectively within architect-led workflows, where automated layout completion is combined with professional judgment and iterative refinement. These directions position usability assessment as a natural next step in the evolution of the framework rather than a prerequisite at the current stage.

A further avenue for future development concerns the integration of FP-MAE into existing architectural production workflows. While the present study focuses on image-based floor plan completion, the raster outputs produced by FP-MAE provide a practical foundation for downstream conversion into vectorized CAD or BIM representations. For example, reconstructed walls, room boundaries, and openings can be extracted and translated into editable geometric elements. Building on this capability, future work will explore lightweight plugins or standalone interfaces that allow architects to sketch partial layouts and receive real-time completion suggestions within familiar CAD or BIM environments. Such interfaces would support interactive acceptance, modification, or rejection of generated elements, ensuring that FP-MAE operates as an assistive component within architect-led workflows. These developments outline a clear pathway toward practical deployment without altering existing design practices.

https://doi.org/10.3390/buildings16030558

Additionally, pretraining with FP-MAE can provide a strong foundation for a range of downstream architectural tasks. Recent studies have shown that building energy performance can be reliably predicted from early-stage representations such as floor plans or conceptual images, indicating that spatial layout encodes meaningful performance-related information [29]. The latent representations learned by FP-MAE are therefore likely to capture generic spatial priors that are not only useful for geometric completion, but also beneficial for performance-oriented tasks. Building on this, future work may explore coupling FP-MAE pretraining with downstream energy prediction models, enabling a unified pipeline that links layout completion with early-stage performance feedback. Beyond energy analysis, the learned representations may enhance tasks such as room type classification, anomaly detection in architectural drawings, and interactive design assistance. This direction aligns with broader machine learning trends, where pretrained models serve as reusable backbones that can be fine-tuned to support diverse, domain-specific applications.

Finally, while FP-MAE primarily focuses on spatial layout completion, we recognize the significance of broader contextual factors such as structural logic, material choices, site orientation, environmental responsiveness, and socio-cultural influences in architectural decision-making. Although these aspects are not explicitly represented in the current model, our framework provides a solid foundation for their future integration. We see meaningful opportunities to incorporate such variables through multimodal inputs, including site data and material constraints, or by linking the model with rule-based systems and simulation-driven components. Through these developments, FP-MAE can progressively evolve into a more comprehensive design assistant that supports context-aware, architect-led workflows.

5.4. Conclusions

In conclusion, FP-MAE represents a significant step forward in the application of self-supervised learning to architectural floor plan generation. By reconstructing masked regions of floor plan images, the model learns both pixel-level details and semantic-level structures, enabling it to produce high-quality, functionally coherent reconstructions. While the current work focuses on reconstructive completion, the learned priors and masked autoencoding strategy offer a foundation upon which future generative floor plan systems may be developed, particularly when combined with additional constraints. The combination of novel architecture, a tailored dataset, and rigorous experimentation highlights the scalability and adaptability of this approach.

While there remain challenges in terms of precision, generalization, and multimodal integration, the progress demonstrated by FP-MAE establishes a strong foundation for future research. More broadly, it illustrates how self-supervised methods can move beyond natural image domains and into specialized fields such as architecture, where the stakes of structural and functional accuracy are particularly high.

As architectural design continues to embrace digital and AI-driven tools, methods like FP-MAE will become increasingly valuable, not as replacements for human creativity, but as collaborators that amplify efficiency, expand possibilities, and enrich the design process.

Author Contributions: Conceptualization, P.L., T.L. and P.Z.; Methodology, J.Z., R.L., T.L., P.Z. and Z.L.; Validation, T.F.; Investigation, P.L. and Z.L.; Writing—original draft, J.Z., R.L. and P.L.; Writing—review and editing, T.L., T.F. and J.Y.; Visualization, J.Y.; Supervision, T.F. and J.Y. All authors have read and agreed to the published version of the manuscript.

Funding: This research received no external funding.

Data Availability Statement: The original contributions presented in this study are included in the article. Further inquiries can be directed to the corresponding authors.

https://doi.org/10.3390/buildings16030558

Acknowledgments: The author gratefully acknowledges University College London (UCL) for supporting the publication of this article.

Conflicts of Interest: The authors declare no conflicts of interest.

References

1. Purcell, A.T.; Gero, J.S. Drawings and the design process: A review of protocol studies in design and other disciplines and related research in cognitive psychology. *Des. Stud.* **1998**, *19*, 389–430. [CrossRef]
2. Hettithanthri, U.; Hansen, P.; Munasinghe, H. Exploring the architectural design process assisted in conventional design studio: A systematic literature review. *Int. J. Technol. Des. Educ.* **2023**, *33*, 1835–1859. [CrossRef]
3. Sami, Z.; Özer, Y.S. The importance of figural and verbal sketches in creativity within the architectural design studio. *Megaron Yildiz Tech. Univ. Fac. Archit. E J.* **2024**, *19*, 539–549. [CrossRef]
4. Li, M.; Wang, C.; Wu, Y.; Santamouris, M.; Lu, S. Assessing spatial inequities of thermal environment and blue-green intervention for vulnerable populations in dense urban areas. *Urban Clim.* **2025**, *59*, 102328. [CrossRef]
5. Vandenhende, K. Mixing Specific and More Universal Design Media to Deal with Multidisciplinarity. *Athens J. Archit.* **2023**, *9*, 319–334. [CrossRef]
6. Lu, S.; Xu, W.; Chen, Y.; Yan, X. An experimental study on the acoustic absorption of sand panels. *Appl. Acoust.* **2017**, *116*, 238–248. [CrossRef]
7. Heckmann, O.; Schneider, F. *Floor Plan Manual: Housing*; Birkhäuser: Basel, Switzerland, 1997.
8. Shi, M.; Seo, J.; Cha, S.H.; Xiao, B.; Chi, H.L. Generative AI-powered architectural exterior conceptual design based on the design intent. *J. Comput. Des. Eng.* **2024**, *11*, 125–142. [CrossRef]
9. Zeng, P.; Yin, J.; Zhang, M.; Shen, Y.; Wang, X. CARD: A cross-modal agent framework for generative and editable residential design. In *Proceedings of the 2025 Conference on Empirical Methods in Natural Language Processing (EMNLP)*; Association for Computational Linguistics: Stroudsburg, PA, USA, 2025; pp. 1–12.
10. Yin, J.; Gao, W.; Li, J.; Xu, P.; Wu, C.; Lin, B.; Lu, S. ArchiDiff: Interactive design of 3D architectural forms generated from a single image. *Comput. Ind.* **2025**, *168*, 104275. [CrossRef]
11. Chen, L.; Song, Y.; Guo, J.; Sun, L.; Childs, P.; Yin, Y. How generative AI supports human in conceptual design. *Des. Sci.* **2025**, *11*, e9. [CrossRef]
12. Zeng, P.; Gao, W.; Li, J.; Yin, J.; Chen, J.; Lu, S. Automated residential layout generation and editing using natural language and images. *Autom. Constr.* **2025**, *174*, 106133. [CrossRef]
13. Karadağ, D.; Ozar, B. A new frontier in design studio: AI and human collaboration in conceptual design. *Front. Arch. Res.* **2025**, *14*, 1536–1550. [CrossRef]
14. Zeng, T.; Ma, X.; Luo, Y.; Ji, Y.; Lu, S. Improving outdoor thermal environmental quality through kinetic canopy empowered by machine learning and control algorithms. *Build. Simul.* **2025**, *18*, 699–720. [CrossRef]
15. Agri, M.E.; Le, A.; Phung, Q. AI integration in architectural design and management: Professionals' perspectives. *Arch. Eng. Des. Manag.* **2025**, 1–16, *ahead of print*. [CrossRef]
16. Yenew, A.B.; Assefa, B.G. From Algorithms to Architecture: Computational Methods for House Floorplan Generation. *SN Comput. Sci.* **2024**, *5*, 589. [CrossRef]
17. Liu, S.; Wang, Y.; Liu, X.; Yang, L.; Zhang, Y.; He, J. How does future climatic uncertainty affect multi-objective building energy retrofit decisions? Evidence from residential buildings in subtropical Hong Kong. *Sustain. Cities Soc.* **2023**, *92*, 104482. [CrossRef]
18. He, K.; Chen, X.; Xie, S.; Li, Y.; Dollár, P.; Girshick, R. Masked autoencoders are scalable vision learners. In *Proceedings of the IEEE/CVF Conference on Computer Vision and Pattern Recognition*; IEEE: New York, NY, USA, 2022; pp. 16000–16009.
19. Huang, W.; Zheng, H. Architectural drawings recognition and generation through machine learning. In Proceedings of the 38th Annual Conference of the Association for Computer Aided Design in Architecture, Mexico City, Mexico, 18–20 October 2018.
20. Lu, Z.; Wang, T.; Guo, J.; Meng, W.; Xiao, J.; Zhang, W.; Zhang, X. Data-driven floor plan understanding in rural residential buildings via deep recognition. *Inf. Sci.* **2021**, *567*, 58–74. [CrossRef]
21. Lv, X.; Zhao, S.; Yu, X.; Zhao, B. Residential floor plan recognition and reconstruction. In *Proceedings of the IEEE/CVF Conference on Computer Vision and Pattern Recognition*; IEEE: New York, NY, USA, 2021.
22. Xu, Z.; Yang, C.; Alheejawi, S.; Jha, N.; Mehadi, S.; Mandal, M. Automatic floor plan analysis using a boundary attention-based deep network. *Int. J. Doc. Anal. Recognit. IJDAR* **2025**, *28*, 19–30. [CrossRef]
23. Abouagour, M.; Garyfallidis, E. GFLAN: Generative Functional Layouts. *arXiv* **2025**, arXiv:2512.16275. [CrossRef]
24. Zeng, P.; Yin, J.; Gao, Y.; Li, J.; Jin, Z.; Lu, S. Comprehensive and Dedicated Metrics for Evaluating AI-Generated Residential Floor Plans. *Buildings* **2025**, *15*, 1674. [CrossRef]

https://doi.org/10.3390/buildings16030558

25. Yin, J.; Zeng, P.; Sun, H.; Dai, Y.; Zheng, H.; Zhang, M.; Zhang, Y.; Lu, S. Floorplan-llama: Aligning architects' feedback and domain knowledge in architectural floor plan generation. In *Proceedings of the 63rd Annual Meeting of the Association for Computational Linguistics (Volume 1: Long Papers)*; Association for Computational Linguistics: Stroudsburg, PA, USA, 2025.
26. Hu, S.; Wu, W.; Wang, Y.; Xu, B.; Zheng, L. GSDiff: Synthesizing Vector Floorplans via Geometry-enhanced Structural Graph Generation. In *Proceedings of the AAAI Conference on Artificial Intelligence*; AAAI Press: Washington, DC, USA, 2025; Volume 39, pp. 17323–17332.
27. Zhong, J.; Li, P.; Luo, R.; Yin, J.; Ding, Y.; Bai, J.; Hong, C.; Deng, X.; Ma, X.; Lu, S. EnergAI: A Large Language Model-Driven Generative Design Method for Early-Stage Building Energy Optimization. *Energies* **2025**, *18*, 5921. [CrossRef]
28. Yin, J.; Zhong, J.; Zeng, P.; Li, P.; Zheng, H.; Zhang, M.; Lu, S. ArchShapeNet: An interpretable 3D-CNN framework for evaluating architectural shapes. *Int. J. Archit. Comput.* **2025**, *23*, 14780771251352965. [CrossRef]
29. Yin, J.; Zeng, P.; Huang, Y.; Sun, H.; Zhong, J.; Hao, T.; Lu, S. AI-empowered prediction of office building energy use from single-view conceptual images for early-stage design. *Appl. Energy* **2026**, *406*, 127289. [CrossRef]
30. Hendrycks, D.; Mazeika, M.; Kadavath, S.; Song, D. Using self-supervised learning can improve model robustness and uncertainty. *Adv. Neural Inf. Process. Syst.* **2019**, *32*, 15663–15674.
31. Liu, X.; Zhang, F.; Hou, Z.; Mian, L.; Wang, Z.; Zhang, J. Self-supervised learning: Generative or contrastive. *IEEE Trans. Knowl. Data Eng.* **2021**, *35*, 857–876. [CrossRef]
32. Liu, Y.; Jin, M.; Pan, S.; Zhou, C.; Zheng, Y.; Xia, F. Graph self-supervised learning: A survey. *IEEE Trans. Knowl. Data Eng.* **2022**, *35*, 5879–5900. [CrossRef]
33. Gui, J.; Chen, T.; Zhang, J.; Cao, Q.; Sun, Z.; Luo, H. A survey on self-supervised learning: Algorithms, applications, and future trends. *IEEE Trans. Pattern Anal. Mach. Intell.* **2024**, *46*, 9052–9071. [CrossRef]
34. Radford, A.; Kim, J.W.; Hallacy, C.; Ramesh, A.; Goh, G.; Agarwal, S.; Sastry, G.; Askell, A.; Mishkin, P.; Clark, J.; et al. Learning transferable visual models from natural language supervision. In *Proceedings of the International Conference on Machine Learning*; PMLR: New York, NY, USA, 2021; pp. 8748–8763.
35. Jia, C.; Yang, Y.; Xia, Y.; Chen, Y.-T.; Parekh, Z.; Pham, H.; Le, Q.; Sung, Y.-H.; Li, Z.; Duerig, T. Scaling up visual and vision-language representation learning with noisy text supervision. In *Proceedings of the International Conference on Machine Learning*; PMLR: New York, NY, USA, 2021; pp. 4904–4916.
36. Baevski, A.; Hsu, W.N.; Xu, Q.; Babu, A.; Gu, J.; Auli, M. Data2vec: A general framework for self-supervised learning in speech, vision and language. In *Proceedings of the International Conference on Machine Learning*; PMLR: New York, NY, USA, 2022; pp. 1298–1312.
37. Huang, Y.; Zeng, T.; Jia, M.; Yang, J.; Xu, W.; Lu, S. Fusing Transformer and diffusion for high-resolution prediction of daylight illuminance and glare based on sparse ceiling-mounted input. *Build. Environ.* **2025**, *267*, 112163. [CrossRef]
38. Sun, H.; Xia, B.; Zhao, Y.; Chang, Y.; Wang, X. Positive Enhanced Preference Alignment for Text-to-Image Models. In *Proceedings of the ICASSP 2025—2025 IEEE International Conference on Acoustics, Speech and Signal Processing (ICASSP)*; IEEE: Piscataway, NJ, USA, 2025; pp. 1–5.
39. Zhou, J.; Wei, C.; Wang, H.; Shen, W.; Xie, C.; Yuille, A.; Kong, T. ibot: Image bert pre-training with online tokenizer. *arXiv* **2022**, arXiv:2111.07832.
40. Devlin, J.; Chang, M.-W.; Lee, K.; Toutanova, K. Bert: Pre-training of deep bidirectional transformers for language understanding. In *Proceedings of the 2019 Conference of the North American Chapter of the Association for Computational Linguistics: Human Language Technologies, Volume 1 (Long and Short Papers)*; Association for Computational Linguistics: Stroudsburg, PA, USA, 2019.
41. Radford, A.; Narasimhan, K.; Salimans, T.; Sutskever, I. Improving Language Understanding by Generative Pre-Training. 2018. Available online: https://openai.com/research/language-unsupervised (accessed on 1 December 2025).
42. Radford, A.; Wu, J.; Child, R.; Luan, D.; Amodei, D.; Sutskever, I. Language models are unsupervised multitask learners. *OpenAI Blog* **2019**, *1*, 9.
43. Sinha, K.; Jia, R.; Hupkes, D.; Pineau, J.; Williams, A.; Kiela, D. Masked language modeling and the distributional hypothesis: Order word matters pre-training for little. *arXiv* **2021**, arXiv:2104.06644. [CrossRef]
44. Shurrab, S.; Duwairi, R. Self-supervised learning methods and applications in medical imaging analysis: A survey. *PeerJ Comput. Sci.* **2022**, *8*, e1045. [CrossRef]
45. Chen, L.; Bentley, P.; Mori, K.; Misawa, K.; Fujiwara, M.; Rueckert, D. Self-supervised learning for medical image analysis using image context restoration. *Med. Image Anal.* **2019**, *58*, 101539. [CrossRef] [PubMed]
46. Huang, S.-C.; Pareek, A.; Jensen, M.; Lungren, M.P.; Yeung, S.; Chaudhari, A.S. Self-supervised learning for medical image classification: A systematic review and implementation guidelines. *NPJ Digit. Med.* **2023**, *6*, 74. [CrossRef] [PubMed]
47. Bao, H.; Dong, L.; Piao, S.; Wei, F. Beit: Bert pre-training of image transformers. *arXiv* **2021**, arXiv:2106.08254.
48. Wang, W.; Bao, H.; Dong, L.; Bjorck, J.; Peng, Z.; Liu, Q.; Aggarwal, K.; Mohammed, O.K.; Singhal, S.; Som, S.; et al. Image as a foreign language: Beit pretraining for vision and vision-language tasks. In *Proceedings of the IEEE/CVF Conference on Computer Vision and Pattern Recognition*; IEEE: New York, NY, USA, 2023.

49. Li, P.; Yin, J.; Zhong, J.; Luo, R.; Zeng, P.; Zhang, M. Segment any architectural facades (SAAF): An automatic segmentation model for building facades, walls and windows based on multimodal semantics guidance. *arXiv* **2025**, arXiv:2506.09071. [CrossRef]
50. Zhong, J.; Yin, J.; Li, P.; Zeng, P.; Zhang, M.; Luo, R.; Lu, S. ArchiLense: A framework for quantitative analysis of architectural styles based on vision large language models. *arXiv* **2025**, arXiv:2506.07739. [CrossRef]
51. Dosovitskiy, A.; Beyer, L.; Kolesnikov, A.; Weissenborn, D.; Zhai, X.; Unterthiner, T.; Dehghani, M.; Minderer, M.; Heigold, G.; Gelly, S.; et al. An image is worth 16x16 words: Transformers for image recognition at scale. *arXiv* **2020**, arXiv:2010.11929.
52. Khan, A.; Sohail, A.; Fiaz, M.; Hassan, M.; Afridi, T.H.; Marwat, S.U.; Munir, F.; Ali, S.; Naseem, H.; Zaheer, M.Z.; et al. A survey of the self supervised learning mechanisms for vision transformers. *arXiv* **2024**, arXiv:2408.17059. [CrossRef]
53. Xie, Z.; Zhang, Z.; Cao, Y.; Lin, Y.; Bao, J.; Yao, Z.; Dai, Q.; Hu, H. SimMIM: A Simple Framework for Masked Image Modeling. In *Proceedings of the 2022 IEEE/CVF Conference on Computer Vision and Pattern Recognition (CVPR)*; IEEE: New York, NY, USA, 2022; pp. 9653–9663.
54. Zhou, J.; Wei, C.; Wang, H.; Shen, W.; Xie, C.; Yuille, A.; Kong, T. iBOT: Image BERT Pre-Training with Online Tokenizer. In Proceedings of the 10th International Conference on Learning Representations, Online, 25–29 April 2022.
55. Zeng, P.; Yin, J.; Zhang, M.; Li, J.; Zhang, Y.; Lu, S. Unified residential floor plan generation with multimodal inputs. *Autom. Constr.* **2025**, *178*, 106408. [CrossRef]
56. Yin, J.; Zeng, P.; Li, P.; Zhong, J.; Thao, T.; Zheng, H.; Lu, S. Drag2Build++: A drag-based 3D architectural mesh editing workflow based on differentiable surface modeling. *Front. Archit. Res.* **2025**, *14*, 1602–1620. [CrossRef]
57. Yin, J.; Zeng, P.; Shen, L.; Zhang, M.; Zhong, J.; Han, Y.; Lu, S. ArchiSet: Benchmarking Editable and Consistent Single-View 3D Reconstruction of Buildings with Specific Window-to-Wall Ratios. In *Proceedings of the IEEE/CVF International Conference on Computer Vision*; IEEE: New York, NY, USA, 2025; pp. 26004–26014.
58. Baldi, P. Autoencoders, unsupervised learning, and deep architectures. In Proceedings of the ICML Workshop on Unsupervised and Transfer Learning, Edinburgh, Scotland, 26 June–1 July 2012. JMLR Workshop and Conference Proceedings.
59. Berahmand, K.; Daneshfar, F.; Salehi, E.S.; Li, Y.; Xu, Y. Autoencoders and their applications in machine learning: A survey. *Artif. Intell. Rev.* **2024**, *57*, 28. [CrossRef]
60. Vincent, P.; LaRochelle, H.; Bengio, Y.; Manzagol, P.-A. Extracting and composing robust features with denoising autoencoders. In *Proceedings of the 25th International Conference on Machine Learning*; Association for Computing Machinery: New York, NY, USA, 2008.
61. Kingma, D.P.; Welling, M. Auto-encoding variational bayes. *arXiv* **2013**, arXiv:1312.6114.
62. Pathak, D.; Krahenbuhl, P.; Donahue, J.; Darrell, T.; Efros, A.A. Context encoders: Feature learning by inpainting. In *Proceedings of the IEEE Conference on Computer Vision and Pattern Recognition*; IEEE: New York, NY, USA, 2016.
63. Van Den Oord, A.; Vinyals, O.; Kavukcuoglu, K. Neural discrete representation learning. *Adv. Neural Inf. Process. Syst.* **2017**, *30*, 6306–6315.
64. Chen, S.; Guo, W. Auto-encoders in deep learning—A review with new perspectives. *Mathematics* **2023**, *11*, 1777. [CrossRef]
65. Wang, Y.; Wang, H.; Zhang, F. Mask autoencoder for enhanced image reconstruction with position coding offset and combined masking. *Vis. Comput.* **2025**, *41*, 7477–7491. [CrossRef]
66. Rodrigues, E.; Gaspar, A.R.; Gomes, Á. Automated approach for design generation and thermal assessment of alternative floor plans. *Energy Build.* **2014**, *81*, 170–181. [CrossRef]
67. Lu, Z.; Li, Y.; Wang, F. Complex layout generation for large-scale floor plans via deep edge-aware GNNs. *Appl. Intell.* **2025**, *55*, 400. [CrossRef]
68. Liu, J.; Xue, Y.; Ni, H.; Yu, R.; Zhou, Z.; Huang, S.X. Computer-Aided Layout Generation for Building Design: A Review. *arXiv* **2025**, arXiv:2504.09694. [CrossRef]
69. Yan, S.; Wu, C.; Zhang, Y. Generative design for architectural spatial layouts: A review of technical approaches. *J. Asian Archit. Build. Eng.* **2025**, 1–21. [CrossRef]
70. Meselhy, A.; Almalkawi, A. A review of artificial intelligence methodologies in computational automated generation of high performance floorplans. *NPJ Clean Energy* **2025**, *1*, 2. [CrossRef]
71. Zeng, P.; Yin, J.; Sun, H.; Dai, Y.; Jiang, M.; Zhang, M.; Lu, S. MRED-14: A Benchmark for Low-Energy Residential Floor Plan Generation with 14 Flexible Inputs. In *Proceedings of the 33rd ACM International Conference on Multimedia*; Association for Computing Machinery: New York, NY, USA, 2025; pp. 11298–11307.
72. Zeng, P.; Yin, J.; Huang, Y.; Zhong, J.; Lu, S. AI-based generation and optimization of energy-efficient residential layouts controlled by contour and room number. *Build. Simul.* **2025**, *18*, 2777–2805. [CrossRef]
73. Merrell, P.; Schkufza, E.; Koltun, V. Computer-generated residential building layouts. *ACM Trans. Graph.* **2010**, *29*, 181. [CrossRef]
74. Wu, W.; Fu, X.-M.; Tang, R.; Wang, Y.; Qi, Y.-H.; Liu, L. Data-driven Interior Plan Generation for Residential Buildings. *ACM Trans. Graph.* **2019**, *38*, 234. [CrossRef]
75. Hu, R.; Huang, Z.; Tang, Y.; Van Kaick, O.; Zhang, H.; Huang, H. Graph2Plan: Learning Floorplan Generation from Layout Graphs. *ACM Trans. Graph.* **2020**, *39*, 118. [CrossRef]

76. Nauata, N.; Chang, K.-H.; Cheng, C.-Y.; Mori, G.; Furukawa, Y. House-GAN: Relational Generative Adversarial Networks for Graph-Constrained House Layout Generation. In *Proceedings of the Computer Vision—ECCV 2020: 16th European Conference*; Springer: Cham, Switzerland, 2020; pp. 162–177.
77. Nauata, N.; Hosseini, S.; Chang, K.-H.; Chu, H.; Cheng, C.-Y.; Furukawa, Y. House-GAN++: Generative Adversarial Layout Refinement Networks. In *Proceedings of the 2021 IEEE/CVF Conference on Computer Vision and Pattern Recognition (CVPR)*; IEEE: New York, NY, USA, 2021.
78. Shabani, M.A.; Hosseini, S.; Furukawa, Y. Housediffusion: Vector floorplan generation via a diffusion model with discrete and continuous denoising. In *Proceedings of the IEEE/CVF Conference on Computer Vision and Pattern Recognition*; IEEE: New York, NY, USA, 2023.
79. Xia, D.; Wu, Z.; Zou, Y.; Chen, R.; Lou, S. Developing a bottom-up approach to assess energy challenges in urban residential buildings of China. *Front. Archit. Res.* **2025**, *14*, 1810–1833. [CrossRef]
80. Zou, Y.; Chen, Z.; Lou, S.; Huang, Y.; Xia, D.; Cao, Y.; Li, H.; Lun, I.Y.F. Accelerating long-term building energy performance simulation with a reference day method. *Build. Simul.* **2024**, *17*, 2331–2353. [CrossRef]
81. Liu, X.; He, J.; Xiong, K.; Liu, S.; He, B.-J. Identification of factors affecting public willingness to pay for heat mitigation and adaptation: Evidence from Guangzhou, China. *Urban Clim.* **2023**, *48*, 101405. [CrossRef]
82. Rahbar, M.; Mahdavinejad, M.; Markazi, A.H.; Bemanian, M. Architectural Layout Design through Deep Learning and Agent-Based Modeling: A Hybrid Approach. *J. Build. Eng.* **2022**, *47*, 103822. [CrossRef]
83. Tang, H.; Zhang, Z.; Shi, H.; Li, B.; Shao, L.; Sebe, N.; Timofte, R.; Van Gool, L. Graph Transformer GANs for Graph-Constrained House Generation. In Proceedings of the IEEE/CVF Conference on Computer Vision and Pattern Recognition, Vancouver, BC, Canada, 17–24 June 2023; pp. 2173–2182.
84. Sun, J.; Wu, W.; Liu, L.; Min, W.; Zhang, G.; Zheng, L. WallPlan: Synthesizing Floorplans by Learning to Generate Wall Graphs. *ACM Trans. Graph.* **2022**, *41*, 92. [CrossRef]
85. Upadhyay, A.; Dubey, A.; Kuriakose, S.M.; Agarawal, S. FloorGAN: Generative Network for Automated Floor Layout Generation. In *Proceedings of the 6th Joint International Conference on Data Science & Management of Data (10th ACM IKDD CODS and 28th COMAD), CODS-COMAD '23*; Association for Computing Machinery: New York, NY, USA, 2023; pp. 140–148.
86. Yin, J.; Zeng, P.; Zhong, J.; Li, P.; Zhang, M.; Luo, R.; Lu, S. FloorPlan-DeepSeek (FPDS): A multimodal approach to floorplan generation using vector-based next room prediction. *arXiv* **2025**, arXiv:2506.21562.
87. Leng, S.; Zhou, Y.; Dupty, M.H.; Lee, W.S.; Joyce, S.; Lu, W. Tell2design: A dataset for language-guided floor plan generation. In *Proceedings of the 61st Annual Meeting of the Association for Computational Linguistics, (Volume 1: Long Papers)*; Association for Computing Machinery: New York, NY, USA, 2023.
88. Zong, Z.; Zhan, Z.; Tan, G. HouseLLM: LLM-Assisted Two-Phase Text-to-Floorplan Generation. *arXiv* **2024**, arXiv:2411.12279v1.
89. Qin, S.; He, C.; Chen, Q.; Yang, S.; Liao, W.; Gu, Y.; Lu, X. ChatHouseDiffusion: Prompt-guided generation and editing of floor plans. *arXiv* **2024**, arXiv:2410.11908.
90. Gueze, A.; Ospici, M.; Rohmer, D.; Cani, M.-P. Floor Plan Reconstruction from Sparse Views: Combining Graph Neural Network with Constrained Diffusion. In *Proceedings of the IEEE/CVF International Conference on Computer Vision*; IEEE: New York, NY, USA, 2023; pp. 1583–1592.
91. Medel-Vera, C.; Britton, S.; Gates, W.F. An exploration of the role of generative AI in fostering creativity in architectural learning environments. *Comput. Educ. Artif. Intell.* **2025**, *9*, 100501. [CrossRef]
92. Swaileh, W.; Kotzinos, D.; Ghosh, S.; Jordan, M.; Vu, N.-S.; Qian, Y. Versailles-FP dataset: Wall detection in ancient floor plans. In *Proceedings of the International Conference on Document Analysis and Recognition*; Springer International Publishing: Cham, Switzerland, 2021.
93. Karadag, I. Machine learning for conservation of architectural heritage. *Open House Int.* **2023**, *48*, 23–37. [CrossRef]

 https://doi.org/10.3390/buildings16030558

buildings

MDPI

Article

Post-Pandemic Trends in Residential Space Design: An Analysis Using Deep Learning and Expert Evaluation

Haewon Lim [1,*] and Hye-Jin Yoon [2]

1 Institute of Symbiotic Life-Tech, Yonsei University, Seoul 03722, Republic of Korea
2 Department of Interior Architecture and Build Environment, Yonsei University, Seoul 03722, Republic of Korea
* Correspondence: woni7883@yonsei.ac.kr; Tel.: +82-2-2123-4663

Abstract

The COVID-19 pandemic has fundamentally transformed residential spaces, yet traditional survey-based approaches face limitations in objectively capturing these changes. This study investigates residential design trends in the Post-pandemic era, defined as the period in which pandemic-induced lifestyle changes have become institutionalized in everyday living environments. Residential interior images were collected from Pinterest and Instagram and analyzed using an image-based deep learning approach combined with expert evaluation. A pretrained convolutional neural network (ResNet50) was employed as a visual feature extractor to quantify three spatial attributes—openness and comfort, flexibility and diversity, and nature-friendliness—across four residential space types: balconies, living rooms, entrances, and bedrooms. The model-generated proportional scores were validated by experts and compared between pre-pandemic and post-pandemic periods. The results reveal dual transformation patterns of functional specialization and increased multifunctionality. Balconies evolved into well-being-oriented spaces with enhanced nature-related features, while living rooms emerged as multifunctional hubs with a substantial increase in spatial flexibility. In contrast, entrances exhibited reduced openness, functioning as hygienic buffer zones. These findings indicate a reconfiguration of spatial hierarchy in post-pandemic housing, where auxiliary spaces gain prominence and traditional primary spaces adopt flexible roles. This study demonstrates the value of image-based deep learning for objectively identifying residential design trends and provides practical implications for resilient housing design in the post-pandemic era.

Keywords: post-pandemic era; deep learning; expert evaluation; residential space; spatial flexibility; residential design

1. Introduction

The COVID-19 pandemic has brought about profound changes in people's lifestyles [1,2], significantly influencing the way residential spaces are planned and utilized. The widespread adoption of remote work, online education, and home-based leisure activities has accelerated the demand for flexible and multifunctional spatial layouts. In addition, heightened concerns over health and well-being have increased the importance of incorporating natural elements and promoting psychological comfort within living environments [3]. For example, living rooms are transforming into multifunctional spaces with open layouts and ample natural lighting, while balconies are evolving into hybrid spaces that blur the boundary between indoors and outdoors. In addition, entrances are being redesigned as quarantine-oriented buffer zones to block viruses and external contaminants. In this way, in the post-pandemic era, the functional boundaries of residential spaces are gradually dissolving, the conventional frames of life and space are being reorganized, and new forms of daily routines and residential patterns are emerging.

In this context, investigating residential design trends in the Post-pandemic era is crucial not only for understanding how spatial configurations have responded to societal changes, but also for providing evidence-based guidance for future housing design. In this study, "residential design trends" refer to recurring spatial configurations, functional arrangements, and visual design features that are collectively observed across residential spaces within a specific socio-temporal context, reflecting shared design intentions and lifestyle adaptations rather than individual preferences. Identifying spatial features that correspond to evolving user needs can support the development of flexible, resilient, and user-centered residential environments capable of accommodating hybrid lifestyles that integrate living, working, and leisure activities.

Previous studies on changes in residential spaces have primarily relied on surveys, in-depth interviews, and field observations [4–6]. Although these methods offer insights into residents' subjective experiences, they are limited in their ability to systematically and quantitatively capture visual and aesthetic characteristics or to identify large-scale spatial trends reflected in built environments. In contrast, the proliferation of social networking services (SNS) and interior design-oriented platforms has enabled the continuous sharing and accumulation of vast numbers of residential interior images. Platforms such as Pinterest and Instagram function as large-scale visual repositories of residential spaces, capturing evolving design practices and everyday spatial adaptations. These platforms are also widely used by Korean designers, developers, and residents as primary sources of design inspiration, reflecting globally shared yet locally adopted residential design trends.

Recent advances in deep learning, particularly in image recognition, provide new opportunities for analyzing design trends through large-scale visual data [7,8]. Convolutional Neural Networks (CNNs) are well suited for this purpose, as they can automatically learn hierarchical visual features from complex images, capturing both spatial composition and object relationships [9–11]. In architectural and interior design research, such capabilities enable the systematic extraction of visual characteristics from residential images, supporting the quantitative analysis of spatial patterns that reflect design intentions and user adaptations. By processing large volumes of visual data, image-based deep learning methods allow researchers to identify recurring spatial features and emerging tendencies, thereby offering an empirical approach to understanding design trends over time.

Accordingly, this study aims to quantitatively compare and evaluate changes in residential space design before and after the COVID-19 pandemic by applying a deep learning-based image analysis algorithm to residential interior images. Residential images were collected from SNS and interior design-oriented platforms, where users and designers continuously share visual records of actual living environments and design outcomes. The research procedure involves extracting visual features from these images and conducting a visual ratio analysis, in which the relative proportions of three spatial attributes—(1) openness and comfort, (2) spatial flexibility and diversity, and (3) nature-friendliness—are quantified and compared across time periods. Unlike conventional methodologies that rely on subjective surveys or qualitative interviews, this approach analyzes large-scale visual datasets using a consistent computational framework, thereby constituting a big data-driven study based on visual information. Through this process, the study seeks to empirically identify the impact of the pandemic on residential design trends and to

 https://doi.org/10.3390/buildings16030589

provide data-driven implications for residential design, architecture, and real estate in the post-pandemic era.

This study addresses the lack of empirical, large-scale methods for identifying how desired residential design attributes have shifted between the pre-pandemic and post-pandemic eras. While prior studies rely largely on surveys or qualitative observations, this research proposes an image-based deep learning approach as an analytical tool to quantitatively capture and compare these temporal design shifts.

2. Research Background

2.1. Changes in Residential Space Functions and Designs

As contactless socializing has become part of the natural transition post-COVID-19, more people have grown comfortable performing a large proportion of their daily activities (e.g., working, learning, shopping, leisure, and socializing) online from home [12]. Accordingly, changes have been made to partially adapt the residential spaces of people who used to frequent coworking spaces or cafes into spaces for learning and working, while adhering to social distancing requirements to minimize the risk of infection. Consequently, with the increased transition of certain activities, including learning, work, and leisure, to home settings, the physical boundaries of residential spaces have expanded [13], requiring the residential space designs to respond to social changes in this new era.

Peters and Halleran (2021) suggested that three factors are crucial in co-living housing planning for populations vulnerable to infectious diseases: social distancing, disconnection from nature, and changing housing functions [14]. Since COVID-19, changes in the frequency of daily living activities within the dwelling have been particularly evident in "caring for family and household members" and "household management," reflecting increased time spent at home [2]. Accordingly, this study does not directly observe or measure daily activities, but instead examines how changes in everyday practices are translated into spatial configurations and design features. By analyzing residential interior images, the study captures the visual and functional adaptations of living spaces that indirectly represent shifts in daily activities and domestic needs.

As the nature of traditional residential spaces has shifted, the resident needs for planning and design have changed, requiring expansion, reduction, separation, and integration of spaces. Accordingly, more studies have suggested the effective utilization of spaces by examining preferences and needs for residential spaces [15,16]. Traditional residential spaces in Korea have a residential function that emphasizes openness, with the living room in the center of the dwelling. That is, the design function of indoor spaces emphasizes the LDK (Living + Dining + Kitchen) format, by locating the living room in the center and connecting the kitchen and dining room [17,18]. Although traditional Korean housing has historically emphasized distinct cultural and spatial characteristics, contemporary residential design in Korea has increasingly adopted globally standardized layouts and design references, particularly those rooted in Western housing models such as the LDK (Living–Dining–Kitchen) configuration. As a result, global interior design platforms and social media channels function not merely as external influences, but as practical reference standards that shape current Korean residential design practices.

Residential functions are categorized as safety, convenience, socialization, relaxation, and multifunctionality; while all residential functions increased after COVID-19, "comfort" experienced the greatest increase. Meanwhile, in the post-pandemic era, multifunctionality refers to the ability of residential spaces to accommodate activities that were traditionally conducted outside the home, including remote work, online learning, indoor exercise, leisure activities, and small-scale social interactions [2].

https://doi.org/10.3390/buildings16030589

2.2. Deep Learning Literature Review

Deep learning is based on artificial neural networks that enable machines to automatically learn hierarchical features from data by simulating the structure of human biological neurons through multiple neural layers [19]. In image analysis, these features may include low-level visual attributes such as edges, textures, and colors, as well as higher-level spatial patterns such as object shapes, layout configurations, and material compositions. Because of this capability, deep learning has been widely applied to image recognition, speech classification, and natural language processing [20].

In architectural and spatial research, image-based deep learning has been used to analyze building façades, interior layouts, and spatial components by extracting visual features related to form, proportion, and spatial organization [21]. In design practice, the integration of information models during the architectural design phase—such as Building Information Modeling (BIM)—has been shown to reduce design errors, including spatial conflicts between structural and mechanical systems, misalignment of building components, and inconsistencies between drawings and specifications. This process, often referred to as design informatization, involves the systematic digitalization and structuring of design information to support decision-making, coordination, and error prevention throughout the design process. In addition, a methodology for identifying patterns by detecting image features has been applied to analyze images of land areas and to effectively design building floor plans [22].

Meanwhile, previous space design research has primarily examined interior design styles by categorizing reference images into predefined style types. Recent deep learning-based approaches have enabled the automatic recognition and evaluation of interior design styles directly from reference images [23]. This allows the derivation of feature relationships through image analysis, and identification of clear furniture and color combination patterns through object detection, color extraction, and network analysis [10]. Furthermore, automatic layouts have been suggested for space design [9] and a model has been designed to find similar products through visual search in image space [24]. The findings of these studies are predominantly grounded in subjective design interpretations, which shape the derivation of conclusions and the formulation of customized design recommendations.

Deep learning techniques can be adopted to respond to residents' lifestyles and needs by analyzing big data regarding individual needs [25] and spatial images, suggesting appropriate space designs for rapidly changing residential functions. The technique has been employed to detect and classify objects in images as well as myriad other research areas. In fact, its applicability has been broadened to fields previously considered subjective, such as emotions, art, and design [11,26–29].

This study analyzed spatial design trends using SNS images based on visual elements. SNS is a platform where users continuously upload photos reflecting the latest trends, so it is easy to secure data in real time and reflect various user perspectives, making it easy to capture popular preferences or lifestyle changes. SNS images are generated and shared directly by residents at the time of space use or renovation, reflecting actual living environments and everyday spatial practices. Because these images are continuously uploaded by a large and diverse user group, the repeated appearance of specific visual elements—such as flexible furniture layouts, integrated workspaces, or indoor greenery—can be interpreted as collective indicators of emerging residential design trends. Thus, SNS-based image data enable the identification of popular preferences and lifestyle changes through large-scale visual pattern analysis.

https://doi.org/10.3390/buildings16030589

2.3. Convolutional Neural Network (CNN)-Based Image Classification

Machine learning models based on Convolutional Neural Networks (CNNs) are among the most widely used deep learning techniques for image recognition and classification [30]. CNNs operate by applying convolutional filters to input images in order to automatically extract hierarchical visual features, ranging from low-level patterns such as edges and textures to high-level semantic features such as object shapes and spatial configurations. For example, in residential interior images, early convolutional layers may capture basic visual elements such as lines, color contrasts, and lighting conditions, while deeper layers identify more complex spatial features, including furniture arrangements, window openings, and the presence of natural elements such as plants.

In 1989, LeCun et al. introduced a CNN-based image classification algorithm for recognizing handwritten digits, which laid the foundation for modern feature extraction and image classification systems [31–34]. Since then, CNN architectures such as AlexNet, VGG, GoogleNet, and ResNet have been developed and widely applied for visual image analysis due to their effectiveness in extracting discriminative features from input images and classifying image categories [30,35].

CNN has been designed for feature extraction and image classification. It contains a convolutional layer that detects image features and analyzes images through multiple filters (kernels) to assess characteristic patterns; the pooling layer lowers the spatial resolution and computation requirement, while the fully connected layer (FCL)—a neural network structure—classifies images based on extracted features. The convolutional operation identifies and extracts the overall image features, and the pooling operation exaggerates the image features to increase the neural network efficiency while improving the result direction of the images to be analyzed and maximizing the morphological features. Finally, the FCL classifies and extracts the features comprehensively, and the output layer presents the classification results [7]. This CNN utilization methodology has been proposed in architectural planning and interior design to improve the classification accuracy of spatial images and analysis [36]. Such studies have classified interior design styles [11] and quantitatively estimated preferences for building patterns [37] based on CNN.

In this study, we modified the Python code from the existing algorithm to optimize and construct the training data set. We then applied collected residential space images from social media to classify and analyze the colors of physical elements such as walls, ceilings, and floors, as well as lighting, furniture, and decorative items, ultimately deriving analytical results.

3. Research Methods

3.1. Research Design

This study was designed to classify and analyze residential space images from the post-COVID-19 period using an image-based deep learning approach. Rather than extracting culturally exclusive or traditional Korean housing characteristics, the study focuses on identifying emerging standardized design tendencies that have been widely adopted in Korean residential spaces through global design circulation.

In this study, the "Post-pandemic" period is defined as beginning in 2020, following the outbreak of COVID-19. Although architectural design and construction generally involve time lags, this study analyzes image-based representations of residential spaces shared on social media, which reflect relatively rapid changes in design intentions, interior configurations, and lifestyle-oriented spatial responses. Accordingly, images posted from 2020 onward are considered appropriate for capturing emerging residential design trends in the Post-pandemic era.

https://doi.org/10.3390/buildings16030589

Image data were collected using Python-based automated scripts that retrieved publicly available residential interior images from social curation platforms, specifically Instagram and Pinterest. The data collection process complied with platform usage policies and focused on images tagged with residential interior-related keywords. A deep learning-based Convolutional Neural Network (CNN) was then employed to classify and quantify the collected residential space images. Among the various CNNs, we employed ResNet50 with standard transfer learning protocols following He et al. (2016) [7]. The model was initialized with ImageNet pre-trained weights, with the final classification layer modified for our three-factor evaluation scheme (openness, flexibility, nature-friendliness). The deep learning model was implemented using Python (version 3.9, Python Software Foundation, Wilmington, DE, USA) with TensorFlow (version 2.x, Google LLC, Mountain View, CA, USA) and Keras (version 2.x, Google LLC, Mountain View, CA, USA) as the primary deep learning frameworks.

The evaluation scale for image classification was divided into three factors: openness and comfort, flexibility [38] and diversity, and nature-friendliness, according to changes in residential functions [39]. Residential spaces were also divided into bedroom, living room, entrance, and balcony for spatial analysis; images of residential spaces before the pandemic and the Post-pandemic era were compared. The specific research methods have been presented in Figure 1.

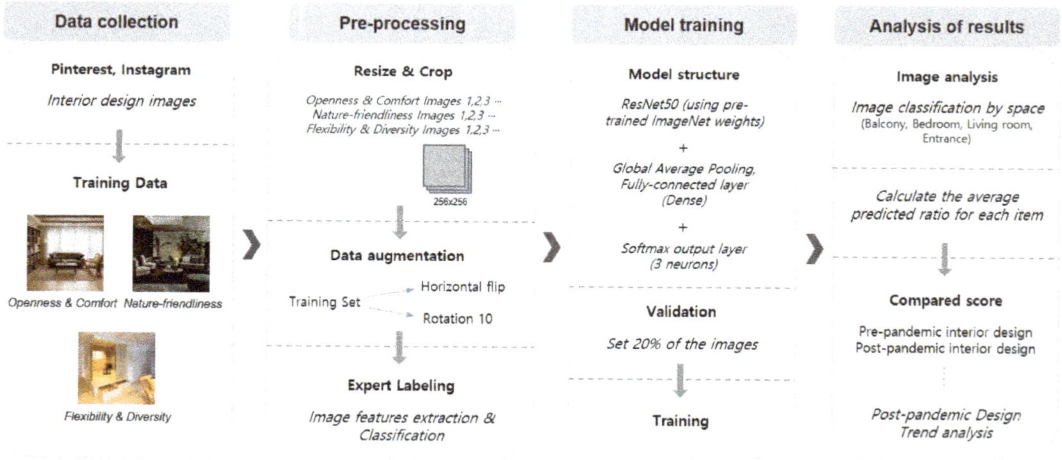

Figure 1. Procedure of Image Deep Learning method.

3.2. *Image Training Dataset*

A total of 625 images, with approximately 200 per keyword, collected from Pinterest were included for residential space image training [40]. For learning progress and performance evaluation, 60% of the collected images were utilized as training data, 20% as validation data, and 20% as test data. The image dataset was divided based on three evaluation scales (i.e., openness and comfort, flexibility and diversity, and nature-friendliness), and the training images were selected by setting each criterion. In particular, spatial flexibility and diversity were not defined by object density or visual clutter. Instead, images were labeled based on the presence of structured spatial configurations, such as partitions, movable or reconfigurable furniture, and clearly implied multifunctional zoning (e.g., work, rest, or storage within a single space). Although visually cluttered spaces may also contain many objects, such environments typically lack coherent spatial organization or functional intent and were not categorized as flexible spaces.

https://doi.org/10.3390/buildings16030589

To ensure consistent feature extraction across images, only images that clearly displayed at least three spatial planes (walls, floor, and ceiling) were selected. This criterion was applied not to emphasize perceived spaciousness, but to ensure that key architectural elements required for spatial interpretation were present in each image. While wide-angle photography is common in interior imagery, images exhibiting extreme lens distortion or artificially exaggerated depth were excluded during the data screening process. Moreover, since the same selection criteria were consistently applied to both pre-pandemic and post-pandemic datasets, potential perceptual bias introduced by photographic techniques is assumed to be systematically controlled across comparative groups.

Examples of images corresponding to the dataset's keywords are provided in Figures 2–4, and the criteria for image selection are clarified. Prior to model training, data pre-processing was conducted to enhance image consistency and suitability for CNN-based analysis. This process included standardizing labeling formats, resizing all images to a fixed resolution of 256 × 256 pixels (horizontal × vertical), and adjusting image proportions to maintain aspect ratio. Images with excessive distortion, noise, or insufficient visual information were excluded to reduce inconsistencies in the dataset [41].

Figure 2. Examples of openness and comfort learning images.

Figure 3. Examples of flexibility and diversity learning images.

Figure 4. Examples of nature-friendliness learning images.

Images with Openness and Comfort had open spaces, large windows, and good ventilation. Bright lighting and colors were selected as the design factors [42]. Data images with flexibility and diversity had images with separated spaces through partitions,

https://doi.org/10.3390/buildings16030589

furniture, and differences in floor level, with more than one function or use of the space. Meanwhile, the data images with nature-friendliness functions included plants on the walls or ceiling within the space or accessories such as pots and flowers: the design color tone was primarily mainly green, and the spaces had natural materials rather than artificial materials [43].

3.3. Training Image Prediction and Performance Evaluation

To train the deep learning model and ensure robust prediction performance, image augmentation techniques were applied to mitigate overfitting and improve generalization, particularly given the relatively limited dataset size [44]. Image augmentation artificially expands the training dataset by applying controlled transformations—such as rotation, horizontal flipping, and noise injection—while preserving the semantic content of the images [45]. These techniques are widely used in CNN-based image analysis to enhance model stability and prevent bias toward specific image compositions.

In this study, Keras' ImageDataGenerator (Keras version 2.x, Google LLC, Mountain View, CA, USA) was used to perform random rotations, flips, and noise additions during training. This approach allowed the model to learn invariant visual features related to spatial structure and design elements rather than memorizing specific photographic viewpoints or compositions.

The trained model outputs three continuous values corresponding to the spatial attributes of openness and comfort, flexibility and diversity, and nature-friendliness. A Softmax activation function was applied at the output layer to normalize these values into proportional scores, representing the relative emphasis of each attribute within a given space. Although these spatial attributes are not conceptually mutually exclusive in architectural practice, the Softmax formulation was adopted to enable consistent comparison of dominant spatial tendencies across different space types and time periods. Accordingly, the predicted values should be interpreted as relative ratio indicators, not as binary or mutually exclusive classifications.

Model performance was evaluated using a confusion matrix based on a test dataset comprising 20% of the total images. The confusion matrix enabled a detailed assessment of classification accuracy by comparing predicted labels with expert-validated reference labels. From this matrix, precision, recall, and F1-score metrics were calculated to assess predictive reliability across the three spatial attributes.

Overall, the model demonstrated high classification performance, indicating that the extracted visual features effectively captured spatial design characteristics relevant to the evaluation criteria. While minor discrepancies were observed in attributes related to spatial flexibility and diversity—likely due to subtle variations in spatial partitioning and furniture-based zoning—the overall performance confirms the suitability of the proposed CNN-based approach for analyzing residential space design trends.

Although the predictability analysis of the evaluated training data had differences per residential function within the space, the model correctly predicted 38, 28, and 36 images per dwelling function, respectively, among a total of 125 images. Moreover, it learned images with an average accuracy of 90% due to training (Table 1). Accuracy indicates that the learning model precisely classified the residential functions within the space in all cases and intuitively evaluated the prediction performance. As the classification performance may differ depending on the data, we confirmed accuracy, precision, recall, and F1 score, which measure the classifier's performance by combining the evaluation metrics' values to assess performance. Precision refers to the prediction of a specific dwelling function within the space that reflects the correct dwelling function in reality. Recall refers to the model's ability to correctly predict the percentage of the corresponding dwelling function. The F1

 https://doi.org/10.3390/buildings16030589

score is a weighted harmonic average of the precision and recall values; this circumvents the skewness of applying a single metric. Table 1 presents the results of calculating each performance metric based on the confusion matrix.

Table 1. Accuracy, precision, recall, and F1-score of the CNN model.

	A (Openness and Comfort)		B (Nature-Friendliness)		C (Flexibility and Diversity)	
	C	B	A	C	B	A
Accuracy	0.87	0.91	0.87	0.93	0.91	0.93
Precision	0.97	0.97	0.86	0.76	0.97	0.76
Recall	0.81	0.97	0.97	0.97	0.97	0.90
F1-Score	0.88	0.97	0.91	0.97	0.97	0.82

Although there were differences per residential function within the space, overall, high performance in precision (0.88) and recall (0.93) was achieved. However, relatively low precision (0.76) was observed in the spatial flexibility and diversity function. Regarding flexibility and diversity, we trained images with space separation using differences in the floor or ceiling, or assessed space division using furniture and partitions; hence, it is assumed that slight differences in space separation and division were not accurately predicted. In general, the F1-score is widely used to evaluate classification performance by balancing precision and recall, particularly in cases of class imbalance. Previous studies have suggested that an F1-score above 0.90 indicates excellent performance, values above 0.80 indicate good performance, and values above 0.50 indicate acceptable or usable performance [46]. For example, Sokolova and Lapalme [47] applied these thresholds when evaluating text and image classification models, demonstrating that models with F1-scores above 0.90 achieved reliable and robust classification results across multiple categories. Based on these criteria, the CNN model employed in this study demonstrated excellent overall performance, with an average F1-score of 0.92.

While the CNN effectively captures visual patterns associated with spatial flexibility, it should be noted that image-based analysis cannot perfectly distinguish functional adaptability from all forms of visual complexity. Therefore, the predicted flexibility scores should be interpreted as relative visual indicators rather than direct measurements of actual spatial use.

3.4. *Training of Residential Space Images*

To identify the design trends of residential spaces in the post-pandemic era, we classified four space images, namely bedroom, living room, entrance, and balcony, by applying them to the learning model. Furthermore, we compared the existing residential space images with the post-pandemic dwelling space images to assess space designs that has changed along with residential functions. In this study, images representing the post-pandemic era were defined as those collected between 2020 and 2022, whereas the pre-pandemic era was operationalized as the period from January 2017 to December 2019, during which housing trends remained relatively stable and were not yet influenced by the pandemic.

We selected images showing residential spaces' walls, floors, and ceilings under the same conditions as the training data, including various interior design factors (e.g., furniture and decoration). Figure 5 provides examples of representative interior design images used in this study. These images reflect contemporaneous residential design characteristics and visual trends commonly observed in recent interior design practices.

In this study, residential space images representing the new normal era were selected based on spatial structures and functional characteristics identified in previous studies on

https://doi.org/10.3390/buildings16030589

post-COVID-19 residential changes [48,49]. Rather than selecting images arbitrarily, we applied space-specific criteria reflecting newly emphasized residential functions.

Figure 5. Examples of residential space design images in the new normal era (from left: balcony, bedroom, entrance, and living room).

Balcony images were selected to represent flexible and multifunctional structures that support diverse leisure and hobby-related activities, such as camping-style setups, indoor gardening, and home exercise, reflecting increased time spent on leisure activities within the home [50,51]. Entrance images were chosen based on their expanded spatial capacity to accommodate storage and management of hygiene-related items, delivery goods, outdoor clothing, and exercise equipment, highlighting their role as buffer zones between indoor and outdoor environments.

Bedroom images were selected when spatial separation or zoning elements were visually identifiable, reflecting the transformation of bedrooms into multifunctional spaces supporting sleeping, studying, and working activities. Living room images were chosen to represent high spatial flexibility and diversity, as these spaces increasingly accommodate overlapping functions such as work, learning, relaxation, communication, and dining, resulting in higher levels of spatial concentration and functional tension [52].

4. Results

4.1. Deep Learning-Based Residential Space Image Analysis

This study applied an image-based deep learning model to classify residential space images according to three visual design attributes: openness and comfort, flexibility and diversity, and nature-friendliness. The trained model assigns normalized relative scores to each attribute based on visual features extracted from the images. These scores do not represent absolute physical measurements or intensities of spatial attributes; rather, they indicate the relative visual prominence of each attribute within a given image and enable comparative analysis across space types and time periods.

For example, in one living room image, the model assigned relative scores of 0.56 for openness and comfort, 0.15 for flexibility and diversity, and 0.32 for nature-friendliness, reflecting the comparative emphasis of these attributes in the visual composition of the space. Table 2 presents representative results for selected residential space images from the pre- and post-pandemic periods.

https://doi.org/10.3390/buildings16030589

Table 2. Relative visual attribute scores of selected residential space images.

Category	Image No.	Openness and Comfort		Flexibility and Diversity		Nature-Friendliness	
		Pre-Pandemic	Post-Pandemic	Pre-Pandemic	Post-Pandemic	Pre-Pandemic	Post-Pandemic
Balcony	1	44%	47%	55%	40%	0%	11%
	2	15%	12%	83%	24%	0%	63%
	3	16%	35%	81%	7%	1%	57%
	4	56%	57%	42%	23%	0%	18%
	5	5%	41%	94%	5%	0%	52%
Bedroom	1	51%	32%	48%	66%	0%	1%
	2	60%	39%	39%	58%	0%	1%
	3	81%	20%	16%	73%	1%	5%
	4	69%	19%	27%	78%	2%	2%
	5	72%	27%	11%	70%	15%	2%
Entrance	1	40%	8%	59%	91%	0%	0%
	2	42%	19%	56%	80%	0%	0%
	3	52%	23%	47%	76%	0%	0%
	4	73%	11%	26%	88%	0%	0%
	5	68%	37%	31%	61%	0%	0%
Living room	1	63%	59%	8%	38%	27%	2%
	2	66%	42%	1%	57%	32%	0%
	3	72%	74%	4%	24%	23%	1%
	4	75%	15%	0%	29%	24%	54%
	5	50%	79%	5%	16%	43%	3%

4.1.1. Pre-Pandemic Era

In the pre-pandemic era, balcony images generally exhibited a combination of openness and comfort and flexibility and diversity, with relatively higher visual emphasis on flexibility and diversity. Bedroom images showed notable levels of openness and comfort and flexibility and diversity, while nature-friendliness appeared at low levels. This limited presence of nature-related attributes may be associated with the occasional inclusion of decorative elements such as plants or green-toned interior finishes rather than explicit nature-oriented design features.

Entrance images displayed patterns similar to those of bedrooms, characterized primarily by openness and comfort and flexibility and diversity, with minimal visual indicators of nature-friendliness. Living room images were dominated by openness and comfort, accompanied by moderate levels of nature-friendliness, while flexibility and diversity were visually less prominent. Overall, residential spaces in the pre-pandemic era tended to emphasize spatial openness and comfort, with limited incorporation of multifunctional or nature-oriented elements.

4.1.2. Post-Pandemic Era

In the post-pandemic era, balcony images showed a pronounced increase in nature-friendliness, alongside sustained levels of openness and comfort. This shift suggests a stronger visual emphasis on incorporating natural elements into balcony spaces compared to the pre-pandemic period. Bedroom images demonstrated a substantial increase in flexibility and diversity, indicating a growing visual representation of multifunctional use, while nature-friendliness remained minimal. Openness and comfort were present at moderate levels.

https://doi.org/10.3390/buildings16030589

Entrance images exhibited a marked increase in flexibility and diversity, accompanied by a slight reduction in openness and comfort, reflecting a visual shift toward multifunctional and task-oriented spatial configurations. Living room images displayed a more balanced combination of openness and comfort and flexibility and diversity, with a limited number of images showing relatively high levels of nature-friendliness. Collectively, these patterns indicate that residential spaces in the post-pandemic era visually emphasize multifunctionality and selective integration of nature-related elements, particularly in semi-outdoor spaces such as balconies.

4.2. Pre- and Post-Pandemic Changes in Residential Design

The CNN-based image analysis revealed differentiated changes in residential space characteristics between the pre-pandemic and post-pandemic periods (Table 3). Balcony spaces showed increased visual representations of openness, comfort, and nature-related elements, indicating a growing emphasis on environmental qualities such as daylight, ventilation, and greenery in post-pandemic images. Bedrooms and entrance areas exhibited marked increases in spatial flexibility and diversity, reflecting their frequent depiction as multifunctional spaces accommodating work, study, storage, and hygiene-related activities. In contrast, openness and comfort decreased in bedrooms and entrance spaces, suggesting a shift toward more enclosed and function-oriented spatial representations. Living rooms showed relatively moderate average changes but displayed increased variability across all evaluated criteria, indicating heterogeneous spatial configurations rather than a uniform design trend. Overall, the comparative results summarized in Table 3 suggest that post-pandemic residential images reflect a redistribution of spatial attributes across domestic spaces, characterized by functional differentiation and diversified visual expressions.

Table 3. Comparison of CNN-predicted spatial design attributes between pre and post pandemic residential spaces.

		Balcony		Bedroom		Entrance		Living Room	
		Mean	**SD**	**Mean**	**SD**	**Mean**	**SD**	**Mean**	**SD**
Openness and comfort	Pre-pandemic	0.27	0.22	0.67	0.12	0.55	0.15	0.65	0.10
	Post-pandemic	0.38	0.17	0.27	0.08	0.20	0.11	0.54	0.26
Flexibility and diversity	Pre-pandemic	0.71	0.22	0.28	0.15	0.44	0.15	0.04	0.03
	Post-pandemic	0.20	0.14	0.69	0.08	0.79	0.12	0.33	0.16
Nature-friendliness	Pre-pandemic	0.02	0.04	0.04	0.06	0.00	0.00	0.30	0.08
	Post-pandemic	0.40	0.24	0.02	0.02	0.00	0.00	0.12	0.24

The deep learning-based image comparison revealed that residential spaces in the post-pandemic era exhibit distinct shifts in functional emphasis (see Table 3 and Figure 6). As visualized in Figure 6, balconies show increased openness and nature-related attributes, whereas bedrooms and entrance spaces tend to appear more enclosed and task-oriented. Flexibility and diversity increased notably in bedrooms, entrances, and living rooms, reflecting the growing demand for multifunctional residential spaces. In contrast, nature-friendliness increased primarily in balconies, indicating a spatially concentrated expression of nature-oriented design responses.

Figure 6 provides a side-by-side visualization of the model-predicted attributes, supporting the quantitative comparisons reported in Table 3.

 https://doi.org/10.3390/buildings16030589

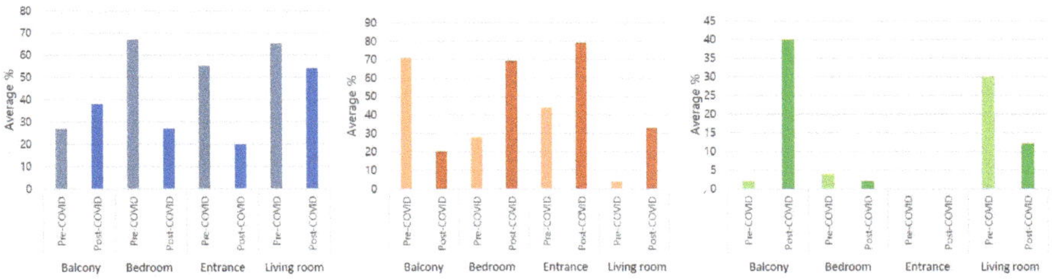

Figure 6. Side-by-side comparison of CNN-predicted spatial design attributes between pre and post pandemic residential spaces.

4.2.1. Changes in Spatial Openness and Comfort

The analysis revealed differentiated changes in openness and comfort across residential spaces between the pre- and post-pandemic periods. Balcony spaces showed an increase in predicted openness and comfort from 0.27 to 0.38 (40.7%), accompanied by a decrease in standard deviation from 0.22 to 0.17. This pattern indicates a relatively consistent shift in how balcony spaces were visually represented in post-pandemic images. The results suggest that balconies were increasingly depicted as spaces emphasizing environmental qualities such as daylight, ventilation, outdoor views, and limited natural elements, which became more salient under prolonged indoor living conditions.

In contrast, bedroom spaces exhibited a substantial decline in openness and comfort, decreasing from 0.67 to 0.27 (59.7%), with a slight reduction in standard deviation (0.12 $\rightarrow$ 0.08). This shift reflects a change in the visual characteristics of bedrooms, where enclosed layouts and function-oriented arrangements were more frequently observed in post-pandemic images. The results suggest that bedrooms were increasingly represented as spaces accommodating work, study, and other task-oriented activities, where spatial enclosure and functional efficiency were visually emphasized.

Entrance spaces also showed a marked decrease in openness and comfort, from 0.55 to 0.20 (63.6%), with reduced variability (SD: 0.15 $\rightarrow$ 0.11). This trend indicates a shift in the visual portrayal of entrances toward more defined and enclosed configurations, consistent with their depiction as buffer zones separating interior and exterior spaces.

Living rooms exhibited a relatively moderate decline in openness and comfort (0.65 $\rightarrow$ 0.54, 16.9%). However, the standard deviation increased substantially from 0.10 to 0.26, indicating greater variability in how openness and comfort were visually expressed across different living room images in the post-pandemic period. This suggests heterogeneous spatial representations rather than a uniform directional change.

4.2.2. Changes in Spatial Flexibility and Diversity

Changes in spatial flexibility and diversity exhibited a pattern distinct from that observed for openness and comfort. Bedroom spaces showed a pronounced increase in flexibility and diversity, rising from 0.28 to 0.69 (146.4%), while the standard deviation decreased (0.15 $\rightarrow$ 0.08). This pattern indicates a consistent increase in the visual depiction of bedrooms as spaces accommodating multiple functions, such as work, study, and leisure activities.

Entrance spaces also demonstrated an increase in flexibility and diversity, from 0.44 to 0.79 (79.5%), with a slight decrease in variability (SD: 0.15 $\rightarrow$ 0.12). Post-pandemic images frequently depicted entrance areas with storage systems, partitioning elements, and functional furnishings, suggesting an expansion of their visually identifiable roles beyond simple circulation.

https://doi.org/10.3390/buildings16030589

Living rooms showed a notable numerical increase in flexibility and diversity from 0.04 to 0.33, accompanied by an increase in standard deviation (0.03 → 0.16). This indicates that while flexibility-related features appeared more frequently in living room images, the degree and manner of their visual expression varied considerably across cases.

In contrast, balconies exhibited a decrease in flexibility and diversity from 0.71 to 0.20 (71.8%), with reduced variability (SD: 0.22 → 0.14). This suggests that post-pandemic balcony images tended to emphasize a narrower range of visually identifiable uses, such as seating or small-scale gardening, rather than multifunctional spatial configurations.

4.2.3. Changes in Spatial Nature-Friendliness

Among all spatial types, balcony spaces showed the most pronounced change in nature-friendliness. The predicted nature-friendliness score increased from 0.02 in the pre-pandemic period to 0.40 in the post-pandemic period, representing the largest absolute increase observed in this study. This change indicates a substantial rise in the visual presence of nature-related elements, including plants, greenery, and outdoor-oriented furnishings, in post-pandemic balcony images.

The accompanying increase in standard deviation (0.04 → 0.24) suggests considerable variability in how nature-related elements were incorporated into balcony spaces. Rather than indicating a uniform design response, this pattern reflects heterogeneous visual expressions across different residential contexts.

In contrast, indoor spaces generally exhibited declining trends in nature-friendliness. Living rooms showed a decrease from 0.30 to 0.12 (SD: 0.08 → 0.24), while bedrooms declined from 0.04 to 0.02 (SD: 0.06 → 0.02). These results indicate that visually identifiable natural elements appeared less frequently in indoor spaces within post-pandemic images, where functional and hygiene-related design features were more prominently represented.

4.3. Expert Evaluation and Methodological Supplementation

To validate the results of deep learning-based image analysis, five architecture and interior design experts with over 10 years of experience conducted expert evaluations focusing on images of the post-pandemic residential space designs. This was used as a cross-validation process to complement the limitations of machine learning-based analysis and assess the consistency between the experts' intuitive judgments and quantitative analysis results. The experts were asked to rate the proportion of each characteristic of each space as a percentage using the same evaluation criteria used in the deep learning analysis (openness and comfort, flexibility and diversity, and nature-friendliness). This approach allowed for verification of the alignment between the directional changes in residential space characteristics identified through deep learning and expert perceptions (Table 4).

Table 4. Results of expert evaluation.

	Balcony	Bedroom	Entrance	Living Room
Openness and comfort	52%	26%	28%	46%
Flexibility and diversity	37%	56%	43%	38%
Nature-friendliness	50%	21%	31%	44%

Expert evaluations generally corroborated the deep learning findings. Balconies were rated highest in openness and comfort (52%), aligning with the observed increase in openness (0.27 → 0.38), and were recognized as key pleasant spaces in the post-pandemic era. Bedrooms received the highest score for spatial flexibility and diversity (56%), strongly supporting the sharp rise identified in the analysis (0.28 → 0.69), with experts agreeing that bedrooms have evolved into multifunctional spaces. Entrance areas were also

https://doi.org/10.3390/buildings16030589

consistently evaluated (43%), reinforcing their recognition as multifunctional zones for disinfection, parcel reception, and buffering. Finally, balconies received the highest rating for nature-friendliness (50%), confirming the deep learning results (0.02 → 0.40) and highlighting their transformation into core spaces integrating indoor gardens, natural lighting, and ventilation.

However, while the expert evaluation indicated a relatively high level of nature-friendliness in living rooms (44%), the deep learning analysis showed a decline in this aspect (0.30 → 0.12). This discrepancy suggests a gap between perception and actual implementation. Experts recognize that living rooms in the post-pandemic era should be designed with nature-friendly elements, yet in practice, such features appear to be limited due to multifunctional requirements and hygiene concerns.

These results do not simply reiterate existing professional knowledge but rather clarify the relationship between expert perceptions and actual design implementation. While experts consistently recognized the importance of openness, flexibility, and nature-friendliness in post-pandemic housing, the image-based deep learning analysis revealed how unevenly these elements are realized across different residential spaces.

For example, although experts rated living rooms as highly nature-friendly, the visual analysis showed a notable decline in nature-related elements in practice. This discrepancy highlights a gap between design intention and real-world application. By quantifying such gaps and identifying which spatial attributes are consistently implemented versus aspirational, this study provides evidence-based guidance that complements professional expertise and supports more targeted and realistic residential design strategies.

4.4. Comprehensive Interpretation of Spatial Change Patterns

Synthesizing the results, the pandemic has generated two contrasting phenomena in residential spaces: functional specialization and multifunctionality. Balconies have been specialized as well-being spaces emphasizing comfort and nature-friendliness, while bedrooms and living rooms have evolved into multifunctional areas accommodating diverse activities.

These changes signify a reconfiguration of spatial hierarchy. The balcony, traditionally regarded as an auxiliary space, has emerged as a core living area, whereas primary living spaces such as bedrooms and living rooms have been redefined as flexible spaces that shift functions depending on circumstances.

Furthermore, variations in standard deviation highlight the growing prevalence of personalized space use. In particular, the substantial increases observed in balconies (SD: 0.04 → 0.24) and living rooms (SD: 0.03 → 0.16; 0.08 → 0.24) indicate that even within the same spatial type, utilization differs considerably according to residents' needs and preferences.

5. Conclusions

This study investigated changes in residential spatial characteristics before and after the COVID-19 pandemic by applying a deep learning-based image analysis framework and expert evaluation. By quantitatively comparing spatial attributes across different residential spaces, the study aimed to identify how the post-pandemic context has influenced residential space design and usage patterns.

Rather than positioning deep learning as the primary contribution, this study demonstrates how an image-based analytical tool can support empirical investigation of residential design transformation in response to societal disruption.

The results reveal that spatial transformations in the post-pandemic era are not uniformly distributed across all residential spaces, but are instead concentrated in specific

https://doi.org/10.3390/buildings16030589

areas such as balconies, bedrooms, and entrance spaces. Among these, balconies exhibited the most pronounced changes across multiple dimensions, including openness, comfort, and nature-friendliness. Rather than reflecting a single standardized design trend, these changes suggest a diversification of balcony usage, responding to increased time spent at home and limitations on outdoor activities. The increased variation observed in nature-related attributes further indicates that residents adopt different strategies depending on spatial conditions and lifestyles. Bedrooms demonstrated a notable increase in spatial flexibility and diversity, supporting the interpretation that they have evolved beyond traditional sleeping functions into multifunctional spaces accommodating work, rest, and leisure. Entrance areas also showed consistent changes, reflecting their emerging role as buffer zones that mediate hygiene, circulation, and transitional activities in response to pandemic-related concerns. In contrast, living rooms and other indoor spaces exhibited relatively modest or even declining changes in nature-related attributes, suggesting that functional efficiency and hygiene considerations may have constrained the incorporation of nature-oriented elements indoors.

Expert evaluations largely supported the deep learning results, particularly regarding the increased multifunctionality of bedrooms and the enhanced nature-friendliness of balconies. However, discrepancies were observed in the assessment of living rooms, where experts expressed higher expectations for nature-oriented design than were reflected in the image-based analysis. This divergence highlights the value of combining computational analysis with expert judgment, as it allows for the identification of gaps between design intentions, professional expectations, and realized spatial configurations.

It is acknowledged that images shared on social media platforms tend to be visually curated and may emphasize aspirational aesthetics rather than everyday functional realities. Accordingly, this study does not interpret social media images as direct representations of daily residential use. Instead, they are understood as visual artifacts that reflect socially shared design intentions, aspirations, and normative expectations of residential spaces at a given time. In this sense, the dataset captures emerging design ideals that influence how residential spaces are planned, renovated, and represented, which constitute a critical dimension of residential design trends in the post-pandemic era.

Several limitations should be noted. First, the analysis is based on visual data and does not directly capture residents' subjective experiences or actual behavioral patterns within residential spaces. Second, cultural and regional factors were not explicitly modeled, which may limit the generalizability of the findings across different housing contexts. Future studies could address these limitations by integrating image-based deep learning with surveys, interviews, behavioral data, or cross-cultural comparisons to further validate the relationship between visual design trends and lived residential experiences. Third, while social media-based image data enables large-scale and timely analysis of housing design trends, reliance on platforms like Instagram and Pinterest can lead to selection bias, as images tend to reflect visually appealing or curated images rather than everyday living environments. Future research could expand data sources to include other design platforms or validate image-based analyses with survey or interview data to enhance their validity.

Despite these limitations, this study demonstrates the potential of deep learning–based image analysis as a complementary methodological tool in residential design research. By quantitatively structuring widely observed yet often intuitively discussed design changes, the findings provide empirical evidence of how residential spaces adapt under societal disruptions. The results offer practical insights for architects, designers, and housing planners seeking to develop adaptable and resilient residential environments in response to future public health crises and lifestyle transformations.

https://doi.org/10.3390/buildings16030589

While this study does not directly propose regulatory or engineering parameters such as Floor Area Ratios (FAR), zoning codes, or HVAC system specifications, the findings provide quantitative spatial evidence that can inform such technical discussions. For example, the increased functional significance of balconies and entrance areas as buffer zones suggests a need to reconsider their spatial allocation, environmental control, and infrastructural support in future housing guidelines. The data-driven identification of space-specific functional shifts offers a foundation upon which architectural regulations, building services planning, and environmental control strategies may be further developed in interdisciplinary research.

Author Contributions: Conception and design, H.L.; analysis and interpretation of the data, H.L.; investigation and resources, H.-J.Y.; data curation, H.L.; the drafting of the paper, H.L. and H.-J.Y.; visualization, H.-J.Y.; revising it critically for intellectual content, H.L.; and the final approval of the version to be published, H.L. and H.-J.Y. All authors have read and agreed to the published version of the manuscript.

Funding: This research was funded by [National Research Foundation of Korea] grant number [RS-2023-00244419].

Data Availability Statement: The data presented in this study are available on request from the corresponding author. The data are not publicly available due to privacy and ethical restrictions related to the use of social media imagery and personal information.

Conflicts of Interest: The authors declare no conflicts of interest.

References

1. Han, D. The Architecture in the "New Normal" era. *Rev. Archit. Build. Sci.* **2020**, *64*, 20–21.
2. Lee, D.Y.; Kwon, O.J.; Kim, J.Y. Changes in Housing Function and Space Preference in the Post COVID Era: Plan Proposal for the Echo Boomer Generation. *J. Korean Hous. Assoc.* **2022**, *33*, 43–53. [CrossRef]
3. Lee, S.; Chang, M. Changes in daily life and quality of life of the elderly due to the COVID-19 pandemic: Focusing on a comparison between single-family and multi-family. *Hum. Ecol. Res.* **2022**, *60*, 163–176. [CrossRef]
4. Stoyanov, G. Human-centered residential architecture in the post-COVID era: Exploring developments and significance. *Athens J. Health Med. Sci.* **2023**, *10*, 227–248. [CrossRef]
5. Hanna, H.A.F. Towards domestic space design in the post-COVID-19 era: A review of relevant literature. *Alex. Eng. J.* **2023**, *73*, 487–503. [CrossRef]
6. Alhadedy, N.H.; Gabr, H.S. Home design features post-COVID-19. *J. Eng. Appl. Sci.* **2022**, *69*, 87. [CrossRef]
7. He, K.; Zhang, X.; Ren, S.; Sun, J. Deep residual learning for image recognition. In Proceedings of the 2016 IEEE Conference on Computer Vision and Pattern Recognition, Las Vegas, NV, USA, 27–30 June 2016. [CrossRef]
8. Chaillou, S. Archigan: Artificial intelligence x architecture. In *Architectural Intelligence: Selected Papers from the 1st International Conference on Computational Design and Robotic Fabrication (CDRF 2019)*; Springer: Singapore, 2020.
9. Wu, W.; Feng, Y. Interior space design and automatic layout method based on CNN. *Math. Probl. Eng.* **2022**, *2022*, 8006069. [CrossRef]
10. Park, B.H.; Son, K.; Hyun, K.H. Interior design network of furnishing and color pairing with object detection and color analysis based on deep learning. In *International Conference on Computer-Aided Architectural Design Futures*; Springer: Singapore, 2021; pp. 237–249.
11. Kim, J.; Lee, J.K. Implementation and Application of Interior Design Style Training Model using Deep Learning. *Korean Inst. Inter. Des. J.* **2020**, *29*, 96–104.
12. Bae, S.; Han, H. A proposal of spatial direction for the efficiency of home work in the homo untact Era–analysis of user behavior of mixed workspace using experience design elements. *Conf. J. Korea Inst. Inter. Des.* **2020**, *22*, 270–275.
13. Birer, E.; Hasgül, E.; Can, E. Transformation of home environments in pandemic: The concept of "life fits into room" in the new normal. *Open House Int.* **2022**, *47*, 87–106. [CrossRef]
14. Peters, T.; Halleran, A. How our homes impact our health: Using a COVID-19 informed approach to examine urban apartment housing. *Archnet-IJAR Int. J. Archit. Res.* **2021**, *15*, 10–27. [CrossRef]
15. Lim, S.; Kim, Y.; Song, S. A Study on the Change of Spatial Use of Unit Housing Floor Plan in the Untact Era—A case of 84 m^2 unit plan of Korea Land and Housing Corporation after 2015. *J. Korea Inst. Spat. Des.* **2021**, *16*, 73–84.

 https://doi.org/10.3390/buildings16030589

16. Yang, H.; Kim, S.A.; Chung, J.S.; Lee, H. A study on the planning of variable housing for supporting working from home in the pandemic—Focusing on the variable space using the smart wall system in apartment building. *J. Archit. Inst. Korea* **2022**, *38*, 3–14.
17. Jung, M.W.; Ko, I.L. A Study on the Cultural Characteristics and Change of Korean Residential Settlement. *J. Archit. Inst. Korea* **1994**, *10*, 73–86.
18. Park, G.O. Changes in housing planning and residential lifestyle. *J. Korean Hous. Assoc.* **2009**, *8*, 43–58.
19. Khosla, A.; Jayadevaprakash, N.; Yao, B.; Li, F.F. Novel dataset for fine-grained image categorization: Stanford dogs. In Proceedings of the CVPR Workshop on Fine-Grained Visual Categorization (FGVC), Colorado Springs, CO, USA, 20–25 June 2011.
20. LeCun, Y.; Bengio, Y.; Hinton, G. Deep learning. *Nature* **2015**, *521*, 436–444. [CrossRef] [PubMed]
21. Deng, J.; Dong, W.; Socher, R.; Li, L.J.; Li, K.; Li, F.-F. Imagenet: A large-scale hierarchical image database. In Proceedings of the 2009 IEEE Conference on Computer Vision and Pattern Recognition, Miami, FL, USA, 20–25 June 2009; pp. 248–255.
22. Kumar, G.; Kumar, A. A Deep Learning Approach for Interior Designing of Apartment Building Architecture using U2 Net. In Proceedings of the 2022 International Conference on Sustainable Computing and Data Communication Systems (ICSCDS), Erode, India, 7–9 April 2022; pp. 1465–1471. [CrossRef]
23. Kim, J.; Lee, J.K. Stochastic detection of interior design styles using a deep-learning model for reference images. *Appl. Sci.* **2020**, *10*, 7299. [CrossRef]
24. Bell, S.; Bala, K. Learning visual similarity for product design with convolutional neural networks. *ACM Trans. Graph.* **2015**, *34*, 1–10. [CrossRef]
25. Seo, Y.M.; Kim, W.K. Information visualization process for spatial big data. *Spat. Inf. Res.* **2015**, *23*, 109–116.
26. Cetinic, E.; Lipic, T.; Grgic, S. A deep learning perspective on beauty, sentiment, and remembrance of art. *IEEE Access* **2019**, *7*, 73694–73710. [CrossRef]
27. Cetinic, E.; She, J. Understanding and creating art with AI: Review and outlook. *ACM Trans. Multimed. Comput. Commun. Appl. (TOMM)* **2022**, *18*, 1–22. [CrossRef]
28. Hu, Z.; Wen, Y.; Liu, L.; Jiang, J.; Hong, R.; Wang, M.; Yan, S. Visual classification of furniture styles. *ACM Trans. Intell. Syst. Technol. (TIST)* **2017**, *8*, 1–20. [CrossRef]
29. Liu, L.; Dzyabura, D.; Mizik, N. Visual listening in: Extracting brand image portrayed on social media. *Mark. Sci.* **2020**, *39*, 669–686. [CrossRef]
30. Krizhevsky, A.; Sutskever, I.; Hinton, G.E. ImageNet classification with deep convolutional neural networks. *Commun. ACM* **2017**, *60*, 84–90. [CrossRef]
31. LeCun, Y.; Boser, B.; Denker, J.S.; Henderson, D.; Howard, R.E.; Hubbard, W.; Jackel, L.D. Handwritten Digit Recognition with a Back-Propagation Network. In *Advances in Neural Information Processing Systems 2 (NIPS 1989)*; Touretzky, D.S., Ed.; Morgan Kaufmann: San Mateo, CA, USA, 1990; pp. 396–404.
32. Wong, W.K.; Yuen, C.W.M.; Fan, D.D.; Chan, L.K.; Fung, E.H.K. Stitching defect detection and classification using wavelet transform and BP neural network. *Expert Syst. Appl.* **2009**, *36*, 3845–3856. [CrossRef]
33. Makantasis, K.; Protopapadakis, E.; Doulamis, A.; Doulamis, N.; Loupos, C. Deep convolutional neural networks for efficient vision-based tunnel inspection. In Proceedings of the 2015 IEEE International Conference on Intelligent Computer Communication and Processing (ICCP), Cluj-Napoca, Romania, 3–5 September 2015.
34. Li, Y.; Zhao, W.; Pan, J. Deformable patterned fabric defect detection with fisher criterion-based deep learning. *IEEE Trans. Autom. Sci. Eng.* **2016**, *14*, 1256–1264. [CrossRef]
35. Jung, S.Y.; Lee, S.K.; Park, C.I.; Cho, S.Y.; Yu, J.H. A method for detecting concrete cracks using deep-learning and image processing. *J. Archit. Inst. Korea Struct. Constr.* **2019**, *35*, 163–170.
36. Lee, S.H.; Lu, N. A methodology of enhancing the accuracy of image classification with CNN. *J. Archit. Inst. Korea* **2020**, *36*, 15–22. [CrossRef]
37. Lee, S.H.; Han, J.H. Estimation of human preference for architectural shape using CNN. *J. Archit. Inst. Korea* **2022**, *38*, 3–11. [CrossRef]
38. Settimo, G.; Bertinato, L.; Bonadonna, L.; D'Ancona, P.; Santarsiero, A.; Soggiu, M.E. *Indicazioni ad Interim per la Prevenzione e Gestione Degli Ambienti Indoor in Relazione Alla Trasmissione Dell'infezione da Virus SARS-CoV-2*; Istituto Superiore di Sanità: Rome, Italy, 2020.
39. Cho, Y.H.; Kim, M.D. A Study on the characteristics of Japanese tradition in the space of Kengo Kuma. In Proceedings of the 2011 Kiid Autumn Conference Proceedings, Seoul, Republic of Korea, 25–29 October 2011; pp. 47–53.
40. Yoon, J.; Ryoo, H.Y. Characteristics of Images in Image-based SNS and User Satisfaction—Focusing on Instagram and Pinterest. *J. HCI Soc. Korea* **2019**, *14*, 5–13. [CrossRef]
41. Pal, K.K.; Sudeep, K.S. Preprocessing for image classification by convolutional neural networks. In Proceedings of the 2016 IEEE International Conference on Recent Trends in Electronics, Information & Communication Technology (RTEICT), Bangalore, India, 20–21 May 2016; pp. 1778–1781.

 https://doi.org/10.3390/buildings16030589

42. Ayoub, L.; Kobayashi, H. The concept of openness in the architectural context. *J. Archit. Plan. (Trans. AIJ)* **2001**, *66*, 305–313. [CrossRef]
43. Yoo, E.; Jang, H.S.; Kim, K.J.; Jung, H.H.; Kim, Y.J. Effect of Green Interior Home on Emotional Psychology of Human. *J. People Plants Environ.* **2015**, *18*, 249–256. [CrossRef]
44. Perez, L.; Wang, J. The effectiveness of data augmentation in image classification using deep learning. *arXiv* **2017**, arXiv:1712.04621. [CrossRef]
45. Taylor, L.; Nitschke, G. Improving deep learning with generic data augmentation. In Proceedings of the 2018 IEEE Symposium Series on Computational Intelligence, Bangalore, India, 18–21 November 2018; pp. 1542–1547.
46. Powers, D.M.W. Evaluation: From Precision, Recall and F-Measure to ROC, Informedness, Markedness and Correlation. *J. Mach. Learn. Technol.* **2011**, *2*, 37–63.
47. Sokolova, M.; Lapalme, G. A systematic analysis of performance measures for classification tasks. *Inf. Process. Manag.* **2009**, *45*, 427–437. [CrossRef]
48. Alawad, A. Adapting and interacting with home design during the COVID-19 pandemic. *Int. Des. J.* **2021**, *11*, 53–63. [CrossRef]
49. Kim, M.K.; Kim, E.J. Apartment Space Planning Directions for Infectious Disease Prevention and Management: Insights Based on Residents' Experiences. *Buildings* **2023**, *13*, 2203. [CrossRef]
50. Aronis, C. The balconies of Tel-Aviv: Cultural history and urban politics. *Isr. Stud.* **2009**, *14*, 157–180. [CrossRef]
51. Aydin, D.; Sayar, G. Questioning the use of the balcony in apartments during the COVID-19 pandemic process. *Archnet-IJAR Int. J. Archit. Res.* **2021**, *15*, 51–63. [CrossRef]
52. Cha, Y.J.; Lee, T. A Proposal of the Appropriate Housing Plan for Young Single-Person Households in the Post-pandemic Era. In Proceedings of the Spring Annual Conference of AIK, Seoul, Republic of Korea, 28–29 April 2022; pp. 160–163.

https://doi.org/10.3390/buildings16030589

buildings

MDPI

Article

Intelligent HBIM Framework for Group-Oriented Preventive Protection: A Case Study of the Suopo Ancient Watchtower Complex in Danba

Li Zhang [1,2], Chen Tang [2], Yaofan Ye [2], Jinzi Yang [2] and Feng Xu [1,*]

[1] School of Architecture and Planning, Hunan University, Changsha 410082, China; 80300009@swun.edu.cn
[2] School of Architecture, Southwest Minzu University, Chengdu 610207, China; 18328396891@163.com (C.T.); 15888242283@163.com (Y.Y.); 15228875548@163.com (J.Y.)
* Correspondence: fengxu@hnu.edu.cn

Abstract

Heritage Building Information Modeling (HBIM) is accelerating the transition from reactive restoration to preventive conservation in architectural heritage management. Nevertheless, research at the heritage-cluster scale remains limited, particularly in terms of multi-source data integration, dynamic value–risk coupling, and lifecycle-oriented decision support. This study proposes an intelligent HBIM-based framework designed to support integrated data processing, automated value–risk assessment, and preventive intervention planning for masonry heritage clusters. The framework is validated through its application to the Suopo Ancient Watchtower Complex in Danba, Sichuan, consisting of 84 polygonal stepped-in stone towers. By integrating 3D laser scanning, unmanned aerial vehicle (UAV) oblique photogrammetry, and historical archival data, a closed-loop workflow is established, spanning data acquisition, parametric semantic modeling, and intervention prioritization. A dedicated parametric component library and hierarchical semantic database tailored to irregular polygonal masonry significantly enhance modeling consistency, semantic coherence, and cross-building reusability. Leveraging the Revit Application Programming Interface (API) and Dynamo, the framework embeds a value–risk model ($P = V \times R$), enabling automated component-level evaluation, real-time visualization of conservation priorities, and one-click generation of intervention lists. Results demonstrate improved modeling accuracy, efficiency, and decision reliability compared with conventional manual workflows. The framework offers a scalable and replicable pathway for sustainable conservation of masonry heritage clusters in high-seismic regions and provides a foundation for future integration with IoT-enabled digital twin systems.

Keywords: Danba watchtowers; heritage cluster; value-risk assessment; intelligent decision support; parametric modeling

1. Introduction

In recent years, architectural heritage preservation has undergone a paradigm shift, moving from reactive "post-event restoration" toward proactive "preventive protection," which emphasizes continuous monitoring, risk assessment, and timely interventions to mitigate potential damage before it occurs [1]. Heritage Building Information Modeling (HBIM) has become the core technical means driving this transformation [2–4]. This global shift is also reflected in UNESCO and ICOMOS guidelines, which highlight that systematic monitoring and risk-oriented preventive measures are essential for safeguarding heritage under the compounded pressures of climate change, natural disasters, and human activities [5].

In China, immovable cultural heritage sites are numerous and diverse, but the overall state of preservation is worrying. The ongoing Fourth National Survey of Immovable Cultural Relics further highlights the grim reality that a large number of heritage sites are at high risk [6]. The traditional passive model relying on restoration is no longer adequate to address complex, multi-scale risks; thus, there is an urgent need to establish an active protection mechanism based on digitalization and intelligence. Against this backdrop, the concept of a "heritage cluster" has been proposed, referring to a spatially contiguous set of heritage assets that share historical functions and construction logic, with interdependent internal structures. Compared with individual buildings, heritage clusters require holistic, cross-building risk control and integrated management, necessitating the development of dedicated, cluster-level digital information frameworks [7].

Globally, HBIM has been widely adopted in fields including geometric reconstruction, damage documentation, structural analysis, and virtual visualization [8–12]. Recent advances in Heritage Building Information Modeling (HBIM) have been largely driven by European research groups. Notably, Oreni and Banfi pioneered ontology-based semantic enrichment frameworks for heritage documentation [13]; Brumana and colleagues developed robust parametric scan-to-HBIM reconstruction workflows [14]; Logothetis investigated interoperability standards and their application in conservation management [15]; and Martínez-Rodrigo integrated HBIM with structural risk assessment to support decision-making in heritage protection [16]. In recent years, the integration of artificial intelligence (AI) has further improved the automation of damage identification and condition assessment [17]. However, existing research still shows significant limitations: most studies focus on individual buildings, leaving cluster-level integration largely unexplored [18]. Similarly, research on Scottish brochs [19], Italian Apennine watchtowers [20], and Himalayan stone tower groups [21] highlights comparable challenges, including seismic vulnerability, material deterioration, and cluster-scale management issues, underscoring the urgent need for integrated HBIM workflows specifically tailored to heritage clusters [22].

The Suopo Ancient Watchtower Group in Suopo Township, Danba County, Ganzi Prefecture, Sichuan Province, exemplifies this need. The settlement comprises 84 stone-built watchtowers, with floor plans ranging from four to thirteen sides, renowned for their outstanding seismic performance and unique Jiarong Tibetan cultural significance, and was listed in the "Tentative List of China's World Cultural Heritage" in 2013 [23]. Located in a high-intensity seismic zone, the site is further challenged by long-term material weathering and increasing tourism pressures, which together pose persistent risks to its structural integrity and cultural value. Similar vulnerabilities and transformation pressures affecting Tibetan-style dwellings and settlements under seismic and environmental constraints have been reported in recent studies [24–26], highlighting the broader relevance of Suopo as a representative case for cluster-scale preventive conservation research.

Motivated by these challenges, this study proposes a cluster-level intelligent HBIM framework for preventive protection, validated through the Suopo Ancient Watchtower Group. The framework achieves systematic management at the cluster scale by integrating multi-source data, semantic–parametric representations, and value–risk-driven intelligent decision-making. It extends HBIM applications beyond individual buildings, providing standardized tools for modeling, enabling cross-building management, and supporting real-time, automated protection decision support [27,28]. This approach significantly enhances management efficiency and sustainability for heritage clusters, laying the groundwork for replicable cluster-level heritage protection strategies [29].

https://doi.org/10.3390/buildings16050995

The remainder of this paper is structured as follows. Section 2 outlines the methodological framework, including multi-source data acquisition, parametric modeling strategies, the value–risk assessment model, and sensitivity analysis. Section 3 presents the implementation results at both component and cluster scales. Section 4 discusses the technical contributions, performance evaluation, limitations, and broader implications in relation to international research. Section 5 concludes the study and highlights directions for future development toward IoT-integrated digital twin systems.

2. Research Methodology

This study establishes an intelligent HBIM-based preventive protection framework for heritage clusters, designed to address the limitations of existing HBIM applications in cluster-scale management, dynamic risk assessment, and decision-making automation. The framework comprises three progressive modules, creating a closed-loop workflow encompassing multi-source data collection, parametric representation, and value–risk-driven intelligent decision-making. During the entire research process, formal approval was secured from the Danba County Cultural Heritage Administration and local communities. Specifically, community members were invited to participate in the process of cultural value identification, thus ensuring the study adheres to ethical standards and respects cultural sensitivity [30]. Considering the widespread use of Autodesk Revit in HBIM practice, the Autodesk Revit 2023 (Autodesk Inc., San Rafael, CA, USA) platform was selected as the core modeling environment for this study. Through the Revit Application Programming Interface (API) and Dynamo (integrated within Autodesk Revit 2023) visual programming interface, the system enables rule-based automation and customization of parametric components. This setup ensures the framework's modules can be effectively implemented and integrated within a cluster-scale HBIM environment.

2.1. Technical Framework

The overall structure of the framework is divided into three main modules (as shown in Figure 1):

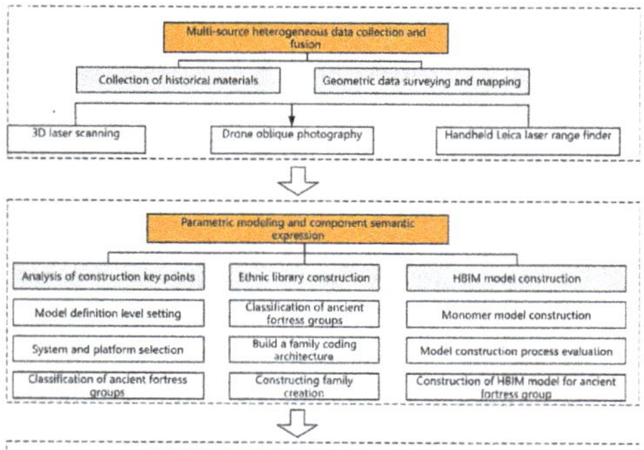

Figure 1. Overall technical framework of the intelligent cluster-oriented preventive HBIM system. Orange boxes represent the three core modules of the framework; gray/white boxes denote specific tasks and sub-processes within each module. Large hollow arrows indicate the main workflow progression between stages, while solid lines show logical connections between components. Dashed borders define the boundaries of each functional module. (Source: Authors' own elaboration).

https://doi.org/10.3390/buildings16050995

2.1.1. Multi-Source Heterogeneous Data Collection and Fusion

Geometric morphology, material properties, damage conditions, and cultural information of the watchtowers are acquired via a combination of 3D laser scanning, unmanned aerial vehicle (UAV) oblique photogrammetry, historical archive collation, and field surveys. Point cloud registration and fusion are implemented using the Iterative Closest Point (ICP) algorithm to ensure the high-precision integration of multi-source data [31].

2.1.2. Parametric Modeling and Component-Level Semantic Representation

A multi-level HBIM model is established on the Autodesk Revit 2023 platform (Autodesk Inc., San Rafael, CA, USA), and a dedicated parametric component library is developed for polygonal stepped-in stone masonry. Semantic information, including materials, construction details, historical maintenance records, and damage information, are embedded at the component level. An alphanumeric coding system is adopted to enable the unified organization and efficient retrieval of models within the cluster.

2.1.3. Value–Risk-Driven Intelligent Management Module

By leveraging Revit API and Dynamo visual programming, the value–risk evaluation model based on the ICOMOS value system and structural and environmental risk factors is deeply integrated into the HBIM system. The core calculation formula is the priority index $P = V \times R$ (where V denotes the comprehensive value score and R denotes the risk coefficient). After experts complete the initial weight calibration, the system can automatically calculate the protection priorities of all watchtowers and their components, conduct real-time color and opacity mapping within the model, and generate emergency intervention lists with one click [32]. This module incorporates a built-in rule engine that supports threshold-triggered alerts and reserves interfaces for Industry Foundation Classes (IFC) and Power Business Intelligence (BI) extensions, allowing future integration of Internet of Things (IoT) sensors—networked devices capable of collecting real-time environmental and structural data—for more advanced dynamic monitoring of heritage components.

2.2. Case Study and Data

The research subject is the Suopo Ancient Watchtower Group in Danba County, Sichuan Province (Figure 2), comprising 84 stone-built watchtowers of diverse configurations (four-cornered, five-cornered, eight-cornered, thirteen-cornered, etc., Figure 3). These watchtowers adopt local dry-laid rubble masonry and feature a typical stepped-in structure with a narrow top and a wider base [33]. Additionally, located in a high-intensity seismic zone, they are continuously threatened by earthquakes, weathering, and rainwater erosion, thus serving as an ideal case for verifying the applicability of the proposed framework.

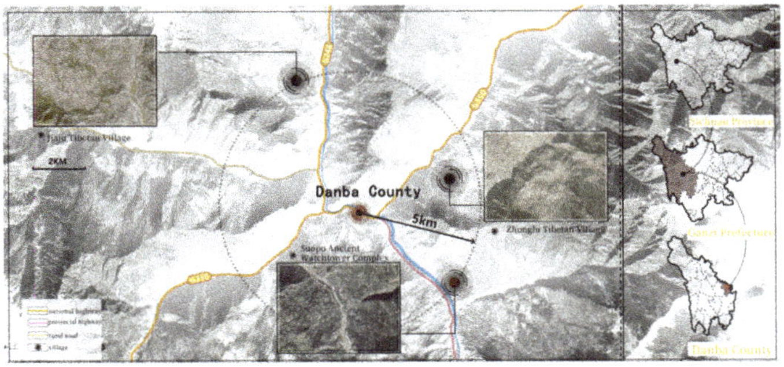

Figure 2. Spatial distribution of Suopo watchtower cluster. The right panel shows the location of Danba County within Ganzi Prefecture and Sichuan Province. The black dots indicate the distribution

https://doi.org/10.3390/buildings16050995

of ancient watchtower clusters and Tibetan villages. The dashed gray circles represent the buffer zones (or monitoring radii) around key heritage sites. The blue and pink lines denote provincial highways and rural roads, respectively. The black arrow with label indicates a distance of 5 km for scale reference. Inset images show detailed views of Jiaju Tibetan Village, Zhonglu Tibetan Village, and the Suopo complex. (Source: Authors' own elaboration).

Figure 3. (**a**) Four-corner watchtower; (**b**) Pentagonal watchtower; (**c**) Octagonal watchtower; (**d**) Thirteen-Cornered Watchtower. (Source: Authors' own elaboration).

Details regarding data collection technologies and their corresponding objectives are presented in Table 1. All the collected data have undergone unified registration, denoising, and coordinate anonymization processes.

Table 1. Data Acquisition Techniques (Source: Authors' own elaboration).

Data Source	Purpose	Method and Instructions
Field Research & Documentary Archives	Reconstruction of Historical and Cultural Information and Damage Conditions	Combining local chronicles with resident interviews to ensure cultural context accuracy
3D Laser Scanning	High-Precision Geometric Data Acquisition	Ground-Based 3D Laser Scanner
Tilted Photogrammetry Using Drones	High-Altitude Perspective and Cluster Layout Information Collection	Five-Lens System with SFM (Structure from Motion) Algorithm-Optimized Reconstruction

2.3. Value and Risk Assessment

The value assessment is grounded in the ICOMOS framework, employing a multi-criteria matrix that encompasses five dimensions: historical, artistic, scientific, social, and cultural. To determine the weights for each criterion, the Delphi method was applied. This structured consensus-building technique involved a panel of 10 experts selected for their diverse expertise and stakeholder representation: five senior researchers in heritage conservation, three officials from cultural heritage management authorities and two specialists in Jiarong Tibetan architecture and culture. This composition ensured interdisciplinary balance and incorporation of both scientific and indigenous knowledge perspectives.

 https://doi.org/10.3390/buildings16050995

The Delphi process consisted of three iterative rounds. In the first round, experts independently assigned initial weights and provided qualitative justification. In the second round, anonymized statistical feedback (mean, median, and range) from the first round was distributed, allowing experts to revise their judgments. The third round confirmed final weights until convergence was achieved, yielding a consistency coefficient $k > 0.8$. Particular attention was paid to the cultural value dimension, where weights were refined in consultation with local community representatives during the field survey, thereby respecting cultural sensitivity and contextual authenticity. The resulting weights are presented in Table 2.

Table 2. Weights of Value Criteria Determined by the Delphi Method (Source: Authors' own elaboration).

Value Dimension	Weight	Primary Rationale (Expert Consensus)
Historical	0.25	Highest priority due to the towers' age and role in regional defense history
Scientific	0.22	Emphasis on unique seismic-resistant masonry techniques
Artistic	0.2	Recognition of distinctive polygonal forms and decorative elements
Social	0.18	Community identity and ongoing cultural practices
Cultural	0.15	Symbolic significance within Jiarong Tibetan traditions
Total	1	—

For the risk assessment, the framework integrates material degradation (e.g., weathering and biological growth), structural vulnerability (e.g., cracks and inclination), and environmental threats (e.g., seismic activity and rainfall erosion). The risk coefficient R (ranging from 0 to 1) is calculated via weighted summation of these factors, with sub-weights calibrated through the same expert panel to maintain consistency.

The priority index is then computed as $P = V \times R$, where V is the weighted comprehensive value score. A value–risk priority matrix is subsequently generated to categorize components and watchtowers into emergency intervention (P0), high-priority monitoring (P1), medium-priority (P2), and routine maintenance (P3). This model is deeply embedded in the HBIM system via Dynamo scripts and Revit shared parameters, enabling automated calculation and real-time visualization of priorities across the entire cluster once expert weights are inputted.

2.4. Sensitivity Analysis of the Value–Risk Priority Model

To further validate the robustness of the priority index formula $P = V \times R$ and justify the adoption of a multiplicative relationship, a sensitivity analysis was conducted. The multiplicative form was selected because it effectively captures the compounded urgency of high-value assets facing high risks, aligning with preventive conservation principles outlined in ICOMOS guidelines [34], where objects with simultaneously elevated value and risk demand prioritized intervention. In contrast to additive models, which may underestimate such synergies, the multiplicative approach ensures that priority escalates non-linearly for critical cases, as supported by similar value–risk matrices in heritage management literature [35].

Sensitivity to uncertainty in value criteria weights was assessed using Monte Carlo simulation (10,000 iterations). Weights for the five value dimensions (historical, artistic, scientific, social, and cultural) were sampled from a Dirichlet distribution with concentration parameters $\alpha = [10, 10, 10, 10, 10]$, simulating minor expert disagreements following Delphi convergence ($\kappa > 0.8$). This distribution centers weights around equal proportions (0.2) while allowing realistic small variations. Comprehensive value scores V were recalculated for each iteration, multiplied by fixed risk coefficients R to generate distributions of P or representative components.

 https://doi.org/10.3390/buildings16050995

2.5. Parametric Modeling

Level of Development (LOD) is used to define the level of geometric and semantic detail in the model. The adaptation of LOD frameworks in HBIM has been recognized as a critical methodological approach to balance the complexity of historical information with computational efficiency [36]. Unlike new constructions, LOD in heritage contexts often integrates geometric accuracy with the "Level of Knowledge" (LoK), encompassing archaeological and stratigraphic data [37]. In this study, a grading strategy corresponding to LOD 100–400 is adopted, where LOD 100 represents coarse conceptual massing, LOD 200 includes generalized system geometry, LOD 300 provides accurate geometry with basic parameters, and LOD 400 represents fully detailed, constructible elements with complete semantic information. To organize the model at the component level, a three-level classification system based on type, material, and construction subclass is established with a unified alphanumeric coding. Contours of irregular polygonal plans are first accurately generated in Rhino before being imported into Revit. Stepped-in walls are implemented via adjustable angle parameters, while regular four-cornered watchtowers are batch-instantiated through templates [38]. This process ultimately develops a parametric component library containing over 100 reusable families, including walls, doors, windows, decorations, and roofs, which supports the efficient assembly and semantic retrieval of cluster-scale models.

3. Results

Based on the proposed intelligent HBIM-based preventive protection framework, this study has completed comprehensive digital modeling, semantic representation, and value–risk analysis for the Suopo Ancient Watchtower Group in Danba, ultimately establishing a cluster-scale digital system for sustainable management. The core outcomes encompass a dedicated parametric component library, a multi-level HBIM database, a unified classification and coding system, and an embedded intelligent decision-making module.

3.1. Core HBIM Outcomes

3.1.1. Parametric Component Family Library

A dedicated parametric component library tailored to the Suopo Ancient Watchtowers has been established on the Revit platform, covering six major categories: walls, foundations, roofs, doors and windows, stairs, and Jiarong Tibetan-style decorations. This library integrates geometric parameters, material properties, historical maintenance records, and damage tags, enabling the precise representation of 3° stepped-in angles, polygonal plans, and decorative details. A three-level coding system (category–type–serial number) is adopted to ensure the unique identification and efficient retrieval of components (Table 3). Successfully adapted to various watchtower configurations ranging from four-cornered to thirteen-cornered, the library provides reusable standard resources for cluster-scale model assembly.

Typical components are detailed as follows:

Wall family: Developed based on system families, it comprises a 400 mm rubble base and a 20 mm yellow mud surface layer. An adjustable 3° stepped-in parameter is incorporated to accurately capture the "narrow top and wide base" characteristics of Tibetan masonry.

Door and window families: A total of 8 window families and 4 door families have been developed. Key parameters include opening width, windowsill height, and frame proportions, with links to on-site images and damage annotations. This design enables the simultaneous expression of both geometric and heritage information (Table 4).

 https://doi.org/10.3390/buildings16050995

Table 3. Component Coding (Source: Authors' own elaboration).

Primary Category	Level 2 Type	Level 2 Number	Level 3 Number	Sample Code	Description
ZQ (Pillar/Wall)	QL (Wall)	1	1	ZQ.QL.01_001	Four-cornered fortified wall foundation
WF (Roof)	DC (Ridge)	2	2	WF.DC.02_002	Thirteen-sided conical ridge
ZS (Decorative)	LWZ (Lawuze)	3	1	ZS.LWZ.03_001	Mountain Flower Pavilion Decorations

Table 4. Parametric families for doors and windows with damage annotation (Source: Authors' own elaboration).

Component Coding	Component Front View	3D View of Component	Component Prototype
Window 01 MLC-SJD-01-1-ZS.CL.01-001	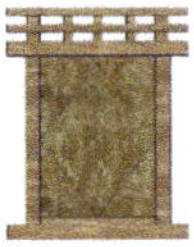		
Window 01 MLC-SJD-01-1-ZS.CL.01-002			
Window 01 MLC-SJD-01-1-ZS.CL.01-003			
Window 01 MLC-SJD-01-1-ZS.CL.01-004			
Window 01 MLC-SJD-01-1-ZS.CL.01-005			
Window 01 MLC-SJD-01-1-ZS.CL.01-006			
Window 01 MLC-SJD-01-1-ZS.CL.01-007			
Window 01 MLC-SJD-01-1-ZS.CL.01-008			

https://doi.org/10.3390/buildings16050995

Decoration families: Covering 13 types of Jiarong Tibetan-style decorative elements (e.g., "Lawoze" and eave carvings), the library restores their dimensions, configurations, and symbolic meanings through image-based surveying and mapping as well as parameter mapping (Table 5).

Table 5. Library of decorative parametric families for Jiarong Tibetan features (Source: Authors' own elaboration).

Component Coding	Component Front View	3D View of Component	Component Prototype
Door 01 M-01	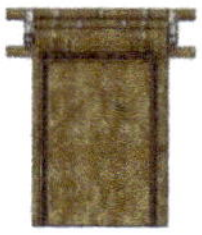		
Door 02 M-02			
Door 03 M-03			
Door 04 M-04			

Currently, this parametric component library contains over 100 reusable families, further demonstrating excellent adaptability to both regular and irregular watchtowers and serving as the foundational standard component resource for the digital modeling of the Suopo Ancient Watchtowers.

3.1.2. Architectural Model Database

An HBIM database covering all 84 watchtowers in Suopo Township has been established, which is divided into two levels: individual building models and cluster models.

Individual building Models: The modeling process involves four key steps: first, point cloud scene initialization; second, coordinate and grid calibration; third, load-bearing system construction; and fourth, the assembly of doors, windows, and accessory components (Figure 4). Damage information is classified into six categories (e.g., plant infestation, spalling, and decay) and graded into three levels (mild, moderate, and severe) based on deterioration rate. RGB color bands are adopted for the visual representation of this damage information [39].

Model accuracy validation showed that the mean geometric deviation between the point clouds and HBIM models was less than 5 mm (verified across 1000 control points). Damage annotation achieved 95% accuracy through manual review.

Cluster models: The database is organized following the hierarchy of "building type—village—individual ID," enabling model retrieval and spatial distribution analysis. For five-cornered, eight-cornered, and thirteen-cornered watchtowers, their planar features are first generated as contours in Rhino before being imported into Revit for model con-

https://doi.org/10.3390/buildings16050995

struction. In contrast, four-cornered watchtowers adopt a template reuse strategy for batch parametric modeling, which significantly improves modeling efficiency (Figures 5 and 6). This database supports cross-model comparison, facilitating the revelation of potential correlations between watchtower morphological characteristics, damage distribution, and seismic activity.

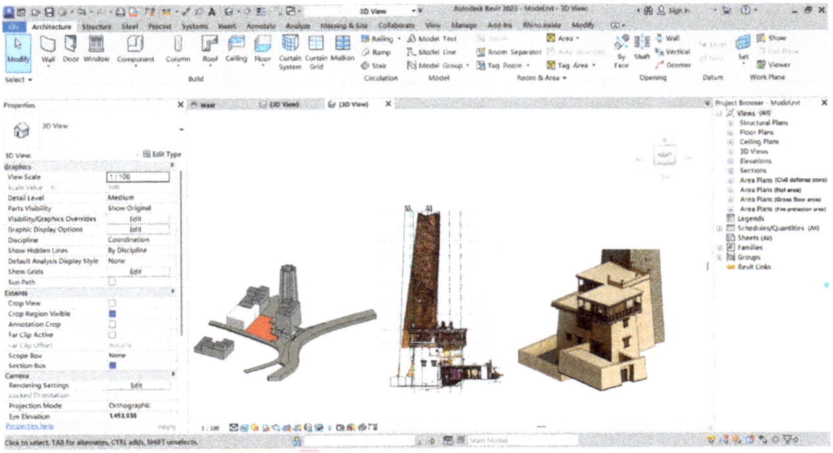

Figure 4. Schematic diagram including site modeling, datum elements and linked point cloud references, and main structural model. The image displays three views: the site layout with surrounding terrain (highlighted in red), the comparison between laser scanning point clouds and the BIM model, and the detailed textured model of the watchtower. The red area represents the specific site context, while gray structures denote the ancient watchtowers. (Source: Authors' own elaboration).

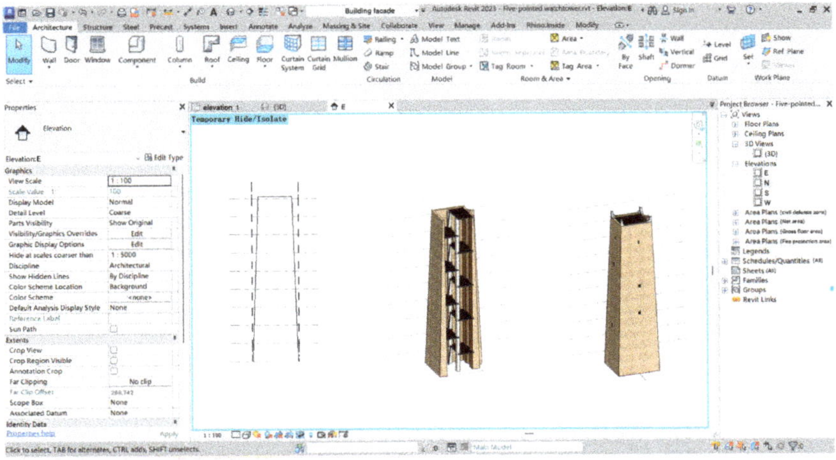

Figure 5. Schematic diagram of the HBIM modeling process in Revit. The three views illustrate: (left) wall height adjustment via 2D elevation profiles; (center) the internal array of columns, staircases, and floor slabs shown in a section view; and (right) the final model with imported door and window components. This sequence demonstrates the parametric construction from basic geometry to detailed architectural elements. (Source: Authors' own elaboration).

https://doi.org/10.3390/buildings16050995

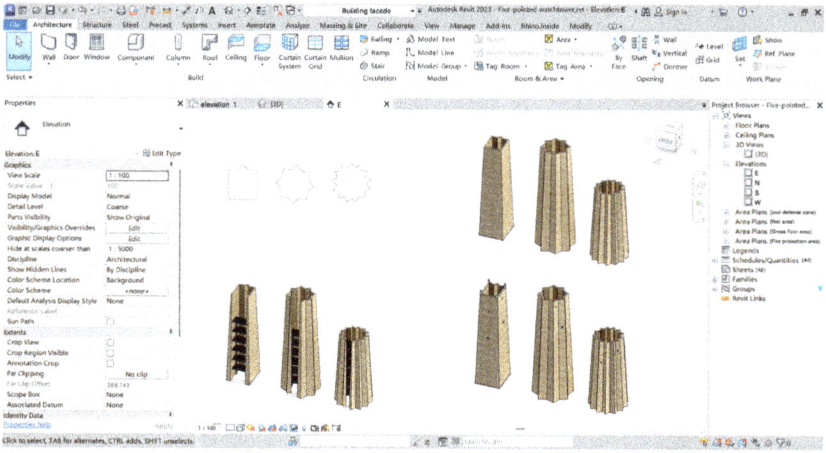

Figure 6. Schematic diagram of modeling variations. The image displays: (top) 2D geometric outlines and initial massing models; (bottom left) sectioned views showing internal component arrays (columns, stairs, floors); (bottom center) wall height adjustments; and (bottom right) the final topped-out structures. These views demonstrate the parametric capabilities for complex masonry geometries. (Source: Authors' own elaboration).

The application of this parametric library has significantly improved modeling efficiency. For a typical thirteen-sided watchtower, modeling time was reduced from approximately 40 h using traditional manual methods to 8 h, representing an efficiency improvement of approximately 80%. Across the 84 watchtowers, the more than 100 family files achieved a reuse rate of 92%, substantially reducing repetitive workload while maintaining geometric and semantic consistency.

3.1.3. Classification and Coding System

A multi-dimensional classification system has been established based on plan form, functional usage, and preservation status. Buildings are uniformly coded according to village name, watchtower configuration, and digitization level (Figure 7), while building components are assigned a three-level coding system based on component location, structural type, and component name (Table 6). Hierarchical coding is adopted to achieve precise identification of component types and data visualization. Taking the stone exterior wall on the west side of the main facade of the Wengdujia Ancient Watchtower in Molo Village as an example, its complete code is "MLC-SJD-01-I_ZQ.QL.01_001." This code denotes: "Molo Village four-cornered watchtower, column-wall section, wall component, stone exterior wall, and the first exterior wall."

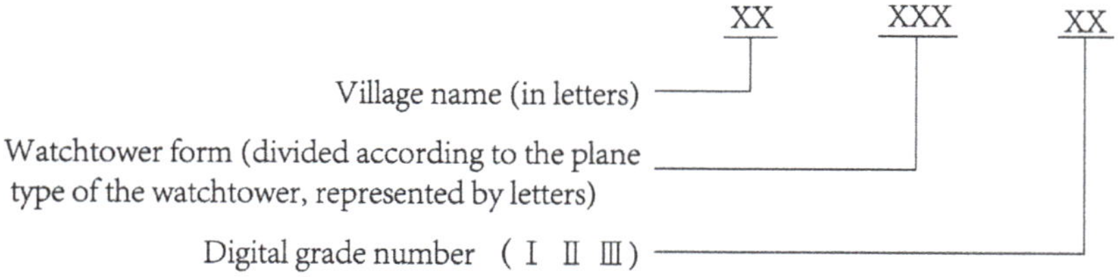

Figure 7. Hierarchical structure of the Suopo watchtower HBIM library (Source: Authors' own elaboration).

 https://doi.org/10.3390/buildings16050995

Table 6. Three-Level Coding System (Source: Authors' own elaboration).

Primary Encoding	Secondary Encoding	Three-Level Coding
Floor LD	Foundation JC	Stone foundation 01
	Basement Floor DB	Stone floor 01 concrete floor 02 wooden floor 03 wooden beam 04
Column wall ZQ	Wall types QL	rubble innerwall 01 rubble inner wall 02
	Column types QL	Structural column 01
Roof WD	Main roof ZW	flagstone layer 01 soil layer 02
	Roof accessor components	White Stone 01
Roof truss WJ	Beam frame U	main beam layer 01 Dense purlin layer 02 Branch layer 03 Wood flooring 03 Wooden beam 04
Stairs LT	single-flight staircase DT Wooden post staircase MT	Stair light 01
Decoration ZS	Category ML	Wooden door 01 Other door components 02
	Window types CL	Wooden window 01 Other window Roof accessory Components 02

Through its hierarchical classification mechanism for building structures, this coding system effectively mitigates the risk of data omission and supports multi-condition intelligent retrieval based on criteria such as configuration, component type and location, risk level, and damage severity. The location and severity of component damage are visually differentiated by color, facilitating the rapid identification of high-risk objects.

3.2. Management and Application Implementation

3.2.1. Information Delivery and Retrieval

Component families are provided in RFA (Revit Family) format, defining reusable parametric elements, while complete models are delivered in RVT (Revit Project) and IFC (Industry Foundation Classes) formats to ensure seamless interoperability across various BIM platforms. A lightweight viewing version is also provided to support mobile and cloud-based browsing. A multi-source data retrieval system based on hyperlinks has been established, enabling the associated access of models with images, texts, and damage records (Figure 8).

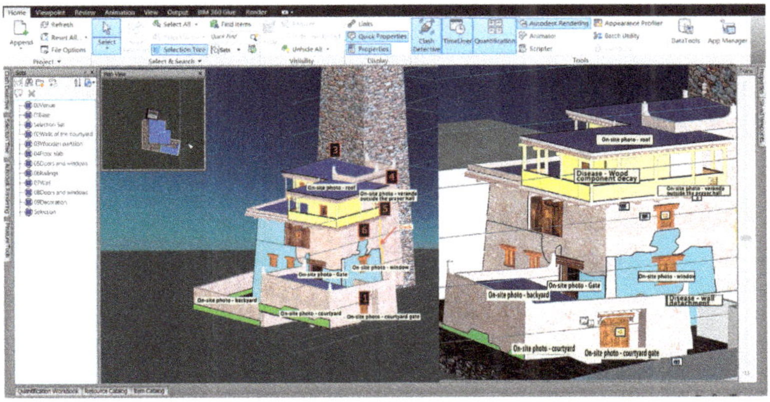

Figure 8. Multi-source information integration in Navisworks. The model visualizes photos, notes, and damage records mapped onto specific components: blue (roofs), yellow (wooden structures),

https://doi.org/10.3390/buildings16050995

cyan (walls), and green (courtyards). Red markers indicate identified defects like masonry cracks. Dual views are provided to show the spatial distribution of these integrated data sources. (Source: Authors' own elaboration) (Source: Authors' own elaboration).

3.2.2. Digital Visualization Display

Immersive navigation (Figure 9) and phased display (Figure 10) have been realized using Autodesk Navisworks Manage 2023 (Autodesk Inc., San Rafael, CA, USA). This system provides technical support for public education and heritage protection promotion.

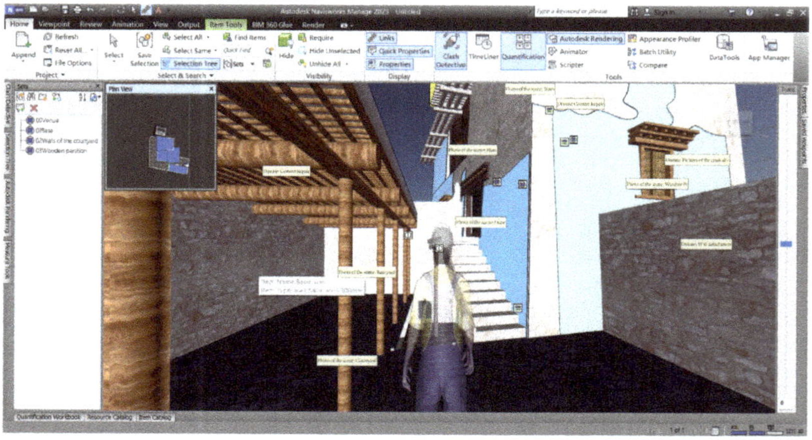

Figure 9. Immersive walkthrough in Navisworks. Immersive walkthrough simulation in Navisworks for virtual heritage inspection. The first-person view (indicated by the avatar) enables navigation as if physically present. Yellow labels display mapped on-site photos and component attributes (e.g., "Photo of the scene: Stairs"), allowing real-time access to multi-source data. This demonstrates visual inspection of detailed elements like wooden beams and stone walls within an integrated digital environment. (Source: Authors' own elaboration).

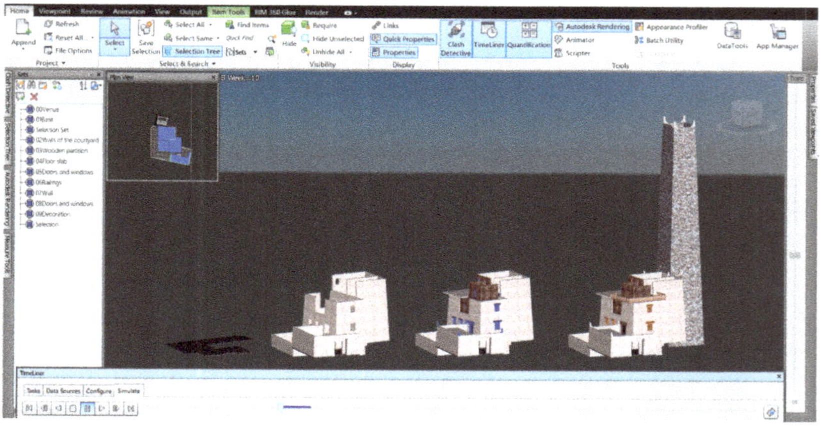

Figure 10. 4D construction sequence simulation of the Wengdu family watchtower, including masonry foundation, masonry wall, partition construction, and blockhouse top construction (Source: Authors' own elaboration).

https://doi.org/10.3390/buildings16050995

3.2.3. Value Assessment Matrix

Value assessment for all watchtowers has been completed based on the ICOMOS framework, and the priority index $P = V \times R$ has been calculated by incorporating risk factors (Table 7). For instance, the "Wall" component exhibits the highest comprehensive value (88) due to its embodiment of traditional dry-stone masonry techniques and historical defensive function, but also the highest risk (0.9) owing to widespread vertical cracks and moisture infiltration observed during field inspection. Conversely, "Other components"—including carved wooden lintels and ritual niches—score high in artistic (19) and cultural (19) value, reflecting intangible heritage aspects, yet show lower physical risk (0.5) as they are often sheltered or recently restored. Weights were determined by a panel of 10 experts through three rounds of the Delphi method, with a consistency coefficient $\kappa > 0.8$. After experts completed the weight calibration, the system automatically ranked the priorities of tens of thousands of components and implemented real-time mapping of material color and opacity within the Revit model (Figure 11). Across the approximately 12,000 major components in the 84 watchtowers, the priority distribution was as follows: P0 (urgent) accounted for 3.2% (384 components), P1 (high) 15.8%, P2 (medium) 42.3%, and P3 (routine) 38.7%. The cluster-scale value–risk intervention list (Table 8) prioritizes components accordingly, from emergency (P0) to routine (P3) maintenance.

Table 7. Protection Priority of an Individual Watchtower (Source: Authors' own elaboration).

Component	Foundation	Wall	Roof	Doors and Windows	Other Components
Historical Value	18	19	17	17	16
Artistic value	14	16	15	17	19
Scientific Value	17	18	16	15	14
Social Value	15	16	15	14	16
Cultural Value	16	18	17	17	19
Comprehensive Value	80	88	80	81	85
Risk Factor (0–1)	0.8	0.9	0.7	0.6	0.5
Protection Priority (P)	64	79	56	49	42

Note: The scoring is based on a 0–20 scale for each criterion. The weights are determined by a panel of 10 experts using the Delphi method (consistency ratio $\kappa > 0.80$). The table shows the representative results for a typical watchtower.

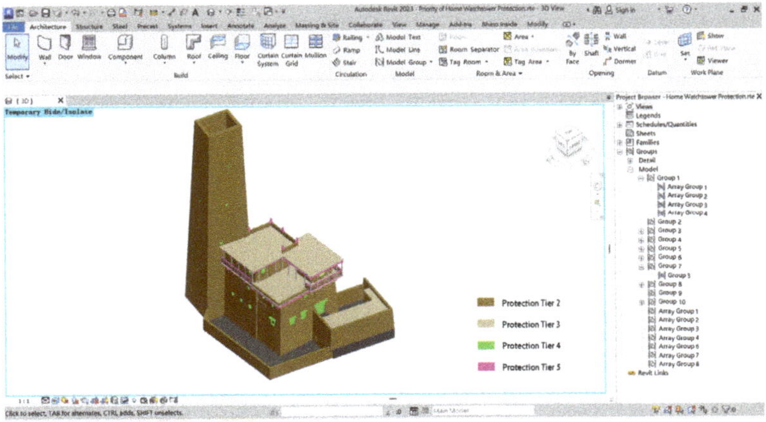

Figure 11. Real-time visualization of conservation priority using material color and transparency mapping (Source: Authors' own elaboration).

https://doi.org/10.3390/buildings16050995

Table 8. Intervention List of 'Value–Risk' Objects for Part of the Watchtower Group (Source: Authors' own elaboration).

Priority Level	Watchtower Code	Component Coding	Value Rating (*V*)	Risk Factor (*R*)	Priority Index ($P = V \times R$)	Primary Risk Diagnosis	Recommended Intervention Types
P0 (Urgent)	MLC-BJD-01-I	_ZQ.QL.01_001	92	0.95	87.4	The structural inclination of the load-bearing wall in the northeast corner exceeds 5°, with cracks continuing to expand.	Structural reinforcement
P1 (High)	ZBC-SJD-02-II	_ZS.ML.01_001	88	0.90	79.2	Upper load compression causes stone cracking	Partial body reconstruction
P1 (High)	NYC-SJD-06-IV	_WJ.DT.03_003	85	0.85	72.3	The wooden structural components of the three-story wooden floor slab are severely decayed, resulting in insufficient load-bearing capacity.	Component Replacement and Anti-Corrosion Treatment
P2 (Medium)	ZBC-SJD-02-III	_WD.FG.01_002	82	0.70	57.4	The decorative surface on the west side of the "Lauze" has weathered and flaked off, with its colors faded.	Surface Cleaning and Weatherproofing
P3 (Routine)	GBC-SJD-03-II	_LD.DB.02_001	65	0.30	19.5	The interior yellow clay plaster floor shows minor wear and is in stable condition.	Daily Maintenance

Note: The same evaluation framework as Table 4. Priority: P0 (Emergency), P1 (High), P2 (Medium), P3 (Routine).

3.3. Sensitivity Analysis

To further evaluate the robustness of the multiplicative value–risk model ($P = V \times R$), Monte Carlo simulations with 10,000 iterations were conducted, introducing plausible variations in expert-assigned weights for the value criteria. The resulting distributions of priority indices P across different component types in a representative watchtower exhibited extremely low variability, with standard deviations below 1.0 and coefficients of variation under 1%, indicating minimal sensitivity to weight fluctuations (Figure 12). Baseline P values, calculated under equal weights, closely matched the medians of the simulated distributions (e.g., walls: ~79; foundation: ~64; roof: ~56), and priority rankings remained invariant throughout all iterations, with critical load-bearing walls consistently holding the highest priority. At the cluster scale, aggregated analyses showed similar stability, with top-ranked objects (e.g., P0-level) retaining their positions in over 99% of iterations. These results confirm that the model reliably identifies high-priority components even under weight uncertainty, providing robust decision support for cluster-scale preventive conservation.

 https://doi.org/10.3390/buildings16050995

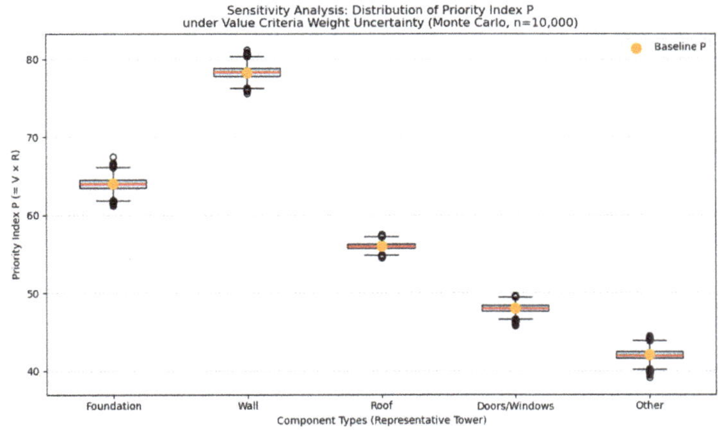

Figure 12. Sensitivity Analysis: Distribution of Priority Index P under Value Criteria Weight Uncertainty (Monte Carlo, n = 10,000). The boxes represent the interquartile range (25th–75th percentiles) of the simulated PP values, while the red horizontal lines indicate the medians. The yellow dots denote the baseline PP values calculated with equal weights, and the black circles represent outliers. The stability of the median relative to the baseline confirms the model's robustness. (Source: Authors' own elaboration).

4. Discussion

The intelligent HBIM framework proposed in this study for cluster-based preventive protection exhibits significant applicability in the digitalization and intelligent management of complex masonry heritage. Compared with existing HBIM applications that primarily focus on individual buildings, this framework achieves the integration of unified data organization, semantic representation, and value–risk coupled decision-making at the cluster scale [40]. It effectively addresses three key limitations in current heritage protection practices: the lack of an overall management mechanism for heritage clusters, inadequate connection between preventive processes and dynamic risk assessment, and insufficient targeted parametric expression for ethnic minority regional architecture.

4.1. Technical Contributions and Innovation

In terms of parametric modeling, the component library developed in this study has successfully adapted to complex configurations such as polygonal plans and stepped-in walls. By leveraging adjustable parameters and a three-level coding system, it enables efficient component reuse and unified cluster-scale management, significantly enhancing the digital expression capability of irregular stone masonry heritage. Compared with recent parametric methods focused on individual objects, this framework exhibits distinct advantages in cross-object semantic consistency and model maintainability [41].

The key innovation lies in the integration of an intelligent decision-making layer. Through HBIM customization tools, the value–risk matrix is embedded into model attributes, enabling automated prioritization, real-time visualization of risk levels, and a feedback-driven decision mechanism. This transforms traditional static HBIM from a documentation tool into an active perception–decision–feedback system, shifting preventive protection from "experience-based judgment" to data-driven decision-making, addressing the gap in automation for preventive conservation [42]. To provide a comprehensive quantitative evaluation of the framework's performance, a comparison between the traditional manual workflow and the proposed HBIM-based approach is summarized in Table 9.

 https://doi.org/10.3390/buildings16050995

Table 9. Performance Comparison Between Traditional and HBIM-Based Workflows (Source: Authors' own elaboration).

Metric	Traditional Manual Workflow	Proposed Framework	Improvement
Single-building modeling time (hours)	35–50	6–12	75–80%
Cluster model consistency (geometric deviation, mm)	20–50	<10	Substantial reduction
Intervention list generation time	Several weeks	<1 min	>99%
High-priority object identification accuracy	Experience-based judgment	Automated + expert calibration	Significant enhancement

4.2. Performance Advantages and Application Effectiveness

Application to the Suopo Ancient Watchtower Group has demonstrated several advantages: (1) cluster-scale parametric modeling reduces repetitive workload while maintaining geometric and semantic consistency across all watchtowers; (2) the hierarchical HBIM database supports multi-condition retrieval, cross-model comparison, and integrated morphological and damage analysis; and (3) the embedded value–risk module provides objective, intuitive guidance for resource allocation and intervention planning.

This framework is particularly suitable for masonry heritage clusters in high-seismic zones, exhibiting high adaptability to environmental constraints. Its modular architecture and intelligent decision-making layer provide strong potential for replication in similar heritage protection projects, extending the applicability of HBIM beyond individual buildings to cluster-level preventive management.

4.3. Limitations and Future Directions

Despite the aforementioned progress, this study still has certain limitations: (1) Due to terrain obstruction, the data integrity of some watchtowers is limited. (2) The current value–risk assessment primarily relies on expert initial weights and phased surveys, and has not yet achieved dynamic updates based on continuous time-series data. (3) Although the system reserves an IoT interface, long-term field validation in actual engineering projects has not been carried out.

Future research will be further advanced in the following directions: (1) Integrate point cloud semantic segmentation algorithms to realize automatic damage identification and annotation. (2) Introduce IoT sensors and time-series data, and combine models such as LSTM (Long Short-Term Memory) to achieve short-term and medium-term dynamic prediction of risk coefficients, with degradation trends visualized through animations within the model. (3) Develop a mobile inspection tool based on Revit API, which supports on-site one-click positioning of high-priority components and pushes intervention recommendations.

All these improvements are based on the reserved interfaces of the existing framework, featuring high feasibility. Moreover, they can further evolve into a complete heritage digital twin system, providing more comprehensive technical support for the intelligent preventive protection of masonry heritage clusters.

Beyond these technical and methodological limitations, issues related to data governance, ethical management, and long-term sustainability also warrant consideration. Ownership of the HBIM models, parametric libraries, and databases is jointly held by the Danba County Cultural Heritage Administration and the local Suopo community, as stipulated in the research approvals. All data were delivered in open, interoperable formats and securely archived by the heritage authority with local backups. Future updates will

https://doi.org/10.3390/buildings16050995

be co-managed to ensure cultural sensitivity and long-term sustainability, in line with ICOMOS principles for ethical digital heritage management.

4.4. Theoretical Significance and Practical Value

At the theoretical level, this study advances HBIM from a digital archiving tool to a preventive intelligent decision-making system, providing a novel technical approach for the protection of ethnic regional architectural clusters. Practically, it establishes a comprehensive digital archive and management platform for the Suopo Ancient Watchtower Group, supporting daily monitoring and decision-making. The modular and scalable design allows potential application to similar masonry heritage clusters worldwide, offering a Chinese solution for sustainable heritage protection and enabling cross-regional cooperation and technology sharing.

Compared with international practices, our framework addresses a critical gap in current digital heritage workflows. While EU-funded initiatives such as PROTHEGO [43] and CHARTER [44] have advanced geohazard monitoring through InSAR and BIM, they primarily focus on externally driven structural risks and offer limited integration of cultural value dimensions as defined by ICOMOS. Similarly, HBIM studies by D'Amico et al. [45] and Bruno et al. [46] demonstrate sophisticated condition assessment for individual monuments but do not scale to interrelated heritage ensembles. In contrast, our approach uniquely couples ICOMOS-aligned cultural values—encompassing historical, artistic, scientific, social, and cultural significance—with physical risk factors within a unified, cluster-scale HBIM environment. This integration enables conservation decisions that explicitly balance significance and vulnerability, transforming HBIM from a static documentation tool into an actionable, intelligent system for preventive conservation. By extending parametric modeling, semantic consistency, and value–risk-driven decision support to the heritage cluster level, the framework provides a replicable, scalable, and practical pathway for managing complex masonry ensembles in high-risk environments—particularly where cultural importance is high but technical and financial resources are constrained.

5. Conclusions

This study proposes and validates an intelligent HBIM-based framework for the preventive conservation of masonry heritage clusters, applying it to the Suopo Ancient Watchtower Group in Danba County, Sichuan Province—a complex of 84 polygonal, stepped-in stone watchtowers. The framework establishes a closed-loop workflow spanning multi-source data integration, parametric modeling, and value–risk-driven decision-making, significantly enhancing the efficiency and responsiveness of cluster-scale heritage management.

The major outcomes of this study can be summarized as follows:

(1) A dedicated parametric component library and unified coding system were developed, enabling efficient reuse and consistent semantic representation across all 84 watchtowers. This provides a practical solution for modeling complex, irregular masonry structures at the cluster scale.
(2) A hierarchical HBIM database was established, supporting multi-level retrieval, cross-building comparison, and correlation analysis of morphology, material behavior, and damage patterns. This database underpins systematic, traceable management of heritage clusters.
(3) The integration of a value–risk priority model ($P = V \times R$) within HBIM enables automated prioritization, real-time visualization, and one-click generation of intervention lists, transforming preventive conservation from subjective judgment into data-driven, intelligent decision-making.

 https://doi.org/10.3390/buildings16050995

(4) The framework demonstrates strong scalability, adaptability, and practical applicability, particularly for masonry heritage clusters in high-seismic zones. Its modular design and intelligent decision-making layer provide a replicable technical paradigm for similar high-risk heritage environments worldwide.

Theoretically and practically, this study advances HBIM from a passive documentation tool to a preventive intelligent decision-making system, offering a novel approach for the sustainable protection of ethnic regional architectural clusters and laying the groundwork for cross-regional cooperation and heritage digital twin development.

Overall, the proposed framework provides a comprehensive, operable, and replicable solution for cluster-scale preventive protection of masonry heritage. With further integration of IoT and AI technologies, it is expected to evolve into a full-fledged digital twin system, offering enhanced monitoring, predictive intervention, and long-term conservation support for complex heritage clusters.

Furthermore, the research demonstrates that the proposed framework effectively supports the entire preventive protection process, from data acquisition to intervention decision-making, providing an operable and replicable paradigm for the sustainable management of masonry heritage in Chinese ethnic minority settlements. With the further integration of IoT and AI technologies, the framework is expected to evolve into a comprehensive heritage digital twin system, offering enhanced monitoring, predictive interventions, and long-term conservation support for complex heritage clusters worldwide.

Author Contributions: Conceptualization, L.Z. and F.X.; methodology, L.Z., C.T. and Y.Y.; software, Y.Y.; validation, C.T. and Y.Y.; formal analysis, L.Z. and J.Y.; investigation, L.Z. and C.T.; resources, F.X.; data curation, C.T. and J.Y.; writing—original draft preparation, L.Z.; writing—review and editing, F.X., Y.Y. and J.Y.; visualization, L.Z. and C.T.; supervision, F.X.; project administration, F.X.; funding acquisition, F.X. All authors have read and agreed to the published version of the manuscript.

Funding: This research was funded by the Natural Science Foundation of Sichuan Province, grant number 2022NSFSC1080. The APC was funded by the authors.

Data Availability Statement: The original contributions presented in this study are included in the article. Further inquiries can be directed to the corresponding author.

Conflicts of Interest: The authors declare no conflicts of interest.

References

1. Vandesande, A. Preventive Conservation Strategy for Built Heritage Aimed at Sustainable Management and Local Development. Doctoral Dissertation, KU Leuven, Leuven, Belgium, 2017. Available online: https://lirias.kuleuven.be/1727568 (accessed on 1 February 2026).
2. Ouan, P.; Hallot, P. Digital twin: Research framework to support preventive conservation policies. *ISPRS Int. J. Geo-Inf.* **2020**, *9*, 244. [CrossRef]
3. Rolim, R.; López-González, C.; Viñals, M.J. Analysis of the current status of sensors and HBIM integration: A review based on bibliometric analysis. *Heritage* **2023**, *6*, 98. [CrossRef]
4. Baik, A. A comprehensive heritage BIM methodology for digital modelling and conservation of built heritage: Application to Ghiqa Historical Market, Saudi Arabia. *Remote Sens.* **2024**, *16*, 2833. [CrossRef]
5. Venkatachalam, T.; Jigyasu, R.; Heron, S.F. A systematic approach for defining thematic groups of World Heritage properties to support the strategic management of threats. *Environ. Chall.* **2022**, *4*, 100538. [CrossRef]
6. State Council of the People's Republic of China. *Circular of the State Council on Carrying Out the Fourth National Survey of Immovable Cultural Relics*; State Council of the People's Republic of China: Beijing, China, 2023. Available online: http://www.gov.cn/zhengce/content/202310/content_6912288.htm (accessed on 1 February 2026).
7. Vuoto, A.; Funari, M.F.; Lourenço, P.B. Shaping Digital Twin Concept for Built Cultural Heritage Conservation: A Systematic Literature Review. *Int. J. Archit. Herit.* **2024**, *18*, 1762–1795. [CrossRef]
8. De Paoli, R.G.; Di Miceli, E.; Giuliani, F. Disasters and Cultural Heritage: Planning for prevention, emergency management and risk reduction. *IOP Conf. Ser. Mater. Sci. Eng.* **2020**, *949*, 012084. [CrossRef]

 https://doi.org/10.3390/buildings16050995

9. Chabuk, M.; Alamiri, S. Risk management and conservation strategies for heritage sites using analytic hierarchy process (AHP). *AIP Conf. Proc.* **2023**, *2651*, 020074. [CrossRef]
10. Chabbi, A.; Jerome, P.; Jigyasu, R.; Kelley, S.J.; Reap, J.K. Tangible risks, intangible opportunities: Long-term risk preparedness and responses for threats to cultural heritage. In *Proceedings of the ICOMOS Scientific Symposium, Beijing, China, 31 October 2012*; ICOMOS China: Beijing, China, 2014. Available online: https://publ.icomos.org/publicomos/technica/9DC1E04186C2FFE4E6963A6B4F3695A6 (accessed on 1 December 2025).
11. Aktürk, G.; Hauser, S.J. Integrated understanding of climate change and disaster risk for building resilience of cultural heritage sites. *Nat. Hazards* **2024**, *121*, 4309–4334. [CrossRef]
12. Rossi, M.; Bournas, D. Structural health monitoring and management of cultural heritage structures: A state-of-the-art review. *Appl. Sci.* **2023**, *13*, 6450. [CrossRef]
13. Banfi, F.; Brumana, R.; Oreni, D. Semantic web and ontology-based HBIM for architectural heritage: Toward a new documentation and management approach. *ISPRS Int. J. Geo-Inf.* **2019**, *8*, 588. [CrossRef]
14. Brumana, R.; Oreni, D.; Raimondi, A.; Georgopoulos, A.; Bregianni, A. From survey to HBIM for documentation, dissemination and management of built heritage: The case study of St. Maria in Scaria d'Intelvi. In *Proceedings of the 2013 Digital Heritage International Congress (DigitalHeritage), Marseille, France, 28 October–1 November 2013*; IEEE: Piscataway, NJ, USA, 2013; Volume 1, pp. 497–504. [CrossRef]
15. Logothetis, S.; Karachaliou, E.; Valari, E.; Stylianidis, E. Open source cloud-based technologies for BIM. *Int. Arch. Photogramm. Remote Sens. Spatial Inf. Sci.* **2018**, *XLII-2*, 607–614. [CrossRef]
16. Martínez-Rodríguez, R.; Fernández, F.J.; Pastor, J.L. HBIM-based risk assessment and decision-making for the preventive conservation of historic buildings. *J. Build. Eng.* **2022**, *45*, 103594. [CrossRef]
17. Calò, A.; Savini, F.; Parrinello, S. A deep learning approach for automatic detection and classification of stone deterioration in historical buildings. *Heritage* **2023**, *6*, 3169–3191. [CrossRef]
18. Barazzetti, L.; Banfi, F.; Brumana, R.; Previtali, M. Creation of parametric BIM objects from point clouds using NURBS. *Photogramm. Rec.* **2015**, *30*, 339–362. [CrossRef]
19. Cavers, G.; Barber, J.; Ritchie, M. The survey and analysis of brochs. *Proc. Soc. Antiqu. Scotl.* **2016**, *145*, 153–176. [CrossRef]
20. Marra, A.; Betti, M.; Bartoli, G. Seismic vulnerability assessment and retrofit strategies for medieval stone watchtowers in the Central Italian Apennines. *Eng. Struct.* **2021**, *243*, 112661. [CrossRef]
21. Darnal, P. Significant Heritages of Upper Mustang and Issue of Conservation. *Dhaulagiri J. Sociol. Anthropol.* **2017**, *11*, 1–23. [CrossRef]
22. Banfi, F.; Brumana, R.; Della Torre, S.; Oreni, D.; Previtali, M.; Barazzetti, L. HBIM for heritage clusters: A review and a conceptual workflow for multi-scale management of archaeological sites and scattered heritage assets. *Remote Sens.* **2023**, *15*, 1901. [CrossRef]
23. International Council on Monuments and Sites China. *China's Tentative List of World Cultural Heritage (2023 Update Launch Edition)*; Media Center of ICOMOS China: Beijing, China, 2023. Available online: http://www.icomoschina.org.cn/content/details92_17268.html (accessed on 1 February 2026).
24. Yang, Q.; Xu, F.; Lu, W.; Yang, Z.; Bai, Y.; Wen, B. Green renovation and multi-objective optimization of Tibetan courtyard dwellings. *Build. Environ.* **2025**, *279*, 113071. [CrossRef]
25. Yang, Q.; Lu, W.; Xu, F.; Luo, X.; Wen, B. A passive strategy for energy-saving retrofitting of courtyard dwellings and its climatic adaptability. *Energy Build.* **2026**, *352*, 116811. [CrossRef]
26. Xu, F.; Bai, Y.; Wen, B.; Xie, W.; Huang, L.; Ou, Y.; Luo, X.; Yang, Q. Contemporary evolution of Tibetan-style dwellings under urbanization: A case study of the Shannan city. *J. Asian Archit. Build. Eng.* **2026**, *25*, 1–18. [CrossRef]
27. Mehranfar, M.; Braun, A.; Borrmann, A. From dense point clouds to semantic digital models: End-to-end AI-based automation procedure for Manhattan-world structures. *Autom. Constr.* **2024**, *162*, 105392. [CrossRef]
28. Firmansyah, H.R.; Sarli, P.W.; Twinanda, A.P.; Santoso, D.; Imran, I. Building typology classification using convolutional neural networks utilizing multiple ground-level image process for city-scale rapid seismic vulnerability assessment. *Eng. Appl. Artif. Intell.* **2024**, *131*, 107824. [CrossRef]
29. Fattore, C.; Buldo, M.; Priore, A.; Porcari, S.; Porcari, V.D.; De Fino, M. A comprehensive overview of heritage BIM frameworks: Platforms and technologies integrating multi-scale analyses, data repositories, and sensor systems. *Heritage* **2025**, *8*, 247. [CrossRef]
30. Grazianova, M.; Mesaros, P. HBIM: The digital transformation of cultural and existing heritage. *MATEC Web Conf.* **2023**, *385*, 01040. [CrossRef]
31. Puerto, A.; Castañeda, K.; Sánchez, O.; Peña, C.A.; Gutiérrez, L.; Sáenz, P. Building information modeling and complementary technologies in heritage buildings: A bibliometric analysis. *Results Eng.* **2024**, *22*, 102192. [CrossRef]
32. Lovell, L.J.; Davies, R.J.; Hunt, D.V.L. The application of historic building information modelling (HBIM) to cultural heritage: A review. *Heritage* **2023**, *6*, 6691–6717. [CrossRef]
33. Huang, Y.Y. Value Evaluation and Protection Strategies of Tibetan-Qiang Stone Tower Architectural Heritage. Doctoral Dissertation, Southwest University of Science and Technology, Mianyang, China, 2023. (In Chinese)

 https://doi.org/10.3390/buildings16050995

34. International Council on Monuments and Sites. ICOMOS Guidelines for Education and Training in the Conservation of Monuments, Ensembles and Sites. Sofia, Bulgaria. 1993. Available online: https://www.icomos.org/images/DOCUMENTS/Charters/education_e.pdf (accessed on 1 February 2026).
35. Michalski, S.; Pedersoli, J.L., Jr. *The ABC Method: A risk Management Approach to the Preservation of Cultural Heritage*; Canadian Conservation Institute & ICCROM: Ottawa, Canada & Rome, Italy, 2016. Available online: https://www.iccrom.org/sites/default/files/2017-12/risk_manual_2016-eng.pdf (accessed on 1 February 2026).
36. Dore, C.; Murphy, M. Current state of the art historic building information modelling. *Int. Arch. Photogramm. Remote Sens. Spatial Inf. Sci.* **2017**, *XLII-2/W5*, 185–192. [CrossRef]
37. Castellano-Román, M.; Pinto-Puerto, F. Dimensions and levels of knowledge in Heritage Building Information Modelling, HBIM: The model of the Charterhouse of Jerez (Cádiz, Spain). *Digit. Appl. Archaeol. Cult. Herit.* **2019**, *15*, e00110. [CrossRef]
38. Hoàng, V.T.; Nguyễn, P.H.T.; Duong, B.L.; Lê, T.T.B.; Võ, Q.H.; Nguyễn, T.Q.H.; Ngô, N.H.; Bae, M.; Jung, Y.; Min, B. 3D scan and HBIM of Thai Hoa Hall for the conservation of Hue's cultural heritage. *Int. Arch. Photogramm. Remote Sens. Spatial Inf. Sci.* **2025**, *XLVIII-M-9-2025*, 587–594. [CrossRef]
39. Zhang, R.; Wang, R.; Liu, X.; Zhao, C. Application of parametric modeling in the construction of historic building information models. *J. Graph.* **2017**, *38*, 144–149. (In Chinese)
40. Huang, W.; Wang, R.; Zhang, R.; Liu, X.; Li, X. Information modeling and knowledge expression for traditional village building clusters based on ontology and GIS. *J. Inf. Technol. Civ. Eng. Archit.* **2021**, *13*, 1–10. (In Chinese)
41. Huang, W.; Zhang, R. Implementation of an automated risk assessment method for ancient buildings based on Revit and Dynamo. *J. Inf. Technol. Civ. Eng. Archit.* **2021**, *13*, 1–9. (In Chinese)
42. Diara, F. Open source HBIM and OpenAI: Review and new analyses on LLMs integration. *Heritage* **2025**, *8*, 149. [CrossRef]
43. Cigna, F.; Tapete, D.; Lee, K. Prothego: Protection of European Cultural Heritage from Geo-Hazards. Project Report. 2018. Available online: https://www.heritageresearch-hub.eu/project/prothego (accessed on 1 February 2026).
44. CHARTER Alliance. *Cultural Heritage Skills Alliance and Action Plan: Recommendations for Sustainable Strategies*; European Commission: Brussels, Belgium, 2024. Available online: https://charter-alliance.eu/wp-content/uploads/2024/11/D5.3-CHARTER-Skills-Strategy.pdf (accessed on 1 February 2026).
45. D'Amico, F.; Gagliardo, S.; Trombetti, T. An integrated UAV–deep learning approach for rapid damage assessment of historic structures. *J. Build. Eng.* **2022**, *51*, 104299. [CrossRef]
46. Bruno, N.; Roncella, R.; Fantini, F. HBIM for the preservation of a historic infrastructure: The case study of the San Michele complex in Padua. *Int. Arch. Photogramm. Remote Sens. Spatial Inf. Sci.* **2021**, *XLVI-M-1-2021*, 133–140. [CrossRef]

 https://doi.org/10.3390/buildings16050995

buildings

MDPI

Article

Integrating Computer Vision and GIS for Large-Scale Morphological Mapping and Driving Force Analysis of Vernacular Courtyard Dwellings

Lihua Liang [1], Xianda Li [1], Shutong Liu [2], Zhenhao Guo [2], Shuo Tang [2] and Baohua Wen [2,*]

[1] School of Architecture, Changsha University of Science and Technology, Changsha 410076, China; lianglihua@csust.edu.cn (L.L.); 25217032578@csust.edu.cn (X.L.)
[2] School of Architecture and Planning, Hunan University, Changsha 410082, China; liu.shutong@hnu.edu.cn (S.L.); zhenhaogzh@hnu.edu.cn (Z.G.); tangshuo@hnu.edu.cn (S.T.)
* Correspondence: wenbaohua@hnu.edu.cn

Abstract

This study develops and applies an integrated methodology that combines deep learning-based computer vision and spatial statistics to automate the large-scale identification and analysis of morphological features in vernacular courtyard dwellings. Focusing on Liangshuaixiu dwellings in Wu'an, southern Hebei, we trained an HRNetV2 semantic segmentation model on high-resolution satellite imagery to identify and extract contours for 134,280 courtyard spaces. Core morphological parameters (area, orientation) were calculated and analyzed using GIS spatial statistics and the geographic detector model. The results show that (1) the computer vision pipeline achieved efficient recognition with satisfactory accuracy (~10% mean error); (2) spatial autocorrelation and hotspot analysis revealed distinct regional patterns, including a west–east increase in average courtyard area; and (3) geographic detector analysis demonstrated that courtyard morphology is shaped by complex interactions between natural and socio-economic factors. While average area and orientation were primarily governed by climate (air pressure, wind, temperature) and topography (elevation), diversity and internal variation were strongly influenced by nonlinear interactions, particularly between natural factors (e.g., wind–aspect) and between natural and human factors (e.g., population–climate). This work provides a scalable, data-driven framework for the quantitative spatial analysis of vernacular architectural heritage, advancing the understanding of building morphology as an outcome of coupled human–environment systems.

Keywords: vernacular architecture; computer vision; geographic information system (GIS); spatial pattern; geographic detector

1. Introduction

1.1. Vernacular Architecture and Courtyard Dwellings

Vernacular architecture refers to indigenous building traditions that emerge spontaneously, shaped by specific regional cultures, climatic conditions, available material resources, and socio-economic structures, typically without the involvement of professionally trained architects [1–4]. Functioning as a wordless local chronicle, it tangibly embodies community memory, environmentally adaptive construction wisdom, and unadorned esthetic values [5–8]. Across the vast rural and urban landscapes of China, courtyard houses stand out as one of the most representative and widely distributed forms of vernacular architecture [9,10]. In particular, the courtyard dwellings of southern Hebei bear the distinct imprint of the North China Plain's natural environment, Confucian ritual principles, clan-based settlement patterns, and local construction techniques developed since the Ming and Qing dynasties [11]. They are characterized by a courtyard-centric layout, buildings enclosing the yard, defined central axes, and a pronounced hierarchical order [12]. These courtyard dwellings are not merely essential living spaces but also concentrated expressions of regional culture, social structure, and ecological intelligence [13,14]. Consequently, a systematic understanding of their spatial distribution patterns and morphological characteristics is not just an architectural pursuit, but a crucial foundation for interpreting the region's traditional settlement landscape, human settlement wisdom, and cultural continuity [15,16].

1.2. Traditional Research Paradigms and Their Limitations

Research on vernacular architecture in southern Hebei and beyond has long been underpinned by methodologies from architecture, historical geography, and sociology. Traditional paradigms typically involve: (1) in-depth fieldwork, measurement, and documentation of representative case studies to obtain precise plan, elevation, and detail data [17–21]; (2) tracing architectural evolution and socio-cultural context by consulting historical documents such as local gazetteers, genealogies, and craftsmen's manuals [22,23]; and (3) classifying, comparing, and summarizing formal characteristics based on collected cases [24–26]. These qualitative approaches have yielded substantial insights, forming the bedrock of our knowledge about traditional building practices and typologies.

However, when confronted with the vast quantity and wide distribution of vernacular architecture, these traditional paradigms reveal significant methodological limitations. First, reliance on manual fieldwork is time-consuming and labor-intensive, making large-scale, comprehensive surveys impractical [27]. Consequently, conclusions are often drawn from a limited number of canonical cases, which, while rich in detail, may introduce sampling bias and fail to capture the full spectrum of architectural diversity. Second, the manual processes of surveying and feature identification are inherently slow, rendering them ill-suited for rapidly processing and synthesizing information from vast repositories of building imagery or map data [28]. Finally, and most critically, traditional methods emphasize qualitative description and typological classification. While valuable for establishing cultural and historical narratives, this focus has left the systematic quantitative analysis of spatial attributes such as courtyard scale, orientation, and proportional relationships relatively underdeveloped [29]. This methodological gap fundamentally limits our capacity to move beyond case-based interpretation and uncover the underlying distribution patterns and morphological regularities that exist at a macro geographical scale.

1.3. Application of Artificial Intelligence in Vernacular Architecture Studies

Recent rapid advances in artificial intelligence (AI), particularly computer vision technologies centered on deep learning, have provided revolutionary tools for the large-scale, automated analysis of the built environment [30]. Their application spans diverse fields, from cultural heritage preservation [31,32] and urban planning [33,34] to architecture analysis [35,36]. Within these domains, a distinction can be drawn between studies focused on architectural style and those centered on spatial analysis. For instance, research in architecture has employed convolutional neural networks (CNNs) for tasks like automated building type classification from street-view or historical photographs [37–39] and even utilized generative adversarial networks (GANs) for architectural style transfer [40–42]. In contrast, work more aligned with remote sensing and spatial analysis has focused on semantic segmentation to extract building elements such as roof outlines from satel-

 https://doi.org/10.3390/buildings16061118

lite imagery [43,44], or on leveraging geospatial data for large-scale urban morphology quantification [45,46].

Applying these techniques to vernacular architecture research holds the potential to overcome the bottlenecks inherent in traditional methods. By processing high-resolution remote sensing imagery and open map data, computer vision approaches can: (1) enable efficient large-scale identification and geolocation of specific building types [47]; (2) automate the extraction of morphological features like building footprints and axial orientations [45]; and (3) support quantitative statistical analysis of massive datasets to reveal previously obscured spatial patterns and correlations [46].

Despite this potential, a critical research gap remains. Existing studies have largely applied AI either to generic historical building classification or to coarse-grained urban morphology analysis. Its systematic use for the detailed mapping and feature analysis of a specific, regionally defined courtyard type, particularly one as culturally significant as the "Liangshuaixiu" dwelling, is nascent. There is a clear absence of an integrated methodological framework that synthesizes advanced computer vision techniques with deep-seated domain knowledge from architecture and cultural geography [48]. Bridging this gap is the central contribution of this paper. This study transcends the boundaries of extant approaches by moving beyond mere classification to a high-precision, quantitative investigation of the courtyard's core spatial morphology. In doing so, it not only aims to establish a comprehensive digital archive for the cultural heritage of southern Hebei but also, through a data-driven lens, to reveal quantitative patterns and spatial heterogeneity in human–environment interactions that have long been obscured by qualitative description. This advancement is intended to propel vernacular architecture research from traditional, case-based interpretation towards a spatial-scientific analysis grounded in large, empirical samples.

1.4. Research Objectives

This research addresses the identified methodological gap by establishing a novel, interdisciplinary framework that integrates architecture, geographic information science, and computer vision. Beyond merely constructing a technical workflow, the central aim is to generate new, empirically grounded knowledge about vernacular architecture that has been inaccessible through traditional methods. The study will explicitly advance professional understanding in three key areas, shifting the discourse from qualitative typology to quantitative, spatially explicit analysis. The specific research objectives are as follows:

(1) To develop an automated identification and feature extraction model. Construct and train a deep learning model adapted to the rural environment of southern Hebei, enabling the automatic detection and contour segmentation of Liangshuaixiu dwelling spaces from satellite imagery, and the batch extraction of core morphological parameters, with a focus on courtyard area and primary orientation angle.

(2) To reveal the spatial distribution patterns of courtyard morphology. Based on the extracted regional-scale dataset of courtyard features, employ spatial statistical methods to systematically delineate the spatial distribution patterns of courtyard area and orientation in southern Hebei. This involves identifying spatial clusters, transitional zones, and anomalies to explore underlying regional differentiation patterns.

(3) To investigate the influence mechanisms of physical geographical factors. Spatially overlay the courtyard morphology dataset with natural environmental variables and conduct correlation analysis. Utilize models such as geographically weighted regression (GWR) to quantitatively identify and assess the degree of influence and spatial heterogeneity of different physical geographical factors on courtyard spatial mor-

 https://doi.org/10.3390/buildings16061118

phology (particularly area and orientation), explaining the causes of morphological variations from a human–environment interaction perspective.

The anticipated outcomes of this research will provide detailed, panoramic data support for the conservation of traditional settlements and architecture in southern Hebei. By fulfilling these objectives, the study will not only generate new, data-driven insights into the vernacular architecture of this specific region but also establish an extensible quantitative methodology for cross-regional comparative studies. Ultimately, this work aims to propel architectural cultural heritage research from a case-based interpretive tradition into a new paradigm grounded in data-intensive, spatially explicit scientific analysis.

2. Materials and Methods

The overall research workflow follows the logic of "Data Acquisition and Processing → Target Identification and Feature Extraction → Spatial Analysis and Mechanism Exploration." It aims to deeply integrate the automated recognition capability of computer vision, quantitative descriptive methods for architectural morphology, and the spatial analysis functions of Geographic Information Systems (GISs, ArcGIS 10.8) to reveal the macroscopic patterns and driving factors of the courtyard morphology of Liangshuaixiu dwellings in the Wu'an region of southern Hebei (Figure 1).

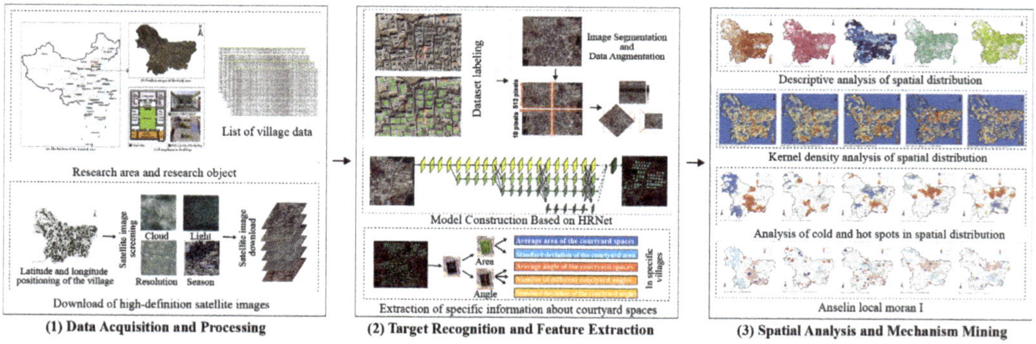

Figure 1. Schematic diagram of the research process.

2.1. Geographical Context and Target Subjects

This study takes all rural settlements within Wu'an City, Hebei Province as the study area (Figure 2). Wu'an is located on the eastern foothills of the Taihang Mountains in southern Hebei, representing a typical transitional zone between the North China Plain farming area and low mountainous/hilly terrain [49]. The area features a rich variety and wide distribution of courtyard house types, with the Liangshuaixiu form being relatively well-preserved and distinct in its characteristics. This makes Wu'an an excellent sample area for studying courtyard dwellings of southern Hebei. The selection of Wu'an balances regional representativeness (representing the core cultural area of southern Hebei), topographic diversity (encompassing plains, hills, and mountains, facilitating environmental adaptability analysis), and data accessibility (availability of clear satellite imagery and fundamental geographic data).

The specific research subject is the courtyard space of traditional dwellings exhibiting a clear Liangshuaixiu layout within the rural settlements of Wu'an. Liangshuaixiu is a variant of the traditional Siheyuan (quadrangle courtyard). It typically refers to the layout where the bedrooms flanking the main north hall extend southward, connecting with the east and west wing rooms. All buildings of the dwelling are connected end-to-end, usually

 https://doi.org/10.3390/buildings16061118

with flat roofs, forming a geometrically regular and highly enclosed courtyard space [50]. This form is widely distributed in the countryside of Handan, Xingtai, and other areas in southern Hebei [46]. In terms of image characteristics, the criteria for identifying a Liangshuaixiu dwelling are: an open-air courtyard enclosed by a main building, two wing buildings, and an opposite building (or courtyard wall), resulting in at least three sides being surrounded by structures. Exclusion criteria include: courtyards that have undergone complete modern reconstruction, courtyards completely obscured by large structures or trees, and courtyards that cannot be clearly interpreted due to poor image quality.

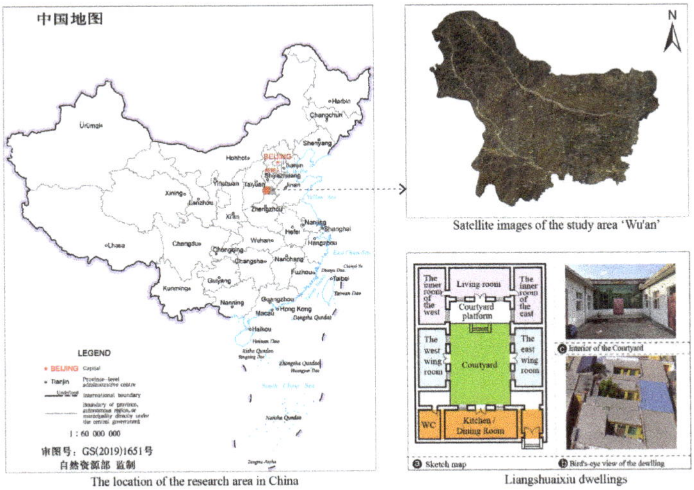

Figure 2. Study area and research subject.

2.2. Satellite Imagery Collection

This study systematically downloaded high-resolution satellite imagery covering all administrative villages within Wu'an City using the "Shuijing Weitu" software (Rivermap V4.3.24). The imagery was primarily from 2009 to the present to reflect the relatively stable recent rural building pattern while avoiding significant loss of traditional forms due to large-scale new rural construction [47]. Priority was given to winter imagery (November to February). During this period, vegetation in northern China is leafless, minimizing tree occlusion of buildings and courtyards, which maximizes visible courtyard area and improves recognition accuracy. All selected imagery met the requirements of being cloud-free, having clear imaging (no severe haze or shadows), and possessing a spatial resolution better than 0.6 m. The downloaded images were mosaicked, cropped (by administrative village), and projected into the CGCS2000 coordinate system. Furthermore, individual villages whose imagery did not meet the quality standards for computer vision recognition were excluded to ensure the final recognition accuracy.

2.3. Computer Vision Technology

To precisely segment courtyard spaces from the massive imagery, a computer vision framework based on deep learning semantic segmentation was constructed. The core algorithm used was HRNetV2 (High-Resolution Network). This network is renowned for its unique architecture that maintains high-resolution feature representations throughout [51]. In semantic segmentation tasks, it is particularly adept at preserving spatial details and geometric structures of targets. The specific advantage of HRNetV2 over conventional encoder–decoder architectures (e.g., U-Net) lies in its parallel multi-resolution

 https://doi.org/10.3390/buildings16061118

subnetwork design. Unlike U-Net, which progressively downsamples and then upsamples, often leading to a loss of fine spatial detail, HRNetV2 maintains high-resolution representations throughout the entire process and repeatedly exchanges information across parallel resolutions. This enables more precise delineation of targets like "courtyards," which often have complex, irregular boundaries and, in some instances, low contrast with surrounding buildings or roads [52]. This architectural choice is therefore critical for achieving the high-fidelity geometric data required for subsequent quantitative morphological analysis [42].

Sample image patches containing typical Liangshuaixiu courtyards were manually selected from the study area imagery. Using the annotation tool LabelMe, pixel-level semantic segmentation annotation was performed, defining three classes: Courtyard, Building, and Background. Annotation was carried out by architecture professionals to ensure that the judgment of "courtyard" conformed to architectural definitions. Ultimately, a dataset containing thousands of annotated courtyard samples was built and divided into training, validation, and test sets.

Within the PyTorch framework (version 2.6.0), transfer learning was performed using a pre-trained HRNetV2 model on the custom dataset. During training, the cross-entropy loss function and the Adam optimizer were employed, and data augmentation (e.g., rotation, flipping, color jitter) was applied to enhance model generalization. The validation set was used to monitor performance and prevent overfitting.

For inference and post-processing, the trained model was applied to the imagery of the entire study area for batch inference, producing a probability map for each pixel belonging to the "Courtyard" class. A threshold (0.5) was applied to convert this into a binary segmentation map. Subsequently, morphological operations (e.g., closing to remove small holes, opening to smooth boundaries) were performed to optimize the segmentation results [47]. Connected component analysis was then used to extract vector polygon files representing the contour of each independent courtyard.

2.4. Calculation of Courtyard Spatial Morphological Parameters

Based on the identified courtyard contour vector data, two core types of morphological parameters were calculated: courtyard area and dominant orientation angle.

2.4.1. Courtyard Area Calculation

(1) Area conversion and calibration

The courtyard area output by the model is based on pixel count. Using the georeferencing information of the satellite imagery (ground distance per pixel), the pixel area was converted to actual ground area in square meters. To verify conversion accuracy, several courtyards with known dimensions were measured on-site, and the results were compared with model calculations for calibration, ensuring systematic error was within an acceptable range.

The model-calculated courtyard area is derived as

$$A_{model} = N \times (GSD)^2 \tag{1}$$

where

A_{model}: Model-calculated courtyard area (m^2).

N: Total number of pixels within the courtyard contour polygon.

GSD: Ground Sampling Distance of the imagery (m/pixel), i.e., spatial resolution.

The absolute error ΔA_i and relative error δ_i for a single sample are

$$\Delta A_i = A_{model,i} - A_{field,i} \tag{2}$$

https://doi.org/10.3390/buildings16061118

$$\delta_i = \left| \frac{\Delta A_i}{A_{field,i}} \right| \times 100\% \tag{3}$$

where

$A_{field,i}$: Field-measured area of the i-th courtyard (m^2).

The Root Mean Square Error (RMSE), characterizing overall accuracy, is

$$RMSE = \sqrt{\frac{1}{m}\sum_{i=1}^{m}(\Delta A_i)^2} \tag{4}$$

(2) Village-scale average courtyard area

Each courtyard was assigned to its respective administrative village. The arithmetic mean of the areas $\overline{A_v}$ of all identified courtyards within a village was calculated as an indicator of the central tendency of courtyard scale for that village:

$$\overline{A_v} = \frac{1}{n_v}\sum_{i=1}^{n_v} A_i \tag{5}$$

where n_v is the number of courtyards in village v.

(3) Village-scale measure of courtyard area consistency

The Coefficient of Variation (CV) was used to measure the dispersion of courtyard areas within the same village, reflecting the uniformity or diversity of courtyard scale in that locality:

$$\overline{A_v} = \frac{1}{n_v}\sum_{i=1}^{n_v} A_i \tag{6}$$

where σ_{A_v} is the standard deviation of courtyard areas in village v. A smaller CV value indicates greater similarity in courtyard areas within the village.

2.4.2. Courtyard Orientation Calculation

(1) Calculation of individual courtyard orientation angle

The Minimum Bounding Rectangle (MBR) was calculated for each courtyard polygon using the minimum area enclosing rectangle method. The direction (azimuth, 0–90°) of the rectangle's long side was defined as the primary orientation of the courtyard. In the context of North China courtyard houses, this direction typically represents the orientation of the main building (the ideal south-facing orientation is 90°). This simplification is theoretically justified by the geometric properties of the Liangshuaixiu form, which is characterized by a highly regular, orthogonal layout. In such cases, the long axis of the MBR reliably corresponds to the principal axis of the entire dwelling complex, making it a robust and efficient proxy for the building's orientation. While this method may be less accurate for irregularly shaped plots, its application to a highly standardized vernacular type ensures a high degree of validity for large-scale analysis.

(2) Village-scale overall orientation calculation

For circular angular data, the average direction was calculated at the village scale. First, each courtyard's angle was converted into a unit vector. The vector sum was calculated, and then the average angle was derived inversely.

$$\bar{r} = \frac{1}{n}\sum_{i=1}^{n} r_i \tag{7}$$

https://doi.org/10.3390/buildings16061118

where

$\bar{r}$: Average resultant length (also known as mean resultant length).
n: Total number of buildings/courtyards.
r_i: Unit vector component for the i-th building.

(3) Village-scale measure of orientation consistency

Village-scale orientation consistency is characterized using two metrics. On the one hand, the number of unique orientation angles within a specific village is calculated to represent angular diversity. The formula is as follows:

$$U = |\{r_i | i = 1 \ldots n\}| \quad (8)$$

where
U: Number of unique values.
r_i: Orientation angle (rotate value) of the i-th building.
i: Index variable, ranging from 1 to n.

On the other hand, the standard deviation of angles is used as a dispersion metric to quantify the deviation of courtyard orientations within a village:

$$s^2 = \frac{1}{n-1}\sum_{i=1}^{n}(r_i - \bar{r})^2 \quad (9)$$

where
s^2: Sample variance (indicating data dispersion).
n: Total number of buildings.
r_i: Orientation angle (rotate value) of the i-th building.
$\bar{r}$: Mean value of the orientation angles.

2.5. GIS Analysis and Geographic Detector

All calculated courtyard morphological parameters (area, orientation) were associated with their spatial location points (courtyard centroids) as attributes, constructing a spatial geodatabase of courtyard morphology.

(1) Spatial distribution characteristics and pattern analysis: Visual Mapping: Thematic maps were generated for the spatial distribution of courtyard area, orientation (discretized into several main directional intervals), and village-level statistical indicators (average area, orientation concentration).

Spatial Autocorrelation Analysis: Global Moran's I was used to determine whether a particular morphological parameter (e.g., courtyard area) across the entire region exhibited a significant spatial clustering pattern [51]. Subsequently, Local Moran's I and Getis-Ord Gi* hotspot analysis were used to precisely identify "High-High" clusters (hotspots), "Low-Low" clusters (coldspots), and spatial outlier areas.

(2) Factor Detection: To explore the driving forces behind the spatial differentiation of courtyard morphology, the Geographic Detector model was introduced. Potential influencing factors (X) were selected, and their continuous variables (e.g., elevation, distance to water) were appropriately discretized. To ensure the robustness and interpretability of our findings, we adopted a theoretically informed and empirically validated approach to discretization: Elevation and Slope were discretized using the natural breaks (Jenks) method. This approach is appropriate as it inherently seeks to minimize within-group variance and maximize between-group variance, effectively identifying meaningful thresholds in the natural landscape where environmental conditions change significantly. The proximity

https://doi.org/10.3390/buildings16061118

variables, such as Distance to Water and Roads, were discretized using quantiles, ensuring a relatively balanced number of samples in each category.

Factor Detector: Used to detect the explanatory power (q statistic) of various influencing factors (e.g., elevation zone, slope zone, aspect category, distance to major water bodies, distance to major roads, mean annual temperature, annual precipitation, village population density, per capita cultivated land area, etc.) on the spatial differentiation of courtyard morphological parameters (e.g., average area, orientation angle). The q-value range is [0, 1]; a larger value indicates stronger explanatory power of that factor [53].

Interaction Detector: Assesses whether the explanatory power for the morphological parameter is enhanced, weakened, or independent after the interaction of any two influencing factors. This helps reveal the complex synergistic influence mechanisms between physical geographical and socio-economic factors.

Through this series of spatial statistical and attribution analyses, this study aims to quantitatively reveal the underlying spatial patterns of Liangshuaixiu courtyard morphology in Wu'an at a macroscopic scale and scientifically identify the underlying natural and human driving factors and their interactions.

3. Results

3.1. Recognition Accuracy and Data Calibration

High-resolution satellite imagery was downloaded for all 450 villages in Wu'an, leading to the identification of 134,280 Liangshuaixiu dwellings. For each village, the average courtyard area, the standard deviation of the area, the average courtyard orientation angle, the number of distinct orientation angles, and the standard deviation of the angles were calculated, as illustrated in Figure 3.

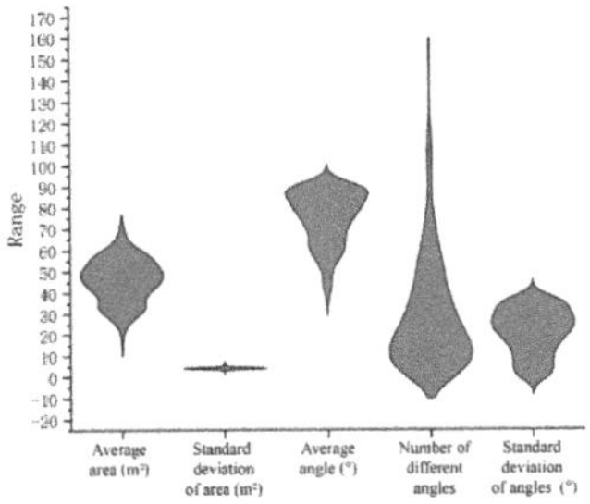

Figure 3. Overall distribution characteristics of data related to courtyard space.

The average courtyard area ranged from 13.51 m^2 to 72.43 m^2, with the majority of values concentrated around 46.83 m^2. The distribution of the area standard deviation was narrower, spanning from 0.96 m^2 to 7.07 m^2 and predominantly clustering around 4.22 m^2. Regarding the average orientation angle, values ranged from a minimum of 33.07° to a maximum of 90.00° (indicating a due south orientation for the main building), with most values centered around 75.30°. The number of distinct courtyard orientation angles per village varied significantly; the maximum observed was 157 (indicating a high degree of variation), while the most uniform village had all buildings sharing the same orientation. The median number of distinct angles was 21. The standard deviation of orientation angles ranged from 0° to 39.62°, with the most frequent values concentrated around 21.01°.

A random sample of 48 Liangshuaixiu dwellings was selected to validate the accuracy of the computer vision recognition results (Figure 4). For courtyard area recognition, the maximum absolute error was +10.09 m^2 (approximately 14.62% of the measured area), while the minimum error was +0.39 m^2. On average, the absolute difference between the

https://doi.org/10.3390/buildings16061118

measured and recognized area values was 4.81 m^2, corresponding to about 10.13% of the average courtyard area. For orientation angle recognition, the largest error was +4.07° (approximately 18.09% of the measured angle), and the smallest error was 0° (for angles consistently identified as 90°). The mean absolute error was 1.99°, representing about 10.97% of the average orientation angle.

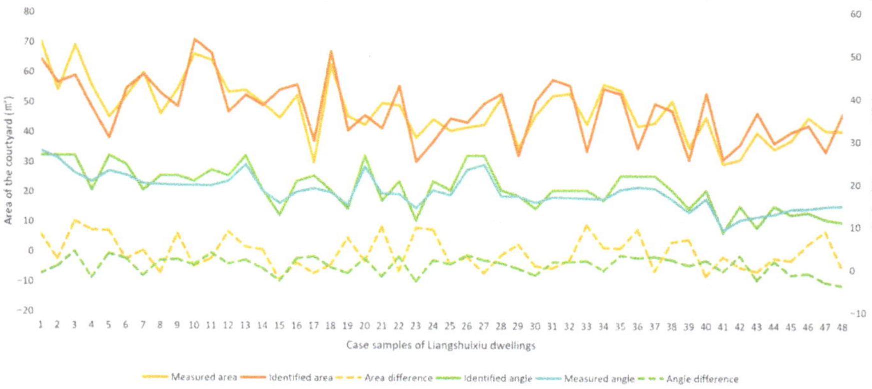

Figure 4. Comparison between predicted results and measured data.

Overall, the average recognition errors for both courtyard area and orientation were approximately 10%, with maximum errors reaching around 18%. This level of accuracy is considered acceptable for the purposes of this study, which focuses on identifying macro-scale spatial patterns and regional trends rather than precisely characterizing individual dwellings. However, the observed systematic overestimation of area, combined with the sample size limitations of the validation set, implies that while the spatial patterns and relative differences reported in subsequent sections are robust, the absolute values of courtyard area should be interpreted with appropriate caution.

3.2. Morphology and Distribution Characteristics of Courtyards

The courtyard area of Liangshuaixiu dwellings exhibits significant variation and distinct geographical distribution patterns, as shown in Figure 5. A general west-to-east gradient is apparent, with smaller courtyards predominantly located in the west and larger ones in the east. Larger courtyards, typically ranging from 58 m^2 to 73 m^2, are clustered in the central part of Wu'an County. In contrast, the average area of courtyards in the west is only 10–20 m^2, while those in the east mostly range between 38 m^2 and 45 m^2.

The results of cold and hot spot analysis further corroborate these observations. Spatial autocorrelation analysis reveals a significant clustering trend for courtyard area size, with a Moran's I index of 0.69 and a z-score of 22.22 (Figure 6). Hot spots (areas with significantly larger courtyards) are concentrated in the central region of the county, whereas cold spots (areas with significantly smaller courtyards) are distributed in the western part.

Furthermore, the standard deviation of courtyard area was calculated for each village to characterize the internal consistency of courtyard sizes (Figure 5). In contrast to the clear gradient observed for average area, the spatial analysis indicates that the consistency of courtyard area is less distinctly patterned. Generally, the standard deviation is slightly lower in the northern regions compared to the south. Spatial autocorrelation analysis for the area standard deviation yielded a Moran's I index of 0.25 and a z-score of 8.20 (Figure 6). This suggests that, although the degree of spatial clustering for the area standard deviation is less pronounced than for the average area, a statistically significant clustering trend still exists. Specifically, cold spots for the area standard deviation are located in the northwest, while hot spots are aggregated in the southern regions.

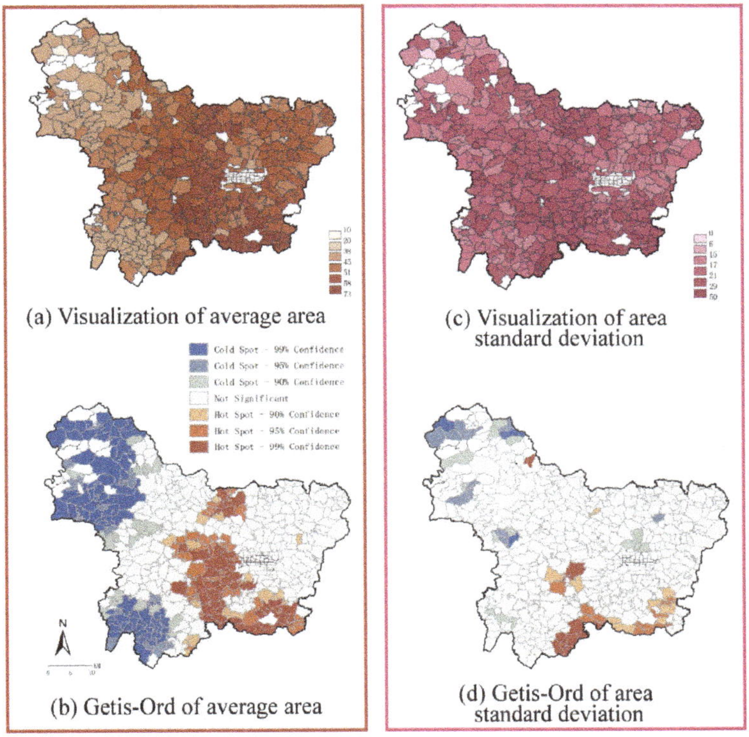

Figure 5. Spatial distribution and hotspot analysis of courtyard area.

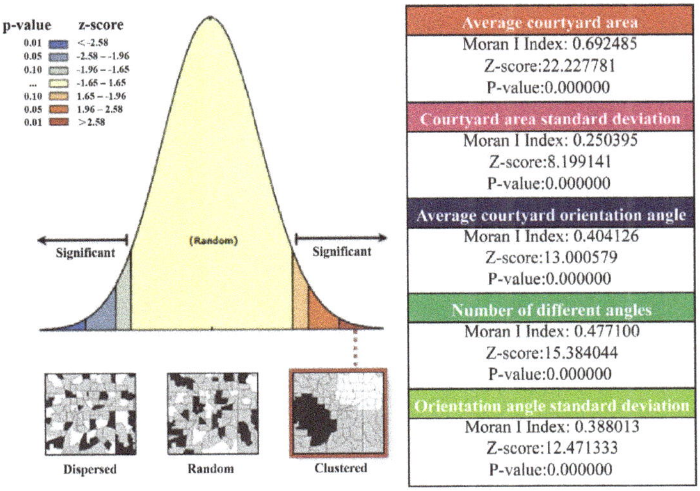

Figure 6. Spatial autocorrelation analysis of courtyard morphology.

Regarding courtyard orientation, layouts oriented due north–south (around 90°) are primarily concentrated in the southeastern part of the study area, particularly surrounding

 https://doi.org/10.3390/buildings16061118

Wu'an county town (Figure 7). A portion of Liangshuaixiu dwellings in the northwest also exhibit orientations clustered around 90°. Overall, villages with the highest average orientation angles (close to due south–north) are aggregated in the southeast, while those with smaller average angles (closer to east–west orientation) are concentrated in the north-eastern part of the study area. Spatial autocorrelation results show a Moran's I index of 0.40 and a z-score of 13.00, indicating that the spatial clustering of the average orientation angle is statistically significant and non-random.

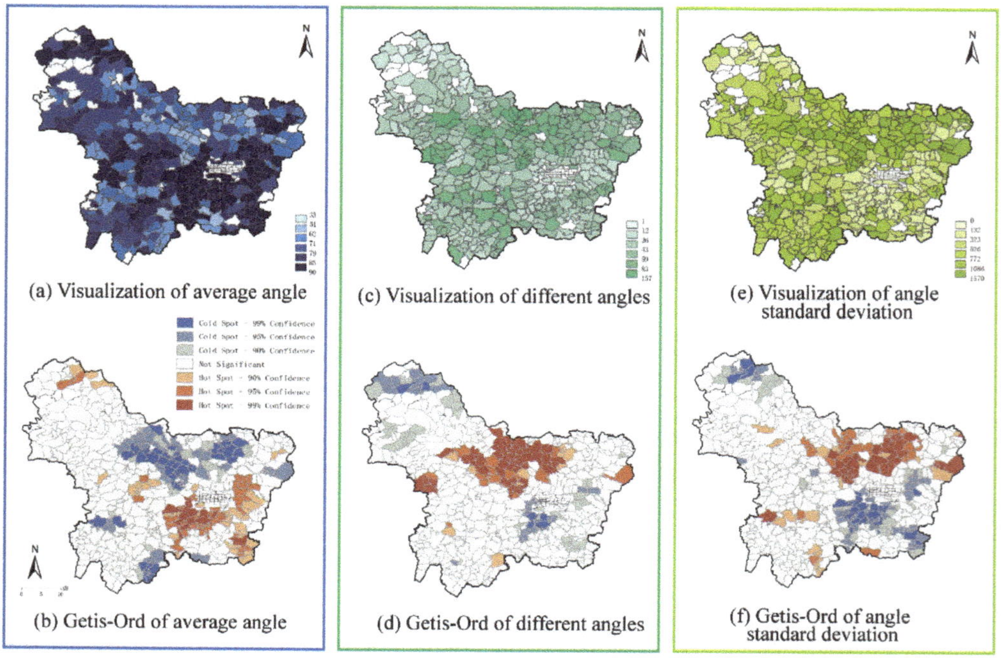

Figure 7. Spatial distribution and hotspot analysis of courtyard orientation angle.

To move beyond this central tendency, the number of distinct orientation angles per village was counted to characterize the diversity in courtyard orientation (Figure 7). Spatially, areas with a higher count and thus greater orientation diversity are mainly located in the peripheral zones at a moderate distance from the county town. Diversity decreases in areas very close to or very far from the town. Cold and hot spot analysis shows that villages with the highest angle counts are concentrated north of the county town, while diversity decreases in the immediate suburbs and the remote northwestern areas. Spatial autocorrelation yields a Moran's I index of 0.47 and a z-score of 15.38, confirming that the spatial clustering of orientation diversity is statistically significant and not random (Figure 6).

Similarly, the standard deviation of courtyard orientation angles was calculated for each village and its spatial distribution was mapped (Figure 7). Overall, the spatial pattern of the orientation standard deviation shows some similarity to that of orientation diversity. Areas with a larger standard deviation are also concentrated in the peripheral zones farther from the county town, with hot spots located north of the town. Conversely, villages with a smaller standard deviation are clustered in the near suburbs and the remote northwest. Spatial autocorrelation analysis for the orientation standard deviation results in a Moran's

 https://doi.org/10.3390/buildings16061118

I index of 0.39 and a z-score of 12.47, demonstrating that its spatial clustering is also statistically significant (Figure 6).

3.3. Exploration of Influencing Mechanisms for Courtyard Morphology

Based on the geographic detector method, this study quantitatively reveals the statistical associations and potential drivers behind the spatial differentiation of various morphological indicators of Liangshuaixiu dwellings in Wu'an City. The results indicate that their spatial patterns are strongly associated with the synergistic interaction between the natural geographical environment and socio-economic factors through complex interplays. The dominant factors and key interactions statistically linked to each indicator are shown in Table 1.

Table 1. Main driving factors for courtyard morphology.

Dependent Variable	Rank	Main Driving Factor (Independent q-Value)	Key Interaction Pair (Interaction q-Value)	Interaction Type
Average courtyard area	1	X11 Air Pressure (0.563 ***)	X11 & X5 Distance to Water System (0.664)	Nonlinear Enhancement
	2	X6 Wind Speed (0.546 ***)	X6 & X2 Aspect (0.628)	Nonlinear Enhancement
	3	X1 Elevation (0.522 ***)	X11 & X16 Resident Population (0.631)	Two-factor Enhancement
Courtyard area standard deviation	1	X6 Wind Speed (0.137 ***)	X14 Population & X7 Min Temperature (0.347)	Nonlinear Enhancement
	2	X1 Elevation (0.129 ***)	X6 Wind Speed & X10 Relative Humidity (0.349)	Nonlinear Enhancement
	3	X18 Cultivated Land Area (0.098 ***)	X1 Elevation & X14 Population (0.266)	Two-factor Enhancement
Average courtyard orientation	1	X7 Min Temperature (0.197 ***)	X7 Min Temperature & X4 Distance to Roads (0.364)	Nonlinear Enhancement
	2	X1 Elevation (0.180 ***)	X6 Wind Speed & X9 Max Temperature (0.404)	Nonlinear Enhancement
	3	X6 Wind Speed (0.177 ***)	X1 Elevation & X12 Precipitation (0.306)	Two-factor Enhancement
Number of different angles	1	X1 Elevation (0.218 ***)	X15 Households & X9 Max Temperature (0.523)	Nonlinear Enhancement
	2	X14 Population (0.206 ***)	X14 Population & X6 Wind Speed (0.507)	Nonlinear Enhancement
	3	X15 Households (0.201 ***)	X1 Elevation & X16 Resident Population (0.483)	Two-factor Enhancement
Angle standard deviation	1	X6 Wind Speed (0.178 ***)	X6 Wind Speed & X2 Aspect (0.342)	Nonlinear Enhancement
	2	X7 Min Temperature (0.166 ***)	X1 Elevation & X12 Precipitation (0.291)	Two-factor Enhancement
	3	X1 Elevation (0.149 ***)	X6 Wind Speed & X7 Min Temperature (0.314)	Two-factor Enhancement

*** indicates $p < 0.001$.

The spatial differentiation of the average courtyard area is primarily statistically associated with climatic and topographic factors. Factor detection shows (Table 1) that air pressure (X11), wind speed (X6), and elevation (X1) have the strongest independent

 https://doi.org/10.3390/buildings16061118

explanatory power, suggesting that regional climatic conditions and basic topography form a foundational background for courtyard scale. Interaction detection further reveals that interactions between natural factors and between natural and human factors show significantly enhanced explanatory power, such as the interaction between air pressure and distance to water systems. This implies that the formation of the average courtyard scale is statistically linked to the coupling of natural background and human activities, with the dominance of natural factors being more prominent.

The spatial pattern of courtyard area standard deviation (internal size variability) is also mainly statistically linked to natural climatic factors, but the independent explanatory power of each factor is relatively weak. Wind speed (X6) and elevation (X1) remain key factors. Notably, cultivated land area (X18), as a socio-economic land use factor, shows significant independent explanatory power. Interactions are widespread and strong (e.g., the interaction between X14 and X7), indicating that the coupling between natural climatic heterogeneity and the distribution of human activities is a statistical pattern shaping the discrete pattern of area.

The spatial differentiation of the average courtyard orientation angle is associated at the independent factor level primarily with extreme temperature and climatic dynamic factors. However, its core driving characteristic lies in the strong interaction effects, especially the reinforced statistical dependency between "human activity location" and "climate". For example, the interaction between "distance to roads" (X4), which is insignificant alone, and "minimum temperature" (X7) yields the strongest explanatory power. This reveals that the distribution of infrastructure significantly regulates the collective preference for courtyard orientation through interaction with local climate conditions.

The spatial pattern of the number of different angles (orientation diversity) exhibits a distinct characteristic of "dual drivers: natural background and human activity". Topographic and climatic factors provide the natural potential for diversity, while population (X14) and household count (X15) show comparable independent explanatory power, indicating that human settlement behavior itself is a core force co-varying with orientation complexity. The interaction network is extremely powerful, particularly the "human–climate" coupling (e.g., the interaction between X15 and X9), suggesting that orientation diversity is statistically associated with the non-linear feedback between population agglomeration and specific climatic conditions.

The spatial differentiation of courtyard angle standard deviation (internal orientation variability) most clearly reflects the strong statistical association with key physical geography processes. In factor detection, wind speed (X6) and minimum temperature (X7) have the strongest explanatory power. Interaction detection clearly points to the coupling of "climatic dynamics and topographic attributes" as the core, such as the interaction between wind speed and aspect having the strongest explanatory power. This essentially reflects a strong statistical link to a "wind–aspect" coupled geographical process. Human factors are not significant independently but show some statistical interaction with natural factors.

In summary, the spatial differentiation of various morphological indicators of Wu'an Liangshuaixiu dwellings shows strong statistical associations with multiple factors. The observed courtyard morphology is statistically complex, reflecting the interplay of a natural system providing context and a human system adapting to it. It is crucial to emphasize that while these statistical dependencies are robust, the methodological framework identifies correlation and co-occurrence, not direct causation.

https://doi.org/10.3390/buildings16061118

4. Discussion

4.1. Computer Vision for Vernacular Architecture

This study demonstrates the significant efficacy of deep learning-based computer vision in the large-scale, automated identification and feature extraction of vernacular courtyard dwellings [47]. The achieved recognition accuracy (average error ~10% for both area and orientation) is acceptable for regional-scale morphological studies, confirming the feasibility of transitioning from labor-intensive manual surveys to AI-assisted mapping [45]. The success hinges on two key factors: first, the use of high-resolution winter imagery minimized occlusion, a crucial pre-processing step for rural building recognition; second, the model was trained on a dataset meticulously annotated by architectural professionals, ensuring that the machine-learned "courtyard" concept aligns with architectural domain knowledge. This pipeline—combining domain-informed data preparation, an appropriate model architecture for preserving spatial details, and expert-validated ground truth—offers a replicable framework for digitizing other vernacular building types [46].

This approach marks a significant methodological advancement over previous research paradigms in vernacular architecture studies. The traditional field survey-based studies, while rich in qualitative detail [19] and historical accuracy [23], are inherently labor-intensive and time-consuming, limiting their scope to small sample sizes [25]. This restriction fundamentally precludes the possibility of capturing the full spectrum of morphological variation across an entire region, leaving unanswered questions about whether documented cases are representative or exceptional [22]. In contrast, our deep learning-based semantic segmentation framework enables, for the first time in this research domain, a comprehensive census-scale analysis of building features across an entire county. It allows for robust spatial statistical analyses to identify meaningful clustering patterns, rather than relying on interpolated or extrapolated estimates from sparse samples [46].

The technical core of this advancement lies in our model architecture selection. HRNetV2 was specifically chosen for its distinctive ability to maintain high-resolution feature representations throughout the entire network hierarchy [47], unlike conventional encoder–decoder architectures that progressively down-sample feature maps to capture semantic context [40], only to later up-sample them for pixel-wise prediction [39]. This down-sampling process, while computationally efficient, inevitably sacrifices spatial precision [43], a critical drawback for delineating fine-grained courtyard boundaries that can be as narrow as 1–2 pixels in satellite imagery. By maintaining parallel streams of varying resolutions and repeatedly exchanging information across them, HRNetV2 produces feature maps that are simultaneously semantically rich and spatially precise.

4.2. Factors Influencing Vernacular Architectural Morphology

The geographic detector analysis reveals a nuanced, multi-layered driving mechanism behind courtyard morphology in Wu'an. Crucially, it moves beyond simplistic single-factor explanations, highlighting the paramount importance of interaction effects.

(1) Natural factors as the dominant baseline

For fundamental attributes like average area and orientation, climatic (air pressure, wind, temperature) and topographic (elevation) factors exhibit the strongest independent explanatory power (q-values > 0.5 for area). This underscores that the basic "footprint" and solar orientation of dwellings are first-order responses to the regional environmental canvas, optimizing for thermal comfort, wind protection, and land use [54].

(2) The primacy of interactions

The most significant finding is that for all morphology indicators—especially those related to variation (standard deviation) and diversity—the explanatory power of factor

 https://doi.org/10.3390/buildings16061118

interactions far surpasses that of any single factor. This is particularly evident in combinations like Distance to Roads × Minimum Temperature for average orientation and Wind Speed × Aspect for orientation variability. These interactions reveal that the built environment is not shaped by environmental or social factors in isolation, but through their coupling. For instance, the strong Household Count × Maximum Temperature interaction for orientation diversity suggests that human settlement density and microclimate co-evolve, leading to more complex and varied building orientations [55].

(3) Socioeconomic factors as amplifiers and modulators

While socioeconomic factors (population, household count, cultivated land) show moderate independent influence on diversity metrics, their most powerful role is as interactive partners with natural factors. They act as amplifiers of natural predispositions or as agents that introduce new layers of complexity in specific environmental settings [46]. This reframes the role of human agency in vernacular architecture from a passive "adapter" to an active "modulator" within environmental constraints [56].

These findings both complement and extend previous research on Chinese vernacular architecture, which has often qualitatively described the influence of feng shui [20], clan structure [23], or topography [48] on dwelling form. By quantitatively mapping these associations across an entire region, our study provides empirical weight to these conceptual frameworks. For example, the interaction between household count and temperature offers a measurable dimension to the long-held notion that social organization and microclimate jointly shape settlement patterns [24].

More broadly, the observed patterns resonate with studies of vernacular settlements worldwide. For instance, the strong influence of topography and climate on core dwelling attributes mirrors findings in Sumatra [57] and Iran [58] contexts, suggesting universal human–environment adaptation principles. However, the specific ways these factors interact, such as the modulating role of road networks on climatic influences, may reflect regionally unique socio-economic histories. This suggests that while the methodology is highly transferable, the resulting interpretations must be grounded in local contextual knowledge [59]. Future comparative studies applying this AI-driven approach across different cultural and geographical regions could help distinguish universal drivers of settlement form from culturally specific ones, thereby enhancing the generalizability of our findings [15].

4.3. *Originality of the Research*

(1) Methodological innovation in architectural analysis

This study establishes a novel, transferable framework that integrates high-resolution semantic segmentation with spatial statistical methods for architectural heritage research. Unlike previous approaches that either conduct small-scale qualitative surveys or apply remote sensing solely for land cover classification, this research adapts cutting-edge computer vision techniques specifically for the fine-grained morphological analysis of vernacular architecture at regional scale. The methodological framework demonstrates how deep learning can bridge the gap between traditional architectural scholarship and geospatial science.

(2) Paradigm shift from typological case studies to empirical census

By enabling the systematic analysis of over 134,000 courtyard units across southern Hebei, this research fundamentally shifts the scale of vernacular architecture investigation. Moving beyond the limitations of representative case selection, it generates the first comprehensive, empirically grounded dataset of courtyard morphology for this region. This data-intensive approach reveals previously undetectable spatial patterns transforming our

https://doi.org/10.3390/buildings16061118

understanding of vernacular architecture from localized typological knowledge to spatially explicit, population-level insights.

(3) Quantitative elucidation of human–environment interaction mechanisms

This research advances beyond simple correlation analyses to quantitatively identify and rank the complex interaction effects among physical geographical factors shaping courtyard morphology. By employing geographically weighted regression and interaction detection methods, it reveals how combinations of natural factors produce spatially heterogeneous effects on architectural form. This provides a more sophisticated model of vernacular architecture as a dynamic human–environment feedback system, empirically demonstrating how traditional dwellings embody adaptive responses to their physical settings.

4.4. Limitations and Future Work

Several limitations should be acknowledged. First, while the computer vision model demonstrated acceptable overall accuracy, the validation process was constrained by a relatively limited sample size (n = 48). This limitation precludes a more granular, stratified analysis of systematic errors across different landscape contexts or building characteristics. Second, the 2D satellite view limits feature extraction to planimetric attributes (area, orientation); three-dimensional features like building height, roof form, and eave details are inaccessible [60]. Third, the temporal scope of this study is fundamentally cross-sectional, based on a composite of satellite imagery primarily from 2009 to the present. This temporal heterogeneity in the source data introduces an unquantified source of potential error. While winter imagery was prioritized to minimize vegetation occlusion, variations in sun angle, shadow length, and image quality across acquisition dates could subtly affect the consistency of courtyard boundary detection and area calculation. Fourth, some potentially important social and cultural variables were not included due to data unavailability [61].

Future research should: (1) incorporate 3D data sources (LiDAR, UAV photogrammetry) to capture volumetric features; (2) employ time-series analysis using historical imagery to track morphological change; (3) apply more complex models (e.g., interaction terms in spatial regression) to further dissect the nature of the identified couplings; and (4) extend this methodology to other cultural regions for comparative studies of vernacular adaptation patterns.

5. Conclusions

This study developed and applied an interdisciplinary methodology combining deep learning-based computer vision, GIS, and spatial statistics to map and analyze the courtyard morphology of Liangshuaixiu vernacular dwellings in Wu'an, southern Hebei, at an unprecedented scale and resolution. The core findings are threefold:

(1) Methodological validation: The HRNetV2-based pipeline proved effective for the automated, large-scale identification and morphological parameter extraction of vernacular courtyards, achieving an accuracy suitable for regional analysis and providing a scalable digital survey tool.

(2) Spatial patterns quantified: The research systematically quantified the spatial distribution of courtyard area and orientation, revealing clear spatial autocorrelation, west–east gradients in size, and complex, non-linear patterns in orientation diversity and variability.

(3) Driving mechanisms decoded: The analysis demonstrated that courtyard morphology is not determined by single factors but emerges from a complex interplay. While natural climatic and topographic factors set the foundational constraints, the observed spatial patterns–particularly regarding diversity and internal variation–are

https://doi.org/10.3390/buildings16061118

predominantly driven by nonlinear interactions between these environmental factors and human socio-economic activities. This underscores vernacular architecture as a dynamic, coupled human-environment system.

This research contributes a significant, high-precision geospatial dataset for the cultural heritage of southern Hebei and offers a transferable, data-driven framework that advances the study of vernacular architecture from qualitative, case-based description towards quantitative, spatial-scientific analysis. It highlights the critical importance of considering factor interactions for understanding landscape form and provides a foundation for informed, evidence-based conservation and regional planning.

Author Contributions: Conceptualization, B.W.; methodology, L.L.; software, L.L.; validation, L.L.; formal analysis, L.L., X.L., Z.G. and S.T.; investigation, B.W. and L.L.; resources, L.L.; data curation, X.L., Z.G. and S.T.; writing—original draft preparation, L.L.; writing—review and editing, L.L.; visualization, L.L. and S.L.; supervision, B.W. All authors have read and agreed to the published version of the manuscript.

Funding: This research was funded by Hunan Provincial Social Science Achievement Evaluation Committee Project, grant number XSP24YBC490; MOE Humanities and Social Sciences Grant, grant number 24YJC850004; SIT Program at Hunan University, S202510532643; National Natural Science Foundation of China, grant number 52578016 and 52108010; Natural Science Foundation of Hunan Province, grant number 2025JJ50234; Science and Technology Program Project of Hunan Province, grant number 2025RC3096.

Data Availability Statement: The original contributions presented in this study are included in the article. Further inquiries can be directed to the corresponding author.

Acknowledgments: The authors have reviewed and edited the output and take full responsibility for the content of this publication.

Conflicts of Interest: The authors declare no conflicts of interest.

References

1. Zerari, S.; Cirafici, A.; Sriti, L. Issues in the Expression of Local Identity in the Saharan Regions of Algeria: In Search of References to Vernacular Architecture. *Conserv. Sci. Cult. Herit.* **2022**, *22*, 181–206.
2. Chohan, A.H.; Awad, J.; Ismail, M.A.; Arar, M.S. Integrating Technology and Heritage Design for Climate Resilient Courtyard House in Arid Region. *Civ. Eng. J.-Tehran* **2024**, *10*, 928–952. [CrossRef]
3. Moscoso-Garcia, P.; Quesada-Molina, F. Analysis of Passive Strategies in Traditional Vernacular Architecture. *Buildings* **2023**, *13*, 1984. [CrossRef]
4. Philokyprou, M.; Michael, A. Environmental Sustainability in the Conservation of Vernacular Architecture. The Case of Rural and Urban Traditional Settlements in Cyprus. *Int. J. Archit. Herit.* **2021**, *15*, 1741–1763. [CrossRef]
5. Su, Y.W.; Li, M.; Cheng, M.S.; Qiang, M.L.; Zhou, X.B. A Study on the Architectural Form and Characteristics of Tusi Manors in the Yunnan-Tibet Region. *Buildings* **2025**, *15*, 1134. [CrossRef]
6. Sharami, H.J.; Hosseini, S.J. Theoretical framework of the Isfahani style: Inspiring sustainable aspects of a vernacular urban development. *Front. Archit. Res.* **2024**, *13*, 349–369. [CrossRef]
7. Sara, F.; Chaymae, B.; Hicham, M.; Sanae, A. Intermediate spaces in Moroccan vernacular architecture: Climatic and cultural challenges. In Proceedings of the 2024 International Colloquium on Vernacular Architecture, a Support for Territorial Development, Rabat, Morocco, 4–5 October 2024; pp. 69–80.
8. Shahamat, H. Formal sustainability in Iran's arid regions: Optimizing thermal performance through vernacular bioclimatic strategies. *Archit. Sci. Rev.* **2025**, 1–18. [CrossRef]
9. Yang, Q.X.; Lu, W.Z.; Xu, F.; Luo, X.H.; Wen, B.H. A passive strategy for energy-saving retrofitting of courtyard dwellings and its climatic adaptability. *Energy Build.* **2026**, *352*, 116811. [CrossRef]
10. He, M.T.; Li, L.X.; Tao, S.M. Sustainable Design Methods Translated from the Thermodynamic Theory of Vernacular Architecture: Atrium Prototypes. *Buildings* **2024**, *14*, 3142. [CrossRef]

https://doi.org/10.3390/buildings16061118

11. Yang, C.; Misni, A. Analysis of Thermal Comfort in Single-Story Courtyard Vernacular Dwellings in Rural China: Passive Design Strategies for Adapting to the Climate. *Buildings* **2025**, *15*, 3964. [CrossRef]
12. Wang, Y.Y.; Agkathidis, A.; Crompton, A. Parametrising historical Chinese courtyard-dwellings: An algorithmic design framework for the digital representation of Siheyuan iterations based on traditional design principles. *Front. Archit. Res.* **2020**, *9*, 751–773. [CrossRef]
13. Rong, W.H.; Bahauddin, A. Heritage and Rehabilitation Strategies for Confucian Courtyard Architecture: A Case Study in Liaocheng, China. *Buildings* **2023**, *13*, 599. [CrossRef]
14. Xu, F.; Bai, Y.; Wen, B.; Xie, W.; Huang, L.; Ou, Y.; Luo, X.; Yang, Q. Contemporary evolution of Tibetan-style dwellings under urbanization: A case study of the Shannan city. *J. Asian Archit. Build. Eng.* **2025**, 1–18. [CrossRef]
15. FLinas, A.; Chithra, K. Exploring Vernacular Architecture: Unravelling Characteristics and Typologies Through Expert Survey. *Scires-It-Sci. Res. Inf. Technol.* **2024**, *14*, 97–110.
16. Dang, X.; Hong, Q.; Liu, W.; Wang, Y. China's heritage governance blueprint: Revisiting evolutionary trajectories, reframing institutional priorities and mapping the national registry. *Habitat Int.* **2025**, *165*, 103541. [CrossRef]
17. Salameh, M.; Touqan, B. From Heritage to Sustainability: The Future of the Past in the Hot Arid Climate of the UAE. *Buildings* **2023**, *13*, 418. [CrossRef]
18. Gamage, W.; Lau, S.; Qin, H.; Gou, Z.H. Effectiveness of air-well type courtyards on moderating thermal environments in tropical Chinese Shophouse. *Archit. Sci. Rev.* **2017**, *60*, 493–506. [CrossRef]
19. Li, Z.X.; Cao, X.; Wang, L. From Vernacular Syntax to Algorithmic Regenerative Design: Semiotic Decoding and Encoding of Kashgar's Earthen Dwellings. *Space Cult.* **2025**, 12063312251371878. [CrossRef]
20. Wang, L.; Yang, D.Y.; Yang, Y.N.; Cui, Y.L.; Pan, H.S. Vernacular Wisdom in Hani Ethnic Courtyard Houses: Architectural Heritage and Construction Systems in the Samaba Terraced Landscape. *Buildings* **2025**, *15*, 3710. [CrossRef]
21. Shetty, S.S.; Patil, S. Vernacular Architecture and Indoor Environmental Satisfaction: A Systematic Review of Influencing Factors. *Architecture* **2025**, *5*, 87. [CrossRef]
22. Feng, H.C.; Xiao, J.L. Dynamic Authenticity: Understanding and Conserving Mosuo Dwellings in China in Transitions. *Sustainability* **2021**, *13*, 143. [CrossRef]
23. Yang, M.J.; Gao, B.; Li, R.W. Spatial Evolution of Narrow-Courtyard Dwellings in Guanzhong Rural Areas of Shaanxi, China, from 1949 to the Present. *Buildings* **2025**, *15*, 4533. [CrossRef]
24. Mekki, S.; Arigue, B.; Santi, G.; Sriti, L.; Pace, V.; Leporelli, E. Tracing the Morphogenesis and Formal Diffusion of Vernacular Mosques: A Typo-Morphological Study of Djebel Amour, Algeria. *Buildings* **2025**, *15*, 4277. [CrossRef]
25. Kamelnia, H.; Hanachi, P.; Moayedi, M. Exploring the spatial structure of Toon historical town courtyard houses: Topological characteristics of the courtyard based on a configuration approach. *J. Cult. Herit. Manag. Sustain. Dev.* **2022**, *14*, 981–997. [CrossRef]
26. Wu, L.Y.; Zhan, Q.C.; Li, Y.J. Three-Tiered Defensive System and Ethnic Fusion: A Study of Architectural Art in Guomari Fortress, Eastern Qinghai. *Buildings* **2025**, *15*, 2218. [CrossRef]
27. Gao, J.N.; Shi, Y.; Cai, Y. Research on the Application of Uav Oblique Photogrammetry to Lilong Housing: Taking Meilan Lane as an Example. In Proceedings of the 29th CIPA Symposium on Documenting, Understanding, Preserving Cultural Heritage—Humanities and Digital Technologies for Shaping the Future, Florence, Italy, 25–30 June 2023; pp. 629–635.
28. Huang, H.; Xie, Y.-Q.; Chen, J.-J.; Liang, S.; Chen, Z.-J. Bioclimatic design strategy of vernacular architecture in the south-east of China: A case study in Fujian, China. *Int. J. Low-Carbon Technol.* **2024**, *19*, 1–17. [CrossRef]
29. Liang, L.H.; Wen, B.H.; Xu, F.; Yang, Q.X. From Poor Buildings to High Performance Buildings: The Spontaneous Green Evolution of Vernacular Architecture. *Appl. Sci.* **2023**, *13*, 10162. [CrossRef]
30. Yazdi, H.; Vukorep, I.; Banach, M.; Moazen, S.; Nadolny, A.; Starke, R.; Bazazzadeh, H. Central Courtyard Feature Extraction in Remote Sensing Aerial Images Using Deep Learning: A Case-Study of Iran. *Remote Sens.* **2021**, *13*, 4843. [CrossRef]
31. Spennemann, D.H.R. Generative Artificial Intelligence, Human Agency and the Future of Cultural Heritage. *Heritage* **2024**, *7*, 3597–3609. [CrossRef]
32. Wang, H.M.; Gong, Y.K.; Zhang, Y.G.; Li, F. Artificial Intelligence for Sustainable Cultural Heritage: Practical Guidelines and Case-Based Evidence. *Sustainability* **2025**, *17*, 9192. [CrossRef]
33. Peng, Z.R.; Lu, K.F.; Liu, Y.H.; Zhai, W. The Pathway of Urban Planning AI: From Planning Support to Plan-Making. *J. Plan. Educ. Res.* **2024**, *44*, 2263–2279. [CrossRef]
34. Kamrowska-Zaluska, D. Impact of AI-Based Tools and Urban Big Data Analytics on the Design and Planning of Cities. *Land* **2021**, *10*, 1209. [CrossRef]
35. Labib, R.; Nagy, Z. The Future of Artificial Intelligence in Buildings. *Ashrae J.* **2023**, *65*.

https://doi.org/10.3390/buildings16061118

36. Li, Y.L.X.; Chen, H.S.; Yu, P.J.; Yang, L. A Review of Artificial Intelligence Applications in Architectural Design: Energy-Saving Renovations and Adaptive Building Envelopes. *Energies* **2025**, *18*, 918. [CrossRef]
37. Zhang, S.F.; Li, M.M.; Zhao, W.F.; Wang, X.Q.; Wu, Q.Y. Building Type Classification Using CNN-Transformer Cross-Encoder Adaptive Learning from Very High Resolution Satellite Images. *IEEE J. Sel. Top. Appl. Earth Obs. Remote Sens.* **2025**, *18*, 976–994. [CrossRef]
38. Wang, Y.J.; Li, S.C.; Teng, F.; Lin, Y.H.; Wang, M.J.; Cai, H.F. Improved Mask R-CNN for Rural Building Roof Type Recognition from UAV High-Resolution Images: A Case Study in Hunan Province, China. *Remote Sens.* **2022**, *14*, 265. [CrossRef]
39. Li, M.H.; Yu, Y.; Wei, H.N.; Chan, T.O. Classification of the qilou (arcade building) using a robust image processing framework based on the Faster R-CNN with ResNet50. *J. Asian Archit. Build. Eng.* **2024**, *23*, 595–612. [CrossRef]
40. Wang, C.C.; Liu, H.H.; Pei, S.C.; Liu, K.H.; Liu, T.J. Modern Architecture Style Transfer for Ruin Buildings. In Proceedings of the 1st IEEE International Conference on Artificial Intelligence Circuits and Systems (AICAS), Hsinchu, Taiwan, 18–20 March 2019; pp. 293–294.
41. Hu, H.; Liang, X.R.; Ding, Y.L.; Shang, Q.S.; Xu, B.; Ge, X.M.; Chen, M.; Zhong, R.F.; Zhu, Q. Semi-supervised adversarial recognition of refined window structures for inverse procedural facade modelling. *ISPRS J. Photogramm. Remote Sens.* **2022**, *192*, 215–231. [CrossRef]
42. Ottoni, A.L.C.; Ottoni, L.T.C. A deep learning approach for cultural heritage building classification using transfer learning and data augmentation. *J. Cult. Herit.* **2025**, *74*, 214–224. [CrossRef]
43. Czerniawski, T.; Leite, F. Automated segmentation of RGB-D images into a comprehensive set of building components using deep learning. *Adv. Eng. Inform.* **2020**, *45*, 101131. [CrossRef]
44. Wong, M.O.; Ying, H.Q.; Yin, M.T.; Yi, X.Y.; Xiao, L.Z.; Duan, W.L.; He, C.C.; Tang, L. Semantic 3D reconstruction-oriented image dataset for building component segmentation. *Autom. Constr.* **2024**, *165*, 105558. [CrossRef]
45. Yazdi, H.; Berenji, S.S.; Ludwig, F.; Moazen, S. Deep Learning in Historical Architecture Remote Sensing: Automated Historical Courtyard House Recognition in Yazd, Iran. *Heritage* **2022**, *5*, 3066–3080. [CrossRef]
46. Wen, B.H.; Yang, Q.X.; Peng, F.; Liang, L.H.; Wu, S.H.; Xu, F. Evolutionary mechanism of vernacular architecture in the context of urbanization: Evidence from southern Hebei, China. *Habitat Int.* **2023**, *137*, 102814. [CrossRef]
47. Wen, B.H.; Peng, F.; Yang, Q.X.; Lu, T.; Bai, B.F.; Wu, S.A.; Xu, F. Monitoring the green evolution of vernacular buildings based on deep learning and multi-temporal remote sensing images. *Build. Simul.* **2023**, *16*, 151–168. [CrossRef]
48. Liu, Q.B.; Shang, B. The Impact of Geomorphological Factors on the Distribution of Typical Dwellings in Northern China. *Rev. Int. Contam. Ambient.* **2019**, *35*, 177–188. [CrossRef]
49. Wen, B.H.; Yang, Q.X.; Xu, F.; Zhou, J.; Zhang, R.P. Phenomenon of courtyards being roofed and its significance for building energy efficiency. *Energy Build.* **2023**, *295*, 113282. [CrossRef]
50. Baohua, W.; Qingxin, Y.; Lihua, L.; Feng, X. Architect's Intervention Approach to the Spontaneous Green Evolution of Vernacular Buildings. In *Design for Climate Adaptation*; Faircloth, B., Zari, M.P., Thomsen, M.R., Tamke, M., Eds.; Springer International Publishing: Cham, Switzerland, 2023; pp. 551–565.
51. HChen, L.; Zhang, L.; Yu, Y.; Wu, C.D.; Hua, T.; Gao, C.L. Photovoltaic Power Station Identification Based on High-Resolution Network and Google Earth Engine: A Case Study of Qinghai Province, Northwest China. *Remote Sens.* **2025**, *17*, 3896.
52. Sun, Q.R.; Wang, X.P. Improved ResUNet Method for Extracting Buildings from Remote Sensing Images. *Laser Optoelectron. Prog.* **2025**, *62*, 0828003.
53. Zhang, M.; Li, Y.C.; Shen, W.F. Research on the analysis of three-dimensional spatial pattern based on multi-scale geographically weighted regression. In Proceedings of the 6th International Conference on Geoscience and Remote Sensing Mapping-GRSM, Qingdao, China, 25–27 October 2024.
54. Alnaim, M.M. The typology of courtyard space in Najdi Architecture, Saudi Arabia: A response to human needs, culture, and the environment. *J. Asian Archit. Build. Eng.* **2024**, *23*, 91–110. [CrossRef]
55. Biradar, V.K.; Mama, S. Vernacular Architecture: A Sustainable Approach. In Proceedings of the National Conference on Sustainable Built Environment, IIT Roorkee, Roorkee, India, 11–12 April 2015; pp. 125–137.
56. Al-Mohannadi, A.; Furlan, R.; Major, M.D. A Cultural Heritage Framework for Preserving Qatari Vernacular Domestic Architecture. *Sustainability* **2020**, *12*, 7295. [CrossRef]
57. Roesler, S. Cross-cultural thermal knowledge: The case of large-scale tobacco barns in Sumatra (Indonesia). In Proceedings of the 6th International Congress on Construction History (ICCH), Brussels, Belgium, 9–13 July 2018; pp. 257–262.
58. Mohamadabadi, H.D.; Ghanbaran, A.H.; Dehghan, A.A. The study of air distribution quality in the summer section of Iranian dry climate houses equipped with wind tower. *Sustain. Cities Soc.* **2022**, *86*, 104095. [CrossRef]
59. Wu, K.; Wang, H.W.; Liu, H.; Yin, M.; Xu, J.H.; Qiang, M.L.; Su, Y.W. A Study on the Inheritance and Differentiation of Spatial Forms of Vernacular Architecture in the Yunnan-Tibet Area. *Buildings* **2025**, *15*, 2087. [CrossRef]

 https://doi.org/10.3390/buildings16061118

60. Eltrapolsi, A.; Mahmoud, K.; Altan, H. A Review of the Geometric Proportions of Shaping a Courtyard of Traditional Architecture in Relation to Human Scale, Tripoli, Libya. *Heritage* **2022**, *5*, 2282–2297. [CrossRef]
61. Al-Mohannadi, A.S.; Furlan, R. The Spatiality of the Vernacular Courtyard House in the Arabian Gulf Region. *Heritage* **2025**, *8*, 268. [CrossRef]

https://doi.org/10.3390/buildings16061118

buildings

MDPI

Article

Human–AI Collaborative Design in Architectural Studios: Evaluating Paradigm Shifts Across the Six Stages of the Design Process

Hend Alana [1,2,*], Mohamed Fikry [1] and Asmaa Hasan [1]

[1] Architecture Engineering Department, Faculty of Engineering, Alexandria University, Alexandria City 21500, Egypt; mfikry@alexu.edu.eg (M.F.); asmaa.elsayed@alexu.edu.eg (A.H.)
[2] Architecture Engineering Department, Faculty of Engineering, Kafrelsheikh University, Kafrelsheikh City 33516, Egypt
* Correspondence: hend.ali23@alexu.edu.eg

Abstract

Artificial intelligence (AI) is increasingly transforming architectural education, shifting design studios toward human–AI collaborative workflows. This study investigates the impact of AI integration across the six stages of the architectural design process: pre-design, conceptual design, schematic design, design development, documentation, and presentation. A mixed-methods approach was adopted, combining survey data from 17 master's degree students with reflective insights from eight faculty members involved in hybrid AI-supported studio environments. AI's influence was evaluated using six indicators: efficiency, creativity enhancement, accuracy, interdisciplinary integration, adoptability, and environmental or architectural impact. The findings indicate that AI is most effective during early design stages, where it supports idea generation, visualization, and rapid iteration. Its impact becomes less pronounced in later technical phases, where human expertise and critical reasoning remain essential. Students perceived AI as a creative catalyst and productivity enhancer, while faculty emphasized its analytical and evaluative potential in supporting informed decision-making. Overall, AI functions most effectively as a complementary partner rather than a replacement for human agency. The study proposes a structured framework to guide ethical and pedagogically sound AI integration within architectural design studios.

Keywords: artificial intelligence; human–AI collaboration; architectural design studios; intelligent decision-making; generative design; design innovation; AI-driven education; hybrid studio environments

1. Introduction

Architectural design studios represent the most critical educational environment in which future architects develop their design competencies, critical thinking abilities, and professional methodologies [1]. As the foundation of architectural education, the studio operates as an experimental platform where students engage in iterative problem-solving, spatial reasoning, and creative exploration within a practice-based learning framework. Beyond skill acquisition, design studios shape methodological thinking and professional identity, making them central to the transformation of architectural pedagogy.

The rapid advancement of artificial intelligence (AI), particularly generative AI (GAI) systems, is introducing a profound shift in how design knowledge is produced, evaluated, and communicated. AI technologies now extend beyond computational drafting assistance to influence ideation, visualization, simulation, and performance-based analysis. Recent research has explored hybrid AI frameworks that integrate analytical and numerical modeling with data-driven techniques to enhance design reliability and performance evaluation. These approaches indicate a shift toward more comprehensive AI integration beyond isolated design assistance tools [2].

Consequently, the architectural studio is increasingly becoming a site of human–AI collaboration rather than purely human-driven design activity. This evolution necessitates a deeper understanding of how AI reshapes learning dynamics, cognitive processes, and design workflows within higher education institutions [3]. Scholars argue that AI can enhance learning and creativity by generating alternative solutions, supporting iterative exploration, and providing immediate feedback that informs decision-making [4].

Nevertheless, the integration of AI into design education remains contested. Concerns persist regarding the potential erosion of students' creative authorship and critical reasoning if excessive reliance on algorithmic outputs diminishes reflective engagement [5]. Moreover, the widespread accessibility of generative AI tools challenges traditional assessment practices and raises questions about academic integrity and evaluation standards [6]. These tensions reflect a broader uncertainty about whether AI acts as an empowering cognitive partner or a disruptive force within design pedagogy.

Recent contributions from the 2025 edition of the JIDA Conference (Jornadas sobre Innovación Docente en Arquitectura) provide significant insights into the pedagogical integration of artificial intelligence within architectural education. For instance, a study by Nicoleta Alexandra Simina explored the role of AI within a Research by Design (RbD) framework, examining its application across multiple stages of the design process, including conceptual exploration, visual iteration, and reflective dialogue. The study adopted a practice-based pedagogical approach, emphasizing learning through action and critical reflection. The findings indicate that AI can function not merely as a generative tool but as a "critical interlocutor" that enhances reflective thinking and supports iterative design development. However, the study also highlights key challenges, particularly the ethical implications of AI use and the risk of diminishing students' independent judgment if not properly guided. These recent JIDA contributions demonstrate a clear shift in architectural pedagogy from viewing AI as a technical aid toward understanding it as an integrated component of the learning process. Nevertheless, most studies remain focused on qualitative and exploratory approaches, emphasizing student experience and reflective practice rather than providing structured, stage-based quantitative evaluation frameworks [7].

Similarly, a study presented at the International Conference of Contemporary Affairs in Architecture and Urbanism investigated the role of AI-assisted tools in architectural design studios within a university setting in Turkey. The research involved a sample of 25 architecture students and applied a comparative methodology between traditional design workflows and AI-supported processes. AI tools were integrated primarily during the conceptual and visualization stages, enabling rapid idea generation and enhanced visual representation. The results indicated a significant improvement in student productivity and engagement, particularly in early design phases, while limitations were observed in later technical stages requiring precision and detailed documentation. Additionally, the study emphasized that excessive reliance on AI could reduce critical reflection if not properly guided by instructors [8].

Despite the growing body of research addressing AI in architecture, most studies tend to focus on isolated tools, specific design phases, or technical capabilities. Limited attention has been given to examining AI integration comprehensively across the entire architectural design process within studio-based learning environments. This gap creates uncertainty

 https://doi.org/10.3390/buildings16071445

regarding how AI influences different stages of design development, how its impact varies across conceptual and technical phases, and how educators can structure meaningful and ethically grounded human–AI collaboration [9].

The central research problem addressed in this study lies in the lack of a comprehensive and stage-based understanding of how artificial intelligence influences the full architectural design process within studio education. While AI tools are increasingly adopted, there is insufficient empirical evidence clarifying their differential impact on creativity, efficiency, decision-making, and critical thinking across the sequential stages of design. Without such understanding, educational institutions risk implementing AI in fragmented or unstructured ways that may either underutilize its potential or inadvertently weaken core design competencies.

Accordingly, this research aims to investigate the impact of artificial intelligence integration across all six principal stages of the architectural design process—pre-design, conceptual design, schematic design, design development, design documentation, presentation, and final critique. By adopting a mixed-method approach, the study evaluates AI's influence through six key indicators: efficiency, creativity enhancement, accuracy, interdisciplinary integration, adoptability, and environmental or architectural impact. The study ultimately seeks to provide a structured framework for human–AI collaboration in architectural studios, supporting intelligent, ethical, and pedagogically sound integration strategies that prepare students for evolving AI-driven professional practice.

2. Literature Review

2.1. *AI as a Pedagogical Tool in Architectural Design Studios*

Several studies have examined the role of AI as a pedagogical tool within architectural education. Researchers suggest that AI can support learning by fostering iterative design processes and enabling adaptive learning environments. For instance, Beyan et al. proposed that AI facilitates iterative learning by offering multiple design alternatives and immediate feedback [4]. Similarly, El Moussaoui and Krois emphasized AI's potential to create adaptive learning environments that shift the educator's role from direct instruction toward guiding reflective learning [10]. A recent case study conducted during the 2024–2025 academic year at Zhejiang University integrated AI into a design studio through a 20 h technical module. Although students demonstrated varying levels of engagement, the study highlighted the importance of developing scalable models for AI-integrated design education [11].

2.2. *Approaches to AI Integration Across the Stages of the Design Process*

Research on AI integration in architectural design studios often focuses on specific stages of the design process, including pre-design, conceptual design, design development, and presentation. This stage-based approach allows for a clearer understanding of how AI supports learning and performance at different points within the architectural workflow.

Beginning with pre-design stage which includes programming activity, AI tools can support students in evaluating the relevance of their design intentions and constructing well-founded arguments to justify their decisions. This contributes to enhancing critical thinking, as students are required to critically assess AI-generated information rather than passively adopting it. A recent study developed hybrid teaching model for a 9-week course involving 24 international students. The course integrated AI technologies into architectural programming to evaluate the impact. The evaluation focused on the effectiveness of AI-assisted teaching which indicated that students developed a deeper understanding of the design process and significantly improved their analytical skills [12].

https://doi.org/10.3390/buildings16071445

The conceptual design is the second stage of the design process which received significant attention from researchers, may be due to the abilities of AI tools in generation. Many studies explored how artificial intelligence can support creativity and idea development during this early stage. For example, a study by Sadek and Mohamed argued that artificial intelligence can be used as a conceptual design tool. Conducted in Fall 2022, it involved 34 architecture students utilizing AI tools to generate inspirational images from narratives which enhanced concept development. Their designs were compared to another group of 50 students using traditional methods. The findings indicated that the designs of AI-assisted students were more diverse and innovative concepts, highlighting AI's potential [13]. In another study, Özorhon et al. depended on the use of AI diffusion models (e.g., Midjourney). It demonstrated how AI tools can enrich creativity and encourage critical design thinking among students [14]. Interior design also garnered attention in this stage, where a study by Karadağ and Ozarm examined the use of AI in interior design education, focusing on its role in enhancing conceptual design through tools like Midjourney. Findings showed that AI had positive impact on creative possibilities and idea development. While students recognize its value, they also stress about the need to address ethical concerns and preserve design authenticity [15].

From another perspective, many studies integrated artificial intelligence in design studios from an environmental perspective, which is regarded as a significant aspect of design development stage. Many studies examined how AI can support sustainable design by analyzing energy use, optimizing building performance, and suggesting environmentally friendly design solutions. This approach highlights the potential of AI to enhance both the educational experience and the environmental responsibility of future architects. A study by Dwijendra et al. examined the integration of AI into architectural education in Bali, focusing on sustainable practices while preserving traditional values. It highlighted how AI tools can enhance sustainable design education and address the challenges of balancing technological advancement with cultural heritage [16]. In Serbia and Montenegro, a study investigated how AI influences final-year architecture students, particularly regarding sustainability. Using surveys and comparative analysis, it shows that students' knowledge about sustainability strongly affects their use of AI tools. The findings provide guidance for refining curricula to better integrate AI and sustainable design in architectural education [17].

However, some researchers focused specifically on the final stage, which includes rendering as essential activity. They studied the ability of AI to improve the quality, speed, and efficiency of rendering processes. For example, Ahmed and Alymani presented a pedagogical approach which incorporated AI generative tools (e.g., AI rendering). This included exploring AI tools that help to automate visualization tasks, making it easier for students and professionals to produce high-quality images and presentations. The results showed increased student engagement in addition to enhancement of learning outcomes [18].

Through a comprehensive review of previous studies, this research aims to provide an inclusive perspective on the overall impact of artificial intelligence (AI) on the entire architectural design process. Rather than focusing on a single stage, it seeks to cover all the six main stages) pre-design, conceptual design, schematic design, design development, design documentation and presentation and final critique (that students typically go through during their design projects.

To achieve the aims of this study, a set of specific research objectives was established to systematically evaluate the educational impact of integrating artificial intelligence (AI) within the architectural design studio. First, the study seeks to explore the influence of AI on each stage of the architectural design process, capturing the perceptions of both

https://doi.org/10.3390/buildings16071445

students and faculty members to gain a comprehensive understanding of its role. Second, it aims to identify how students and instructors perceive the effectiveness and usefulness of AI tools in organizing, supporting, and facilitating the design workflow. Third, the research examines which stages of the design process are perceived as being most or least effectively enhanced by AI, considering levels of engagement, satisfaction, and consensus among participants. Finally, the study investigates potential challenges and limitations associated with AI-assisted design learning, addressing both pedagogical considerations and practical constraints within the studio environment. Collectively, these objectives provide a structured framework to assess the integration of AI in architectural education and its impact on the learning and creative process.

3. Methodological Framework

The research methodology focused on evaluating AI's impact within a hybrid architectural design studio that combined physical and digital learning environments. It evaluates AI impact through perceptual and educational performance indicators rather than measurable built outcomes. Data were collected from students and instructors through questionnaires, project evaluations, and observations. This approach enabled comparison between literature-based expectations and actual student performance. Data included both quantitative and qualitative measures to capture comprehensive insights into learning outcomes and design quality across sequential studio phases.

Analytical Matrix as an Evaluation Tool

To systematically evaluate the impact of AI, an analytical matrix was developed that links the six stages of the architectural design process (pre-design, conceptual design, schematic design, design development, design documentation, and presentation) with six evaluation indicators: efficiency, creativity, accuracy, AI integration, adoptability, and environmental/architectural impact (see Table 1). The initial two-dimensional matrix, grounded in previous studies, served as a theoretical framework to assess performance at each stage. This matrix was then refined into a three-dimensional model using empirical findings from the studio, connecting the evaluation tools directly to the observed outcomes.

The six indicators were selected to capture pedagogical and professional considerations. Efficiency evaluates workflow, time management, and productivity; creativity reflects innovative and diverse design thinking; accuracy measures technical reliability. AI integration examines the depth of AI use as a tool, collaborator, or assistant; adoptability considers usability and ease of implementation; and environmental/architectural impact reflects AI's role in sustainable and context-responsive design. Together, they provide a structured framework for assessing AI's dynamic influence on learning outcomes and design quality throughout the studio process.

The matrix was developed based on previous studies, which indicate that AI's impact varies by stage. In pre-design, AI strongly enhances efficiency but moderately affects creativity and accuracy. During conceptual design, AI's influence peaks, supporting both efficiency and creativity. In schematic design, AI emphasizes performance analysis and accuracy, while creativity is somewhat constrained by functional priorities. Design development shows high impact on efficiency, accuracy, and adoptability. In contrast, design documentation demonstrates limited creative engagement but high technical accuracy. Finally, in presentation and final critique, AI strongly enhances visualization, rendering, and communication. Overall, AI evolves from analytical support in early stages, through creative facilitation in the middle, to technical precision in later stages, forming a dynamic and integrated influence in architectural studios.

https://doi.org/10.3390/buildings16071445

Table 1. Two-dimensional evaluation matrix (source: Authors).

		Measurement Indicators					
		Efficiency	**Creativity**	**Accuracy**	**AI Integration**	**Adoptability**	**Environmental/Architectural Impact**
Stages of Design Process	Pre-design	AI tools boost efficiency by speeding up site analysis, program assessment, and data processing [19,20]	AI supports initial idea generation, providing diverse scenarios, though human analytical input remains essential [19,21]	Data accuracy relies on input quality and requires human verification for reliability [22,23]	AI supports early-stage decisions through data analysis and predictions [19,24]	Analytical and research tools can be easily incorporated into pre-design curricula [25]	AI helps assess environmental and contextual factors without directly shaping the design at this stage [26,27]
	Conceptual Design	AI speeds up the creation of design alternatives, improving decision-making in the conceptual phase [19,21]	Generative AI enhances creativity by offering diverse and novel design solutions during conceptual exploration [28,29]	Conceptual outputs need human refinement to meet project goals and constraints [19,21]	Generative design involves high AI engagement, shaping initial forms and spaces [19,23]	Adopting AI tools requires some training, but integration into studios is practical and achievable [24]	AI supports early sustainable design by guiding initial environmental performance considerations [26,30]
	Schematic Design	AI simulations help evaluate design alternatives, enhancing efficiency in spatial and functional assessments [19,27]	Creativity is partly directed toward functional performance rather than purely conceptual innovation [28,31]	Integrating spatial and energy analysis improves the accuracy of schematic layouts and early performance predictions [21,32]	At this stage, AI focuses more on analytical evaluation than on generating forms [32,33]	Effective use of simulation and evaluation tools requires technical proficiency [24]	AI supports environmental performance evaluation, guiding designs toward better sustainability outcomes [26,34]
	Design Development	Efficiency is maximized through the integration of building systems, detailing, and optimized workflows [21,23]	Creativity is focused on material and system innovation rather than overall form [22,29]	AI tools enhance accuracy in documenting and coordinating complex design elements [23,35]	AI supports analytical evaluations and detail optimization [35,36]	These tools are easily adopted in both academic and professional design development [23,25]	AI-supported optimization can improve environmental and material efficiency, reducing waste [26,37]
	Design Documentation	Automating drawings, schedules, and specifications greatly enhances documentation efficiency [19,23]	This stage is mainly execution-focused, with limited room for creative exploration [22,35]	AI enhances the accuracy of construction documentation, reducing human error [23,38]	AI is mainly used for automated detailing and schedule generation [12,27]	Adoption is high due to practical benefits and ease of integrating AI into documentation workflows [23,24]	Enhanced documentation quality indirectly supports environmental performance by minimizing material waste and construction errors [36,37]
	Presentation and Final Critique	AI speeds up the creation of visual presentations, 3D renderings, and interactive models, improving efficiency in communicating design intent [22,38]	AI enhances visual communication, enabling richer and more expressive architectural storytelling [28,39]	The accuracy of representations depends on input quality and requires human verification [22,38]	AI plays a significant role in rendering, AR/VR, and generative visualization [22,39]	These tools are easily adopted, allowing students to use AI for more impactful presentations [39]	Improves understanding of environmental and architectural impacts through clear visual representation [26,40]

Strong Relation; Moderate Relation; Weak Relation.

https://doi.org/10.3390/buildings16071445

4. Case Study Application

4.1. Sample

This research investigates the impact of artificial intelligence (AI) on the architectural design process across its various stages through a quasi-experimental approach. The study involved a purposive sample of 17 master's degree students and eight faculty members from the Department of Architectural Engineering at Kafrelsheikh University, Egypt.

The study was conducted during the spring term of 2025 as part of the course titled Integrated Architectural Design Studio, which provided a suitable academic environment for applying AI tools within real design tasks and reflective discussions. Master's degree students were specifically chosen over undergraduates due to their advanced academic experience and their ability to critically evaluate design-related issues, including the potential impact of AI integration. This selection ensures the reliability and depth of the feedback collected, as these students have completed foundational design courses and participated in multiple design studios, equipping them to assess AI tools' integration with informed awareness and analytical insight.

4.2. Method

The study employed previously completed academic design projects that participants had developed during their architectural studies without the use of AI. To ensure the relevance and comparability of the data, participants were required to select projects completed within the last three academic years, typically corresponding to advanced stages of architectural education, where students possess a higher level of design maturity and technical competence. Each participant selected a prior project—such as a cultural center or exhibition complex that served as the basis for a renewed design process incorporating AI tools.

This approach enabled a direct comparison between traditional design methods and AI-assisted workflows across the same six design stages. By repeating equivalent design tasks and activities, the study was able to systematically identify the benefits and challenges introduced by AI integration. Throughout the course, participants were closely monitored, and their progress was documented across all stages, providing a structured framework for evaluating AI's impact on the design process. To ensure consistency and reliability, the study defined specific activities associated with each stage, along with the expected outputs, forming a reference framework for evaluation. As illustrated in Table 2, three essential activities were identified for each of the six design stages.

Table 2. Stages of design process and its related activities (source: Authors).

Stages of Design Process	Activities
Pre-Design (Programming) Focus: Understanding the project requirements and site constraints	Research and Analysis: Collecting information about the site, context, client needs, and regulations.
	Site Analysis: Evaluating site conditions, including climate, topography, and existing structures.
	Program Development and Space Requirements: A documented architectural program that guides the conceptual design stage.
Conceptual Design Focus: Refining design concept	Brainstorming: Developing a wide range of design ideas and possibilities.
	Sketching and Diagramming: Creating rough sketches and diagrams to explore spatial relationships and forms.
	Initial Models: Building simple physical or digital models to test ideas.

 https://doi.org/10.3390/buildings16071445

Table 2. *Cont.*

Stages of Design Process	Activities
Schematic Design (SD) Focus: developing the chosen design concept	Space Planning: Developing preliminary floor plans and layouts.
	Massing Studies: Exploring the building's form and its impact on the site.
	Conceptual Renderings: Creating visual representations of the design.
Design Development (DD) Focus: Adding detail to the design and integrating technical aspects	Detailed Drawings: Developing more detailed floor plans, elevations, and sections.
	Refinement of Spatial Layout and Form: Developing the approved schematic design into more detailed and accurate spatial configurations
	Material Selection: Choosing materials and finishes for the project.
Design Documentation (DC) Focus: Preparing detailed drawings and specifications	Drawings Documentation: Producing detailed architectural drawings, including plans, sections, elevations, and details.
	Integrating Environmental and Structural Aspects: Ensuring that the design is both sustainable and structurally efficient.
	Specifications: Writing detailed descriptions of materials, workmanship, and installation methods.
Presentation and Final Critique Focus: Finalizing the design and presenting it	Final Models and Renderings: Creating detailed models and high-quality renderings to convey the design.
	Presentation Boards: Assembling visual materials that effectively communicate the design.
	Final Critique: Receiving critical input from faculty, peers, and external reviewers.

4.3. Data Collection and Analysis

To ensure a coherent and reliable assessment of AI's educational impact, the six evaluation indicators were systematically aligned with three main measurement tools: student questionnaires, project reviews, and studio observations. This structure was intended to establish a clear and meaningful connection between each indicator and its most relevant source of evidence as shown in Table 3, and these indicators were measured using a five-point Likert scale (1 = strongly disagree, 5 = strongly agree). Efficiency and adoptability were evaluated through student questionnaires, as these aspects depend on students' personal experiences, perceptions of productivity, and willingness to engage with AI tools.

Creativity and environmental or architectural impact were assessed through project reviews, enabling instructors to judge the originality and contextual quality of the design outcomes. Accuracy was measured using studio observations, as technical precision and adherence to professional standards require expert input. Also, AI integration was analyzed through studio observations, providing real-time insights into how effectively AI tools were embedded within each stage of the design process. This structured mapping created a balanced methodology that combined subjective and objective perspectives, integrating students' experiential feedback with faculty evaluations and observational evidence to offer a comprehensive understanding of AI's role in the architectural design studio.

 https://doi.org/10.3390/buildings16071445

Table 3. Primary measurement tools for every indicator (source: Authors).

Evaluation Indicator	Primary Measurement Tools	Rationale
Efficiency	Student Questionnaire	Efficiency was evaluated based on improvements in time management, workflow speed, and overall productivity resulting from the use of AI tools. The assessment considered students' ability to complete design tasks more effectively across different project stages.
Creativity	Project Review	Creativity was evaluated through a structured project review using a standardized rubric to ensure reliability. The assessment focused on the originality of design concepts, the diversity of approaches, and the level of innovation demonstrated in spatial organization, form, and overall design solutions. Each project was scored by multiple reviewers independently evaluated the work to enhance inter-rater reliability and reduce subjectivity.
Accuracy	Structured Studio Observation	Accuracy was evaluated through faculty observations focusing on the technical precision, consistency, and reliability of AI-assisted design outputs. The assessment examined the alignment between design intent and final representations, as well as the reduction in technical errors across different project stages.
AI integration	Structured Studio Observation	The assessment considered the breadth and depth of AI use across different design stages, the level of critical engagement with AI-generated outputs, and the degree to which AI tools were integrated into the overall design workflow.
Adoptability	Student Questionnaire	Adoptability was evaluated through students' feedback on usability, accessibility, and their willingness to continue using AI tools in future design projects. The assessment reflected overall acceptance of AI within the studio environment.
Environmental and architectural impact	Project Review	This indicator was assessed through a project-based analytical review, combining qualitative judgment focusing on how AI-supported designs responded to environmental and contextual factors.

4.4. Strategy and AI Tools Used in the Study

This study adopted a hybrid, design-studio-based methodology for 14 weeks, during which the design process stages were distributed accordingly. As shown in Table 4, the six design stages were arranged sequentially with the AI tools used, allowing for accurate monitoring and evaluation throughout the course period. Throughout the course, AI-driven platforms were introduced alongside digital and traditional tools. The purpose of this approach was to provide students with advanced resources that can enhance their design ability, while preserving the irreplaceable role of human judgment, intuition, and critical thinking in the design process.

The integration of artificial intelligence tools in the studio was designed to complement rather than replace conventional design methods. Therefore, AI-driven platforms were introduced alongside commonly used digital tools and traditional design practices such as sketching, diagramming, and conceptual modeling. The objective of this approach was to provide students with advanced technological resources that could enhance design exploration, analysis, and visualization while preserving the essential role of human judgment, creativity, intuition, and critical thinking within the architectural design process.

 https://doi.org/10.3390/buildings16071445

Table 4. Workflow of the design studio in conjunction with the AI tools used (source: Authors).

	Week Number	Traditional Tools	Digital Tools	Out Put	AI Tools Used
	Week 1	Introduction Lecture			
Pre-design	Week 2	Site analysis Manual sketches	Google Earth GIS; AutoCAD 2024 (Site Plans) Revit (Site Context)	Site analysis Data collection Problem identification	Chat GPT (data collection & analysis) Microsoft Designer (concept images) AI GIS tools (environmental analysis)
Conceptual Design	Week 3, 4	Hand sketches Physical models	Sketch Up Rhino Grasshopper	Initial design concept Sketches and diagrams	Microsoft Designer (quick ideation) Canva AI Ideogram AI Playground AI (concept images)
Schematic Design	Week 5, 6, 7	Manual plans Group discussions	AutoCAD Revit	Developed design concept, zoning, initial plans	Planner 5D AI (space layouts) Room GPT (layout suggestions)
Design Development	Week 8, 9, 10	Manual detailing Area schedules	AutoCAD Revit	Detailed architectural drawings	Autodesk Forma AI (solar, wind & environmental analysis) Krea.ai (design alternatives—basic use)
Design Documentation	Week 11, 12	Manual construction docs Material schedules	Revit (Construction Docs) AutoCAD (Details)	Architectural drawings supported by structural system	Basic AI floor plan checkers (validation only) Microsoft Copilot 2024 (text & documentation support)
Presentation and Final Critique	Week 13, 14	Printed boards PowerPoint	Photoshop Illustrator InDesign	Final project presentation	Canva AI (presentation boards) Gamma.app (presentation generation) Runway ML (simple video) ChatGPT 2024 (project narrative & explanation)

To ensure consistency and methodological clarity, a set of selection criteria was established for identifying the AI tools used in this study. The selection process was guided by several considerations. First, the tools needed to be relevant to architectural design activities, meaning that they could support tasks such as data analysis, concept generation, environmental analysis, spatial organization, visualization, or presentation. Second, the selected tools had to be accessible and easy to learn, ensuring that students could use them effectively within the limited duration of the studio experiment.

Third, preference was given to tools that allow rapid generation of design alternatives, enabling students to explore multiple design options within a short period of time. Fourth, the tools needed to support different stages of the design process, ensuring that AI integration could be evaluated across the entire workflow rather than being limited to a single design phase. Finally, the tools were selected based on their availability as online platforms or widely accessible software, which reflects the types of tools that students can realistically adopt in educational environments.

Figure 1 presents samples of interfaces of selected AI tools that were used in study during the six stages of the design process.

https://doi.org/10.3390/buildings16071445

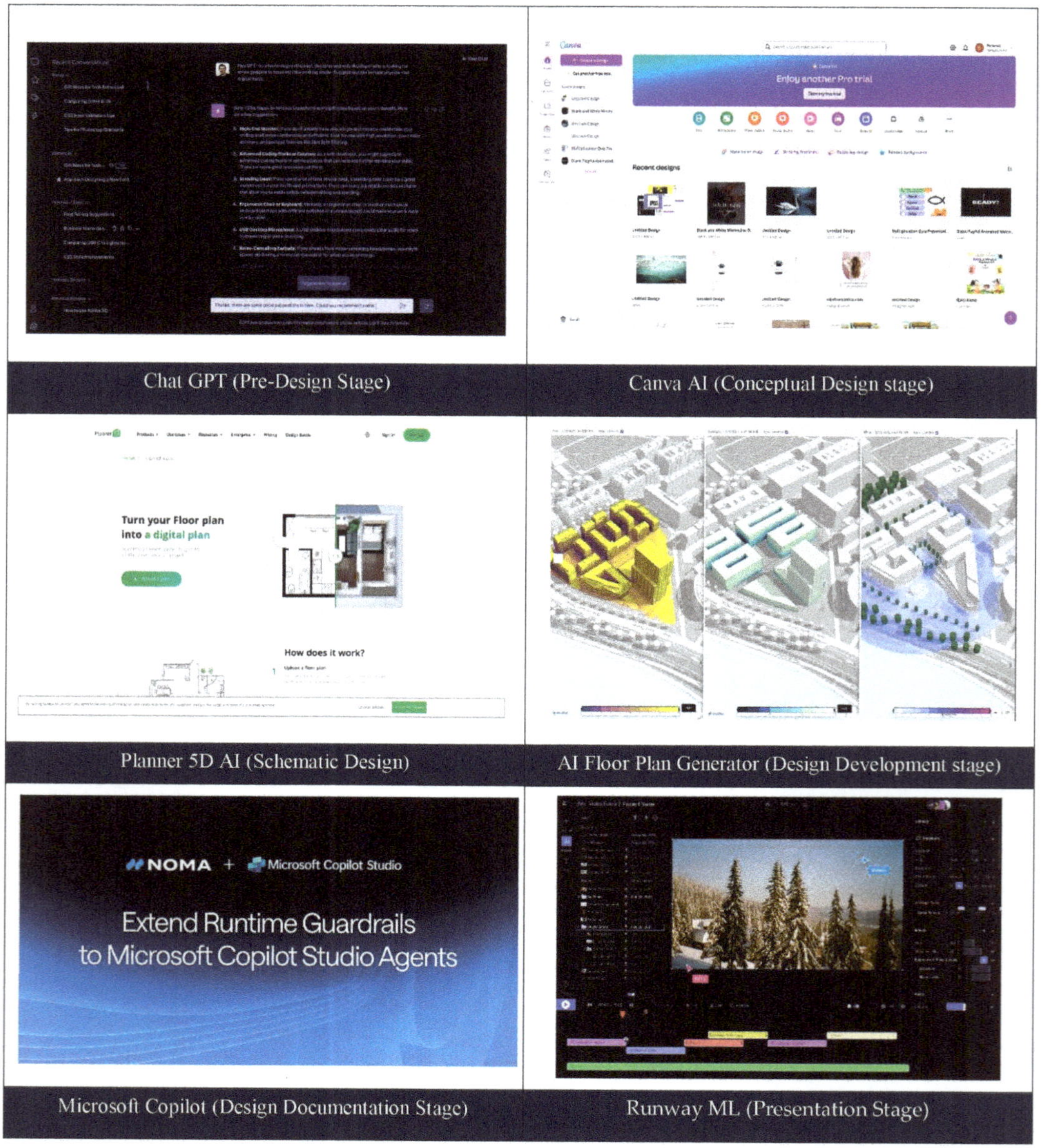

Figure 1. Interface of Selected AI tools that were used in study (tool interface). Source: Authors.

Figure 2 presents selected student design outputs, showing earlier work using traditional methods alongside outputs produced during the case study with AI assistance, reflecting the progression of the architectural design process from the pre-design stage to the final presentation. The displayed materials include site analysis, initial sketches, developed design concepts, design development drawings, design documentation supported by structural systems, and final project presentations. These outputs demonstrate how AI-supported tools were integrated across different stages of the studio.

 https://doi.org/10.3390/buildings16071445

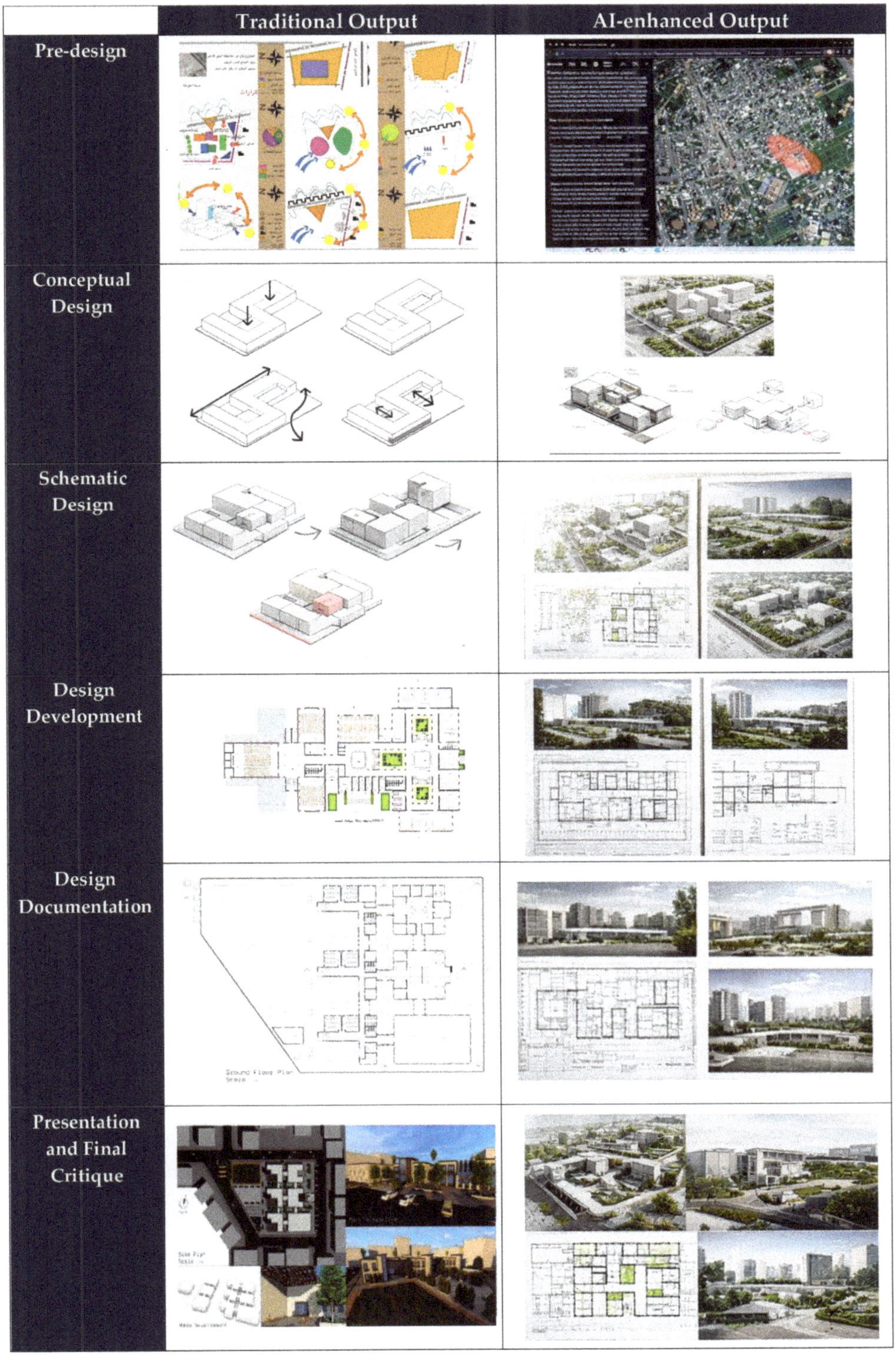

Figure 2. Student project outputs: traditional vs. AI-assisted (source: Authors).

https://doi.org/10.3390/buildings16071445

5. Results

This section presents the findings of the study on the impact of AI-assisted tools in architectural design education. The results were analyzed across the six project stages using the six evaluation indicators. Data were collected from multiple sources, including student surveys, faculty assessments, and final project reviews, and were measured using a five-point Likert scale. The analysis includes mean scores, standard deviations, and comparative assessments with prior studies to provide a comprehensive understanding of AI's influence on both student performance and perception throughout the design process.

As shown in Figure 3, in the Pre-design stage, efficiency (4.2) and adoptability (4.4) were high, confirming AI's effectiveness in site analysis, data processing, and early contextual understanding. Creativity (3.6) and accuracy (3.5) remained moderate, indicating that AI serves mainly a supportive role at this stage. The Conceptual Design stage recorded the highest creativity (4.8), along with very high efficiency (4.6) and AI integration (4.7), confirming AI's strong influence in early ideation and form generation, as predicted in the theoretical framework.

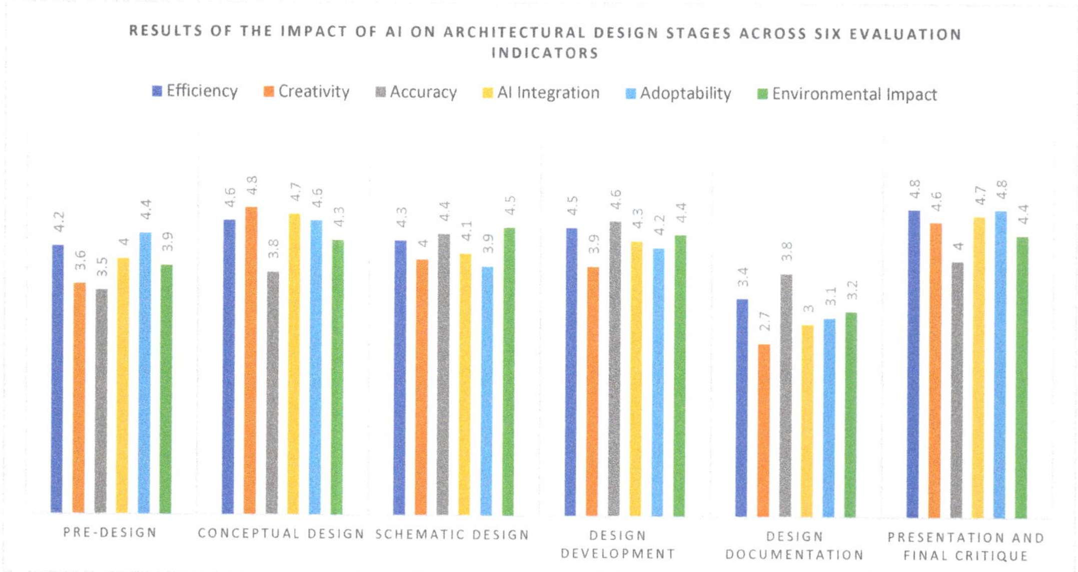

Figure 3. Impact of AI on architectural design stages across six evaluation indicators (source: Authors).

In the Schematic Design phase, accuracy (4.4) and environmental impact (4.5) improved, reflecting AI's shift toward performance-based evaluation, while creativity (4.0) was moderate, showing functional and environmental constraints increasingly guide design decisions. During Design Development, efficiency (4.5) and accuracy (4.6) remained high, emphasizing AI's role in workflow optimization, coordination, and technical precision. Creativity (3.9) slightly decreased, suggesting innovation is now focused on materials, systems, and technical solutions rather than overall form. The Design Documentation stage showed the lowest scores: efficiency (3.4), creativity (2.7), and AI integration (3.0), indicating students struggled to effectively apply AI at this technical stage. Manual drafting and instructor guidance remained essential. Finally, the Presentation and Final Critique stage achieved peak performance, with efficiency (4.8), creativity (4.6), AI integration (4.7), and adoptability (4.8), confirming that AI visualization, rendering, and storytelling tools significantly enhance design communication and visual impact.

https://doi.org/10.3390/buildings16071445

The results of mean and standard deviation in (Figure 4), indicate clear variations in the impact of AI across the different design stages. The highest overall mean score was recorded at the Presentation and Final Critique stage (M = 4.55, SD = 0.31), highlighting the strong role of AI in visual communication, rendering, and final presentation quality. This was closely followed by the Conceptual Design stage (M = 4.47, SD = 0.37), where AI significantly supported idea generation and creative exploration. The Design Development stage also showed a high mean value (M = 4.32, SD = 0.25), indicating effective use of AI in refining and technically developing design solutions. The Schematic Design stage demonstrated a similarly positive impact (M = 4.20, SD = 0.24), reflecting stable AI support during mid-level design decisions. In contrast, the Pre-design stage recorded a slightly lower mean (M = 3.93, SD = 0.34), as AI was mainly used for preliminary analysis and early exploration. The lowest mean score was observed in the Design Documentation stage (M = 3.20, SD = 0.37), confirming that AI has limited effectiveness in highly technical drafting and construction documentation tasks. Overall, the relatively low standard deviation values across all stages indicate a high level of consistency in participants' evaluations.

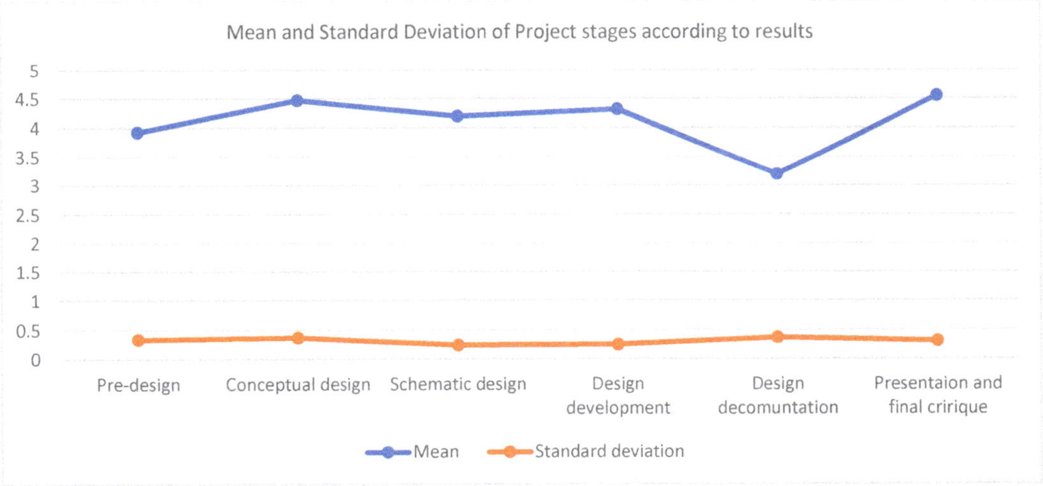

Figure 4. Mean and standard deviation of project stages according to results (source: Authors).

6. Discussion

In the Pre-design phase, students reported high usefulness of AI for organizing information, conducting research, and generating preliminary ideas. Survey results showed high Likert ratings for efficiency and adoptability, which faculty feedback and project reviews confirmed. Figure 2 shows a mean of 4.2 (SD = 0.6), indicating consistent performance and suggesting that AI effectively supports early-stage planning and conceptual clarity.

During the conceptual design phase, perceptions were more varied. Students valued AI for creativity and idea exploration, though some questioned its ability to fully support conceptual innovation. Faculty noted differences in originality and coherence. Figure 2 shows a mean of 3.9 (SD = 0.7), reflecting variability, particularly in creativity, highlighting that AI aids visualization but cannot replace individual creative thinking.

In the design development phase, AI improved workflow efficiency and technical detailing, with high Likert scores for efficiency and ease of use. Some students faced challenges integrating complex elements. Faculty observed moderate variation in performance.

 https://doi.org/10.3390/buildings16071445

Figure 4 shows a mean of 4.0 (SD = 0.8), emphasizing that AI supports process efficiency but cannot replace technical skill or judgment.

The design documentation phase showed the greatest variability. Students reported lower scores for documentation quality and adoptability, indicating difficulties in producing comprehensive records. Faculty reviews confirmed these challenges. Figure 2 shows the lowest mean of 3.4 (SD = 0.9), particularly affecting documentation and presentation, demonstrating that AI alone cannot ensure consistent quality.

Finally, in the presentation and final critique phase, students found AI highly useful for visualization, rendering, and preparation. Faculty observed consistent presentation quality. Figure 4 shows a mean of 4.1 (SD = 0.5), confirming AI's effectiveness in enhancing visual communication and final presentation outcomes.

The findings of this study reveal a differentiated impact of AI integration across the architectural design process, highlighting that its effectiveness is not uniform but strongly stage-dependent. The conceptual design and schematic design stages emerged as the most positively influenced phases, particularly in terms of creativity, visualization, and the ability to rapidly explore multiple design alternatives. This can be attributed to the generative and iterative nature of AI tools, which align closely with the exploratory character of early design thinking. These results are consistent with recent research in architectural education, such as the work of Fatmanur Atalay, which emphasizes the role of AI in enhancing idea generation, supporting design exploration, and enabling students to efficiently evaluate multiple design scenarios [8].

In contrast, the design documentation stage demonstrated the lowest level of improvement, reflecting the inherent limitations of AI in tasks requiring high levels of technical accuracy, standardization, and detailed construction knowledge. At this stage, students relied more heavily on manual skills, professional conventions, and instructor guidance, indicating that AI currently functions as a supportive rather than a substitutive tool in technically demanding phases. This divergence across stages underscores the need for a structured and pedagogically guided integration of AI within architectural education. While AI significantly enhances creativity and efficiency in early and presentation stages, its role in later technical phases remains constrained, requiring critical human oversight to ensure accuracy and reliability. Overall, these findings reinforce the argument that AI should be positioned not as a universal solution, but as a context-sensitive tool whose value depends on the nature of the design task and the stage of the process.

Comparative Matrix Analysis: Literature vs. Experimental Results

To better understand the results, the outcomes of the design studio experiment were added to be three-dimensional matrix, as shown in Table 5, and was reviewed alongside the initial analytical matrix that had been developed from earlier studies (Table 1). This step helped reveal the points where the theoretical expectations matched what actually happened in the studio and where they did not. Through this comparison, the study offers a clearer and more grounded view of how AI functions not only as a theoretical concept, but also as a practical and experiential tool that shapes students' learning throughout the architectural design process.

The comparative analysis between the literature-based expectations and the experimental results reveals both strong convergence and notable deviations in the role of artificial intelligence (AI) across the architectural design studio stages. Overall, the findings confirm that AI is most influential during the early conceptual and final presentation phases, while its impact remains comparatively limited during the technical documentation stage.

https://doi.org/10.3390/buildings16071445

Table 5. Three-dimensional matrix based on experimental results (source: Authors).

Stages of Design Process	Efficiency	Creativity	Accuracy	AI Integration	Adoptability	Environmental/Architectural Impact
	Measurement Indicators					
Pre-design	AI helps during data gathering and contextual analysis, allowing designers to make more informed decisions in the early stages of the project.	AI-generated concept visuals can help spark early design ideas, but they still need human refinement to achieve coherence and convey a clear design intention.	AI can improve site understanding and analysis, but its results still need to be checked and verified by humans to ensure accuracy.	AI tools were smoothly incorporated into analytical tasks, improving both efficiency and clarity.	Students found both text- and image-based AI tools to be intuitive and easy to use throughout the design process.	AI and GIS tools helped with early environmental and contextual analysis, enhancing students' understanding of the site and the relevance of their design decisions.
	4.2	3.6	3.5	4.0	4.4	3.9
Conceptual Design	AI sped up the ideation process and made it easier to quickly generate design forms.	AI tools fostered creative exploration and supported the generation of multiple conceptual alternatives.	Maintaining conceptual alignment still relied on instructor feedback to ensure clarity and coherence in the design.	A high level of integration was achieved, with AI tools effectively supporting digital sketching and early-stage visualization.	Students reported high levels of enjoyment and engagement when working with generative visual AI tools.	Generative AI tools promoted sustainable form-finding and encouraged the exploration of passive design strategies.
	4.6	4.8	3.8	4.7	4.6	4.3
Schematic Design	AI facilitated efficient testing of space layouts and assessment of functional performance.	Creativity was guided by AI-generated performance feedback, which helped refine design decisions.	AI improved spatial accuracy while also supporting more informed environmental considerations in the design process.	The effective integration of AI depended on students' technical skills and their familiarity with the tools.	Successful AI integration relied on students' technical skills and their comfort in using the tools.	Energy simulation tools improved the designs' lighting and ventilation performance.
	4.3	4.0	4.4	4.1	3.9	4.5
Design Development	AI helped speed up the detailing process and enabled smoother integration of structural logic.	Innovation was most evident in the selection of materials and the design of building systems.	AI enhanced consistency in drawings and helped coordinate different design elements more effectively.	AI integration was feasible, but its effective use required guidance from instructors.	Students adapted quickly and effectively to using generative visual AI tools.	AI-assisted optimization of structures and materials contributed to reducing construction waste.
	4.5	3.9	4.6	4.3	4.2	4.4
Design Documentation	The partial automation of tasks helped improve overall workflow efficiency.	At this stage, the focus was more on technical precision than on creative exploration.	AI-assisted clash detection proved useful, but manual drafting remained the primary method.	Integration was limited, with AI use mostly remaining at a basic level.	Students faced challenges in effectively applying AI tools for documentation tasks.	AI played a moderate role in addressing environmental considerations.
	3.4	2.7	3.8	3.0	3.1	3.2
Presentation and Final Critique	AI significantly reduced the time needed to prepare presentations.	AI tools enhanced storytelling, rendering, and video-based design communication.	Visual outputs still required manual editing and instructor guidance to ensure accuracy.	AI tools played a key role in producing the final project deliverables.	Students enthusiastically embraced AI-based visualization tools throughout the design process.	AI visualization tools improved the representation of environmental factors and enhanced spatial perception.
	4.8	4.6	4.0	4.7	4.8	4.4

Results according to five-point Likert scale

https://doi.org/10.3390/buildings16071445

The proposed three-dimensional matrix is structured along three axes:

(1) Design stages;
(2) Evaluation indicators;
(3) Data sources (student surveys, faculty assessment, and project evaluation).

This structure allows for a multi-layered analysis of AI impact across both process and performance dimensions.

- Efficiency

Previous studies emphasized that AI significantly enhances workflow efficiency, particularly in pre-design, conceptual, and documentation stages through automation, simulation, and BIM-based processes [19,23]. The experimental results strongly support this assumption. High efficiency scores were recorded during Conceptual Design (M = 4.6) and Presentation & Final Critique (M = 4.8), indicating that students benefited greatly from AI in accelerating ideation, visualization, and project delivery. However, a noticeable decline in efficiency appeared during the Design Documentation stage (M = 3.4), suggesting that students still struggle to fully exploit AI tools for highly technical drafting tasks, despite the strong emphasis on automation in the literature.

- Creativity

The literature consistently highlights the creative potential of generative AI, particularly in the conceptual phase [28]. This expectation was strongly validated by the experimental findings, where Conceptual Design recorded the highest creativity score (M = 4.8), followed closely by Presentation & Final Critique (M = 4.6). These results demonstrate that AI not only supports idea generation but also enhances architectural storytelling and visual expression. In contrast, creativity dropped sharply during Design Documentation (M = 2.7), aligning with previous studies that describe this phase as execution-oriented rather than exploratory [22].

- Accuracy

The literature suggests that AI improves analytical accuracy but still requires human verification [23,32]. This position is strongly reflected in the experimental data. Accuracy steadily increased from Pre-design (M = 3.5) to Design Development (M = 4.6), indicating that AI is more reliable when design information becomes structured and technically defined. During Presentation & Final Critique (M = 4.0), accuracy remained high but continued to depend on manual refinement, reinforcing the literature's emphasis on the complementary role of human judgment.

- AI Integration

The literature describes AI integration as stage-dependent, with higher levels during generative and simulation phases and lower levels during documentation [19]. The experimental findings confirm this pattern. High integration was observed in Conceptual Design and Final Presentation (both M = 4.7), where AI supported visualization, form generation, and digital communication. Conversely, integration dropped during Design Documentation (M = 3.0), demonstrating that AI adoption in technical documentation is still limited in educational practice despite its theoretical potential.

- Adoptability

While earlier studies predicted that AI adoptability would depend heavily on user expertise and training, the experimental data revealed consistently high levels of student acceptance, particularly in Pre-design (M = 4.4) and Final Presentation (M = 4.8) stages. This indicates a higher level of confidence and openness toward AI tools among students than what was previously anticipated in the literature. The lowest adoptability score was again

https://doi.org/10.3390/buildings16071445

recorded in Design Documentation (M = 3.1), reflecting practical challenges in applying AI to rigid technical workflows.

- Environmental and Architectural Impact

The literature characterizes AI's role in environmental performance as emerging and primarily analytical [26]. The experimental results support this view while also indicating moderate progress. Environmental impact scores were relatively high in Schematic Design (M = 4.5), Design Development (M = 4.4), and Final Presentation (M = 4.4), where simulation, optimization, and visualization tools were actively used. However, the lower value in Design Documentation (M = 3.2) suggests that environmental intelligence remains underutilized during final technical production.

To enhance the methodological rigor of the study and ensure the validity of the findings, a set of statistical analyses was conducted, including Spearman's rank correlation coefficient, Cronbach's alpha, and the Friedman test. These non-parametric methods were deemed appropriate given the ordinal nature of the Likert-scale data and the relatively small sample size ($n = 17$).

Spearman's rank correlation coefficient was used to explore the relationships between the six evaluation indicators (efficiency, creativity, accuracy, adoptability, environmental impact, and AI integration). The results indicated the presence of moderate correlations between certain indicators, particularly between efficiency and adoptability, as well as between creativity and AI integration. Importantly, no excessively high correlations were observed, which suggests that each indicator captures a distinct yet related dimension of AI's impact on the architectural design process.

To assess the reliability of the evaluation framework, Cronbach's alpha was calculated, yielding a value of approximately $\alpha \approx 0.78$. This indicates an acceptable level of internal consistency, confirming that the selected indicators collectively provide a reliable and coherent measure of performance while maintaining conceptual independence among variables.

Furthermore, the Friedman test was employed to examine differences across the six design stages. The results revealed statistically significant variations ($p < 0.05$), demonstrating that the influence of AI is not uniform but varies across different phases of the design process. This finding reinforces the idea that AI plays a more prominent role in certain stages, particularly those associated with conceptual exploration and visual communication.

The ranking derived from the Friedman analysis is consistent with the descriptive findings, where the Presentation and Final Critique stage demonstrated the highest level of AI impact, followed by the Conceptual Design stage, while the Design Documentation stage recorded the lowest impact. These results highlight that AI tools are most effective in visually oriented and ideation-driven stages, whereas their influence is more limited in highly technical and documentation-intensive phases.

In general, the experimental findings largely validate the trends reported in previous studies, particularly regarding the strong role of AI in enhancing efficiency, creativity, and visualization in early and final project stages as shown in Table 6. However, the results also reveal a clear gap between theoretical expectations and practical implementation, especially in the Design Documentation stage, where AI's technical potential is not yet fully realized in studio-based education. Furthermore, the high levels of adoptability and integration observed among students indicate that AI is being embraced more rapidly in academic environments than anticipated in the literature, suggesting a shift in digital design culture within architectural education.

https://doi.org/10.3390/buildings16071445

Table 6. Evaluation of AI Impact on student design performance: expected vs. observed outcomes (source: Authors).

		Expected Effect Based on the Literature	Observed Effect (Experimental Results)	Interpretation
Indicators	Efficiency	High—AI expected to enhance productivity and workflow	High—Students reported improved time management and faster iteration	Confirms literature; AI supports efficiency in early stages
	Creativity	High—AI anticipated to expand design exploration	High—Participants found AI to significantly inspire idea generation	Experimental results exceed expectations, showing deeper creative engagement
	Accuracy	Moderate—AI tools support analysis but depend on user skill	Moderate—Precision improved slightly but still relied on human judgment	Consistent with literature; AI remains a supportive analytical tool
	AI integration	Increasing—Adoption expected to grow with accessibility	High—Students integrated AI widely in early and final stages	Shows faster adoption than anticipated in literature
	Adoptability	Variable—Predicted to depend on user experience	High—Students showed strong willingness to continue using AI	Surpasses earlier predictions; indicates growing confidence with AI
	Environmental and architectural impact	Emerging—AI expected to have limited environmental influence	Moderate—Some progress in contextual analysis but still developing	Partial improvement: AI use in environmental analysis remains early-stage

The findings of this study extend beyond identifying the differential impact of AI across design stages and point toward the necessity of a structured human–AI collaboration framework within architectural studios. The results demonstrate that AI contributes most effectively during early ideation and visualization phases, where it enhances exploratory thinking, rapid iteration, and alternative generation. In contrast, later technical stages continue to rely on human judgment, critical reasoning, and professional responsibility.

This stage-sensitive distribution of influence suggests that AI integration should not be uniform across the design process but strategically aligned with pedagogical objectives and cognitive demands at each phase. Rather than positioning AI as a replacement for human creativity, the evidence supports a complementary partnership model in which AI augments analytical capacity and generative exploration, while human designers retain authorship, ethical responsibility, and critical evaluation.

Accordingly, the study advocates for a structured integration framework grounded in three principles: calibrated stage-based application, faculty-guided critical mediation, and ethical awareness embedded within studio culture. Such a framework enables architectural education to transition toward an intelligent yet human-centered paradigm, ensuring that AI functions as a cognitive collaborator that strengthens, rather than diminishes, reflective design practice.

Recent advancements in AI integration within the built environment extend beyond educational applications toward hybrid modeling frameworks that combine analytical, numerical, and data-driven approaches. For instance, recent studies demonstrate how AI techniques can be integrated with physics-based models and experimental validation to enhance both the reliability and interpretability of design systems. Such approaches

 https://doi.org/10.3390/buildings16071445

highlight the potential of AI not merely as a generative or assistive tool, but as part of a comprehensive decision-support framework that bridges simulation, performance evaluation, and design optimization. This perspective suggests that while the current study focuses on educational studio contexts, future developments could extend AI integration toward more performance-driven and professionally applicable architectural design processes [2].

7. Conclusions

This study investigated the integration of artificial intelligence (AI) within architectural design studios and its impact across the six key stages of the design process. The findings indicate that AI had the most significant influence during the early and expressive stages (pre-design, conceptual design, and presentation) where it enhanced creativity, efficiency, and innovation. Its impact was more limited during the technical stages, such as design development and documentation, highlighting the need for better alignment between AI tools and advanced design skills.

Both students and faculty members acknowledged AI's value in education, though from different perspectives. Students highlighted its creative and time-saving benefits, while faculty emphasized its analytical and reflective potential. These complementary viewpoints suggest that AI is most effective when used to support, rather than replace, human creativity and critical judgment.

The study concludes that a balanced and structured approach is essential to fully leverage AI's educational benefits in design learning. When applied thoughtfully, AI can serve as both a creative partner that expands imagination and a pedagogical assistant that supports reflection and precision. This research contributes to the ongoing discussion on digital transformation in architectural education and provides a foundation for fostering a more adaptive, ethical, and human-centered design pedagogy in the age of artificial intelligence. The findings should be interpreted within the context of architectural education and not overgeneralized to professional practice without further validation.

Author Contributions: Conceptualization, H.A.; Methodology, A.H.; Software, A.H.; Validation, H.A.; Formal analysis, M.F. and A.H.; Investigation, M.F.; Writing—review & editing, H.A.; Visualization, M.F.; Supervision, H.A. and M.F. All authors have read and agreed to the published version of the manuscript.

Funding: This research received no external funding.

Data Availability Statement: The original contributions presented in this study are included in the article. Further inquiries can be directed to the corresponding author.

Conflicts of Interest: The authors declare no conflicts of interest.

References

1. Ceylan, S. Artificial Intelligence in Architecture: An Educational Perspective. In Proceedings of the 13th International Conference on Computer Supported Education (CSEDU 2021), Online, 23–25 April 2021.
2. Fulgione, M.; Palladino, S.; Esposito, L.; Sarfarazi, S.; Modano, M. A multi-stage framework combining experimental testing, numerical calibration, and AI surrogates for composite panel characterization. *Buildings* **2025**, *15*, 3900. [CrossRef]
3. Cudzik, J.; Nyka, L. Artificial intelligence in architectural education—Green campus development research. *Glob. J. Eng. Educ.* **2024**, *26*, 20–25.
4. Beyan, E.V.P.; Rossy, A.G.C. A Review of AI Image Generator: Influences, Challenges, and Future Prospects for Architectural Field. *J. Artif. Intell. Archit.* **2023**, *2*, 53–56.
5. Oxman, R. Thinking difference: Theories and models of parametric design thinking. *Des. Stud.* **2017**, *52*, 4–39. [CrossRef]
6. Moorhouse, B.L.; Yeo, M.A.; Wan, Y. Generative AI tools and assessment: Guidelines of the world's top-ranking universities. *Comput. Educ. Open* **2023**, *5*, 100151. [CrossRef]
7. Simina, N.A. IA en la enseñanza de arquitectura: Límites y potencial desde el Research by Design. In *Jornadas sobre Innovación Docente en Arquitectura*; Polytechnic University of Catalonia, Polytechnic Digital Initiative: Barcelona, Spain, 2025.

 https://doi.org/10.3390/buildings16071445

8. Atalay, F. Artificial Intelligence in Architectural Education: New Learning and Design Approaches. In Proceedings of the International Conference of Contemporary Affairs in Architecture and Urbanism-ICCAUA, Antalya, Turkey, 8–9 May 2025; Volume 8, pp. 343–355.
9. Korra, C.; Sadhana, A.; Reddy, A.R.K.; Yelagandula, M.; Vemula, L. Transformative Approaches in Architectural Education: Leveraging Artificial Intelligence for Enhanced Design, Creativity, and Technical Integration. *Int. J. Transcontinental Discov.* **2022**, *9*, 33–43.
10. El Moussaoui, M.; Krois, K. Architectural Pedagogy in the Age of AI: The Transformation of a Domain. In *Annual Conference of the European Association for Architectural Education*; Springer Nature: Cham, Switzerland, 2024. [CrossRef]
11. Wang, J.; Shi, Y.; Chen, X.; Lan, Y.; Liu, S. Teaching with Artificial Intelligence in Architecture: Embedding Technical Skills and Ethical Reflection in a Core Design Studio. *Buildings* **2025**, *15*, 3069. [CrossRef]
12. Jin, S.; Tu, H.; Li, J.; Fang, Y.; Qu, Z.; Xu, F.; Liu, K.; Lin, Y. Enhancing Architectural Education through Artificial Intelligence: A Case Study of an AI-Assisted Architectural Programming and Design Course. *Buildings* **2024**, *14*, 1613. [CrossRef]
13. Sadek, M.; Mohamed, N.A.G. Artificial Intelligence as a pedagogical tool for architectural education: What does the empirical evidence tell us? *MSA Eng. J.* **2023**, *2*, 133–148. [CrossRef]
14. Özorhon, G.; Nitelik Gelirli, D.; Lekesiz, G.; Müezzinoğlu, C. AI-assisted architectural design studio (AI-a-ADS): How artificial intelligence join the architectural design studio? *Int. J. Technol. Des. Educ.* **2025**, *35*, 1999–2023. [CrossRef]
15. Karadağ, D.; Ozar, B. A new frontier in design studio: AI and human collaboration in conceptual design. *Front. Archit. Res.* **2025**, *14*, 1536–1550. [CrossRef]
16. Dwijendra, N.K.A.; Dewi, N.M.E.N.; Hendrawan, F.; Dinata, R.D.S.; Pranajaya, I.K.; Suryani, N.K. Integrating Artificial Intelligence in Architectural Education for Sustainable Development: A Case Study in Bali. *Eng. Technol. Q. Rev.* **2024**, *7*, 49–57. [CrossRef]
17. Komatina, D.; Miletić, M.; Mosurović Ružičić, M. Embracing artificial intelligence (AI) in architectural education: A step towards sustainable practice? *Buildings* **2024**, *14*, 2578. [CrossRef]
18. Ahmed, A.; Alymani, A. Integrating Artificial Intelligence Rendering Tools in Design Integrating AI as teaching methods in architectural education. In Proceedings of the 42nd Conference on Education and Research in Computer Aided Architectural Design in Europe (eCAADe), Nicosia, Cyprus, 11–13 September 2024. [CrossRef]
19. Jang, S.; Roh, H.; Lee, G. Generative AI in architectural design: Application, data, and evaluation methods. *Autom. Constr.* **2025**, *174*, 106174. [CrossRef]
20. Adewale, B.A.; Ene, V.O.; Ogunbayo, B.F.; Aigbavboa, C.O. Application of artificial intelligence (AI) in sustainable building lifecycle; a systematic literature review. *Buildings* **2024**, *14*, 2137. [CrossRef]
21. Li, Y.; Chen, H.; Yu, P.; Yang, L. A review of artificial intelligence in enhancing architectural design efficiency. *Appl. Sci.* **2025**, *15*, 1476. [CrossRef]
22. Alshahrani, A.; Mostafa, A.M. Enhancing the use of artificial intelligence in architectural education–case study Saudi Arabia. *Front. Built Environ.* **2025**, *11*, 1610709. [CrossRef]
23. Zhang, C.; Zou, Y.; Dimyadi, J. A Systematic Review of Automated BIM Modelling for Existing Buildings from 2D Documentation. In *ISARC. Proceedings of the International Symposium on Automation and Robotics in Construction*; IAARC Publications: Irving, TX, USA, 2021. [CrossRef]
24. Nag, A.; Boricha, J.; Sarkar, A. Architectural Education: AI Integrative Challenges and Prospects. In *Effective Instructional Design Informed by AI*; IGI Global Scientific Publishing: Hershey, PA, USA, 2025; pp. 383–408.
25. Novoselchuk, N.; Shevchenko, L.; Mass, E. Artificial intelligence in Architecture and education: Potential, tendencies, perspectives. In *Artificial Intelligence: An Era of New Threats or Opportunities*; OKTAN PRINT s.r.o.: Prague, Czechia, 2023; pp. 125–136.
26. Manmatharasan, P.; Bitsuamlak, G.; Grolinger, K. AI-driven design optimization for sustainable buildings: A systematic review. *Energy Build.* **2025**, *332*, 115440. [CrossRef]
27. Cortiços, N.D.; Zheng, X.; Duarte, C.C. The Impact of Artificial Intelligence on Architecture: A Comprehensive Analysis of AI Software Tools and Their Global Adoption. In *Proceedings of the International Conference on Building Materials and Construction*; Springer: Berlin/Heidelberg, Germany, 2025; pp. 152–169.
28. Arisman, A.; Widiastuti, I.; Indraprastha, A.; Sudradjat, I. Creativity in generative design: The impact of architects' control over geometric parameters in early-stage form-finding using genetic algorithms. *Int. J. Archit. Comput.* **2025**, 14780771251340204. [CrossRef]
29. Petrova, M.; Kuhnen, C. Artificial Intelligence as a Tool for Individual and Collaborative Creativity in Design Education. *Des. Technol. Educ. An Int. J.* **2025**, *30*, 86–101.
30. Albukhari, I.N. The role of artificial intelligence (AI) in architectural design: A systematic review of emerging technologies and applications. *J. Umm Al-Qura Univ. Eng. Archit.* **2025**, *16*, 1457–1476. [CrossRef]
31. Choudhury, M.M.; Eisenbart, B.; Kuys, B. Artificial intelligence (AI) in the design process—A review and analysis on generative AI perspectives. *Proc. Des. Soc.* **2025**, *5*, 631–640. [CrossRef]

32. Ji, Y.; Wang, W.; He, Y.; Li, L.; Zhang, H.; Zhang, T. Performance in generation: An automatic generalizable generative-design-based performance optimization framework for sustainable building design. *Energy Build.* **2023**, *298*, 113512. [CrossRef]
33. Zeytin, E.; Kösenciğ, K.Ö.; Öner, D. The Role of AI Design Assistance on the Architectural Design Process: An Empirical Research with Novice Designers. *J. Comput. Des.* **2024**, *5*, 1–30. [CrossRef]
34. Matter, N.M.; Gado, N.G. Artificial intelligence in architecture: Integration into architectural design process. *Eng. Res. J.* **2024**, *181*, 1–16. [CrossRef]
35. Sacks, R.; Girolami, M.; Brilakis, I. Building information modelling, artificial intelligence and construction tech. *Dev. Built Environ.* **2020**, *4*, 100011. [CrossRef]
36. Attia, A.R. The impact of integrating artificial intelligence and Building information modeling (BIM) systems on the development of construction methodologies. *J. Umm Al-Qura Univ. Eng. Archit.* **2025**, *16*, 1537–1554. [CrossRef]
37. Saad, S.; Haris, M.; Ammad, S.; Rasheed, K. AI-assisted building design. In *AI in Material Science*; CRC Press: Boca Raton, FL, USA, 2024; pp. 143–168, ISBN 1003438482.
38. Bghdadi, M.; Zairul, M. A Thematic Review on Artificial Intelligence (AI), Virtual Reality (VR), and Augmented Reality (AR) in Architecture Education. *Alam Cipta Int. J. Sustain. Trop. Des. Res. Pract.* **2024**, *17*, 55–66.
39. Rodriguez, J.K.C.; Yali, J.B.A.; Torres, V.S.M. Technology and architecture: Impact of artificial intelligence and virtual reality on the perception of architectural design. *Civ. Eng. Archit.* **2025**, *13*, 637–652. [CrossRef]
40. Muslu, O.; Koçyiğit, R.G. Artificial intelligence in the context of photorealism in architectural visualization. *Contexto* **2025**, *19*, 15–32. [CrossRef]

 https://doi.org/10.3390/buildings16071445

buildings

MDPI

Article

Leveraging Generative AI for High-Fidelity 360° Spatial Images: Methodological Validation for Use as Experimental Stimuli

Yoojin Han * and Joowon Jeong

Department of Interior Architecture and Built Environment, Yonsei University, Seoul 03722, Republic of Korea
* Correspondence: yoojin79@yonsei.ac.kr; Tel.: +82-10-2721-2753

Abstract

Despite its efficiency, the structural integrity and geometric accuracy of artificial intelligence (AI)-generated imagery used in environmental psychology experiments have not been sufficiently validated. This study investigated the methodological validity and substitutability of generative AI-generated 360° images as experimental stimuli for indoor environmental research. Using a three-stage framework, we generated base panoramas with controlled structural parameters, integrated greenery via AI-based inpainting, and conducted multifaceted validation through objective quality metrics and expert assessments. Quantitative results confirmed high technical integrity, indicating that structural distortions at panoramic stitching points were effectively minimized. Furthermore, the AI-generated stimuli maintained stable visual quality across varying greenery densities. Expert evaluations confirmed that the AI-driven approach significantly outperforms conventional 3D modeling, particularly in terms of presence and realism. By achieving high usability and spatial integrity scores, we established a novel standard for employing generative AI to create high-fidelity virtual environments for architectural and psychological research.

Keywords: AI-generated images; generative AI; indoor environments; experimental stimuli; 360° panoramic images; spatial images

1. Introduction

In contemporary indoor environmental research, space is recognized not merely as a physical backdrop but as a complex environmental stimulus—defined in this study as a controlled visual setting designed to evoke specific psychological and physiological responses [1,2]. While natural elements like greenery are essential variables for emotional restoration, their application in virtual reality (VR) experiments has been frequently hindered by the high technical costs and extensive time required for conventional 3D rendering [3,4]. This study addresses the methodological constraints inherent in the creation of conventional stimuli by proposing a generative AI-based workflow that ensures both efficiency and scientific rigor.

Currently, 360° panoramic imagery is a standard format for providing immersive spatial stimuli [5]. However, traditional production processes—involving sequential modeling, texturing, and lighting—limit the diversity of experimental conditions and make it difficult to maintain visual consistency while rapidly altering specific environmental variables [6]. Although several studies have attempted to utilize AI in this field [7–11], empirical validation of whether AI-generated panoramas can maintain the architectural rigor and consistency required for scientific experiments, compared with conventional 3D rendering, remains insufficient.

Building on this objective, although previous research has primarily applied generative AI for visual ideation and design exploration, its application as a controlled experimental tool in spatial research remains insufficiently examined. We argue that, in experimental contexts, spatial images are not merely visual representations but function as stimuli that require high levels of reliability, reproducibility, and perceptual validity. In contrast to exploratory design contexts where visual inspiration is prioritized, experimental settings demand that every visual element be strictly controlled to ensure that participant responses are triggered by intended variables rather than unintended AI artifacts. However, the extent to which AI-generated 360° panoramic images can satisfy these requirements has not been thoroughly validated.

To bridge this gap, the primary objective of this research is to validate the effectiveness of AI-generated 360° panoramic images as experimental stimuli for indoor environmental psychology. We focus on three key dimensions: (1) evaluating the precision of text-to-image (T2I) models for architectural environments, (2) examining the capacity for systematic greenery manipulation across multiple levels and configurations, and (3) establishing methodological validity through a multi-layered verification framework. In this framework, diffusion-based T2I models are adopted as the most effective technical instruments to achieve high fidelity and precise variable control; concurrently, their performance is rigorously verified beyond technical Image Quality Assessment (IQA) metrics through structured perceptual evaluations by architecture and design experts. By adopting the igroup Presence Questionnaire (IPQ) and a multi-dimensional quality assessment framework derived from generative AI literature, we verify whether these AI-generated 360° environments possess the architectural integrity, greenery fidelity, and overall usability required for immersive psychological experiments.

The academic contribution of this study lies in its shift from using AI for exploratory design ideation to systematic stimulus production for controlled experiments. We present a methodology that drastically reduces the time and labor typically required for manual 3D modeling while maintaining the scientific rigor—specifically reliability, reproducibility, and strict variable control—essential for empirical research. Crucially, the absence of such rigor leads to unreliable experimental comparisons and misattribution of perceptual responses, compromising the credibility of spatial research. By overcoming these limitations and the inefficiencies of traditional methods, this study validates the potential for researchers to develop diverse, high-quality 360° experimental environments with significantly improved efficiency.

2. Literature Review

2.1. Generative AI for Spatial Image Generation and Experimental Visual Stimuli

Recent studies on architectural and interior designs have increasingly explored the use of generative AI as a tool for producing spatial images during the early stages of design development, particularly for concept exploration and visual ideation [12]. Unlike conventional visualization workflows that rely on manual modeling and rendering, generative AI enables rapid image synthesis based on abstract inputs, allowing designers to externalize, develop, and refine spatial concepts at an early conceptual level without the need for labor-intensive manual processes [13].

Text-to-image generation models have been widely adopted in architectural research owing to their ability to translate linguistic descriptions into visual representations of space. Existing studies have demonstrated that prompt-based interactions enable designers to articulate abstract spatial attributes, including atmosphere, materiality, lighting conditions,

https://doi.org/10.3390/buildings16091679

and stylistic references, through natural language, which are then synthesized into spatial images using diffusion-based models [12,14]. This approach supports exploratory design processes by enabling rapid iteration and comparison of alternative spatial expressions without requiring predefined geometric models. From an experimental perspective, this property also allows the explicit specification and controlled variation in spatial attributes through structured linguistic inputs.

By contrast, image-to-image (img2img) generation approaches produce spatial variations by transforming existing reference images while partially preserving their underlying structure. Horvath and Pouliou [13] report that img2img workflows, such as textures, lighting artifacts, and compositional biases, tend to retain unintended visual elements embedded in the source image. These inherited visual features may hinder experimental control and limit the clarity of spatial manipulation, particularly when systematic variation in visual conditions is required; this limitation becomes critical in experimental scenarios, where the isolation of specific variables requires precise and independent control over visual attributes.

Several studies have emphasized that generative AI-based spatial images are shaped by prompt content and the selection of visual descriptors related to material surfaces, volumetric composition, scale perception, and stylistic references. Jeong et al. [15] demonstrated that fine-tuned diffusion models can learn domain-specific visual vocabularies, including interior materials, color palettes, and furniture styles, through keyword-based training, thereby enabling more consistent control over spatial appearance. Similarly, Paananen, Oppenlaender and Visuri [12] reported that architecture students often employ biophilic and nature-inspired descriptors, such as plants, wood, and organic forms, in text prompts to support imaginative exploration and creative ideation during early-stage design tasks.

From a technical perspective, diffusion-based generative models have become the dominant framework for spatial image synthesis owing to their stability and ability to produce coherent global structures [7,16]. Unlike earlier generative models, diffusion models iteratively refine images through probabilistic denoising processes that recover structured signals by progressively removing Gaussian noise, thereby improving structural consistency and reducing visual artifacts [17]. This characteristic has expanded the applicability of generative AI from artistic image production to spatially structured architectural representations [16]. While diffusion models improve overall image quality and structural coherence, the level of controllability in experimental situations is determined not just by the model itself, but also by how inputs are structured and limited. In this context, "text-based generation" refers to the input modality that provides spatial descriptions, whereas the diffusion model refers to the generative architecture that synthesizes the images. These two dimensions are conceptually distinct: one governs how spatial intent is specified, and the other governs how images are computationally generated.

Despite these advancements, existing architectural applications of generative AI primarily focus on ideation and visual communication rather than on controlled experimental usage. Previous works have focused on creative support and stylistic exploration, where outputs are typically judged in terms of visual plausibility instead of experimental rigor. In such contexts, spatial images must maintain consistency across conditions while enabling precise manipulation of target variables. Accordingly, the extent to which AI-generated spatial images can ensure reliability, reproducibility, and perceptual validity under these conditions has not been thoroughly investigated, despite the fact that these are critical requirements for valid experimental comparison.

https://doi.org/10.3390/buildings16091679

2.2. 360° Panorama Images and the Use of Generative AI

360° panoramic images provide continuous visual coverage of spatial environments and have been widely employed in spatial and environmental research as immersive and ecologically valid experimental stimuli [5]. By enabling users to perceive an environment from all directions, panoramic imagery offers a closer approximation of real-world spatial experiences than conventional perspective images.

Previous studies on virtual and immersive environments have demonstrated that panoramic visual stimuli significantly influence the visual attention, arousal responses, and perceptual engagement of users. Kim and Lee [3] showed that 360° virtual retail environments elicit gaze patterns and physiological responses comparable to those observed in physical spaces. Similarly, Lee et al. [4] reported that overlaying 3D models onto panoramic images within augmented reality (AR) environments facilitates effective comparison of architectural design alternatives, supporting the validity of panoramic imagery as a spatial evaluation medium.

Despite these advantages, the production of panoramic images has conventionally relied on resource-intensive workflows, including 3D modeling, 360° camera capture, panoramic stitching, and manual post-processing [4,10,18]. These processes require specialized expertise and substantial labor, limiting scalability and constraining the systematic manipulation of visual variables while maintaining consistent spatial structure across experimental conditions, which is significant for controlled experimental research.

To address these limitations, generative AI has recently been employed for the automated generation and modification of 360° spatial images. Diffusion-based generative approaches have demonstrated the capacity to synthesize panoramic imagery with improved global spatial coherence, enabling the generation of multiple visual conditions within a shared spatial framework [17]. This capacity indicates the potential of generative AI to aid in achieving both efficiency and experimental control in spatial stimulus generation.

In parallel, recent improvements in computer vision have led to the design of text-based panoramic image generation techniques which deal with spatial continuity and geometric distortion phenomena of 360° images. Recent studies have proposed generation strategies that enhance consistency across different viewpoints, enabling panoramic images to maintain coherent spatial structures throughout the full field of view. For instance, Kalischek et al. [9] proposed a cube map-based generation approach that improves the continuity between adjacent views and reduces visible seams and distortions. Zhang et al. [8] further demonstrated that integrating the global spatial context with localized perspective information supports more stable and spatially coherent panoramic environments. In addition, Ni et al. [11] demonstrated that parameter-efficient fine-tuning methods enable the generation of high-quality panoramic images with limited model adaptation, indicating the feasibility of producing controlled spatial stimuli without extensive computational resources.

Despite these technical advances, most studies have primarily evaluated generative performance in terms of visual realism, distortion reduction, and structural consistency. However, these criteria do not directly address the requirements of experimental research, where spatial stimuli must maintain consistency across conditions while enabling precise manipulation of target variables. As a result, the empirical validation of the AI-generated panoramic images as such controlled experimental stimuli, especially compared with traditional panoramas or 3D-rendered surroundings, remains insufficiently examined. In contrast, this study investigates whether AI-generated panoramic photos can support controlled modification of environmental variables while retaining spatial consistency between conditions, allowing them to be used as legitimate experimental stimuli.

https://doi.org/10.3390/buildings16091679

3. Method: Generation of 360° Panoramic Spatial Images Using Generative AI

3.1. Terminology and Definitions

To ensure methodological rigor and address potential ambiguities, this study establishes clear operational definitions for its core concepts. Table 1 summarizes the distinction between the conceptual environment, the generated visual artifacts, and the technical processes involved. By separating the 'environmental stimulus' (the conceptual intent) from the 'spatial stimulus' (the visual output), this framework provides a structured approach to validating generative AI as a reliable tool for indoor environmental research.

Table 1. Operational definitions of key terminology.

Category	Term	Operational Definition in This Study
Concept	Environmental Stimulus	The physical and sensory attributes (e.g., wood tones, greenery density) designed to elicit psychological or physiological responses in indoor environmental research.
Artifact	Spatial Stimulus	The specific 360° panoramic image generated by AI and presented to participants as the visual proxy for the virtual environment.
Process	Stimulus Production	The systematic technical workflow encompassing prompt engineering, diffusion-based image generation, and post-optimization.
Mechanism	Text-to-Image (T2I)	A generative synthesis approach that creates visual content strictly based on textual descriptions, ensuring precise control over experimental variables.
Evaluation	Semantic Alignment	The degree of correspondence between the intended research variables (input prompts) and the resulting visual content (output images), quantified via CLIP scores.

3.2. Tool Selection for 360° Panoramic Spatial Images

Skybox AI (Model 4, Blockade Labs, Indianapolis, IN, USA), a generative AI service that produces 360° panoramic images using text prompts, was selected as the primary stimulus generation tool. This tool was selected due to its capability to directly generate 360° equirectangular panoramic images with stable global coherence, which is essential for maintaining spatial continuity across experimental conditions. It has been increasingly adopted as a background generation tool in virtual production pipelines and extended reality content development [19]. While text-based panoramic generation offers superior visual coherence despite potential spatial ambiguities, img2img-based workflows are unsuitable for controlled VR environments due to persistent source image artifacts; thus, this study exclusively employed text-driven generation, supplemented by post-processing to ensure structural consistency and minimize noise.

Although Skybox AI stably generates spatial structures, its ability to place discrete objects—like plants—while maintaining consistent lighting and scale remains limited. Specifically, the "Remix" function does not support fixed random seeds, rendering it challenging to precisely control object placement across experimental conditions. To address this, vegetation elements were incorporated via post-processing. The Gemini 3 Flash Image model (codenamed Nano Banana 2; Google, Mountain View, CA, USA), accessed via the Envato platform (Envato, Melbourne, VIC, Australia), was employed to insert elements into the generated panoramas. This tool supports visually coherent object insertion within 360° environments while preserving lighting consistency and spatial realism, ensuring suitability for experimental stimulus construction.

https://doi.org/10.3390/buildings16091679

3.3. Condition Setting for 360° Panoramic Spatial Image Generation

3.3.1. Derivation of Architectural Characteristics of Public Areas in Mixed-Use Facilities

Before stimulus production, architectural characteristics of domestic mixed-use facilities were examined to establish a neutral spatial typology. Specifically, we conducted an extensive analysis involving field surveys, photographic documentation, spatial analysis, and a comprehensive review of online spatial data focused on public common areas within domestic mixed-use facilities. These characteristics support experimental neutrality and generalizability, rather than association with specific buildings. The derived characteristics and analytical categories are summarized in Table A1.

3.3.2. Construction of Controlled Stimulus Environment

To establish a baseline environment, we developed three versions by varying material conditions while maintaining consistent spatial structures and lighting: white, light wood, and dark wood (Table A2). The selection of these three specific material-tone conditions was directly informed by the results of our prior field analysis, which identified them as the most representative and prevalent finishes in the common areas of domestic mixed-use facilities. The white version uses light and white-toned finishes common in domestic mixed-use facilities, with neutral configurations to avoid specific program interpretation. The light wood version incorporates warm wood finishes while restricting color range and application to prevent wood from becoming the dominant visual element. The dark wood version reflects a premium atmosphere, while the material hierarchy and furniture quantity are controlled to avoid interpretation as a hotel lounge. Spatial structure, circulation, and lighting were controlled across all stimuli (Table 2). This strategy minimized unintended AI-generated scene transitions and suppressed non-essential visual differences.

Table 2. Common environmental control conditions applied to all stimuli.

Category	Item	Control Specification
Spatial conditions	Spatial structure	Central vertical void combined with repetitive horizontal slabs
	Floor configuration	Simultaneous perception of two to three floors
	Circulation	Central open atrium with peripheral circulation
	Balustrades	Transparent glass balustrades with light-toned metal frames
	Lighting	Fully artificial lighting with uniform illumination
	External elements	Exclusion of exterior views, natural daylight, and skylights
	People & Decorations	Complete exclusion of people, greenery, and installations
Camera parameters	Camera position	Fixed (eye-level)
	Field of view	±40° horizontal field of view
Image specifications	Projection type	360° equirectangular (2:1)
	Resolution	8K

3.4. Prompt Writing Strategy and Optimization

Trial generations were conducted to examine Skybox AI's language processing characteristics. Skybox AI assigns substantial weights to initial prompt conditions and operates with strict input length constraints. Prompts were constructed using ~1200 characters, placing core architectural elements—void configuration, lighting, and slab geometry—at the beginning, followed by material and atmospheric descriptions. When large public spaces were specified, the system automatically generated sky elements; thus, constraints were re-

 https://doi.org/10.3390/buildings16091679

peated throughout prompts to reinforce exclusion. A photorealistic rendering configuration (realistic, m3 advanced) was selected to approximate actual visual perception.

Negative prompts were limited to 480 characters. Applying identical negative text across all stimuli was insufficient, as uniform criteria either suppressed material characteristics or failed to block unintended interpretations. Therefore, negative prompts used a shared base with material-specific adjustments. This process was refined through repeated visual inspection, adding exclusion items only when necessary and removing items affecting spatial coherence.

To ensure methodological clarity and reproducibility, a representative prompt used for generating the base panoramic environments is presented below. The prompt design follows a hierarchical structure: it begins with spatial configuration and geometric constraints to stabilize the global structure, followed by material specifications and atmospheric details to refine the visual characteristics.

- Positive Prompt: "A large central atrium inside a contemporary mixed-use commercial complex. The viewpoint is at human eye level on the basement floor. A central vertical void defines the atrium, with two to three upper levels visible around the perimeter. Upper floors form continuous horizontal slabs with consistent thickness, clearly supported by aligned columns. Materials follow a refined beige and light-brown commercial palette. Railings are continuous clear glass with slim light-toned metal handrails. The atrium is fully enclosed below ground with no skylights, exterior views, or visible sky. Lighting is entirely artificial. The space is empty, with no people, vegetation, or decorative installations".
- Negative Prompt: "red, blue, green vivid colored paintings, paintings, people, crowds, silhouettes, plants, greenery, trees, sky, skylight, translucent ceiling, glass roof, exterior view, windows to outside, black doors...".

3.5. Spatial Image Generation and Validation

3.5.1. Evaluation Metrics

To evaluate the quality of the AI-generated 360° indoor panoramas, we employed five metrics covering semantic alignment, geometric integrity, and structural continuity at the seams. To account for the omnidirectional nature of panoramic images, each panorama was divided into 20 normal field-of-view (NFoV) images. Metrics were calculated for each view, and the average score was used as the final indicator.

The suitability of the generated images was evaluated using Contrastive Language-Image Pre-training (CLIP) scores to quantitatively evaluate the semantic alignment between prompts and generated images using a contrastive CLIP model [20]. Higher scores indicated better alignment with the user's intent. The structural integrity of the 360° panoramic images was evaluated using the straight-line deviation (SLD) metric, which quantifies geometric distortion by calculating the distance between detected edge pixels and their corresponding idealized straight lines. Based on the "straight-line constraint" principle [21], we measured the deviation of edge pixels from idealized Hough-transformed lines. Lower values indicated superior structural preservation. Continuity of the generated panoramas was assessed using seam mean squared error (MSE), which measures the average squared difference between pixel intensities at the junction, peak signal-to-noise ratio (PSNR) to assess the ratio between the maximum possible power of a signal and the power of corrupting noise, and structural similarity index (SSIM), which evaluates the degradation of structural information by modeling the perceived change in luminance and contrast [22]. Seam MSE and PSNR assess pixel-level discontinuity at the interface [23], where high PSNRs and low MSEs signify seamless transition and high-intensity consistency. SSIM evaluates perceptual continuity by modeling human visual sensitivity to luminance, contrast, and structural

 https://doi.org/10.3390/buildings16091679

patterns [24]. Unlike pixel-based error metrics, SSIM captures the preservation of local structural information across junctions; values approaching 1.0 indicate the visual integrity of the 360° representation.

3.5.2. Results of Spatial Images Generation and Evaluation

The white, light wood, and dark wood stimuli were generated as base environments reflecting only architectural and material conditions. All stimuli were 360° panoramic images with similar spatial types, structural principles, lighting, circulation, and viewpoints. The quantitative results are presented in Table 3.

Table 3. Quantitative evaluation results.

ALT.	Images	Scores	
White		CLIP Score	0.309
		Relative SLD (%)	0.050
		Seam MSE	328.190
		Seam PSNR	22.970
		Seam SSIM	0.752
Light wood		CLIP Score	0.359
		Relative SLD (%)	0.093
		Seam MSE	104.820
		Seam PSNR	27.930
		Seam SSIM	0.840
Dark wood		CLIP Score	0.319
		Relative SLD (%)	0.040
		Seam MSE	305.160
		Seam PSNR	23.290
		Seam SSIM	0.847

The dark wood variant exhibited the highest geometric precision (SLD: 0.040%), whereas the light wood variant showed higher distortion (0.093%). Although light wood (0.359) exhibited superior semantic fidelity, all results exceeded the 0.3 threshold, indicating high semantic alignment. This threshold is established as a benchmark where CLIP scores demonstrate a strong correlation with human perceptual judgment, confirming that the generated imagery accurately reflects the input prompts [25]. However, seam metrics

https://doi.org/10.3390/buildings16091679

revealed significant performance gaps. The white variant showed acceptable geometric stability (SLD: 0.050%) but high seam discontinuity (MSE: 328.190). Conversely, light wood exhibited the most refined stitching quality (MSE: 104.820, PSNR: 27.930). Based on SSIM, dark wood (0.847) exhibited the highest visual and structural continuity. The dark wood version was selected for the final experimental control. Despite the light wood variant's superior semantic alignment and surface continuity, the dark wood version achieved exceptional geometric precision (SLD: 0.040%), which is vital for accurate spatial reconstruction and minimizing visual distortion variables. With high perceptual integrity (SSIM: 0.847), the dark wood variant provides the most stable, mathematically consistent foundation for spatial analysis and subsequent studies.

4. Systematic Manipulation of Greenery on 360° Panoramic Spatial Images Using Generative AI

4.1. Criteria for Greenery Insertion

After generating 360° interior scenes, indoor greenery was introduced using a post-processing workflow. Viewpoints, camera positions, equirectangular geometry, architectural layouts, materials, lighting, and spatial proportions remained constant across all versions. Vegetation consisted of low-salience foliage species, primarily *Epipremnum aureum*, with limited use of *Dracaena*. Greenery was integrated exclusively into existing architectural surfaces, such as walls, columns, and balustrades, while freestanding, floor-based, and ceiling-mounted elements were excluded. Due to generative AI inpainting constraints, the final version was rendered at 4K resolution.

4.2. Greenery Manipulation Strategies for Comparative Analysis

The five configuration types were derived based on primary architectural surfaces (walls, columns, and balustrades), which differ in spatial prominence and visual exposure within the panoramic field of view. These configurations were designed to examine how the placement of greenery across different architectural elements influences spatial perception while preserving a consistent underlying spatial structure. They represent distinct spatial distribution patterns of greenery, enabling comparison between localized and distributed interventions, while the three density levels allow incremental assessment of perceptual impact without altering the underlying spatial structure. The three greenery density levels (low, medium, and high) represent incremental increases in visual exposure, enabling the assessment of perceptual responses across a controlled range of greenery intensity under uniform spatial conditions. The overall experimental framework, including the fixed spatial conditions and controlled greenery manipulations, is summarized in Figure 1.

Accordingly, five configurations were defined based on primary surface location: wall only (V1), column only (V2), balustrade only (V3), column–balustrade (V4), and wall–column–balustrade systems (V5). Independent of the version-based greenery distribution stimuli, a separate set of panoramic images was generated to examine the perceptual effects of greenery intensity. Greenery intensity was operationalized at low, medium, and high levels, with application locations limited to column surfaces and inner balustrade edges. Differences between levels were achieved solely by adjusting vertical reach, continuity, and perceptual prominence. Low levels represent minimal greenery, characterized by limited application on selected columns' lower sections and a single thin continuous linear band along balustrades. Medium levels increase vertical reach to mid-column height and introduce continuous linear bands across visible balustrade segments. Finally, high levels further intensify repetition across columns and balustrades without full spatial enclosure, extending vertically toward the ceiling (while stopping short of it) and increasing balustrade continuity. Greenery density levels were defined as follows: low (limited

https://doi.org/10.3390/buildings16091679

vertical application and minimal continuity), medium (moderate vertical extension and continuous distribution), and high (extended vertical reach with repeated distribution across surfaces).

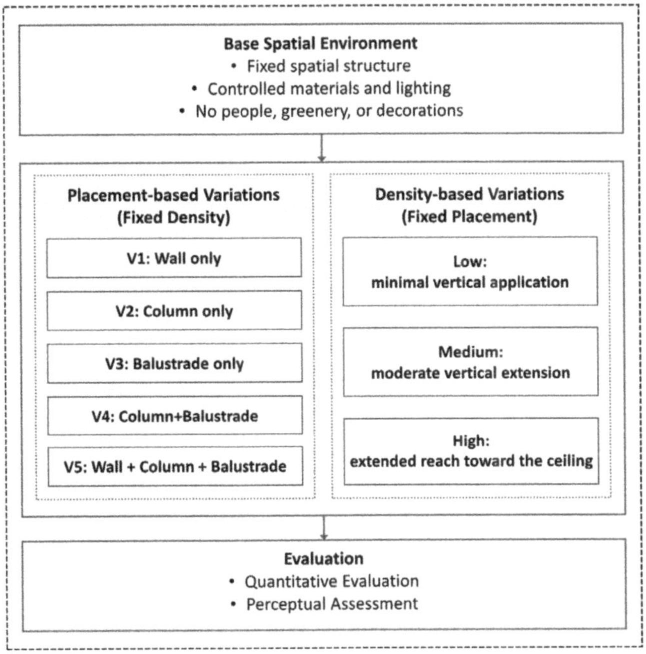

Figure 1. Experimental framework illustrating the fixed base environment and the systematic manipulation of greenery placement (V1–V5) and density (low-high) for perceptual evaluation.

4.3. Greenery Integration and Validation

4.3.1. Evaluation Framework and Methodology

To evaluate the quality of the image outputs modified by generative AI, a comprehensive assessment framework was established using both full-reference (FR) metrics that compare the output to a ground-truth image and no-reference (NR) IQA metrics that evaluate quality without a baseline. Structural integrity of the original image was primarily assessed using the SSIM, while learned perceptual image patch similarity (LPIPS) was simultaneously used to quantify perceptual distance in accordance with human visual judgment [26]. This evaluation was further extended to assess artifacts and naturalness through the analysis of Blind/Referenceless Image Spatial Quality Evaluator (BRISQUE) and Natural Image Quality Evaluator (NIQE), which quantify the absence of artificial distortions. This was complemented by the quantification of technical and aesthetic excellence via Multi-scale Image Quality transformer (MUSIQ) and aesthetic scores. CLIP–IQA, an IQA method based on the CLIP model, was integrated into the pipeline to cross-verify visual quality in terms of semantic consistency and high-level conceptual alignment between the source and generated outputs.

4.3.2. Greenery Insertion Results

The quantitative performance of the generative modifications across various experimental configurations is presented in Table 4. The data present a comparative analysis of structural fidelity, measured by SSIM and LPIPS, along with technical quality and aesthetic

 https://doi.org/10.3390/buildings16091679

assessments. These metrics serve as an empirical foundation for identifying the optimal generative parameters within each experimental category.

Table 4. Evaluation results on set of generated panoramic images.

Group		SSIM (↑)	LPIPS (↓)	BRISQUE (↓)		NIQE (↓)		MUSIQ (↑)		Aesthetic (↑)		CLIP-IQA (↑)	
		M	*M*	*M*	*SD*	*M*	*SD*	*M*	*SD*	*M*	*SD*	*M*	*SD*
Orig.		-	-	34.362	3.136	8.505	1.064	63.285	7.559	4.971	0.594	0.669	0.076
Ver1	1	0.808	0.094	36.140	4.179	7.686	1.488	56.669	6.791	4.550	0.576	0.444	0.048
	2	0.791	0.134	33.285	6.016	7.569	1.536	56.317	6.731	4.540	0.567	0.443	0.054
	3	0.791	0.132	34.484	4.965	7.702	1.531	56.919	7.110	4.530	0.601	0.440	0.056
Ver2	1	0.779	0.123	34.800	4.200	7.588	1.416	57.617	6.850	4.469	0.551	0.457	0.058
	2	0.787	0.095	36.768	3.491	8.034	1.496	57.381	7.267	4.461	0.545	0.476	0.058
	3	0.794	0.100	35.608	4.107	7.695	1.503	57.343	7.186	4.476	0.552	0.457	0.057
Ver3	1	0.795	0.139	31.715	7.192	7.399	1.677	56.665	6.166	4.537	0.563	0.455	0.060
	2	0.820	0.075	37.214	4.527	7.959	1.489	56.905	7.161	4.470	0.541	0.458	0.073
	3	0.824	0.075	36.727	4.869	7.916	1.313	57.008	7.082	4.485	0.587	0.473	0.079
Ver4	1	0.755	0.178	33.625	5.128	7.612	1.590	56.616	6.284	4.509	0.557	0.434	0.059
	2	0.776	0.125	34.465	4.781	7.453	1.449	56.427	6.721	4.456	0.527	0.438	0.061
	3	0.775	0.140	31.394	6.890	7.547	1.566	56.236	6.403	4.445	0.486	0.426	0.065
Ver5	1	0.739	0.198	29.613	8.140	7.561	1.581	57.401	6.299	4.477	0.522	0.430	0.051
	2	0.784	0.144	33.899	5.060	7.622	1.390	55.577	6.446	4.458	0.490	0.426	0.060
	3	0.758	0.181	32.579	5.978	7.564	1.706	56.602	6.723	4.476	0.569	0.432	0.061
Low	1	0.779	0.123	34.800	4.200	7.588	1.416	57.617	6.850	4.469	0.551	0.457	0.058
	2	0.798	0.093	36.753	4.292	7.622	1.166	56.355	6.412	4.421	0.518	0.445	0.080
	3	0.794	0.103	35.597	4.212	7.682	1.455	56.111	6.719	4.465	0.525	0.442	0.072
Med	1	0.755	0.178	33.625	5.128	7.612	1.590	56.616	6.284	4.509	0.557	0.434	0.059
	2	0.800	0.079	37.206	3.300	7.826	1.429	57.807	7.323	4.513	0.550	0.461	0.061
	3	0.771	0.141	32.185	6.288	7.264	1.613	55.895	6.231	4.437	0.488	0.438	0.067
High	1	0.739	0.198	29.613	8.140	7.561	1.581	57.401	6.299	4.477	0.522	0.430	0.051
	2	0.778	0.124	32.122	6.010	7.535	1.354	56.706	6.750	4.445	0.512	0.431	0.063
	3	0.756	0.157	31.194	6.651	7.539	1.558	56.948	7.339	4.460	0.526	0.450	0.067

4.3.3. Selection of Optimal Results by Experimental Group

By analyzing the trade-offs between structural fidelity and generative quality across all experimental groups (Versions 1–5, and Low, Medium, and High), the following optimal candidates were identified for each category:

In the quantitative assessment for determining the optimal generative outcomes across diverse experimental configurations, each specimen was systematically identified based on its capacity to balance structural fidelity with generative quality.

Specifically, Ver1-1 demonstrated exceptional fidelity, yielding a group-leading SSIM of 0.808, whereas Ver2-3 was prioritized for its superior perceptual alignment (LPIPS = 0.100) relative to the same series. Most significantly, Ver3-3 emerged as the overall optimal output across the entire dataset, attaining a peak SSIM of 0.824 and a minimum LPIPS of 0.075, indicating the near-optimal preservation of the semantic essence of the source. Furthermore, Ver4-2 was recognized for maintaining a stable SSIM of 0.776 despite the increased complexity of generative modification. Ver5-2 was selected owing to its superior structural preservation (SSIM = 0.784) and performance on non-reference quality metrics. Collectively, these results signify the highest level of adherence to established quantitative

 https://doi.org/10.3390/buildings16091679

benchmarks by effectively suppressing generative artifacts while maintaining the integrity of the original visual information.

Within the density iterations, High-3 was designated as the representative for its category because it achieved a more harmonized distribution across multiple quality metrics than other candidates in the high-variance group. Concurrently, Low-2 and Med-2 exhibited minimal perceptual distortion (LPIPS = 0.093) and optimal synergy between robust structural similarity (SSIM = 0.800) and technical aesthetic excellence (Aesthetic = 4.513), respectively. Table 5 presents the representative optimal images selected from each experimental group. To provide clear visual evidence of the AI's precision, each entry includes the final output and a Difference Map. The Difference Map highlights the specific pixels modified from the baseline environment, demonstrating the capability to maintain architectural integrity while precisely manipulating independent variables (i.e., greenery).

Table 5. Selected images by experimental group.

Group		Images	Difference Map
	1		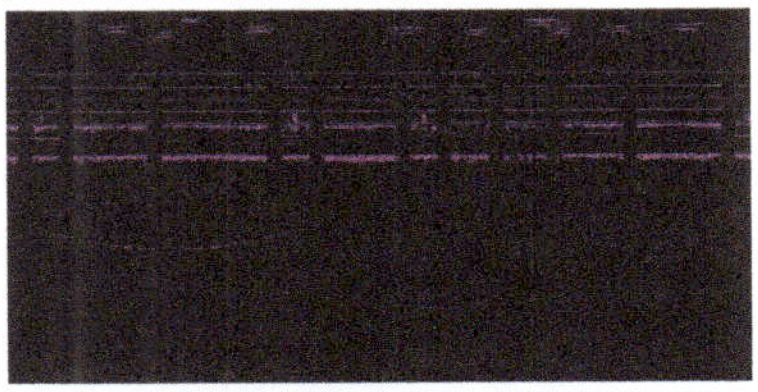
	2		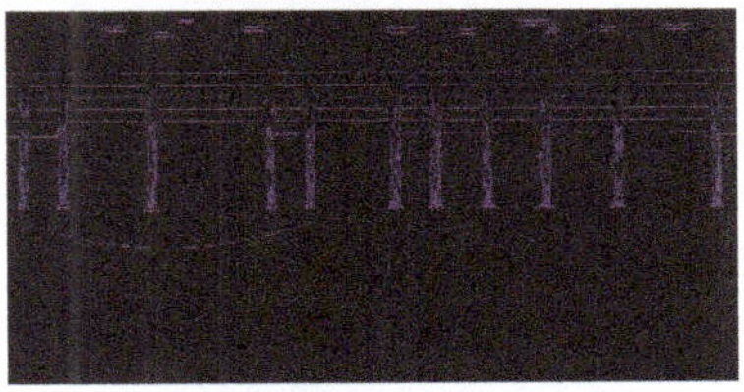
Ver	3		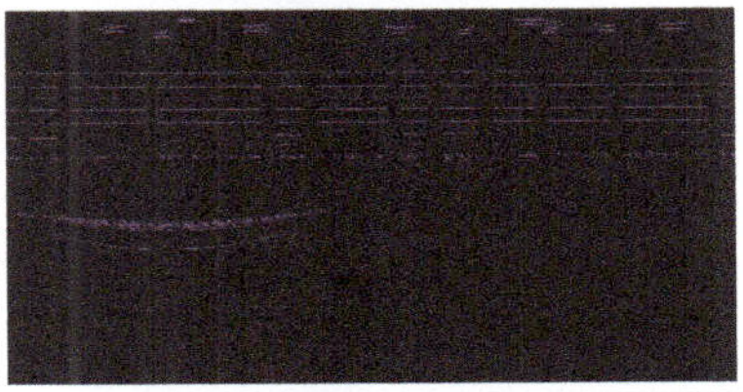
	4		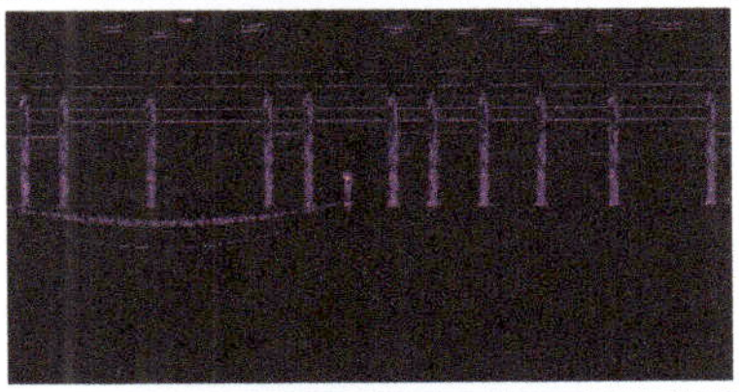
	5		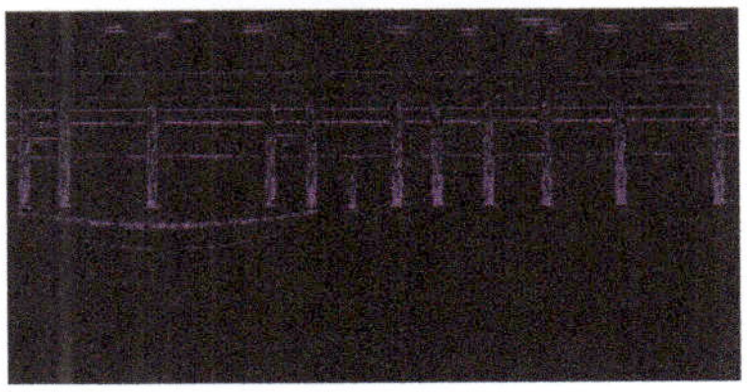

https://doi.org/10.3390/buildings16091679

Table 5. *Cont.*

Group		Images	Difference Map
Density	Low		
	Med		
	High		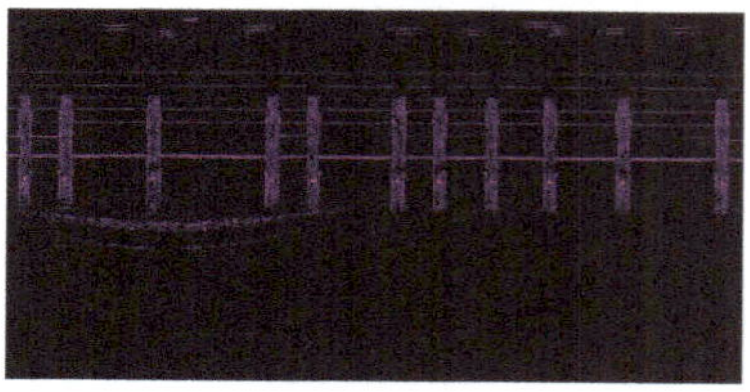

4.3.4. Perceptual Verification via VR-Based Assessment

In AI-generated 360° indoor imagery, conventional IQA metrics alone cannot fully capture the nuanced perceptual characteristics of omnidirectional environments [26–28]. While automated algorithms provide a technical baseline, determining the structural integrity and spatial plausibility remains a high-level cognitive task. Therefore, this study employed an expert-based evaluation as a final perceptual verification stage to complement the technical data.

To bridge the gap between automated metrics and human perception, a structured perceptual verification was conducted with seven senior experts (four architectural designers and three researchers) with over ten years of professional experience. For a controlled comparison, conventional 3D reference stimuli were developed using SketchUp and Enscape, applying identical environmental parameters—including spatial scale, lighting intensity, and material properties—to match the AI-generated environments (Table A3). The generated images were presented via Meta Quest 3 HMDs to ensure an immersive, high-fidelity spatial experience.

Experts evaluated both environments using a seven-point Likert scale, ensuring methodological consistency with the IPQ [29]. The evaluation of Presence revealed a substantial performance gap: AI-generated stimuli achieved a significantly higher mean score (6.143) compared to conventional modeling (4.397) (Table 6). To determine statistical significance, a Wilcoxon signed-rank test was performed on the aggregated presence scores. The results confirmed that AI-generated stimuli evoked a statistically significant higher level of spatial presence ($Z = -2.3664$, $p = 0.018$), proving that the proposed workflow achieves superior perceptual realism that surpasses traditional manual modeling standards.

https://doi.org/10.3390/buildings16091679

Table 6. Comparative analysis of mean presence scores: AI-generated vs. traditional modeling.

Dimensions	Sub-Dimensions	AI-Generated (*M*)	Modeling (*M*)	Difference
Presence	General Presence	6.429	4.286	+2.143
	Spatial Presence	6.429	4.714	+1.715
	Involvement-1	5.857	4.571	+1.286
	Involvement-2	5.714	4.000	+1.714
	Involvement-3	6.286	4.857	+1.429
	Involvement-4	6.000	4.143	+1.857
	Realism-1	6.714	4.000	+2.714
	Realism-2	6.286	4.857	+1.429
	Realism-3	5.571	4.143	+1.428
Total		6.143	4.397	+1.746

Beyond Presence, to evaluate the specific performance of the generative AI workflow, we established a multi-dimensional framework derived from established generative AI literature [7,30–33]. This framework comprised three domains: (1) Architectural Quality, (2) Greenery Quality, and (3) Usability as an experimental stimulus (detailed in Table A4). The evaluation functioned as a technical audit; a high level of descriptive consensus was observed among the experts, confirming that the AI-generated stimuli meet the rigorous standards required for empirical research. Based on this framework, the AI-generated environments were further evaluated across specific quality metrics to verify their technical validity (Table 7). Within the Architectural Quality dimension, 'Space function' achieved the highest score (6.429), indicating that the AI accurately reflects the intended architectural purpose. Both 'Text-to-image alignment' and 'Visual consistency' scored 6.286, demonstrating the reliability of the system in translating descriptive prompts into coherent 360° visuals. In the Greenery Quality dimension, while 'Design details' (5.571) and 'Greenery details' (5.429) received slightly lower ratings, they still exceeded the scale's median, confirming high overall fidelity. Finally, the Usability score of 6.000 serves as a critical benchmark, confirming that the experts considered these virtual spaces sufficiently robust for use as empirical research stimuli.

Table 7. Expert assessment scores for AI-generated 360° panoramic images.

Dimensions	Items	Score (*M*)
Architectural quality	Visual quality	5.429
	Space function	6.429
	Text-to-image alignment	6.286
	Design details	5.571
	Visual consistency	6.286
Greenery quality	Text-to-greenery alignment	5.911
	Greenery details	5.429
Usability	Usability	6.000

5. Discussion and Conclusions

The empirical results of this study support the methodological soundness and technical validity of generative AI-driven 360° images as experimental stimuli. Specifically, the

https://doi.org/10.3390/buildings16091679

ability to maintain environmental consistency while manipulating greenery elements via inpainting addresses a major challenge in spatial perception research.

The primary strength was revealed through the evaluation of quantitative metrics across different materials and greenery densities. In the first phase of space generation, the seam SSIM and PSNR values reached 0.847 and 27.930, respectively. These results are particularly significant as the seam area in equirectangular projections typically suffers from the highest distortion and lower SSIM values compared to the global average, yet our score of 0.847 surpasses the low 0.8 range identified as the critical threshold for eliminating perceptible ghosting artifacts and structural discontinuities [34]. The PSNR of 27.930 exceeds typical acceptable thresholds for generative outputs, where complex textures often lower numerical scores, confirming high signal precision. This indicates that the generated images maintain stable pixel-level correspondence and minimal noise at stitching boundaries. Such results are competitive with recent studies [34,35], verifying that the proposed approach delivers robust reconstruction quality consistent with current 360° image synthesis standards.

Furthermore, the second phase involving greenery integration demonstrated remarkable stability. The stability of SSIM (0.739–0.824) and Aesthetic scores (consistently above 4.4 on a scale of 1–10) across different greenery densities confirms that AI-based inpainting enables precise variable manipulation without reducing the underlying spatial quality. This level of aesthetic integrity is consistent with results reported in recent 360-degree panoramic studies [35,36], demonstrating that it ensures the visual consistency required for immersive environments. Even under varying greenery densities and surfaces, the stability of the MUSIQ (55.577–57.807) index demonstrates that AI can maintain high-fidelity visual standards regardless of experimental complexity. Notably, these scores are highly meaningful as they fall within the stable mid-to-high range reported in the original study [37], indicating professional-grade visual integrity despite inherent spherical distortions. The minimal variance in this metric further confirms the robustness of the generation process, ensuring uniform aesthetic quality across diverse spatial conditions.

The reliability of this approach was further supported by expert assessment, resulting in a significant increase in general presence (6.429) and visual realism (6.714) compared with the 4.286 and 4.000 scores of 3D conventional modeling, respectively. This discrepancy shows that AI-generated stimuli can more effectively overcome the limitations of visual artificiality by synthesizing complex lighting, subtle shadows, and realistic material textures, which typically require extensive computational resources and time for conventional modeling. Unlike previous studies that relied on static 2D AI images, this research demonstrates that 360° panoramic AI stimuli can maintain high spatial presence (6.429), enabling users to develop the psychological state of being "inside" the space.

This study offers a validated AI-generative approach that significantly reduces technical barriers to creating high-fidelity virtual stimuli, moving beyond the costly and rigid nature of conventional 3D modeling. The high text-to-greenery alignment (5.911) indicates that nuanced experiments on biophilic design can be conducted by controlling specific elements with high accuracy. For practitioners, the high usability (6.000) and space function (6.429) scores imply that AI can be used as a pre-occupancy evaluation tool to simulate user reactions to public space designs before actual construction. This convergence of subjective expert satisfaction and objective quality metrics confirms that the proposed three-stage framework offers a scientifically rigorous alternative to high-cost physical photography or complex 3D simulations, particularly for studies requiring precise control over environmental variables. Despite these strengths, this study has certain limitations. Although the visual consistency (6.286) was rated high, the current AI workflow may still produce minor artifacts in complex architectural geometries. In addition, the reliance on static 360° images

 https://doi.org/10.3390/buildings16091679

limits the evaluation of the movement of dynamic user within the space. Furthermore, the generative process may be subject to biases from prompt engineering and a reliance on specific AI tools, which presents challenges for reproducibility. As results can vary across different generative models or versions, future research should explore the generalizability of this workflow across diverse platforms to mitigate model-specific uncertainties.

In conclusion, this study validates the methodological feasibility of using generative AI for creating high-fidelity 360° environments, confirming the technical and psychological validity of generative AI-driven 360° stimuli. The AI-generated stimuli achieved higher scores in professional evaluations, markedly surpassing the scores recorded by conventional modeling methods. By integrating objective quality metrics such as SSIM, PSNR, and CLIP-based assessments with subjective expert feedback, this study confirmed that AI can produce experimental stimuli that are both aesthetically superior and scientifically rigorous. The key findings highlight that AI-driven methodologies enable high visual consistency and precise text-to-greenery alignment, thereby enabling the manipulation of environmental variables with unprecedented flexibility. The high scores in the space function and presence dimensions reinforce the potential of AI to generate psychologically valid virtual representations of complex public spaces. This study offers a high-efficiency, low-cost paradigm for spatial perception studies, paving the way for future indoor environmental research utilizing AI-generated VR stimuli for more diverse and scalable experimental designs.

Future studies would focus on integrating these AI-generated 360° environments into real-time VR engines to facilitate interactive navigation. Additionally, testing the framework across a broader range of complex public facilities, such as transit hubs and healthcare environments, will further validate its generalizability. Finally, a comparison of psychological responses related to AI-generated stimuli and actual physical environments will provide definitive proof of the substitutability of this innovative method.

Author Contributions: Conceptualization, Y.H.; methodology, Y.H.; software, Y.H. and J.J.; validation, Y.H.; formal analysis, Y.H.; investigation, Y.H.; resources, Y.H.; data curation, Y.H. and J.J.; writing—original draft preparation, Y.H. and J.J.; writing—review and editing, Y.H.; visualization, Y.H. and J.J.; supervision, Y.H.; project administration, Y.H.; funding acquisition, Y.H. All authors have read and agreed to the published version of the manuscript.

Funding: This work was supported by the National Research Foundation of Korea (NRF) grant funded by the Korean government (MSIT) (No. RS-2024-00360680).

Data Availability Statement: The data that support the findings of this study are available from the corresponding author, Y.H., upon reasonable request.

Conflicts of Interest: The authors declare no conflicts of interest.

Appendix A

Table A1. Architectural characteristics of public common areas in domestic mixed-use facilities.

Analysis Category	Summary of Key Characteristics
Spatial Type	Public common areas in domestic mixed-use facilities (e.g., department stores, large commercial complexes)
Method of Spatial Analysis	Field surveys, photographic documentation, spatial analysis, and online data review
Spatial Structure	Central vertical void penetrating multiple floors

 https://doi.org/10.3390/buildings16091679

Table A1. *Cont.*

Analysis Category	Summary of Key Characteristics
Spatial Form	Predominantly rectilinear configuration
Horizontal Elements	Repetitive slabs of uniform thickness
Structural System	Regular slab–column structural configuration
Balustrade Configuration	Transparent glass balustrades with light-toned metal frames
Daylighting Condition	Fully enclosed interior space with exclusion of external views
Lighting Environment	Uniform artificial lighting using indirect illumination
Material Characteristics	Neutral-toned interior finish materials

Table A2. Summary of material control strategies by stimulus version.

Category	White	Light Wood	Dark Wood
Material Basis	White plaster, light-toned stone	Light beige and light wood	Dark-toned wood combined with stone and metal
Referenced Spatial Characteristics	Neutral finishes commonly observed in public areas of mixed-use facilities	Warm material impression typical of underground common areas	Premium atmosphere of high-end mixed-use facilities
Risk of AI Auto-Interpretation	Low	Risk of being interpreted as retail or café space if wood use is excessive	Risk of being interpreted as hotel or lounge program
Control Strategy	Restriction of color contrast and surface texture	Limitation of color range and proportion of wood application	Maintenance of material hierarchy and minimization of furniture
Target Spatial Perception	Neutral public atrium	Warm but non-program-specific public space	High-end yet clearly commercial public space

Table A3. AI-generated and conventional modeling-based 360° panoramic images.

AI-Generated Image	Conventional Modeling-Based Image

https://doi.org/10.3390/buildings16091679

Table A4. Expert perceptual assessment items.

Dimensions	Items	Description
Presence	General presence	The virtual space felt like a real place rather than an image or simulation.
	Spatial presence	I felt as if I was really inside the space shown in the 360° environment.
	Involvement	I had a strong sense of "being there" in the environment.
		I was fully engaged with the environment during the experience.
		I paid more attention to the environment than to the real world around me.
		I felt deeply immersed in the virtual environment.
	Realism	The environment looked visually realistic.
		The spatial layout and depth felt similar to a real indoor space.
		The lighting and materials appeared natural and believable.
Architectural quality	Visual quality	The environment is aesthetically pleasing and free of obvious errors.
	Space function	The design meets its intended purpose.
	Text-to-image alignment	The 360-panoramic image matches the text description (prompt).
	Design details	The design elements are thoughtfully designed, with a reasonable layout and composition.
	Visual consistency	The 360-panoramic images maintain a high level of visual consistency.
Greenery quality	Text-to-greenery alignment	The greenery of the space aligns with the provided text description (prompt).
	Greenery details	The arrangement and composition of the greenery elements reflect a high level of intricacy and thoughtfulness in their design.
Usability	Usability	The quality of this virtual space is sufficient to be used as actual research stimuli.

References

1. Ulrich, R.S. View through a window may influence recovery from surgery. *Science* **1984**, *224*, 420–421. [CrossRef] [PubMed]
2. Kaplan, R.; Kaplan, S. *The Experience of Nature: A Psychological Perspective*; Cambridge University Press: New York, NY, USA, 1989.
3. Kim, N.; Lee, H. Assessing consumer attention and arousal using eye-tracking technology in virtual retail environment. *Front. Psychol.* **2021**, *12*, 665658. [CrossRef] [PubMed]
4. Lee, J.K.; Lee, S.; Kim, Y.C.; Kim, S.; Hong, S.W. Augmented virtual reality and 360 spatial visualization for supporting user-engaged design. *J. Comput. Des. Eng.* **2023**, *10*, 1047–1059. [CrossRef]
5. Shinde, Y.; Lee, K.; Kiper, B.; Hasanzadeh, S. A Systematic Literature Review on 360° Panoramic Applications in the Architecture, Engineering, and Construction (AEC) Industry. *J. Inf. Technol. Constr.* **2023**, *28*, 405–437. [CrossRef]
6. Zhu, Y.; Fukuda, T.; Yabuki, N. A mixed reality design system for interior renovation: Inpainting with 360-degree live streaming and generative adversarial networks after removal. *Technologies* **2024**, *12*, 9. [CrossRef]
7. Yang, W.; Wang, C.; Liu, L.; Dong, S.; Zhao, Y. Advancing interior design with AI: Controllable Stable Diffusion for panoramic image generation. *Buildings* **2025**, *15*, 1391. [CrossRef]
8. Zhang, C.; Wu, Q.; Gambardella, C.C.; Huang, X.; Phung, D.; Ouyang, W.; Cai, J. Taming Stable Diffusion for text to 360° panorama image generation. In Proceedings of the 2024 IEEE/CVF Conference on Computer Vision and Pattern Recognition (CVPR 2024), Seattle, WA, USA, 17–21 June 2024; pp. 6347–6357.
9. Kalischek, N.; Oechsle, M.; Manhardt, F.; Henzler, P.; Schindler, K.; Tombari, F. Cubediff: Repurposing diffusion-based image models for panorama generation. In Proceedings of the Thirteenth International Conference on Learning Representations (ICLR 2025), Singapore, 24–28 April 2025.
10. Lee, J.K.; Kim, Y.; Shin, E.; Choo, S.; Cha, S.H. An AI-assisted approach for creating and archiving interior design references using 360-degree panoramic images. *Archit. Sci. Rev.* **2025**, *68*, 506–518. [CrossRef]

https://doi.org/10.3390/buildings16091679

11. Ni, J.; Zhang, C.B.; Zhang, Q.; Zhang, J. What makes for text to 360-degree panorama generation with Stable Diffusion? In Proceedings of the IEEE/CVF International Conference on Computer Vision (ICCV 2025), Honolulu, HI, USA, 19–23 October 2025; pp. 16555–16564.
12. Paananen, V.; Oppenlaender, J.; Visuri, A. Using text-to-image generation for architectural design ideation. *Int. J. Archit. Comput.* **2023**, *22*, 458–474. [CrossRef]
13. Horvath, A.-S.; Pouliou, P. AI for conceptual architecture: Reflections on designing with text-to-text, text-to-image, and image-to-image generators. *Front. Archit. Res.* **2024**, *13*, 593–612. [CrossRef]
14. Akyildiz, E.C. An analysis of text-to-image generative models as creativity support tools. *Int. J. Arts Technol.* **2025**, *15*, 257–282. [CrossRef]
15. Jeong, H.; Kim, Y.; Yoo, Y.; Cha, S.; Lee, J.-K. Gen AI and interior design representation: Applying design styles using fine-tuned models. In Proceedings of the 23rd International Conference on Construction Applications of Virtual Reality (CONVR 2023), Florence, Italy, 13–16 November 2023; pp. 950–957. [CrossRef]
16. Li, C.; Zhang, T.; Du, X.; Zhang, Y.; Xie, H. Generative AI models for different steps in architectural design: A literature review. *Front. Archit. Res.* **2025**, *14*, 759–783. [CrossRef]
17. Chen, J.; Zheng, X.; Shao, Z.; Ruan, M.; Li, H.; Zheng, D.; Liang, Y. Creative interior design matching the indoor structure generated through diffusion model with an improved control network. *Front. Archit. Res.* **2025**, *14*, 614–629. [CrossRef]
18. Pramalystianto, A. Study of image resolution in virtual reality panorama Technology 360 in comfort of interior visualization. *Int. J. Archit. Urban.* **2023**, *7*, 244–250. [CrossRef]
19. Song, J.; Guo, H.; Zhang, L.; Wang, Z.; Yip, D. Expanding virtual production frontiers: AI-driven workflows for enhanced cinematic creation. In Proceedings of the 18th International Symposium on Visual Information Communication and Interaction (VINCI '25), Linz, Austria, 1–3 December 2025; pp. 1–5. [CrossRef]
20. Radford, A.; Kim, J.W.; Hallacy, C.; Ramesh, A.; Goh, G.; Agarwal, S.; Sastry, G.; Askell, A.; Mishkin, P.; Clark, J.; et al. Learning transferable visual models from natural language supervision. In Proceedings of the 38th International Conference on Machine Learning, Online, 18–24 July 2021; Volume 139, pp. 8748–8763. Available online: https://proceedings.mlr.press/v139/radford21a.html (accessed on 10 January 2026).
21. Devernay, F.; Faugeras, O. Straight lines have to be straight. *Mach. Vis. Appl.* **2001**, *13*, 14–24. [CrossRef]
22. Szeliski, R. Image alignment and stitching: A tutorial. *Found. Trends Comput. Graph. Vis.* **2007**, *2*, 1–104. [CrossRef]
23. Wang, Z.; Bovik, A.C. Mean squared error: Love it or leave it? A new look at signal fidelity measures. *IEEE Signal Process. Mag.* **2009**, *26*, 98–117. [CrossRef]
24. Wang, Z.; Bovik, A.C.; Sheikh, H.R.; Simoncelli, E.P. Image quality assessment: From error visibility to structural similarity. *IEEE Trans. Image Process.* **2004**, *13*, 600–612. [CrossRef]
25. Hessel, J.; Holtzman, A.; Forbes, M.; Le Bras, R.; Choi, Y. Clipscore: A Reference-Free Evaluation Metric for Image Captioning. In Proceedings of the 2021 Conference on Empirical Methods in Natural Language Processing, Online and Punta Cana, Dominican Republic, 7–11 November, 2021; pp. 7514–7528.
26. Zhang, R.; Isola, P.; Efros, A.A.; Shechtman, E.; Wang, O. The unreasonable effectiveness of deep features as a perceptual metric. In Proceedings of the 2018 IEEE/CVF Conference on Computer Vision and Pattern Recognition (CVPR), Salt Lake City, UT, USA, 18–22 June 2018; pp. 586–595. [CrossRef]
27. Tran, H.T.; Ngoc, N.P.; Pham, C.T.; Jung, Y.J.; Thang, T.C. A subjective study on QoE of 360 video for VR communication. In Proceedings of the IEEE 19th International Workshop on Multimedia Signal Processing (MMSP), Luton Bedfordshire, UK, 16–18 October 2017; pp. 1–6. [CrossRef]
28. Hai Uyen, T.T.; Kwon, O.J.; Choi, S.; Hussain, I. Subjective assessment of 360° image projection formats. *IEEE Access* **2020**, *8*, 33588–33599. [CrossRef]
29. Schubert, T.; Friedmann, F.; Regenbrecht, H. The experience of presence: Factor analytic insights. *Presence Teleoper. Virtual Environ.* **2001**, *10*, 266–281. [CrossRef]
30. Shao, Z.; Chen, J.; Zeng, H.; Hu, W.; Xu, Q.; Zhang, Y. A new approach to interior design: Generating creative interior design videos of various design styles from indoor texture-free 3D models. *Buildings* **2024**, *14*, 1528. [CrossRef]
31. Shi, M.; Seo, J.; Cha, S.H.; Xiao, B.; Chi, H.L. Generative AI-powered architectural exterior conceptual design based on the design intent. *J. Comput. Des. Eng.* **2024**, *11*, 125–142. [CrossRef]
32. Jiang, J. Enhancing interior design and space planning via human–machine intelligent interaction for artistic cognition. *Sci. Rep.* **2025**, *15*, 32344. [CrossRef]
33. Kuang, Z.; Zhang, J.; Li, Y.; Fukuda, T. Preserving architectural heritage in urban renewal: A Stable Diffusion model framework for automated historical facade generation. *npj Herit. Sci.* **2025**, *13*, 256. [CrossRef]
34. Li, J.; Yu, K.; Zhao, Y.; Zhang, Y.; Xu, L. Cross-reference stitching quality assessment for 360 omnidirectional images. In Proceedings of the 27th ACM International Conference on Multimedia, Nice, France, 21–25 October 2019; pp. 2360–2368.

 https://doi.org/10.3390/buildings16091679

35. Wu, Z.; Watson, D.; Tagliasacchi, A.; Fleet, D.J.; Brubaker, M.A.; Saxena, S. 360Anything: Geometry-Free Lifting of Images and Videos to 360°. *arXiv* **2026**, arXiv:2601.16192. [CrossRef]
36. Luo, R.; Wallingford, M.; Farhadi, A.; Snavely, N.; Ma, W.C. Beyond the Frame: Generating 360° panoramic videos from perspective videos. In Proceedings of the IEEE/CVF International Conference on Computer Vision (ICCV 2025), Honolulu, HI, USA, 19–23 October 2025; pp. 14336–14345.
37. Ke, J.; Wang, Q.; Wang, Y.; Milanfar, P.; Yang, F. MUSIQ: Multi-scale image quality transformer. In Proceedings of the IEEE/CVF International Conference on Computer Vision (ICCV 2021), Online, 11–17 October 2021; pp. 5148–5157.

https://doi.org/10.3390/buildings16091679